CHINA IN INTERNATIONAL SOCIETY SINCE 1949

ST ANTONY'S SERIES
General Editors: Alex Pravda (1993–97), Eugene Rogan (1997–), both
Fellows of St Antony's College, Oxford

Recent titles include:

Mark Brzezinski
THE STRUGGLE FOR CONSTITUTIONALISM IN POLAND

Peter Carey (editor)
BURMA

Stephanie Po-yin Chung
CHINESE BUSINESS GROUPS IN HONG KONG AND POLITICAL
CHANGE IN SOUTH CHINA, 1900–25

Ralf Dahrendorf
AFTER 1989

Alex Danchev
ON SPECIALNESS

Roland Dannreuther
THE SOVIET UNION AND THE PLO

Noreena Hertz
RUSSIAN BUSINESS RELATIONSHIPS IN THE WAKE OF REFORM

Iftikhar H. Malik
STATE AND CIVIL SOCIETY IN PAKISTAN

Steven McGuire
AIRBUS INDUSTRIE

Yossi Shain and Aharon Klieman (editors)
DEMOCRACY

William J. Tompson
KHRUSHCHEV

Marguerite Wells
JAPANESE HUMOUR

Yongjin Zhang and Rouben Azizian (editors)
ETHNIC CHALLENGES BEYOND BORDERS

St Antony's Series
Series Standing Order ISBN 0–333–71109–2
(outside North America only)

You can receive future titles in this series as they are published by placing a standing order.
Please contact your bookseller or, in case of difficulty, write to us at the address below with
your name and address, the title of the series and the ISBN quoted above.

Customer Services Department, Macmillan Distribution Ltd
Houndmills, Basingstoke, Hampshire RG21 6XS, England

China in International Society since 1949

Alienation and Beyond

Yongjin Zhang
Senior Lecturer
Department of Political Studies
University of Auckland
New Zealand

Senior Associate Member
St Antony's College
Oxford

palgrave

in association with
ST ANTONY'S COLLEGE, OXFORD

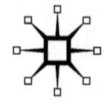

© Yongjin Zhang 1998

All rights reserved. No reproduction, copy or transmission of this publication may be made without written permission.

No paragraph of this publication may be reproduced, copied or transmitted save with written permission or in accordance with the provisions of the Copyright, Designs and Patents Act 1988, or under the terms of any licence permitting limited copying issued by the Copyright Licensing Agency, 90 Tottenham Court Road, London W1P 0LP.

Any person who does any unauthorised act in relation to this publication may be liable to criminal prosecution and civil claims for damages.

The author has asserted his right to be identified as the author of this work in accordance with the Copyright, Designs and Patents Act 1988.

Published by
PALGRAVE
Houndmills, Basingstoke, Hampshire RG21 6XS and
175 Fifth Avenue, New York, N. Y. 10010
Companies and representatives throughout the world

PALGRAVE is the new global academic imprint of
St. Martin's Press LLC Scholarly and Reference Division and
Palgrave Publishers Ltd (formerly Macmillan Press Ltd).

Outside North America
ISBN 0-333-60726-0

Inside North America
ISBN 0-312-21540-1

This book is printed on paper suitable for recycling and made from fully managed and sustained forest sources.

A catalogue record for this book is available from the British Library.

Library of Congress Cataloging-in-Publication Data
Zhang, Yongjin.
China in international society since 1949 : alienation and beyond / Yongjin Zhang.
p. cm — (St. Antony's series)
Includes bibliographical references and index.
ISBN 0-312-21540-1
1. China—Foreign relations—1949– I. Title. II. Series
DS777.8.Z39 1998
327.51—dc21   98-17293
                                                       CIP

Transferred to digital printing 2003

Printed and bound in Great Britain by
Antony Rowe Ltd, Chippenham and Eastbourne

Contents

List of Figures and Tables	vi
Preface	vii
Introduction	1
1 The Past as a Prologue	7
2 Isolation or Alienation?	17
Was China in isolation?	18
Was there isolationism in Chinese foreign policy?	31
China's alienation from international society	41
3 Mutual Legitimation	59
The 'China breakthrough' reconsidered	62
The process of mutual engagement	73
The limits of the 1970s	91
4 Changing Perceptions	99
The international system	102
War and peace	107
Revolution and development	113
Dependence and inter-dependence	118
5 Political Socialisation	126
Transcending ideology in international relations	127
UN peacekeeping: from condemnation to participation	138
Arms control: the limits of progress	150
Human rights contentions	177
6 Economic Integration	194
The trade nexus	197
China and global capital markets	208
From IMF to GATT and APEC	225
Conclusion: China in post-Cold War International Society	244
Notes	252
Bibliography	306
Index	330

List of Figures and Tables

FIGURES

2.1	Sino-British trade, 1949–59	40
3.1	China's foreign trade, 1970–79	84
3.2	Sino-Japanese trade, 1970–79	85
3.3	Sino-American trade, 1972–79	86
6.1	China's foreign trade, 1986–95	202
6.2	International capital inflows into China, 1979–95	209
6.3	Foreign direct investment in China, 1986–96	220
6.4	Long-term capital outflows from China, 1991–95	223

TABLES

2.1	China's foreign trade, 1950–59	39
2.2	China's trade with Western Europe, 1960–66	40
5.1	Status of implementation of the major multilateral arms control agreements by five major nuclear powers, 31 December 1981	152
5.2	Status of implementation of some major multilateral arms control agreements, by five major nuclear powers, 31 December 1992	153
5.3	China's arms sales to the developing world, 1988–92	167
6.1	China's foreign trade, 1979–85	199
6.2	Percentage of exports to GDP of China, Brazil and Australia 1979–85	200
6.3	China's foreign trade, 1986–95	202
6.4	China's exports and GDP, 1986–95	203
6.5	China's engineering and labour service contracts with foreign countries, 1979–95	207
6.6	Net disbursements of World Bank loans to China, 1990–94	213
6.7	Loans to China received from foreign governments and international organisations, 1991–95	213
6.8	China's foreign and Eurobond issues, 1982–85	216
6.9	International bond issues by selected developing counties, 1985–90	217
6.10	China's international bond issues, 1991–94	217
6.11	Foreign direct investment in China, 1986–96	219
6.12	Long-term capital outflows from China, 1991–95	222

Preface

In an unusual intervention in the studies of Chinese foreign policy recently, James Rosenau notes a prevailing rejection of 'the applicability of general theory' of IR (International Relations) in explaining and interpreting contemporary China's international relations. While scathingly critical of China specialists' antipathy towards IR theory, he asserts that 'we have no choice ... but to place China in a larger theoretical context'.[1]

The antipathy is, in fact, mutual. There seems to be a curious conspiracy among international theorists and China specialists about the studies of international relations of contemporary China. IR theory and, for that matter, IR theorists, seem to have maintained a respectful distance from contemporary China. Studies of China's international relations and Chinese foreign policy, on the other hand, seem to have reciprocated, if only inadvertently, with inexplicable recalcitrance to being theorised about. Small wonder it is that there should be an earnest plea for greater efforts by IR theorists and China specialists in 'linking the study of Chinese foreign policy with its parent discipline of international relations'.[2]

This study is a venture in modifying that mutual antipathy by placing the study of China's international relations since 1949 in the general theoretical framework of international society tradition normally associated with the English School of International Relations. It is an attempt to integrate the study of China's past with its present, and of China in world politics with China in the international economy. It is also the continuation of a personal endeavour started in my earlier book *China in the International System, 1918–1920: the Middle Kingdom at the Periphery* to seek to understand China's international behaviour in the tumultuous twentieth century world politics.[3]

Such is not an easy enterprise. In undertaking and finishing this enterprise, my intellectual debts to a large number of individuals and institutions are great. It would not be possible to list all of them here and many would in fact prefer to remain anonymous. I would like to acknowledge my thanks to Wolfson College, Oxford, where the idea of this study was first conceived while I was a Junior Research Fellow there, to St Antony's College, Oxford, for offering an inspiring environment for me to finish this final draft, to the Chinese Academy of Social Sciences for its help during my various research trips to China and to the Department of Political Studies of Auckland University for institutional support.

Adam Roberts has never failed to provide encouragement and stimulation for me to finish this study, whether when I was in town or down under. To him I am immensely grateful. I am also indebted to two anonymous readers of an earlier draft for valuable suggestions of revision and to Rosemary Foot for sponsoring my Senior Associate Membership at St. Antony's College at the final stage of my writing.

Finally, my greatest debt goes to my wife, Shanping and my daughter, Jessie for their love and understanding and for Jessie's putting up with my inability to explain clearly to her what this book is all about.

Introduction

In the post-Cold War and post-Communist international order, China continues to present as much a puzzle as a paradox, challenging those who seek to understand contemporary China. Politically, the Chinese Communist Party (CCP) has survived the internal upheaval of 1989 associated with the bloodshed in Beijing. It seems also to have withstood the shocking assault of the collapse of Communism in Eastern Europe and the former Soviet Union, although uncertainties regarding China's political future are still underlined by the passing of Deng Xiaoping. The Leninist state is now presiding over an increasingly liberalising economy. Stunning economic growth in China in the last few years, however, has not been accompanied by democratisation but by political stagnation and repression. China is now widely perceived as a rising power with its rapid economic modernisation. It is at the same time a state beset by socio-economic problems of mammoth proportion unleashed precisely by the very process of its economic modernisation. Further, whereas China is often seen as the engine of growth for the Asia Pacific in the years towards the next millennium, the perception of China as a threat in the region, with an irredentist agenda and undefined strategic intentions, continues to prevail in many quarters.

In the wider international context, the paradox is even more obvious, yet less observed. The People's Republic of China (PRC) has been a permanent member of the UN Security Council since 1971, and has been universally acknowledged as a great power in world politics. It has been a member of the International Monetary Fund (IMF) and the World Bank since 1980. Yet, its ten-year prolonged negotiations to regain its membership in the General Agreement on Tariffs and Trade (GATT) fell through. It is now excluded from the newly established World Trade Organisation (WTO). Its future membership of WTO remains an open-ended question today. This is so in spite of the fact that China has been the eleventh largest trading nation in the world since 1992, and is the largest trading partner among developing economies with members of the Organisation for Economic Cooperation and Development (OECD). The exclusion of China is paradoxical also because in 1995 China's foreign trade consisted of over 40 per cent of its GNP, and that in the revised wisdom of the World Bank and the IMF, China is now either the second or the third largest economy in the world.

Such a paradox indicates plainly an anomaly in China's position in the global international society. It also suggests profoundly ambivalent relations between China and the post-Cold War international society. Continual denial of China's full membership in the international community has recently been voiced by the United States. Speaking to the Japan National Press Club on 25 January 1995, Deputy Secretary of the State Strobe Talbott claimed that 'we believe China cannot be a full partner in the world community until it respects international obligations and agreements on human rights, free and fair trading practices, and strict controls on the export of destabilising weapons and military technology'.[1]

This statement underlines a crucial question central to our understanding of China's international relations: whither China in the global international society? This is particularly significant because in the wake of the end of the Cold War, the substance of international relations has been changing rapidly and profoundly and the rules of world politics and international economy are being frequently rewritten in large and small ways. The world-wide movement towards democratisation, the theoretical propositions of democratic peace and of the homogeneity of international society, the issues of deep integration in the international economy,[2] to name but a few, have all compounded the question of China's position in the post-Cold War international society, especially in view of the stagnation of political reforms in China.

Any cursory and brief survey of the existing literature on modern China's foreign relations published in the last 50 years is likely to reveal one perpetual theme which seems to have been immortalised in the study of modern China – namely, China *vis-à-vis* the changing world. The studies *China's Response to the West, China's Entrance into the Family of Nations* and *The Chinese View of Their Place in the World* are probably representative of the intellectual pursuit of this central theme in the 1950s and the 1960s respectively.[3] They address the questions related to the collapse of the Chinese world order in the late nineteenth century, the trauma of China's dislocation in the fast-changing world around China, and its quest for its rightful place in the European-dominated international system. They examine the encounter with and conflicts between the two civilisations mainly in the late nineteenth century and the early decades of this century. In the 1970s, *The World and China, 1922–1972, China and the World since 1949, and China, the United Nations and World Order* are typical of the perspective from which most studies of the same central theme are pursued.[4] There is an important and essential difference, however. The cultural dimension which characterises the previous studies of China's relations with the world is sidelined. China is increasingly studied simply as a nation among nations. These studies discuss Communist China as a revolutionary challenger to the prevailing international order and investigate the PRC's behaviour in the United Nations after its eventual return to the family of nations. This thesis of China *vis-à-vis* the world has its justifiable rationale. For one thing, there had been a distinctive Chinese world order for millenniums before the expansion of the European international system into East Asia brought about its collapse.[5] For another, until the 1970s, China's full incorporation into the international system was at best transient.

In the 1980s, the same topical theme is approached from yet another perspective. China is examined as a member of the world community and the Chinese economy evaluated in the global perspective.[6] The entry of China into the world economy and into the international economic organisations are subjects of such seminal works as *China's Entry into the World Economy, China in the Global Community* and *China's Participation in the IMF, the World Bank and GATT: Toward a Global Economic Order*.[7] Increasingly, China is being studied as an integral part of the whole of the universal international society. The thesis of China *vis-à-vis* the world, however, persists. There has been a strong reassertion, in fact, of this theme following the end of the Cold War.[8] The perception of China as culturally 'the other' is famously and strikingly presented in Samuel Huntington's 'Clash of Civilisations?'[9]

The intensive intellectual interest in the subject of China's place in and relations with the expanding international society points to a simple fact. The perpetual theme of China *vis-à-vis* the world transcends all Chinese revolutions, the Republican, the Nationalist and the Communist, in this century. It is a perpetual theme also because it has transcended the Cold War. That probably explains why China before 1949 has long been taken as a classical case to be examined in the studies of cultural and civilisational conflicts in international society. That also underlines intensive debates as to whether and in what sense China has 'rejoined' the world since the 1980s.

This study seeks to address this same perpetual theme, but by introducing a new and different theoretical perspective. It employs the notion and theory of international society normally associated with the English School of International Relations in an attempt to reinterpret aspects of China's international relations since 1949. This is not the place to elaborate or even to summarise various theoretical arguments about the notion of international society.[10] It may be helpful, however, to quote what has now become a classical definition of international society by Hedley Bull.

A *society of states* (or international society) exists when a group of states, conscious of certain common interests and common values, form a society in the sense that they conceive themselves to be bound by a common set of rules in their relations with one another, and share the working of common institutions.[11]

Further, without trying to prejudice the international society tradition of the English School, it should be pointed out that it is analytically useful to look at the expansion of international society as both a historical growth, and also a socialisation or contractual process.[12] Such a perspective yields significant insights into China's international behaviour through examining China's gradual inclusion and integration into international society both as a non-European state and as a revolutionary power. It informs us of important lessons which have bearings on how international society could best cope with the rise of China.

With the vantage of the post-Cold War perspective, the examination of China in international society since 1949 demonstrates a unique case. The reasons are simple yet powerful. In the last 40-odd years, few countries have experienced changes in its foreign relations as tumultuous as China has and few nations have embarked upon a more turbulent quest than that of China in search of its rightful place in the universal international society. No other nation except China was excluded from the United Nations and other international organisations for more than two decades in the post-war years. No other country except China was forced, as much as it opted, out of the prevailing international economic order for almost three decades after 1949. No other power except China was many times subjected to the blackmail of nuclear threat by both the United States and the former Soviet Union. For all these reasons, China's isolation and alienation from, and its socialisation and integration into, international society have left their marks on the evolution of the global international society since 1949.

The uniqueness of China's case is also seen in its constant challenge to the legitimacy of the existing international system, advocating either revolutionary transformations or radical reforms of the system in the 1960s and the 1970s. Equally important is how international society has responded to the China challenge and how it has exercised pressures and influences to bring China around to accept and to conform to standards, rules and norms universally acknowledged by members of the society of states. More fascinatingly, therefore, China's opening to the outside world since 1979 and the inclusion of China into the international political system and the world economy in the 1980s and the 1990s presents itself as a unique example of how a revolutionary state and a traditionally self-sufficient and 'socialist' economy has been gradually yet inexorably incorporated into the present-day international society. The implications of this inclusion for changes of the Chinese society and for the international relations in general are still open to interpretation. The ambivalent position that China occupies in the post-Cold War international society, as both an insider and an outsider, remains to be addressed.

This study is therefore a systematic investigation of China's changing political as well as economic relations since 1949 with international society. In terms of its theoretical orientation, as suggested earlier, it locates itself squarely in the notion and theory of international society. It is an attempt to suggest a different approach to look at China's international relations and to interpret China's foreign policy behaviour since 1949. It is also an effort to address questions associated with the transformation of the European-dominated society of states into the global international society today and its travail in incorporating China, a revolutionary power and a non-European civilisational state, into its embrace. Bilateral relations between China and other countries are examined only in this context. The investigation is conducted from essentially two perspectives. One is the perspective of China's continued quest for its full membership and rightful place in the global family of nations, a quest started when the European-dominated international system expanded to incorporate China in the mid-nineteenth century. It therefore emphasises the continuity of one central theme underlining modern China's international relations. The other is the perspective of how international society as a whole has responded to China's quest and how constraints and incentives offered by the changes or lack of change of the international system have influenced the direction in which this changing relationship has been developing.

Specifically, Chapter 1 traces the historical process through which China was brought into the global international society up to 1949. Chapter 2 seeks to reinterpret China's anomalous position in international society in the 1950s and the 1960s. The central contention here is that it is alienation rather than isolation that is characteristic of China's position in international society in the period. On the basis of this reinterpretation, Chapter 3 examines the process of mutual legitimation between China and international society in the 1970s and reassesses the significance and outlines the limits of China's return to international society in the decade. Chapter 4 is a study of China's changing perceptions of some key international institutions which occurred in the 1980s. Chapter 5 uses several case studies such as China and international peacekeeping and human rights contentions between China and other members of international society to illustrate the progress and limits of China's political socialisation into international society in the 1980s and the 1990s. Chapter 6 explores the gradual integration of China into the world economy since 1979 as part of its integral behaviour in international society. The chapters look at both the changes in Chinese domestic politics and transformations of the international system/society for explanations of both the anomaly of China in the international system in earlier decades and China's gradual political socialisation and economic integration into the global international society since 1979. The conclusion summarises my central argument and discusses the uneasy position that China occupies in the post-Cold War international society.

1 The Past as a Prologue

At the 1988 Cyril Foster Memorial Lecture, Sir Geoffrey Howe, then the British Foreign Secretary, spoke of China's 'rejoining the rest of the world'.[1] To characterise the process of China's integration into international society in the 1980s as a process of 'rejoining' the world, however, begs three general assumptions. First, China had been a member of international society; second, there was a period when China was ostracised; and third, China is being reintegrated into the contemporary universal society of states. All three assumptions are to be examined rigorously. This inquiry starts with a review of the historical process through which China was drawn into the universal international society.

CHINA VERSUS THE WORLD

Two themes have been expounded most often in the studies in both the history of European expansion into East Asia and that of China's external relations. One is the world image in the minds of the Chinese and the Chinese world so ordered. From ancient times, China was conceived by the Chinese as the centre of the universe and the civilisation *per se*. Imperial China saw the outer limits of the world as sinking away into vague and uninteresting barbarities. For most Chinese, the outside world faded into increasing vagueness and fantasy and ended in *terra incognita*. It is little more than a truism to state that the geographical environment in which China found itself and the indigenous nature of the East Asian civilisation conditioned the Chinese image of the outside world. Virtually cut off from substantial contacts with other cultures in the world, China, as the world state and as the civilisation, developed and flourished for centuries. Culturally, politically, ideologically and materially, China was a totally self-sufficient entity. It is certainly true that the ethnocentric world image was not unique to the Chinese. To say that China as it was had no means of adjusting its world image simply misses the whole point. The truth is that up to the end of the eighteenth century, there was no need for China to modify its image of the world. This is probably a better explanation of why most of China's historical contacts with other cultures were so fleeting and did not even result in any substantial and accurate information about the aliens.[2]

The Chinese image of the world was further buttressed by the existence and the nature of a tribute system elaborately built up over two millenniums by the Chinese Empire. The system was the expression of China's political, economic and cultural relations with other states or societies of the Chinese culture and its periphery. The Chinese emperor, the Son of Heaven, stood at the apex of this hierarchical order and ruled China's known world by the Mandate of Heaven. Bilateral relations between China and other states were strictly conducted in the framework and through the institutions constructed and controlled by the Chinese and by the ethical standard of Confucianism. In other words, the Chinese lived in a world so ordered by China. China's cultural superiority justified, in the minds of the Chinese, such a world order, which in turn reinforced the sense of the superiority of Chinese culture. The Chinese world order, however, operated for China to interact with rather than integrate other states and political communities of Central and East Asia. The tribute system, which achieved its classic form in the Ming (1368–1644) and Qing (1644–1912) dynasties, constituted a policy of controlled apartness between China and other communities participating in the Chinese world order. This policy was 'central to all the philosophical assumptions, cognitive perceptions, customs, and institutions'[3] of the last phase of the classic Sino-centrism.

The most eloquent expression of China's self-satisfaction with its world order and with its political and material cultures and the most blatant indication of China's ignorance of the outside world and its lack of interest in other cultures were found, as so often quoted, in the classical example of the lofty and condescending edict by Emperor Qian Long to King George III in 1793.[4] Lord Macartney was told that the first British embassy to the Celestial Empire was dispatched to China, because the King of England was 'so inclined' towards the Chinese civilisation. The British request to send a trade representative resident in the Chinese capital was for Emperor Qian Long, however, 'not in harmony with the state system of our [the Qing] dynasty and will definitely not be permitted' and 'the territory under the control of the Celestial Court is very large and wide. There are well established regulations governing tributary envoys from the outer states to Peking.' Further,

> The Celestial Court has pacified and possessed the territory within the four seas ..., the virtue and prestige of the Celestial Dynasty having spread far and wide, the kings of the myriad nations come by land and sea with all sorts of precious things. Consequently there is nothing we lack... . We have never set much store on strange or ingenious objects, nor do we need any more of your country's manufactures.[5]

TRIBUTE SYSTEM VERSUS TREATY SYSTEM

The other theme is, of course, how this world order crumbled and how China was incorporated into the European-dominated international system as it expanded across the globe. By the middle of the nineteenth century, China's traditional world had been invaded by a hitherto largely unfamiliar enemy, the West, represented first and foremost by the British. The Chinese government exercised every available means of power, politics and persuasion to bring the British into conformity with the institutions of the Chinese world order, but to no avail. The British cannons battered China open for international commerce with the 1842 Treaty of Nanjing. On the face of it, the conflict resulted from the fact that China's traditional trading practice as embodied in the tribute system had become increasingly incomprehensible and irrational in terms of nineteenth-century Western capitalist assumptions. In effect, it was the collision of two world systems. The expanding European international system which had set out to encompass all states and political entities on the planet clashed with the so-called East Asian international system. It was little realised at the time that the European expansion as a historical process was to engulf the entire Chinese world order and was to initiate the transformation of Imperial China, a world unto itself, into a sovereign member of the international system of states which originated in Europe.

China's trauma began when the Sino-centric Empire was removed progressively, yet swiftly, to the periphery of a more universal world order. Whereas before 1840, Imperial China dictated all terms in its relations with all the other political entities, including the European states, it was now forced to meet every term dictated by the European powers in its international relations. War was then a justifiable instrument of the European expansion to place the world under the blessings of the European civilisation and to cast the world in the European image. The European powers did not hesitate in exercising this instrument in imposing their order upon Imperial China. Two 'Opium Wars' were forced on China. The British fought the first in 1840. The Treaty of Nanjing of 1842 opened five Chinese coastal cities as treaty ports for Western commerce. The British and the French joint expedition fought the second in 1860. By the Treaty of Tianjin of the same year, China was compelled to accept a common practice of European diplomacy: a resident mission in the capital.

Between 1840 and 1860, other treaties were signed between the Empire and Western powers. The British obtained the Supplementary Treaty of Bogue on 8 October 1843. In 1844, the Americans signed the Treaty of

Wangxia in July, and the French, the Treaty of Whompoa in October. The Russians not only became a signatory to the Treaty of Tianjin but also signed the Treaty of Peking in November 1860, firmly establishing Imperial Russia as one of the treaty powers in China. By virtue of the 'most favoured nation' clause included in all the above-mentioned treaties which automatically granted any privilege conceded to one power to all powers, these bilateral treaties constituted a single system, the so-called 'treaty system' in China. By 1860, the treaty system was in place, and operated to regulate China's relations with European powers. The system survived, though not without modifications and amendments, until 1943 when, in the thick of the Second World War, the British and the Americans had to agree to scrap the system *in toto* in order to give China, their ally in a total war against a ferocious enemy, the fascists, an equal place in the forthcoming United Nations.

With the treaty system and all its ramifications, European powers not only dismantled China's classic tribute system but also established their collective domination in China. They denied China the exercise of its sovereignty in matters like the organisation of its foreign trade and its export and import tariffs. They also wrung from China such privileges as extraterritoriality, consular jurisdiction and freedom to preach in China's interior. Later, Western domination of the Empire was to find its expression in their 'scrambles for concessions', their leased territories and their spheres of influence. The subjection of China in world politics was the hallmark of China's international relations in the second half of the nineteenth century.

Parallel to China's subjection in world politics was the transformation of the Empire's institutions and statecraft in dealing with its foreign relations. This is a further witness to the total collapse of the Sino-centric world order. In a short span of 20 years, from 1860 to 1880, Imperial China's foreign relations institutions were brought into conformity with the diplomatic practice of the European society of states. The foreign diplomatic representation in the capital, Beijing, was accepted in 1861. Zongli Yamen as a centralised organ to handle China's foreign affairs – a prototype Foreign Office – was set up in the same year. In 1864, China 'discovered' the efficacy of international law. In the same year, China for the first time appealed to international law in settling a dispute involving the Prussian seizure of three Danish merchant ships in Chinese territorial waters during the Prussian–Danish War. It succeeded.[6] More significantly, China belatedly dispatched its first resident diplomatic mission abroad in London in 1877.[7]

CHINA'S ENTRY INTO INTERNATIONAL SOCIETY

The evolution of this pattern of political, economic and military relations between China and the Western powers under the treaty system turned out to be historically a process in which China was drawn into the European-dominated international system. In other words, it was a process in which the European system of states superseded the East Asian world order. By then, European expansion, which had begun in the fifteenth century, had already engulfed other regional international systems (the Arab-Islamic one, for example) which could be dated further back in history and had once existed side by side with the European states system. In the second half of the nineteenth century, a universal international system with European dominance was emerging and was the expression of economic and political unification of the globe. It seems absurd today that, in the late nineteenth century and the early decades of this century, some well-established non-European political communities such as China, Japan, the Ottoman Empire and Persia should have had to satisfy the European powers in a qualification test in order to be admitted as a full member of the expanding family of nations. However bitter it was for non-European states, their entry into the emerging universal international society was a historical experience and was conditioned on the approval of the European states as original members of that society.

Much more must to be added to this statement. First, up to the end of the eighteenth century, the expanding European international society was still an exclusive club of European states and states of European culture. The inclusion of the Spanish colonies in the Americas at the beginning of the nineteenth century presented little problem in matters of admission. The real challenge was the incorporation of states belonging to culturally heterogeneous systems – that is, non-Christian and non-European states.

Second, when European expansion encountered other regional international systems of different civilisations and cultures in the eighteenth and nineteenth centuries, it developed a set of rules and institutions exclusively for governing its relations with non-European states and polities. Thus,

> the rules and institutions which the Europeans spread to Persia and China in the nineteenth century were those which they had evolved with the Ottomans (e.g. capitulations, consulates with jurisdictions over their nationals) rather than those in use within itself (e.g. free movement and residence virtually without passports).[8]

Third, it was European expansion that unified the world and shaped the foundations of the global international society today. It was European institutions, such as sovereign states, resident diplomatic missions and international law, that were gradually accepted as common institutions governing relations between states. In the late nineteenth century, European powers were in such a dominant position in the international system that they did not only dictate terms of their relations with non-European states but also decided collectively whether or not to extend to a particular non-European state the benefits of membership of the originally exclusive club of European nations. In what can be now regarded as the classic period of international relations – that is, from 1878 to 1914 – the standard of 'civilisation', either as a set of unspoken assumptions or obligatory terms explicitly expressed by publicists, served for the European powers as the test of admission of non-European states into their exclusive club.[9]

Last but not least, non-European states and political communities aspired to full membership of the expanding European society of states. Whether willingly or unwillingly incorporated, non-European polities strove to take their place in the European-dominated international system. They painstakingly modified their foreign relations institutions so as to bring them into conformity with the European standard and norms. They tacitly gave consent to rules of the European international system by actively seeking the protection of their interest by those rules. The expression of their aspiration to full membership of the expanding European international society was also found, for example, in their domestic political, social and institutional reforms to narrow down the differences between them and the European states as independent political entities.

The entry of non-European states into international society is a multifaceted phenomenon to be studied. How each non-European state eventually took its place in that society is an entirely different story. There is no doubt that by the treaty system, sustained political, economic and cultural relations were established between China and the European states. China was involved, albeit against its will, in the expanding international system. The treaty system, however, also crippled China's full rights as a sovereign state, thus reducing China to a 'semi-colony'. It is true that by 1880, the traditional Chinese statecraft and institutions dealing with foreign relations had been transformed and brought largely in line with European practice. This did not and could not, however, ensure an acceptance of China by European members into the expanding international society. The absence of perception of common interest and common values in the existing international order was obvious. Equally important was the absence of cooperation between China and the European states in the then existing common international institutions.

This was clearly registered by leading international publicists at the time. In expounding the principles of the natural law school in matters of political recognition, Lorimer insisted that only 'partial political recognition' should be extended to 'old historical States of Asia' such as China and Persia.[10] Holland, on the other hand, claimed that China was brought only to the 'outer court of the charmed circle' at the end of the nineteenth century.[11] Wilson argued that since China did not enjoy full sovereignty, it became one of political communities which had 'all the attributes of states, in the sense of public law and from the point of view of political science and yet lack[ed] full international statehood'. By the same token, it was not 'recognised by the "Family of Nations" as stated in the full sense of international law.'[12]

China achieved its full sovereignty much later than its entry into international society. By the end of 1920, with its membership in the League of Nations, China was tacitly admitted by the European powers into the emerging global international society.[13] A combination of circumstances and factors had decisive impact on China's entry. First, in the first decade of this century, the educational, military, judicial and government organisational reforms were carried out by the Imperial Chinese government. These reforms significantly lessened the gaps between China and European states as political entities. The process of convergence culminated in the Republican Revolution in 1911. That revolution changed irrevocably China's body politic. To the disappointment of many Chinese, however, the establishment of the Republic did not automatically secure for China full membership of the family of nations. As Sun Yat-sen declared in January 1912 in his capacity as Provisional President of the Republic, China must try its best to 'carry out the duties of a civilised nation so as to obtain rights of a civilised nation'.[14]

Second, the outbreak of the First World War signalled the collapse of the European balance of power. It was the beginning of the transformation of the global international system. The dynamic principle of national self-determination promoted by Woodrow Wilson, and also by Lenin, was a fundamental challenge to the legitimacy of the pre-war international order and it was to change both the face and the structure of the international system. The establishment of the League of Nations represented a positive step to incorporate all states and political communities, whether African, American, Asian or European, into a framework of international political and economic cooperation for peace and order. The principle of collective security in the League's Covenant was not only the renunciation of the legitimacy of the balance of power system but also presupposed involvement of all political communities in a structure of global peace and war. The League also amounted to the first formal recognition by all states of an international community transcending not only nation-state but also the European society of states.

Third, China actively participated in the reconstruction of international order in the post-war years. Its assertive diplomacy found its expression in the Paris Peace Conference, where China refused to sign the Versailles Treaty with three provisions detrimental to its sovereignty in Shandong.[15] After the war, China also set out to take a series of initiatives to regulate its foreign relations on the principles of equality, reciprocity and mutual respect of sovereignty. On 3 December 1919, China signed a Treaty of Friendship with Bolivia after its firm rejection of an earlier Bolivian proposal to obtain consular jurisdiction. This is the first time in modern Chinese history that China had signed a bilateral treaty with a foreign nation on the principles of equality and reciprocity. It was the end of an era. Never again did China sign any 'unequal treaties' with any foreign nations. Concurrently to be reckoned with were Chinese initiatives to dismantle the structure of the Russian treaty rights and privileges in China.[16]

After the First World War China began to interact with the world in an unprecedented manner. The incorporation of China into the emerging international society was, however, characterised by China's demand that principles and values universally acknowledged by European nations as governing international relations should equally be applied to China's foreign relations. The treaty powers, mostly the original members of the European society of states, were now on the defensive. The democratisation of the international system as embodied by the League of Nations created an international milieu favourable to China's search for its rightful place in international society. China's membership in the League of Nations, and its election into the League Council with the support of Britain and France in 1920, were expressions of a tacit concession by the original members to grant China membership in the emerging international society. As some leading publicists were soon to spell out, the post-war international system manifested a 'disposition not to insist upon over-rigorous standards in respect to area or civilisation as conditions of membership in the international community', and the maintenance of an exclusive club of 'civilised' states 'no longer corresponds to the main facts of contemporary life.'[17] In the fourth edition (the first after the post-war peace settlement) of Oppenheimer's majestic *International Law* edited by MacNair in 1928, it was explicitly stated that, before the First World War, 'the position of such states as Persia, Siam, China and Abyssinia, and the like, was doubtful'. However, since 'China and Siam took part in the World War on the side of the Allied and Associated powers, and subsequently represented at the Peace Conference at Paris', and since 'Abyssinia, China, Persia, and Siam are now all members of the League of Nations', 'it is impossible to deny that they are now international persons and Members of the Family of Nations'.[18]

MEMBERSHIP IN QUESTION

China's entry into international society was by no means smooth sailing. Nor did China's membership in that society, reluctantly and tacitly conceded, change China's semi-colonial status. The treaty system continued its operation, though not without modifications. The treaty powers, no doubt, responded to changes in China in the inter-war years. However, they still arrogated to themselves the right to intrude into China's internal affairs when they felt their interests threatened. The American and British gunboats' bombardment of Nanjing in March 1927 and the Japanese invasion of Northeast China (Manchuria) in September 1931 are two examples. It was another titanic international struggle – the Second World War – and China's involvement in this anti-fascist war that were to bring about swift changes to all of this. In the preparations for the Cairo Conference at which Roosevelt, Churchill and Chiang Kai-shek were to meet, the two principal treaty powers, Great Britain and the United States, finally agreed in January 1943 to give up their special rights and privileges in China granted by the treaty system. It was an expedient to remove 'one of the obstructions to complete political equality among the United Nations'.[19]

This was followed by China's signing of the Four-Nation Declaration on General Security on 30 October 1943 in Moscow, together with the United States, Great Britain and the Soviet Union. China also attended the Dumbarton Oaks Conference in late 1944 and eventually became one of the five permanent members of the Security Council of the United Nations. China was now not only recognised as a 'civilised' member of international society but was also given at least symbolically the title and status of a great power in that society. The myth of making China a 'great power' may have its root in Roosevelt's infatuation with China or the American need to contain the Soviet influence after the war. Churchill might have had a point in dismissing the idea of China acting as a great power as 'an absolute farce', considering the realities of China's internal politics and of China's influence in international affairs at the time.[20]

These factors should not obscure the fact that by then there seemed to be no question whatsoever of China's full membership in the reconstructed international society emerging from the Second World War.

None the less, this was not the end of the anomaly in China's position in international society. The fact is that the international order in East Asia envisaged at the Yalta Conference by the Big Three, the United States, Britain and the Soviet Union, virtually assigned China a place not as a power but as a testing ground for the 'cooperation and understanding' of the Big Three in the post-war years. China was considered 'a prize for exploitation' by the Big Three.[21] It is true that the Big Three at Yalta agreed to accept the principle of China's territorial integrity, to refrain from interfering in Chinese domestic politics, and to continue to deal with the Nationalist government of Chiang Kai-shek. But it is also true that it was at Yalta that the United States and Great Britain secretly offered the Soviet Union a prize at the expense of China to induce the latter to enter the war against Japan in the last, and possibly the bloodiest, phase of the Second World War. It has been well-known that Roosevelt and Churchill agreed that Manchuria would, after the end of the war, be turned into a Soviet sphere of influence.[22] Two other latter developments, unseen at Yalta, would further throw into question China's membership in the post-war international society: the beginning of the Cold War, which quickly crystallised the bipolarisation of the world in the late 1940s; and the emergence of New China with the Chinese Communists in power in 1949. For another 20-odd years after 1949, China was rather excluded from than included in the family of nations.

2 Isolation or Alienation?

> From now on, our nation will join the great family of peace- and freedom-loving nations of the world.
>
> *Mao Zedong, 21 September 1949*

To all intents and purposes, the establishment of the People's Republic of China in October 1949 is one of the most significant events in twentieth-century world politics. It helped reshape the political and strategic balance in the post-war international system, and has since exercised profound and lasting influence in the evolution of international relations in the second half of the twentieth century. The PRC entered international politics, however, at a critical juncture in world history. By October 1949, the bipolarisation of the world was already crystallised by the division of Europe in the wake of the Berlin Crisis and the establishment of the North Atlantic Treaty Organisation (NATO). Nuclear confrontation between the two superpowers was taking shape with the explosion of the Soviet atomic bomb in July 1949. A titanic struggle between two ideologies, communism and capitalism and between East and West, was in the making. The emergence of the PRC in such a divided world had profound implications for its place in post-war international society.

Indeed, in the first two decades of its existence, the PRC was excluded from the United Nations and was largely outside the existing international economic order. China was sometimes regarded as a 'bogy' in world politics. It is very often argued that the abnormality of China was China's isolated status in the world. The assumption and contention that China was in isolation underline many studies of China's foreign relations of the period.

This chapter revisits and challenges the conventional wisdom that China was in isolation in the international system. It argues that the exclusion of the PRC from the United Nations and many other international organisations and China's limited contact with the world economy did constitute realities of international life in the 1950s and the 1960s. The China anomaly did exist in international relations. It is, however, not the isolation but the alienation of China from international society that characterises the anomalous position of China in that society in the 1950s and the 1960s.

WAS CHINA IN ISOLATION?

On the eve of proclaiming the establishment of the PRC, Mao Zedong made two proud announcements at the First Plenary Session of the Chinese People's Political Consultative Conference on 21 September 1949:

> Our nation will never again be a nation insulted by others. We have stood up. ... The era in which the Chinese people were regarded as uncivilised is now over. We will emerge in the world as a highly civilised nation.
>
> From now on, our nation will join the great family of peace- and freedom-loving nations of the world.[1]

Mao's proclamation of the end of an era in Chinese history has been proved true. His pronouncement about the PRC's entering the family of nations, however, remained for the next 20 years an aspiration expressed rather than a prospect fulfilled. The PRC was excluded from the United Nations from 1949 to 1971. The international legitimacy of the PRC was not accorded by a majority of members of the international community until the 1970s. The anomalous position of the PRC in international society in that period constitutes one of the greatest anomalies in the history of international relations of this century.

The China anomaly

The conventional wisdom in explaining this China anomaly is that China was in isolation in international society.[2] The picture of China's isolation is very often presented, not without detailed variations, as follows. Ideologically, Sino–American confrontation in the 1950s and the 1960s and Sino–Soviet polemics since 1958 had progressively isolated China from both superpowers and consequently from both blocs in world politics. It culminated in so-called 'revolutionary isolation' in the early years of the Cultural Revolution (1966–68) when China saw itself as the 'revolutionary bastion against imperialism, revisionism and all reactionaries'.[3] Politically, the PRC had been more of an outsider to the international community. It had been excluded from the UN system until 1971. By the same token, the PRC had also been kept out of almost all other intergovernmental organisations (IGOs). By the end of 1969, the PRC had established diplomatic relations with only 50 countries, most of which were socialist and newly independent states. At one stage during the Cultural Revolution, the PRC had only one ambassador residing abroad:

namely, Huang Hua in Cairo in 1969.[4] Its legitimacy in international society was more denied than acknowledged.

Economically, the PRC, though not fully autarchic, did not share any pattern of inter-dependence with the international economy as most other countries did. It had pursued a development strategy of self-reliance in order to build an integrated national economy. Apart from Soviet economic assistance in the 1950s, the PRC did not have any foreign investment and did not accept any significant international credit. Indeed, the PRC declared with self-righteousness in 1968 that the country had not a penny of foreign debt. Foreign merchandise trade in 1970 was $4.59 billion,[5] or only 5.53 yuan per capita.[6] Moreover, partly as a consequence of its exclusion from the UN, the PRC did not and could not have membership of the key international economic organisations such as the International Monetary Fund or the World Bank. China's participation in the international economic order was nothing but minimal.

Socially, China 'drew down the Bamboo Curtain between itself and the non-Communist world. It nearly isolated Chinese intellectuals and Christian communities from the West.'[7] Apart from a short period in the 1950s, even exchange and dialogue between Chinese and foreign scientists were strictly controlled by the Chinese government. The discourse between Chinese society and the outside world was progressively being cut off. The PRC sent very few students abroad to study in the 1960s. It accommodated very few 'foreign experts' in science and in education in China. To have a foreign friend could bring unpleasant consequences. Even the traditional international migration from South China to Southeast Asia had been stopped. To complete this picture of isolation with a glaring example, the PRC was not a member of the International Olympic Committee until 1980 and did not participate in the Olympic Games until 1984. Such isolation, some further argue, largely resulted from China's chosen policy of isolationism in its foreign relations.[8]

These arguments cannot be dismissed lightly. The relegation of the PRC to isolation in international society in the 1950s and the 1960s is, however, at best a half truth and is usually misleading. It is a half truth because an apparent fact that the PRC had fewer interactions politically, economically and socially with other members of international society than it should have had does not and cannot in itself warrant such a claim. Geldenhuys recently argued that there are two kinds of isolation – self-imposed and enforced – in international relations. In his words, self-imposed or defensive isolation is 'a protective strategy designed to shield the particular state against perceived harmful influences from outside', whereas enforced isolation or ostracism 'is by design a punitive measure applied against the offending state' and a 'means by which a group of states or the international community at large exerts pressure on that state'.[9] The crucial question in examining the claim that China was in isolation is therefore how and to what extent China's isolation was self-imposed or collectively enforced.

It is misleading because, as the hard facts will show, the PRC was not in such isolation as was commonly alleged and presented. It is true that the force of circumstances in the international system then prevented the establishment of diplomatic relations between the PRC and some members of the international community. Yet, the PRC's relations and links with members of international society were substantial and extensive, especially with the decolonisation process in the late 1950s and early 1960s. Further, the PRC's interactions with the international political system were both sustained and consistent, albeit in their own fashion. If the PRC was in isolation as alleged, how and why was such isolation constantly seen by the leading powers in the international system as a threat to the international political order in the 1950s and the 1960s? It is misleading also because underlying such a relegation is an unwarranted and invalid assumption; that is, that international society dominated by the two superpowers held a benevolent attitude towards the PRC, which, when giving up its alleged isolationism, would be readily embraced by international society that had always welcomed it with open arms. Later developments in the 1970s certainly did not vindicate this assumption.

The United States and the China anomaly

If we walk down the familiar path of the United States' policy towards the PRC in the 1950s and the 1960s, evidence is abundant that isolation of the PRC constituted the core of both changes and continuity of the American China policy in the period.[10] Jonathan Pollack wrote in the early 1990s that Nixon/Kissinger's breakthrough with China signalled 'the end of a twenty-year effort [by the United States] to isolate China'.[11] Before the establishment of the PRC, the United States and the Soviet Union had already been locked in the deadly combat of the Cold War. The Truman Doctrine was, as Baruch claimed, 'tantamount to a declaration of ... an ideological war' against Communism.[12] Kennan, on the other hand, called for a containment policy which was 'to confront the Russians with unalterable counter-force at every point where they show signs of encroaching upon the interests of a peaceable and stable world'.[13] Historians may continue to disagree as to whether the Cold War and containment had extended to the Asian rim as a whole before the Korean War.[14] It is nevertheless clear from NSC (National Security Council) 41 of 18 February 1949 that at the prospect of a complete victory of the Communists in China, the Truman administration had already considered isolating China completely from the non-Communist world as an alternative policy in order to choke the Chinese Communist regime.[15] This is because of 'the absence of an instrument in China, the United States support of which could bring about defeat or containment of Chinese Communism'.[16]

Arguably, the American China policy manifested a degree of ambivalence and ambiguity from early 1949 to the beginning of the Korean War in mid-1950.[17] To the Truman administration, the defeated and discredited Kuomintang (KMT) regime now on the island of Taiwan was more of an embarrassment and a liability than an asset. Political considerations nevertheless argued against abandoning it completely. The Americans were loath to accept a Communist government on the mainland unless it was an inevitability. Privately, Truman and Acheson (later, even Dulles and Eisenhower) both harboured a belief, not incorrectly as it turned out to be, that a rift between the Chinese and the Soviet Communists was a not too distant possibility. They both had the intention to apply, under right circumstances, a 'wedge strategy' to explore and speed up the rift.[18] Time, however, was not on their side. While Truman and Acheson were 'waiting for the dust to settle', things moved fast, perhaps too fast. Mao pronounced his 'lean-to-one-side' policy on 30 June 1949, proclaimed the establishment of the PRC on 1 October, and proceeded on his trip to Moscow and met Stalin on 16 December 1949. Less than two months later, on 6 February 1950, the Sino–Soviet Treaty of Friendship, Alliance and Mutual Assistance was signed by Zhou Enlai for China and A. Vyshinsky for the USSR.[19] Was this sufficient proof that international Communism was monolithic? Was Communism not one and indivisible?

Up to mid-1950, New China seemed to be making 'a successful debut in the world',[20] with its recognition accorded by the Soviet Union and many East European countries, as well as some Asian countries, including India. Great Britain also recognised the PRC in January 1950. Then came the Korean War. The Korean War, among other things, legitimised the extension of a full-scale Cold War and containment to East Asia. It helped sanction the implementation of NSC 68, which Walter LaFeber called 'one of the key historical documents of the Cold War'.[21] NSC 68 for every practical purpose extended the application of the Truman Doctrine worldwide and provided justification for the United States to act as the world's policeman in order to deter Communism. More importantly, NSC 68 sanctioned 'an immediate and large-scale build-up in our [American] military and general strength and that of our [American] allies to right the power balance'.[22] In the next 20 years, it served as the basis and justification for the American military build-up around the PRC's periphery to hem in Chinese Communism. The containment after the Korean War, in Ambrose's vivid description, was to make sure that 'if any communist showed his head on the free side of the line, someone – usually an American – would be there to shoot him'.[23]

The Korean War also enabled the United States to make the PRC an international outlaw. After China crossed the Yalu and fought the American boys in bloody battles, the United States manoeuvred its hegemonic position in the United Nations and engineered a resolution by the General Assembly on 1 February 1951, branding the PRC as an aggressor. A total trade embargo against the PRC was then introduced. The PRC's membership in the United Nations was put indefinitely into abeyance.[24] As Acheson reasoned, 'a claimant for seating cannot shoot his way into the UN and cannot get in by defying the UN and fighting its forces'.[25] The Korean War had thus also produced a political climate in which the United States was also able to rally its allies in implementing its policy of treating the PRC as an international pariah, as foreshadowed in NSC 41.

If there was any ambivalence and ambiguity at all in the American China policy before the Korean War, its China policy emerging out of the Korean War was anything but ambiguous. The rise of McCarthyism and domestic debate as to who was responsible for the 'loss of China' further ensured the orientation of American China policy. The four fundamentals of its China policy – non-recognition of the PRC, total support of Taiwan, opposition to seating Beijing at the United Nations, and the American trade embargo against the PRC – underwent little change in the rest of the 1950s and the 1960s. In fact, the Americans showed no disposition to alter them. They constituted four pillars of a general policy of isolating the PRC in international society to the maximum extent possible. Ironically, the KMT government on Taiwan, which had almost been written off as a liability by the American policy makers not long before, became an asset now. The support of the KMT government was made the pivot of the American China policy. Only by maintaining the KMT government on the island of Taiwan could the Americans legitimise their non-recognition of the PRC. Only by dismissing the government in Beijing as the legitimate government of China could the United States reject the PRC's claim to China's seat in the UN and the Security Council.[26] Only by denying the PRC its legitimacy as an international actor could the United States justify its policy of ostracising the PRC from international society.

The American strategy in Asia during and after the Korean War aimed specifically at militarily containing the PRC. From the latter half of 1951 to

1953, what Gilpin called 'the open-ended expansion of American commitment all over the world'[27] led the United States to sign a security treaty with the Philippines, the Anzus agreement with Australia and New Zealand, the mutual security treaty with Japan, and a defence treaty with South Korea. In December 1954, it concluded a mutual defence treaty with Taiwan shortly after the South East Asian Treaty Organisation (SEATO) was created on 8 September by the Manila Pact signed by the United States, Great Britain, France, Australia, New Zealand, Thailand, the Philippines and Pakistan. By so doing, the United States did not only create but was also committed to a network of military pacts on the entire East Asian periphery of mainland China.[28] In May 1957, the Americans installed on Taiwan Matador missiles capable of carrying tactical nuclear weapons against the mainland. By 1959, the United States had nuclear-armed forces operating from bases in Korea, Japan and Okinawa, all targeted at the PRC.[29] These security arrangements made under the guidance of policies dubbed by some critics as 'pactomania'[30] underwent only minor changes in the 1960s. If anything, the direct military involvement of the United States in Vietnam only reinforced these arrangements on the PRC's perimeters. The United States 'starting from the idea of damming up communism, gave itself as a prime objective, in a manner that was almost obsessive, the responsibility of preventing an accession to power of communist parties'.[31] It is therefore not unnatural that the PRC had consistently maintained in the 1950s and the 1960s that the main thrust of its foreign policy was to break the 'American military encirclement of China'.

American hegemony and omnipotence in the international system in the 1950s and the 1960s enabled the United States to deny, if not dictate, the China policies of its allies which were deemed to contradict the American policy of isolating the PRC to the maximum extent possible. There was virtually an extraterritorial reach of American control over its allies in Western Europe and elsewhere on matters concerning their China policies. In September 1952, the United States successfully introduced the so-called 'China differential' into the embargo lists imposed on export of strategic items to Communist countries. The China Committee (ChinCom) was established within the Paris Coordinating Committee for Exports of Strategic Materials (CoCom, consisting of 13 NATO countries and Japan) to monitor this embargo, which was acknowledged to be much more severe than that imposed on the Soviet Union and its Eastern European allies.[32] The so-called 'China differential' was unilaterally dropped only in 1957 first by Great Britain (followed by France and West Germany) against the wishes of the United States.[33]

As late as 1964, even after French recognition of the PRC, America's European allies still had very limited political leverage *vis-à-vis* the United

States in their China policies. While confidential bilateral talks between the PRC and West Germany about a trade agreement were going on in Berlin, Chancellor Erhard, on his official visit to the United States, had to go out of his way to assure the American public and the world that West Germany had no intention to recognise the PRC, nor had it any intention to conclude any official trade agreement with the PRC.[34]

> The American pressure against normalisation [of relations between the PRC and Western European countries] was much too great to permit them [Western European countries] to follow France. The majority of them, in fact, continued to support Washington in its Asian policy and in its policy of keeping China out of the United Nations.[35]

Canada, on the other hand, remained 'a reluctant adversary' of the PRC until 1970.[36] For similar reasons, Australia and New Zealand did not recognise the PRC until December 1972.[37] Nixon candidly admitted in 1973 that the estrangement between the United States and the PRC 'had global ramifications that went far beyond our [US–China] bilateral relationship'.[38]

Japan was another classical example. Throughout the 1950s and the 1960s, Japanese policy towards the PRC was fashioned under the shadow of American China policy. It was under explicit American pressure that the Yoshida government signed a peace treaty with Taiwan on 18 April 1952, recognising Taipei as the legitimate government of China.[39] Japan was also compelled to join the CoCom and the ChinCom in 1952, thus participating in strategic embargo against the PRC.[40] By and large, the Liberal-Democratic Party (LDP) had to and did adopt an official China policy posture consistent with the United States' position in the Sino–American conflict. In spite of traditional cultural and economic ties and the desirability of the China market for Japan's economic recovery, only private and unofficial trade was permitted to go on between Japan and the PRC. From 1952 to 1958, four private trade accords with Japanese government blessings were signed between Japan and the PRC.[41] Both the Japanese government and the LDP insisted that there was a 'separation of politics and economics'[42] in their trade policy towards China and that such trade did not signify any political and diplomatic recognition of the PRC. Sino–Japanese trade increased only dramatically in the mid-1960s when the Japanese foreign policy became more imaginative and assertive. Japan, however, continued to follow the Americans in their non-recognition of the PRC and in their opposition to seating the PRC at the United Nations. In 1971, Japan was the only major power to co-sponsor the ill-fated

American motion which proposed that a two-thirds majority be required to expel Taiwan.[43] 'The United States policy aimed at isolating the PRC', as was argued in a recent study of Sino–Japanese relations, 'was particularly important during the Korean War, but continued well into the late sixties and remained an important, if not the most important, factor in many Japanese policy decisions concerning the PRC.'[44] The natural consequence was that the anomalous pattern of interactions between Japan and the PRC in those two decades was 'characterised by a mixture of diplomatic, ideological, and strategic conflicts and economic and cultural cooperation'.[45]

The American policy of isolating the PRC had its bitter manifestations at the United Nations.[46] The hegemonic position of the United States at the United Nations enabled the Americans to manipulate what is arguably the greatest anomaly in the history of the UN; namely, the exclusion from this global organisation of the PRC with around one-fourth of the world's population. Denying the PRC the status and prestige associated with membership of international society had dire consequences for post-war international society as a whole. This, and the implications of excluding the PRC from multilateral diplomacy, will be discussed shortly. Suffice it here to note that from 1951 to 1960, the United States evoked the UN decision to denounce the PRC's 'aggression' in Korea to block any efforts to bring into discussion the seating of the PRC at the United Nations. In 1961, faced with a diminishing majority and its declining dominance at the United Nations, the United States had to resort to the rules of procedure at the United Nations to block the PRC's entry. At the sixteenth session of the UN General Assembly, it engineered a resolution to the effect that the restoration of the PRC's representation was an 'important question' requiring a two-thirds majority vote for a decision under Article 18 (2) of the Charter. In the early 1960s, President Kennedy even went out of his way to pledge secretly to Chiang Kai-shek in Taiwan that the United States would use its veto at the UN Security Council to keep Beijing out of the United Nations.[47] It is not without good reason that China proclaimed that the restoration of the PRC's legitimate seat at the United Nations in 1971 signalled the 'ultimate bankruptcy of the American policy of isolating China in, and excluding China from, international society'.[48]

There may be different interpretations as to the success or failure of the US China policy in the 1950s and the 1960s. It is indisputable, however, that the American China policy and its global ramifications were largely responsible for the PRC's relative exclusion from the world community, and its separation especially from the West. In Raymond Aron's words, the United States had simply 'quarantined Red China'.[49] It is small wonder that 'containment without isolation' should be proposed as a major step in liberalising the American China policy in the mid-1960s.[50] Richard Nixon's voice in *Foreign Affairs* in 1967 that China should no longer be treated as a pariah was almost a solo among the American political leaders at the time, and was not taken seriously until two years after when he became the US president in 1969.[51] It is Nixon who acknowledged that China lived 'in angry isolation'[52] 'partly due to its own attitude and preoccupation with internal problems, and *partly to the policies of the outside world, most importantly by the United States*'.[53] China's isolation, if any, was more of an intended result of particular American policies than of China's own choice.

The Soviet Union and the China anomaly

The problem of the PRC's position in international society was further compounded by Sino–Soviet relations. The Sino–Soviet Friendship, Alliance and Mutual Assistance Treaty of February 1950 formalised a relationship characterised by Lowell Dittmer as 'socialist dependency' of China upon the Soviet Union.[54] Equally importantly, the Sino–Soviet alliance treaty gave China a sense of belonging to the community of socialist countries. Less than a decade later, however, increasingly acrimonious polemics between the CCP and the CPSU (the Communist Party of the Soviet Union) was brought into the open. As Dittmer observed, 'China's sense of having its identity securely anchored in the socialist community and value system had become unhinged.' 'The seeds for this alienation', Dittmer argued, 'were sown in the famous "secret speech" Khrushchev delivered to the Twentieth CPSU Congress in February 1956.'[55]

In the late 1950s, the CCP's departure from the Soviet developmental model and Beijing's deviation from Moscow's foreign policy line were clearly pronounced. Both the Bucharest Conference of World Communist Parties in 1960 and the Moscow talks between Deng Xiaoping and Suslov in 1963 did not see any serious efforts by either the CCP or the CPSU for compromise and reconciliation. Rather, they represented two points of no return in the relationship between the CCP and the CPSU.[56] On 16 July 1960, Khrushchev suddenly announced that the Soviet government was to unilaterally scrap 600 inter-governmental contracts with China and was to withdraw all Soviet experts working in China within one and half months.[57] In September 1963, *People's Daily* and *Red Flag* jointly published an editorial, 'The Origin and Development of the Differences between the Leadership of the CPSU and Ourselves – Comment on the Open Letter of Central Committee of the CPSU'.[58] The polemics between the CCP and the CPSU exploded into open and direct attack on each other. From

Isolation or Alienation? 27

September 1963 to July 1964, the CCP published nine commentaries on its differences with the CPSU on a broad range of ideological controversies.

Repeated attempts were made by the CPSU to ostracise the CCP from the international Communist movement, while the relationship between China and the Soviet Union changed from qualified friendship to tempered hostility.[59] Those efforts and the uncompromising position held by the CCP gradually put the CCP into an ideologically isolated position in that movement. Further, the seemingly inter-party ideological controversies quickly soured the inter-state relations. The sudden and unheralded withdrawal of Soviet experts and contracts in 1960 was but an expression of the overspill of ideological controversies into the bilateral relations between the states. Sino–Soviet trade also plunged sharply after 1963. Given the Soviet predominance in Eastern Europe, it was only natural that the relations between the PRC and the Soviet client states there deteriorated rapidly. China's trade with Eastern Europe dwindled.

If the American China policies predetermined by the Sino–American ideological confrontation were largely responsible for the PRC's relative isolation from the non-Communist world, the Sino–Soviet polemics which gradually resulted in the ideological isolation of the CCP in the international Communist movement certainly estranged the PRC from most socialist bloc countries. By the beginning of the Cultural Revolution in 1966, when extreme radicalism prevailed in the domestic politics of China and Chinese foreign policy was at its most militant, the PRC only had nominal relations with the Soviet Union and its client states in Eastern Europe. Its membership in the socialist camp was put into serious question. In the early 1970s the Chinese leadership would claim that the socialist camp no longer existed and the two camps division of the existing international system was replaced by the three worlds composition.

Modifying the China anomaly

Even if it could be conceded that there was relative isolation of the PRC from the two blocs dominated by two superpowers, that isolation should not be overemphasised. Whatever merits the relegation of the PRC to isolation may have, it fails to take full account of, or purposely ignores, the evidence that the PRC had developed, as the circumstances allowed, substantial and sustained relations, political and diplomatic as well as economic and commercial, with members of international society. Allen Whiting argued in the late 1980s that

> China's rapidly expanding relations with European, African and Asian countries [in the 1950s and the 1960s] obviated much of the substantive,

if not the symbolic, deprivation of remaining outside of the United Nations. Expanded foreign trade provided access to European and Japanese technology, diluting the impact of the American embargo.[60]

The PRC also participated in the construction of international order in Asia and contributed to shaping strategic relations of the global international system. This is all the more significant, for they were achieved in spite of the American policy of isolating the PRC in the international community and in spite of the Sino–Soviet ideological estrangement. This can best be seen at least in the following aspects.

First, let us look afresh at the chart of the PRC's international trade. It is true that self reliance, not inter-dependence, was characteristic of the Chinese economy in the two decades under consideration. The PRC's foreign trade played a role not as a leading but as a balancing sector of the economy. In quantitative terms, both the volume and the value of the PRC's foreign trade constituted only a small per centage of the national economy. The Chinese economy was essentially self-sufficient in nature. It is also true that the Soviet Union and the Eastern-bloc countries were dominant in the PRC's foreign trade during most of the 1950s. The PRC in its first three years (1949–52) markedly reorientated its direction of foreign trade. For example, in 1952, its imports from the non-Communist countries fell to 20.6 per cent, and exports to them, to 33.3 per cent of its total foreign trade value.[61]

Nevertheless, this is too narrow a reading of the evidence. One may ask to what significant extent inter-dependence as we understand it today characterised economic relations between the industrialised world and the developing countries at the time. One may indeed question the possibility and feasibility of foreign trade playing a role as the leading sector of such a continental, underdeveloped and traditional economy as the PRC had inherited. One may also argue that in qualitative terms, the small per centage of PRC's imports did supply the PRC with much-needed capital goods, which gradually increased the PRC's capacity to export, and accordingly also import. Finally, the reorientation of the PRC's direction of foreign trade was at least as much Beijing's choice as the result of the *force majeure* at work at the height of the Cold War.

A wider reading of the evidence reveals a different picture. In 1952, the value of the PRC's exports had surpassed that of China's exports just before the Second World War.[62] By 1954–55, the PRC's imports and exports surpassed China's pre-Communist peak levels in 1928 and 1929 in terms of absolute value.[63] The value of the PRC's foreign trade grew rapidly and almost without interruption from 1950 to 1959. Between 1952 and 1959, its imports and exports more than doubled.[64] In 1959, its foreign trade 'grew much more rapidly than total world trade, trade of all underdeveloped countries, or trade of all Asian countries as a group'.[65] Of particular significance is the fact that with the gradual easing of trade embargoes after the Korean armistice, the PRC's trade with the West increased almost continuously up to the natural-disaster-ridden year of 1960. Imports from non-Communist Europe quadrupled between 1953 and 1958, the year in which more than 20 per cent of PRC imports were from Western Europe.[66] It must be remembered that the PRC did not, and could not, have full diplomatic relations with most of its trading partners in Western Europe. Nor did the PRC have even a semi-official resident trade mission in many of those countries. Viewed against this background, the implications of such a development are more telling.

As Sino–Soviet relations deteriorated in the 1960s, the PRC initiated another sharp reorientation of its foreign trade. Already in 1963, 66.5 per cent of the PRC's imports were from non-Communist states and 54.9 per cent of its exports were taken by those countries. In comparison, in 1954, the respective figures were 17.4 per cent for imports and 27.2 per cent for exports.[67] In 1965, Japan replaced the Soviet Union as PRC's leading trading partner. In 1969, the PRC's trade with the capitalist economies in the West rose to 75 per cent from 37 per cent in 1955.[68]

More important in the context of our concern here is probably the geographical spread the of PRC's foreign trade in the two decades under discussion. The two radical reorientations of the PRC's foreign trade constitute only one aspect. The other aspect is that the PRC traded with 70 or so countries and regions in all continents – Asia, Africa, America, Europe and Oceania.[69] It had cultivated economic relations with both Communist and non-Communist countries and with both industrialised and developing nations. Given the nature of the state monopoly of foreign trade, the PRC's foreign economic policy can hardly be qualified as 'isolationist'. Any claim of the PRC's 'isolation' has to be modified by this evidence.

Second, the Euro-centric or West-centric view of the international system tends to misrepresent the fact that, over the two decades in question, the PRC had developed extensive links, political as well as economic, with countries of the Afro-Asian world. This fact (in addition to the fact that the PRC had relations with socialist-bloc countries) contradicts the idea of the relegation of the PRC to isolation. Even if there was a degree of validity in the claim that the PRC was diplomatically isolated from the West, this 'isolation' should not be described as PRC's isolation *in toto* from international society as a whole. Mao's identification of an 'intermediate zone', which included most of Asia and decolonised Africa, directed the main thrust of Chinese foreign policy to this area in the late 1950s and the 1960s. Development of the widest possible and most sustainable relations of all kinds with these countries was precisely the PRC's strategy, in order to counter the American policy of isolating China. Credit must be given to the PRC's claim for the success of such a strategy when, with the overwhelming support of Third World countries, it was seated in both the General Assembly and the Security Council of the United Nations in 1971.

From 1949 to 1955, only 24 countries established full diplomatic relations with the PRC.[70] The Bandung Conference in April 1955 provided the PRC with a much-needed opportunity to get in touch with leaders of Afro-Asian countries. It is largely owing to the personal initiatives taken by Zhou Enlai at the Bandung Conference that a breakthrough was made. Zhou Enlai's talks with Nasser, the Egyptian Prime Minister, resulted eventually in the establishment of diplomatic relations between the two countries in May 1956. Egypt became the first African and Arab country to recognise the PRC.[71] It was followed in the next three years by Yemen, Morocco, Algeria, and the Sudan in Africa, and by Syria, Ceylon, Cambodia and Iraq in Asia. The decolonisation process of sub-Saharan Africa started in the late fifties offered the PRC further diplomatic leverage. The PRC quickly seized the initiative to declare its full support of those independence movements. It also accorded swift recognition to most newly independent countries and entered into negotiations for establishing diplomatic relations. Starting with Guinea in October 1959, 12 newly independent sub-Saharan African states had established diplomatic relations with the PRC by 1965. The official account of the PRC's diplomatic history hailed the decade from 1956 to 1965 as seeing the 'second upsurge in the establishment of diplomatic relations' between the PRC and other countries.[72] In contrast, between 1955 and 1970, no other country in the capitalist West, with the exception of France which established diplomatic relations with the PRC on 27 January 1964, was added to the list of 52 countries which had diplomatic relations with the PRC in 1970. Of the 52, more than 30 were Afro-Asian countries, whereas Cuba was the only Latin American country. The PRC had thus successfully exploited what Hedley Bull called 'the revolt against the West' in the decolonisation period to expand its links with new members of international society.[73]

There are two other equally significant aspects of the PRC's sustained and extensive relations with the Afro-Asian world: namely, the PRC's involvement with the national liberation movements particularly in Africa, and its foreign aid programme to Asian and African countries. The PRC not only offered moral support to the national liberation movements in, for example, Angola, Mozambique, Zimbabwe and South Africa; it also provided military aid and the training of military officers to these movements.[74] The PRC officially launched its foreign aid programme as early as 1953. From 1953 to 1965, its aid commitments to Afro-Asian countries (excluding North Korea, North Vietnam and Mongolia) were $815 million.[75] By the beginning of 1965, 19 non-Communist Afro-Asian countries had received aid from the PRC, ranging from Afghanistan to Zaïre.[76]

Third, even with its legitimacy and full membership in international society temporarily denied by the United States and its allies, the PRC's participation in the construction of the international order and its contribution to the changing regional balance of power and global strategic relations were undeniable. It would not be too difficult to argue that such events as the Sino–Soviet alliance, the Korean War and consequent Sino–American confrontation, and the Sino–Soviet split had dictated changes in the foreign policy and international strategy not only of China but also of other leading powers in the international system. By the same token, they had helped shape the post-war international system in general and the international strategic milieu in particular. At a lower level, even the PRC's exclusion from the UN did not make it possible to exclude it from international conferences on regional issues. The PRC, together with Great Britain, France, the United States and the Soviet Union, was invited to two Geneva conferences, one in 1954 on Indo-China and the other in 1962 on Laos. It has been well acknowledged that the PRC's conciliatory attitude at the Geneva Conference of 1954 and its success in persuading Ho Chi-minh and Pham Van Dong to accept conditions less favourable to North Vietnam than they had expected were indispensable to the final conclusion of the Geneva agreements on Indo-China.[77] The strategic breakthrough in Sino–American relations in 1971–72 was also attributable to the American desire to involve the PRC positively in ending the Vietnam War.

More subtly, perhaps, the Korean War armistice commission at Panmunjom, the two Geneva Conferences, and the Sino–American ambassadorial talks from 1955 onwards first at Geneva and then at Warsaw kept in existence diplomatic contacts between the PRC and the United States, the hegemon of the international system at the time. These diplomatic dialogues contributed to the effective management of the two Taiwan Strait crises by both the United States and the PRC. Equally, they played a positive role in preventing the two sides from engaging in direct military confrontation in the Vietnam War. They thus helped produce 'the establishment and relative stabilisation of a balance of power system in the Far East'.[78]

WAS THERE ISOLATIONISM IN CHINESE FOREIGN POLICY?

Another conventional proposition, though less convincing and less popular, was that there was isolationism in Chinese foreign policy. Such isolationism, it was claimed, was mostly responsible for the PRC's anomalous position in international society. Most manifestly, the Chinese revolutionary isolationist foreign policy was seen in the following aspects. First, the PRC pursued a confrontational approach to its international relations, particularly in the 1960s, opposing both the United States and the Soviet Union, the two dominant powers in the international system. The 1960s also witnessed periodical outbursts in the PRC's denunciation of the United Nations.[79] Second, the PRC deliberately fostered a strategy of self-reliance in its economic development, which posited that the nation's interest would be best served and promoted by minimal dependence on international economy. By implication, the PRC would not have interactions with international economy more than was absolutely necessary for its survival. Third, the PRC purposely and effectively closed its door to the outside world and cut off its cultural ties and other institutional links with most Western countries. Fourth, it developed an independent strategic thinking. This isolationism, it was further contended, was imbedded in Mao's ideology. It follows logically that China after Mao witnessed either 'the end of isolation' or a trend 'towards the end of isolationism'. Historical analogy was also frequently used to substantiate this claim. Communist China had inherited the Middle Kingdom syndrome from Imperial China. The only difference, it was claimed, was that Communist China did not see itself as the self-proclaimed centre of the world *civilisation* but the epicentre of the world *revolution*.[80]

What isolationism?

The first problem with the claim of isolationism in Chinese foreign policy is that those who have made such a claim are 'imprecise in their terminology', as in many other historical studies.[81] Those who have made the claim have never bothered to define what isolationism in the Chinese context really means. That leads to confusion and misunderstanding. Isolationism, in the studies of international relations, generally refers to 'the policy of non-involvement in the affairs of other nations by the abstention or withdrawal of a nation from international agreements, treaties and commitments' (*Encyclopaedia Britannica*). That policy may result either from a nation's geographic insularity, or from its preoccupation with domestic affairs, or from its preference. It is further stipulated that isolationism is a policy chosen by a nation which believes that such a policy would serve its best interest. *Fortress Britannica* and the *Fortress Americana* refer respectively to the 'splendid isolation from its position of superiority' by Great Britain from the Continent in the nineteenth century,[82] and to the traditional American policy in international affairs outside the Northern Hemisphere up to the Second World War. They are two prime, classical examples of isolationism.[83]

Isolationism as such, it can be argued persuasively, had never been a chosen policy of the PRC in international relations in the 1950s and the 1960s. Arguably, the exception should be made of the two years from late 1966 to late 1968 when domestic turmoil during the peak of the Cultural Revolution required next to total preoccupation of the CCP with China's internal affairs. Evidence is otherwise at best scanty that the PRC chose initially to isolate itself from the international community. For the government of the newly established PRC, to gain international acceptance and full legitimacy in international society demanded no less than a vigorous and assertive foreign policy in the face of the formidable circumstances of the bipolarisation of the world in the Cold War, the American policy of non-recognition of the PRC, and the existence of a rival Kuomintang government in Taiwan, which was still widely recognised and still occupied China's seat at the United Nations. For such a new regime as the PRC, isolationism was never, by any stretch of the imagination, even an option in its policy in world politics.

The historical analogy between Communist China and Imperial China, on the other hand, was over-stretched. More significantly, it missed out the crucial point of the internationalist outlook of the Communist ideology of a world Revolution. The Chinese revolution, the CCP consistently held, constituted one part of the world revolution. The Chinese Revolution aimed to create, in Mao's words, 'conditions in which classes, state power and political parties will die out naturally and mankind will enter the realm of Great Harmony'.[84] The CCP also professed an international proletarian solidarity. Unlike the previous empires in Chinese history, therefore, the PRC did not try to seclude itself from the outside world. On the contrary, from the very first day, it was trying to reach out to the world and to other members of the international community. In a simple comparison, the Chinese Communists, when coming to power in 1949, were probably the most outlooking and internationally-minded among all the ruling elites in Chinese history.

Mao Zedong and initiation of the foreign policy of the PRC

Michael Hunt has relegated Mao Zedong to the cosmopolitan tradition in China's foreign relations.[85] Indeed, it is in the spirit of that tradition that Mao set the course of New China's foreign policy even before the complete military victory of the People's Liberation Army on the mainland.

On 19 January 1949, in a document entitled 'The CCP's Central Committee's Instructions on How to Conduct Foreign Affairs', Mao personally added that the newly established People's Republic would not recognise any embassy, legation or consulate of any capitalist countries recognised by the KMT government until New China negotiated with those countries for the establishment of diplomatic relations. Accordingly, diplomatic personnel from those countries would only be treated as foreign residents in China. In March, Mao further elaborated another important foreign policy of New China – that is, that New China should eliminate all prerogatives and influences of imperialist countries in China *before* establishing diplomatic relations with them.[86] In June, while a CCP delegation headed by Liu Shaoqi was making a secret visit to Moscow,[87] Mao declared in a dramatic fashion that New China was to 'lean to one side'. These three policy decisions were later dubbed as 'start anew', 'put our house in order before inviting the guests', and 'lean to one side'. Their purpose was to have 'a clean break with the diplomacy of semi-colonial Old China' and to safeguard 'the independence and sovereignty of New China'.[88] Such foreign policies are certainly more nationalist than 'isolationist'. The crux of these policies was that New China and the Chinese Communists would insist on establishing diplomatic relations on their own terms, especially with the capitalist West and 'imperialist' countries.

As early as 28 April 1949, Mao personally instructed Deng Xiaoping, Chen Yi and Liu Bochen, whose forces had now occupied the Nationalist capital Nanjing, that 'if the United States and Great Britain sever their [diplomatic] relations with the KMT, we could consider establishing diplomatic relations with them'.[89] In June 1949, four months before Mao Zedong declared the establishment of the PRC, the winning Chinese Communists already publicly expressed their desire and willingness 'to discuss with any foreign government the establishment of diplomatic relations' and to 'have friendly co-operation with the people of all countries and to resume and expand international trade in order to develop production and promote economic prosperity'.[90] It is often purposely neglected that even in his 'lean-to-one-side' speech, Mao expressed Communist China's willingness to 'do business' with the United States, Britain and other capitalist countries.[91]

In September, on the eve of the birth of the PRC, the Chinese People's Political Consultative Conference at Beijing adopted a key document entitled 'The Common Programme'. Included in it were several provisions concerning the foreign policy of New China which are of significance to our discussion. It was publicly stated in 'The Common Programme' that,

Isolation or Alienation? 35

On the basis of equality, reciprocity and mutual respect of sovereignty and territorial integrity, the Central Government of the People's Republic of China is willing to negotiate for establishing diplomatic relations with all foreign countries which have severed their relations with the KMT reactionaries and have adopted a friendly attitude towards the People's Republic of China.[92]

It was further declared that 'the People's Republic of China is willing, on the basis of equality and mutual benefit, to restore and develop commercial and trade relations with *all* foreign governments and peoples'.[93] Most important of all, Mao Zedong, in his capacity as Chairman of the Central Government of the People's Republic of China, declared on 1 October 1949 on the rostrum of Tiananmen that

this government is the sole legitimate government representing all peoples of the People's Republic of China. This government is willing to establish diplomatic relations with governments of all foreign countries which abide by the principles of equality, reciprocity and mutual respect of sovereignty and territorial integrity.[94]

It is clear from these statements that the PRC had a two-pronged policy regarding its relations with foreign countries. On the one hand, while insisting on the precondition that any state wishing to establish diplomatic relations with the PRC must withdraw its recognition of the KMT government, the PRC was eager to gain international recognition by entering into normal diplomatic relations with members of the international community. As revealed recently, even the lean-to-one-side policy, Mao himself asserted, was to 'help compel [the capitalist] countries to recognise China unconditionally and help [us] to abrogate old treaties and sign new agreements'.[95] On the other hand, fully aware of the complications of recognition in a bipolarised world of a full-scale Cold War, the PRC was ready and willing, pending normal diplomatic relations, to have commercial and trade relations with countries all over the world. Mao, on his way to Moscow on 22 December 1949, explicitly cabled his instruction to Beijing that,

In preparing a trade agreement with the Soviet Union, we must take the whole situation into account and plan accordingly. Of course, the Soviet Union is the most important partner. But we should also prepare ourselves to do business with Poland, Czechoslovakia, Germany, *Britain, Japan and the United States*. We should have a general idea about the business scope and the volume of trade [with those countries].[96]

New China's aspiration to be accepted by international society was further expressed in Zhou Enlai's repeated calls for the United Nations to accept the emissaries sent by the PRC to replace the KMT representatives. Three times in two months from mid-November 1949 to mid-January 1950, Zhou Enlai, in his capacity as Premier and Foreign Minister of the newly founded PRC, sent telegrams to Secretary-General Trygve Lie and the United Nations at Lake Success, demanding the immediate ouster of the KMT delegation from the world organisation and its subsidiaries.[97] At the same time, the government of the PRC also cabled other international organisations, including the IMF, the World Health Organisation (WHO), the International Labour Organisation (ILO), the United Nations Educational, Scientific and Cultural Organisation (UNESCO) and the United Nations Food and Agriculture Organisation (FAO), demanding the acceptance of the PRC representation. The argument was that since the KMT government had lost its legitimacy in law as well in fact to represent the Chinese people, the United Nations should immediately expel the KMT representative and accept the PRC ambassador.[98]

These foreign policy initiatives were not responded to positively by members of international society dominated by the United States, most of whom remained at least ambivalent about the emergence of Communist China. One prevailing argument against recognising the PRC at the time was the assumption that the new regime would not fulfil its international obligations even if it was accorded international recognition. Furthermore, the Sino–Soviet Alliance and the PRC's relations with other socialist countries, interpreted through the mirror of the Cold War politics, did not necessarily signal the PRC's willingness to conduct state-to-state relations on principles commonly accepted by international society as a whole. However, the assumption that recognition of the PRC would not make it fully accountable on the international scene had never been put to test. By denying the legitimacy of the PRC in international society on this assumption, the United States and its allies were courting the unaccountability of the PRC for its actions in that society.

From Geneva to Bandung

What is revealing regarding China's accountability in the international system is the PRC's participation in the Geneva Conferences on Korea and Indo-China in 1954 and the Bandung Conference in 1955. In both cases, the PRC did not shun any international responsibilities incurred but sought to be actively involved in regional and world affairs. China's diplomacy at both international conferences disputes the claims of isolationism in Chinese foreign policy.

As mentioned earlier, the success of the Geneva Conference on Indo-China in 1954 was at least partly attributable to China's conciliatory attitude.[99] The significance of China's participation in the Geneva Conference, however, lies elsewhere. On the one hand, it was the first *de facto*, if not *de jure*, recognition of the PRC by the United States and its allies as a legitimate player in world politics. It also accorded, probably unwittingly, great power status to the PRC. Furthermore, it was an acknowledgement that the PRC was indispensable in the solution of the regional conflicts around its periphery, an acknowledgement that was to be more explicitly and emphatically made later by the United States in disentangling itself from the Vietnam War. On the other hand, if, as the official Chinese diplomatic history records with approbation, the PRC's attendance at the 1954 Geneva Conference was the first international recognition of the PRC as a great power,[100] then, it was the first time that the PRC enjoyed the privilege and the glory of being a great power, however illusional it might be, in the international system. Equally importantly, such a status and privilege carried with it the heavy burden of responsibility bestowed upon great powers to the international system. The Geneva Conference can be regarded as the very beginning of the PRC's basic understanding of this point. Chinese diplomacy at the conference supports this argument.

The attendance and the policies of the PRC at the Bandung Conference of 1955 is altogether a different story. It was at Bandung that the PRC, jointly with India, sponsored the adoption of the so-called five principles of peaceful coexistence. It was at Bandung that the PRC reached out to Africa, as in the case of Sino–Egyptian relations. It was also at Bandung that Zhou Enlai proposed direct contact between the PRC and the United States to reduce regional tensions.[101] Such a proposal bore fruit, in spite of the ongoing hostility between the two countries, when Sino–American ambassadorial talks opened in Geneva in August 1955.[102] The vaguely defined 'spirit of Bandung' as shown in the PRC's diplomatic initiative is anything but isolationism.

There is more than a symbolic significance in Chinese diplomacy at Bandung. Bandung signalled the formation of what James Mayall called 'a revisionist alliance' of the Afro-Asian world, the underlying collective purpose of which was to 'restructure international society'.[103] It is also the beginning of China's alignment with this 'revisionist alliance' in challenging the existing international order. China's Third World policy in later years had its origin in this alignment. The PRC's experience at both Geneva and Bandung was valuable for its future international relations not because of its participation *per se*, but because through its involvement the PRC had acquired two different perspectives of the international system: the top-dog perspective in Geneva, and the under-dog perspective in Bandung.

Certainly, the allegation that after the Bandung Conference China sought 'to become the leader of a new international of the underprivileged' and asserted 'its claim to a leading world role outside the UN and in defiance of the UN's principal members'[104] was at odds with the claim that China pursued isolationism in its international relations. Indeed, with the radicalisation of the PRC's domestic politics in the late 1950s and the 1960s, China as a revolutionary power launched a fierce attack on the existing international order presided over by the two superpowers. From the PRC's presence in Africa to its effective use of trade as a 'weapon' to develop and consolidate its relations with non-Communist Asian countries,[105] and from its support for militant neutralism to its revolutionary united front strategy against the 'dual adversary', the United States and the Soviet Union, we find more proofs of, to borrow Harold Hinton's words, 'China's turbulent quest' for its place in the international system than of an isolationist policy in its international relations.[106] The united front strategy, for example, was incompatible with an isolationist mentality, to say the least.[107] The alleged 'export of revolution' by China through its support of national liberation movements certainly contradicts the claim of an isolationist foreign policy.

Further, those who made the claim must be aware that the whole rationale of the American policy of containing China was that a Chinese expansionism existed. Communist China, it was contended, aimed at step-by-step domination of Asia and was dedicated to the promotion of Communism by violent revolution. In particular, the United States justified its involvement in Vietnam by repeatedly indicating that Vietnam was 'the testing ground for Chinese-inspired wars of national liberation and "Chinese expansionism"'.[108] Clearly, such an image of a revolutionary power reaching out to challenge the *status quo* of the existing international system does not fit in well with that of an isolationist China. The tensions between the two claims are all too obvious and irreconcilable. Expansionism simply cannot be squared with isolationism.

The claim of isolationism in Chinese foreign policy can be further disputed. Immediately prior to and in the wake of the Sino–American *rapprochement* in 1972, many Western countries and their American allies rushed to recognise and normalise their relations with China. China virtually embraced almost all of them. In the two years after 1972, full diplomatic relations were established between China and almost all industrialised countries, except, ironically, the United States.

Economic isolationism?

Even China's adoption of a self-reliance strategy in its economic development should not be readily taken as evidence of isolationism. As has been discussed earlier, the PRC's adoption of self-reliance in developing its economy was not entirely its own choice. The US-led trade embargo and the sudden withdrawal of Soviet specialists and technicians in 1960 are at least as responsible. For example, barter trade was adopted by the PRC early in the 1950s partly to avoid the complications of making settlements in American dollars in its foreign trade, which arose from the trade embargo imposed on the PRC by the United States.[109] Not until May 1971 did the United States relax its currency control and permit the PRC to use American dollars for international settlement.[110] One recent study on China's initial engagement with the capitalist international economy in the early 1950s detailed the difficulties of that relationship.[111]

China's foreign trade in the 1950s, as argued previously, saw a rapid growth in spite of the trade embargo imposed by the United States. According to Chinese statistics, exports from the PRC increased from $0.552 billion in 1950 to $2.261 billion in 1959, while imports to the PRC grew from $0.583 billion to $2.12 billion. The average annual growth rate of PRC's foreign trade in 1950–52 was 30.8 per cent, and from 1953 to 1957, 9.8 per cent.[112]

At the same time, China's trade with Western Europe increased from $161 million in 1950 to $651 million in 1959.[113] Sino–British trade, for example, increased substantially from 1949 to 1959, although there were frequent fluctuations (see Figure 2.1).

Still more important, it must be remembered that self-reliance, the Chinese always insisted, did not in any way rule out the participation of a foreign economy in the PRC's economic construction. External assistance was regarded as a necessary complement to the self-reliance strategy. In

Table 2.1 China's foreign trade, 1950–59 (in million US dollars)

	1950	1951	1952	1953	1954	1955	1956	1957	1958	1959
Exports	552	757	823	1 022	1 146	1 412	1 645	1 597	1 981	2 261
Imports	583	1 198	1 118	1 346	1 287	1 733	1 563	1 506	1 890	2 120
Total	1 135	1 955	1 941	2 368	2 433	3 145	3 208	3 103	3 871	4 381

Source: *Zhongguo Duiwai Jingji Maoyi Nianjian*, 1989, p. 299.

Figure 2.1 Sino–British trade, 1949–59

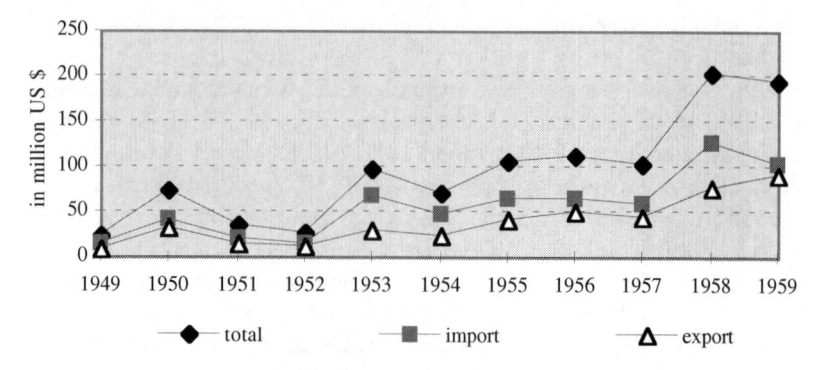

Source: Dong Zhikai, *Jishen Guoji Shichang de Jianxin Qibu* (A Difficult Start to Get into the International Market), p. 176.

Table 2.2 China's trade with Western Europe, 1960–66 (in million US dollars)

1960	1961	1962	1963	1964	1965	1966
640.4	339.2	337.4	364.5	452.0	697.5	866.0

Source: Kapur, *Distant Neighbours*, p. 62.

fact, this was the entire rationale behind the PRC's expanding trade with the West at the height of its self-reliance period in the 1960s. From 1960 to 1966, China traded with a total of 17 Western European countries, from Austria to West Germany (see Table 2.2).[114] In 1964, China's trade with non-Communist countries was such that the Economist Intelligence Unit in London sponsored a publication entitled *The Foreign Trade of Communist China: Its Impact on the Free World*.[115]

There is also foreign economic aid to take into account of. According to a study by Wolfgang Barkte in 1975, from 1956 when China's foreign economic aid programme was launched to 1973, China offered a total of $3384 million loans to more than 30 countries, half of which had been already used by the end of 1973. Of this total, 48.8 per cent went to Africa, 32 per cent, to Asia, 13.2 per cent to the Near/Middle East, 4.7 per cent to Latin America, and 1.3 per cent to Europe.[116]

This is certainly not to deny that there were restrictive practices in China's policy towards the international economy. For example, borrowing from the international capital markets was strictly prohibited. Neither is this to argue that China's interactions with many other economies were not minimal. It is questionable, however, whether there was a deliberate policy of economic isolationism in China's development strategy.

To conclude, a caution must be heeded. To argue that there was no isolationism in the PRC's foreign policy does not imply that some of its policies did not create circumstances in which the PRC found itself increasingly separated and isolated from the international community. Moreover, the argument by no means denies that relative isolation of the PRC from the West did exist.

In fact, the argument has raised rather than answered a series of key questions. What is the essence of this China anomaly, if it is not isolation? How, why and to what extent was the PRC's own foreign policy and domestic politics in the period responsible for its anomalous position in international society? The greatest drawback in describing China as isolation and isolationist is its failure to account for the reasons why such isolation was perceived to have presented such a challenge to the international order in the 1950s and the 1960s. In other words, what those claims have failed so conspicuously to account for are the following two questions: why should China have exerted such an impact on the development of the international system in its isolation period; and how and to what could this isolation be attributed? Even if isolation is descriptive in China's position, it is by no means interpretative. Moreover, those claims hinder rather than help our understanding of later changes of China's international relations since 1971. Isolation is a too convenient yet not altogether a convincing explanation of the anomaly of the PRC's position in international society. The other two aspects of this anomaly, confrontation and contention, have been left largely unexplained. In other words, isolation is at least an inaccurate, if not an entirely false, explanation of China's anomalous position in the society of states. The question then arises: if not isolation, then what?

CHINA'S ALIENATION FROM INTERNATIONAL SOCIETY

> Speaking generally, punishment hardens and numbs, it produces concentration, it sharpens the consciousness of alienation, it strengthens the power of resistance.
>
> *Friedrich Nietzsche*

Although scholars and students of international relations sometimes differ sharply in interpreting Chinese foreign policy in the 1950s and 1960s, they generally agree that the PRC's position in international society in the two decades under consideration is a great anomaly. Further, this anomaly is marked by the PRC's relative separation (or isolation, if one prefers) from the existing international society, by its confrontational approach to international relations, and by its contention in challenging as well as rejecting the prevailing international order. Isolation as a fact or as a policy, however, fails to either describe or explain this anomaly properly. China's relative isolation cannot be entirely attributed to its own policies. The mutual unacceptability between China and the prevailing international order was equally responsible for this anomaly.

If the China anomaly is not that of isolation, how can we then describe, and, more importantly, interpret, China's relative isolation from the West? If there was no isolationism as such in Chinese foreign policy, what would best account for the China anomaly and its persistence in international politics for 20-odd years? I would argue that China was not isolated, but *alienated* from international society. Isolation, if it existed, is but one expression of this alienation.

Alienation in international relations

'Alienation' is not an unfamiliar word in the discourse and studies of international relations. The late Hedley Bull asserted that the Third World 'is alienated from the Western states not simply because of the latter's lack of high-mindedness but because of their overwhelming power'.[117] A book jointly edited by two eminent international historians, Chihiro Hosoya and Ian Nish, is entitled *Anglo-Japanese Alienation, 1919–1952*. In his book *On Diplomacy*, James Der Derian devotes one whole chapter to the discussion of the demarcation of diplomacy by alienation between states.[118] He also contended that 'the existence of a diplomatic culture only becomes self-evident, and subject to inquiry, when the values and ideas of one society are estranged from another'.[119] Deon Geldenhuys discussed in his study of isolated states 'sporadic bouts of alienation' between allies and adversaries alike in international relations.[120] David Armstrong in his most recent study of revolution and world order argues specifically that 'the profoundly ambiguous, if not entirely paradoxical' relationship between a revolutionary state and international society indicates that the revolutionary state is 'alienated to some degree from the society within which it finds itself: the society of states'.[121] Other formidable thinkers on international relations, like Martin Wight and Raymond Aron, also touched on the concept of alienation.[122] The *Dictionnaire de la Terminologie du Droit International* offers a definition of alienation in international law as follows:

Terme designant pour un Etat le fait de renoncer à un droit, à une compétence, d'ordinaire en faveur d'un autre Etat ou d'une institution internationale. Terme employé surtout dans l'expression 'alienation territoriale' pour designer le fait pour un Etat de renoncer en faveur d'un autre Etat à sa souveraineté sur un territoire determiné.[123]

More frequently, of course, one reads of 'alienation' in newspaper reports on world affairs.

It would be a gross mistake to assume that familiar words are better understood. The fact is just the contrary. This familiarity, unfortunately, hinders, rather than helps, cognitive understanding of the term in its usage in studying international relations. Because of its rich origins, the definition of alienation is often fuzzy at best, if not vague. One may speak of economic alienation, or social alienation, or religious alienation, or psychological alienation or political alienation. Great minds such as Grotous, Rousseau, Hegel and Marx all offered formidable conceptualisation and theorisation of alienation related to their own theories and studies.[124] The precise meaning of the term differs and largely depends on the context. As a result, the near omnipotence of the term enables anyone to dip in and out of its multiple meanings to serve their purpose. The dire consequence is that very few students of international studies who have employed the term in their works have bothered to define 'alienation'. On the assumption that the term is familiar and therefore well understood and that the context conditions the interpretation, they have virtually left their readers at the mercy of the context and their own (mis)understanding of the word.

There is no attempt here to generalise and define what 'alienation' means precisely in the field of international studies. That amounts to attempting the impossible. Raymond Aron long ago issued his warning that 'this ambiguity in "international relations" is not to be imputed to the inadequacy of our concepts: it is an integral part of reality itself'.[125] The fuzzy edge of the definition of 'alienation' is part of that reality. What I shall attempt to do is to define what is meant by 'alienation' in this study, and further, what is meant by a state's 'alienation' from international society. We will confine our attention to this particular alienation.

Two basic meanings of 'alienation' suggested in its etymology and morphology are recorded in the second edition of the *Oxford English Dictionary* (OED). *Alienate* means, in an older sense, 'to transfer to the ownership of another'. It means, in a more modern sense, 'to make estranged, to estrange, or turn away the feelings or affections of any one'. 'Alienation' in the first sense has been widely used in international law. As indeed the quote above indicates, transference of some of its rights and territories by one state to another is referred to as alienation of its sovereignty. Alienation in such a sense, however, is not our concern here. In general, alienation in this study takes on the other basic meaning which the word most commonly conveys in political studies. Alienation means the state of otherness or apartness or the sense of being in a state of otherness or apartness.[126] To be more specific, alienation of one state or one group of states from another means that cordial relations between the two have been broken and friendly feelings towards each other have been turned into bitterness and hostility. By the same token, the two are becoming more and more unwelcome and averse to each other. Because of the feelings of alienness to each other, a perceptible distance or complete separation is purposely kept by one from the other in their mutual relations. Such alienation is not only naturally accompanied by greatly reduced contacts, but also more often leads to confrontation and conflicts between the two.

What is then meant by a state's alienation from international society? The present-day universal international society, as defined by Hedley Bull and Adam Watson, is

> a group of states (or, more generally, a group of independent political communities) which not merely form a system, in the sense that the behaviour of each is a necessary factor in the calculations of the others, but also have established by dialogue and consent common rules and institutions for the conduct of their relations, and recognise their common interest in maintaining these arrangements.[127]

It follows that alienation of a state from international society happens first when that state does not regard or is perceived not to regard as binding a set of common rules regulating relations between member states; second, when that state withdraws or is prevented from sharing in the working of common institutions; and third, when that state does not hold that it has any stake, or interests, as the others do, in maintaining the existing order within that society. By the same token, an alienated state tends to present challenges to commonly accepted values, rules and conventions that sustain the existence of international society. It inclines to develop hostility towards common international institutions. It is also likely to have a different perception of the nature of the prevailing international order and the justice administered by that order in regard in particular to itself. In international society, as in any other societies, the elusive perception of justice is bound up with the causes of alienation. In Armstrong's words, 'if a revolutionary state finds itself at odds with international society, a threat to order is a probable consequence'.[128] Alienation is therefore often accompanied by violent confrontations and conflicts.

Further, alienation may be an act or the result of an act. Alienation of a state may result from the actions of other member states, or from that state's chosen policies. In the former case, that state is alienated, in spite of itself, by and from other member states. In the latter case, that state alienates itself, either wittingly or unwittingly, from other member states. The two aspects are mutually reinforcing. The more a state is alienated from other members of the universal international society, the more it tends to alienate itself further from that society, and vice versa. It is also very often the case that alienation of a state results not from an intention of a policy, but from the interpretation by the said state of others' policy intentions.

It is only natural that a state's alienation from international society begins when it is or it feels as if it is being treated as a pariah. Such an alienation is then first and foremost characterised by mutual perception of alienness. The estranged state has a sense of not belonging and feels excluded, while the majority of member states regard the estranged one alien to rules and conventions sustaining the international order. Second and consequently, such alienation is marked by absence of cooperation leading to confrontation between the alienated and the others. Third, it finds its expression in the alienated state(s) challenging the existing institutions and prevailing international order. Tensions are usually the hallmarks of the relations between the alienated state(s) and other members of international society. In Raymond Aron's vivid characterisation, 'How does one live according to reason if the other, the alien, the foreigner whether remote or nearby may burst into one's world at any moment?'[129] Fourth, alienation is usually followed by a process of de-alienation, or reconciliation and accommodation, whereby the alienated returns to and is in turn accommodated and embraced by international society again. The process of de-alienation of a state in international society is mostly initiated and completed by and through changes in that state's domestic politics, or changes in the international system, or as is more often the case, changes in both.

The classical examples of such an alienation of great powers from international society in this century are the Soviet Union in the late 1910s and the 1920s, and Germany and Japan in the 1930s and the 1940s. Martin Shaw, in his most recent critique of the notion of international society, noted that discussions of international society have their 'favourable historical periods', but also 'rather noticeable absences'. He went on to observe that 'it is rather difficult, as even Bull himself acknowledges, to see Hitler's Germany and Stalin's Russia as bound by common norms of international society'.[130] In fact, they were not, precisely because they were powers alienated from international society. One common denominator underlying these three cases is the clear rejection of the prevailing international order by these alienated states, either from the perspective of a revolutionary power, as with the former Soviet Union, or from the perspective of dissatisfied, or revisionist, powers, in the case of Germany and Japan. The rejection was *in toto* and uncompromising. It was backed up by their fundamentally different conceptions of the world order. It was further accompanied by an attempt to modulate the world in their own images. The Soviet Russia tried it through a world socialist revolution in the interwar years; Germany, by a devastating and doomed war to conquer Europe and the world; whereas Japan struggled violently through its condemned failure to establish a 'Greater East Asian Co-prosperity Sphere', the last two during the Second World War.

The de-alienation process of these three powers was both violent and lengthy. In the case of the Soviet Union, arguably its accommodation into international society happened only after it explicitly gave up the notion of a world-wide socialist revolution and contented itself with 'socialism in one country', and in the wake of drastic changes in the international system in the 1930s.[131] The full integration of the former Soviet space into the global international society was made possible only after the collapse of the former Soviet Union in 1991. For Germany and Japan, an unprecedentedly destructive total war, which almost engulfed the whole world, had to be fought and won by the Allies to destroy German fascists and Japanese militarists. International order had to be rebuilt and the domestic political structures of both alienated states had to be thoroughly overhauled before they could be accepted back into international society.

The international system and China's alienation

Three brief observations are due here before we discuss fully the stages of China's gradual alienation from international society after 1949. All three observations are concerned with what I call 'systemic factors'. The first one discusses the 'prohibitive' nature of the international system in 1949 when the PRC was established. The second concerns itself with structural changes in the international system in later years, particularly the 'enlargement of international society through the creation of states'.[132] The third suggests effects of systemic exclusion of China from multilateral diplomacy.

First, the configuration of the international system in 1949 was, to say the least, not propitious in accommodating Communist China into international society. By 1949, political, ideological and strategic clashes between the two superpowers had been crystallised after two years of intense Cold War and the division of Europe. World politics was highly dichotomised. Immediately before the establishment of the PRC in October 1949 such events took place as the prolonged first Berlin Crisis, the creation of NATO, and the end of the American nuclear monopoly with the explosion of the first Soviet atom bomb. Such tensions between the rigidly divided world had probably pre-empted any possibility of New China as a Communist state to be accommodated into the American-dominated international society. Given the nature of the Chinese Revolution, the ideological constraints were too great to ignore for both China and the United States. The PRC, in other words, was caught in a systemic framework already created within which it had to make its choice. Indeed, the domination of the international system first by the United Sates and later by both the United States and the Soviet Union, and the system of states so structured, were one constant and most important, if not the most important, systemic factor in effecting and also sustaining PRC's 20-odd years' alienation from international society.

Second, it must be noted that in the 20 years of China's alienation from international society, the international system underwent some structural changes. Decolonisation was in full swing in the 1950s and the 1960s. A large number of new states emerged from ex-colonies of European powers, first in Asia and then in Africa. This extension of boundaries of international society is significant in several ways in looking at China's alienation from international society. First, it modified China's isolation from both superpower-dominated camps by creating space for China. The 'intermediate zone' as identified by Mao became the expanse where China could manoeuvre. Second, nationalism and anti-colonialism made it possible for Revolutionary China to find allies against the domination by the West. China cultivated that possibility diligently. China's alignment with the 'revisionist alliance' of Afro-Asian nations discussed previously is a good example, however loose the alignment may be. Curiously, these two aspects of structural change helped sustain China's confrontations with both superpowers, hence its alienation from international society. Third, and most significantly, it is such a structural change that eventually brought the PRC into the UN. By eroding the hegemony of the United States in the UN, the international society as embodied in that global organisation was made more accommodative. As the number of Asian and African states increased in the UN membership, the numbers game in the UN General Assembly was turned in favour of China, which led eventually to the admission of the PRC at its 26th General Assembly in 1971, and hence the beginning of accommodation of China into the global international society.

Finally, it must be argued that the total and systemic exclusion of China from multilateral diplomacy expressed in the denial of the PRC membership in the UN had double adverse effects on China's relationship with international society. On the one hand, the denial of the PRC's legitimacy by excluding it from the global international organisation and its affiliates undoubtedly reinforced the PRC's sense of being treated as a pariah in international society. On the other, by denying the PRC a place in the global multilateral diplomacy network, the international community also deprived itself of an effective means to mediate the PRC's estrangement.[133] The systemic exclusion of China from multilateral diplomacy, among other things, must be seen as the single most important factor in sustaining China's 20 years' alienation from international society. It is particularly deplorable that such a denial took place when multilateral diplomacy flourished in the post-war years, which gave more substance to both the notion and the existence of a global international society.

There are other inherent political and historical constraints for both the PRC and the United States in their foreign policy options. For one thing, it has been observed that in China's foreign relations, as in its domestic affairs, 'the past wields its power over the present'.[134] This is particularly true of New China in 1949. A 'profound sense of humiliation'[135] entertained by the Chinese after 100 years' sustained contact with the West after the Opium War in 1839 and the commitment of the Chinese Communist Revolution severely limited New China's foreign policy options. For another, the American involvement in the Chinese civil war supporting the KMT against the Chinese Communists, and the widespread frustration in the United States at the 'loss of China', hampered the Truman administration's efforts even to engage the emerging Communist regime in dialogue.

Five phases in China's alienation

This is, however, not to argue that the alienation of China from international society was predetermined by the systemic factors discussed above. Those factors, it must be admitted, did set up parameters and produce constraints from which it was difficult for China to escape in its interactions with the international system. Nevertheless, it is through a process of action and reaction between China and dominant members of the international system that China's alienation was taking place and was hardening. China's domestic politics also had its due impact on this process.

In retrospect, the PRC's estrangement from international society comprised five phases, each building upon another and reaching its climax in the mid-1960s. The initial period of the PRC's alienation was characterised by mutual suspicion and mistrust between the People's Republic and the United States, the predominant power in the international system. This estrangement had its global ramifications. For the Americans, Communist China could only 'lend itself to the aims of Soviet Russian imperialism and attempt to engage in aggression against China's neighbours'.[136] Two years before Mao's 'lean-to-one-side' speech, Washington, in leading an anti-Communist crusade in 1947, already assigned a prospective Communist China a place in world politics which was 'closely aligned politically, economically, and militarily with the USSR', firmly anchoring a Communist-led China in the United States' enemy camp.[137] Six months earlier, in announcing the so-called Truman Doctrine, Truman had declared that 'At this moment in world history nearly every nation must choose between alternative ways of life'.[138] That is to say, every nation must choose either to go with the American-led free world or to fall behind the Soviet 'Iron Curtain'. Mao's declaration of New China's lean-to-one-side policy in June 1949, therefore, merely fulfilled Truman's prophecy. In the zero-sum game of the Cold War, however, America's 'loss of China' could only be a net gain for the Soviet Union. The Sino–Soviet Friendship, Alliance and Mutual Assistance Treaty signed in Moscow in February 1950 was seen by the United States as a confirmation of the worst scenario it had envisaged. New China was not only under a 'foreign yoke' now.[139] It was also, in Dean Rusk's words, 'a Slavonic Manchukuo on a larger scale.'[140]

It is all too easy to see today that such a perception of Communist China is ideologically heavily tinted and distorted. In 1949, however, such a perception in ideological terms led the United States to taking measures to alienate the emerging new regime in Beijing from the international community. Even before Mao announced that New China would lean to one side, the United States had started to orchestrate a policy of non-recognition of Red China. The State Department in May 1949 had approached various foreign ministries of non-Communist countries all over the world to discourage them from according recognition to a prospective Chinese Communist government. Earlier in February 1949, Washington had suggested to London that the Cold War restraints governing Western trade with the Soviet Union and its satellites be extended to Chinese Communists. Within the framework of NATO, a policy of trade embargo against New China was in place by November 1949, which was to last more than 20 years. It is therefore not New China's lean-to-one-side policy and the Sino–Soviet Alliance Treaty which sealed off the possibility of any constructive relations with the United States and its Western allies, as some

American scholars sought to interpret. The fact is that they only provided convenient pretexts for the United States to implement, and impose on its allies, its policies of ostracising the new regime in Beijing politically and economically from the American-dominated international system. In the post-war contests between the two camps, the United States was 'moved by their almost instinctual anti-Communist reflexes, but also by the way the Cold War was developing' in making its policies towards Communist countries.[141] The trap of a cycle of rhetoric and response in the process of implementing the Truman Doctrine did not only restrict the Truman administration's flexibility in dealing with Moscow, as Geddis rightly argued.[142] In 1949, it also severely limited Truman's foreign policy options in dealing with Communist China.

For the Chinese Communists, the United States, in spite of its anti-colonial history and rhetoric, had participated, together with other European imperialist powers and Japan, in humiliating and exploiting China for a century. Like all other imperialist powers, therefore, the United States also stood for what the Chinese Communist Revolution was principally directed at: the imperialist domination of China. More than any other imperialist power, American imperialism was perceived as the mortal arch-enemy of the Chinese Communist Revolution, because of American policies of supporting Chiang Kai-shek and suppressing the CCP either by 'mediation' or by providing military and logistical aid to the KMT in the Chinese civil war and because of the possibility of American direct military intervention in the Chinese Revolution. In January 1949, Mao issued an instruction to his military commanders that, 'when making strategic plans, we have always taken into consideration the possibility of the direct American military occupation of some coastal cities to fight directly with us. Such consideration should not be discounted now.'[143]

The Chinese civil war, in Mao's words, was waged 'in reality by the United States' and 'a war in which the United States supplies the money and guns and Chiang Kai-shek supplies the men to fight for the United States and slaughter the Chinese people'.[144] The continual American military aid to the KMT even after the complete victory of the Chinese Communists on the mainland and the United States' refusal to accord any recognition, *de jure* or *de facto*, to the new regime in Beijing were seen as America's continued interference in China's internal affairs by other means. The relentless American anti-Communist stance in the Cold War world politics only helped to reinforce this interpretation. Mao warned in September 1949 that

> The imperialists and their running dogs, the Chinese reactionaries, will not resign themselves to defeat in this land of China. They will con-

tinue to gang up against the Chinese people in every possible way. ... Furthermore, if they still hanker after adventures, they will send some of their troops to invade and harass China's frontiers.[145]

Interestingly, a recent official history of China's diplomacy since 1949 justifies the PRC's lean-to-one-side policy not on the ground of the ideological homogeneity of Communism, but on the necessity of defending the newly born People's Republic. The paramount concern of the Communist leadership in China in 1949, it is claimed, was not China's ideological commitment to Communism nor to the Soviet Union, but the possible imminent, American-led armed intervention in the Chinese Revolution. This apprehension was largely drawn from the historical precedent of imperialist armed intervention in Soviet Russia in 1918–20 in the wake of the success of the October Revolution, because the imperialists – in particular, the American imperialists – 'would not resign to their defeat in the Chinese revolution'. It is forcefully stated that 'it is the possibility of an armed intervention in the Chinese revolution by imperialist powers that dictated the necessity [for the PRC] to unite with other socialist countries'.[146] As early as January 1949, several months before the PLA crossed the Yangtze River, Mao Zedong had already warned the CCP's politburo of possible American military intervention in occupying coastal cities. Throughout 1949, the possibility of an American military intervention in China loomed large in the CCP's decisions on its military strategy.[147] The historical irony here is that it is primarily the perceived imperialist hostility, principally the American hostility, towards the Chinese Communist Revolution that drove the Chinese Communists into alliance with the Soviet Union.

Incidents involving American diplomatic personnel and Western interests in China in this initial period were both the cause and the effect of the PRC's alienation.[148] In the eyes of the Americans, the detention and eventual expulsion of Angus Ward, the American Consul-General in Shenyang, was one example of 'calculated mistreatment of American diplomatic and consular personnel then remaining in China'[149] and was against the international conventions on diplomatic immunity. Interpreted in the framework of American legal culture, the forceful requisition of the American military barracks in Beijing, and the CCP's statement in 1947 that they refused to recognise any international agreement concluded by the KMT government after 1946 was tantamount to New China's repudiation of its international obligations. From the Chinese Communist point of view, all foreign diplomats accredited to the defeated KMT government were now reduced to the status of foreign residents in China, since New China did not recognise any of the diplomatic relations the KMT government had established.[150]

Angus Ward, then, was merely an American resident in China. The unilateral requisition of foreign military barracks in Beijing and Tianjin and confiscation of some Western economic interests were natural steps to eliminate the foreign privileges and influence in China. These incidents were frequently invoked later to justify the United States' non-recognition of the PRC, because the CCP had given 'no indication of their willingness to undertake the type of responsibilities which are required of international obligations which normally devolve upon a government'.[151] For the Chinese, however, those actions were taken to carry out their foreign policies of 'starting anew' and 'putting our house in order before inviting guests'. Further, just as Scalapino would argue in the 1970s, even if it was true that Chinese Communists gave no indication of their willingness to live up to minimal obligations implicit in recognition of the PRC, 'this question was largely untested when testing was possible'.[152]

The second phase in China's alienation was dominated by the Korean War. To the Chinese, the rolling-back of the North Korean Army across the 38th Parallel by American-led forces, the American decision to eliminate North Korea as a separate political entity, the talk about Pyongyang as the 'first Iron Curtain capital' to be liberated, and later General MacArthur's cry for 'no substitute for victory' – all were unmistakable indications that the worst scenario of imperialist armed intervention in the Chinese Revolution was unfolding. Truman's decision to send the Seventh Fleet to the Taiwan Strait was only a prelude to an American adventurist attempt to overthrow militarily the Communist government in Beijing. From America's perspective, 'all inspiration for the Korea action came from Moscow'.[153] The Chinese decision to intervene in the Korean War was 'against the interests of the Chinese people and on behalf of Russian colonial policy in Asia'.[154] The Korean conflict was then part of the so-called 'Kremlin's design for world domination', as Paul Nitze elucidated in NSC 68, through the destruction of government and society of the non-Soviet world. Acheson warned the visiting British Prime Minister Attlee in December 1950 that the Korean problem was 'part of a pattern. After Korea, it would be Indo-China, then Hong Kong and then Malaya.'[155] The domino theory was taking shape.

It is certainly true that the bloody fighting between the Chinese People's Volunteers and the Americans on the Korean peninsula created lasting enmity and apprehension between the two nations. It is, however, those policies which the Korean War enabled the United States to implement that crystallised the PRC's further alienation from international society. The PRC was branded an aggressor in a UN document because it was fighting the United Nations forces, whose commander, General

MacArthur, took orders from Washington instead of the UN headquarters in New York; and because it was fighting on the side of North Korea, an outright aggressor condemned by the United Nations. The PRC was thus made an international outlaw, and an outcast from the family of nations. A full trade embargo against the PRC was then introduced, implemented and maintained for many years to come. The PRC's legitimate claim to its seat in the United Nations was rejected. The American policy of non-recognition of the PRC was fully justified. The relative diplomatic isolation of the PRC, though not to the extent desired by the Americans, was in effect for at least a few years. The Korean War helped the Americans to exile the PRC almost irretrievably from the American-dominated international system. Sino–American relations emerging out of the Korean War were, as succinctly summarised by Harry Harding, 'at once remote, hostile and apprehensive'. After the Korean War, 'China and the United States confronted each other, at a distance, as implacable adversaries'.[156] There could not be better description of the mutual alienation between the United States and the PRC.

In the middle of the Korean War, Acheson, when urged to negotiate with the Chinese for a settlement, had argued with Attlee that the United States could not negotiate with the Chinese, simply because the Chinese would 'ask for recognition of their government, for a seat in the United Nations Security Council, and for concessions on Formosa'. To meet these demands would, in his view, spell disaster for the free world.[157] By implication, these issues were non-negotiable with the Chinese Communists. The PRC must be excluded from the United Nations and its legitimacy must be denied. That constituted in fact part of the United States' global strategy to contain Communism. The denial of the PRC's UN membership and its exclusion from the multilateral diplomacy network effectively cut the PRC adrift, as it were, from the international system.

The third phase in China's alienation was marked by crises and border wars in and around the PRC. It is generally acknowledged that the PRC adopted a conciliatory attitude at the Geneva Conference on Korea and Indo-China, which contributed to the solution of the first Indo-China crisis. Zhou Enlai's flexibility at the Bandung Conference did not go unnoticed. It is also widely noted that Vice-Premier Chen Yi in a report to the CCP's Eighth Party Congress in September 1956 affirmed that the PRC's policy of peaceful co-existence equally applied to the United States. The PRC also signed in 1960 friendship and mutual non-aggression treaties with its three non-Communist neighbours: Burma, Cambodia and Afghanistan.

The period was, however, also marred, probably more noticeably to the international consciousness, by crises from Tibet to the Taiwan Strait, and by the Sino–Indian border war. The Chinese Communists have consistently maintained even today that their military actions against the offshore islands during the two Taiwan Strait crises in 1955 and 1958 respectively were entirely China's internal affairs. They were merely 'punishing the Chinese reactionaries for signing the Taiwan Defence Pact with the United States' in the first crisis, and trying to assert Chinese sovereignty over the offshore islands so as to 'frustrate the American conspiracy of creating two Chinas' in the second.[158] In the grim world of the Cold War, there was little appreciation of, let alone sympathy for, the PRC's position on these issues. Through the prism of the bipolar world, such use of force was Communist aggression against the free world pure and simple. The Eisenhower administration went as far as to threaten the use of nuclear weapons to resolve the crises.

The Chinese crushing of the Tibetan rebellion in 1959 and the Sino–Indian border war in 1962 were seen as Chinese expansionism in action. Coupled with the CCP's support of the Communist insurgents in Southeast Asian nations, this new expansionism was simply 'Peking's drive for empire', that is, to establish a *Pax Sinica* in Asia.[159] Although not many people entirely agreed with Dulles in perceiving the Chinese Communists as 'much more violent and fanatical, much more addicted to the use of force than the Russians are or have become',[160] the perception of the PRC as an active, expanding power was not uncommon among members of the international community. It is easy today to see that these analyses and interpretations of the PRC's policies and actions are not entirely correct, if not altogether false. Some would argue later that 'China is not judged to be aggressive because of her actions; she is presumed to be aggressive because she is communist'.[161] It is also not difficult, with hindsight, to refute Dulles' allegation that 'China is engaged in a long range struggle to destroy the way of life of the free countries of the world and to bring about the global domination of communism'. That was no more than trying to cast China in the devil's role. It is possible to argue that some of those actions reflected China's legitimate security concerns around its periphery and that 'Mao was treating foreign relations as basically non-ideological'.[162] However, the PRC's policies, and especially the interpretation of them in the Cold War context by some other members of international society, did create such an image of a war-mongering Beijing regime engaged in subversion, aggression, expansion and military conquest of its neighbours, further alienating the PRC from international society. It is small wonder that Nixon should remark in 1973 that his administration in 1969 'inherited two decades of mutual estrangement and hostility [between the United States and China]'.[163]

The fourth phase in China's alienation was dominated by the Sino–Soviet polemics. Of many ramifications of the Sino–Soviet dispute, ideological differences were at least not at the heart. There was certainly an element of personality clash between Khrushchev and Mao Zedong. However, what was profoundly at issue was the conflict of national interests of the two powers and the contention between the two for power and status.[164] The acrimonious arguments which marked their strategic divergence in approaching international crises, such as the Iraq–Jordan–Lebanon crisis and the second Taiwan Strait crisis of 1958, were as much the reflection of their different perceptions of the changing international strategic landscape as that of different evaluations of what was at stake for their nations in the emerging new order. The Soviet Union, a *status quo* power now, insisted that nuclear armaments, the balance of terror, had fundamentally changed the international political process. The cautious Soviet approach to international crises was to lead to some measures of *détente* between the two superpowers, a prelude to the peaceful coexistence of the two blocs. That was compatible with Soviet national interests. For the PRC, the world around it had not changed much. Taiwan and the offshore islands were still 'occupied' by American imperialists. The imperialist threat to China's security and integrity was as real as ever. The PRC was still not recognised as a legitimate actor in international politics and was largely insulated from the international economic system. How could the PRC – still a have-not nation – be expected to live with such an international order?

The Soviet attempt to reach *détente* with the United States, the CCP believed, was the beginning of the Soviet collusion with the United States to dominate the world. Worse still, the CCP was convinced that the Soviet Union was pursuing its global strategy of *détente* with the United States at the expense of Chinese interests. Khrushchev was reluctant to support the Chinese position during the second Taiwan Strait crisis in August 1958, for fear that it would involve the Soviet Union in direct military conflict with the United States. His belated warning to Eisenhower against any American military attack on mainland China came only after he had received guarantees from the Chinese leadership that the PRC itself would take all the consequences of the crisis and, after the PRC agreed to negotiate, to resolve the crisis.[165] One year later, Khrushchev raised the matter again in a surprise visit to Beijing immediately following his Camp David meeting with Eisenhower in September 1959. Khrushchev complained to Mao and Zhou on 2 October that the bombardment of two offshore islands, Jinmen and Mazu [Quemoy and Matsu], 'presented a problem' for the Soviet Union and 'created an atmosphere of a great war'. More irritating to Mao and Zhou was the fact that Khrushchev suggested that the PRC renounce the use of force against Taiwan in order to reduce international tensions. He even implied that the PRC could consider allowing the temporary independence of Taiwan.[166]

The CCP's conviction was further strengthened by two incidents before Khrushchev's visit to the United States. In August 1959, the first armed skirmish occurred along the Sino–Indian border. On 9 September, just a few days before Khrushchev's visit to the United States, Tass issued a statement on the Sino–Indian border dispute, which seemingly emphasised Moscow's neutrality in the dispute but in fact 'was partial to India', the Chinese believed. During Khrushchev's talk with Mao and Zhou on 2 October, he was said to have 'made unwarranted charges' against China on the Sino–Indian border conflict.[167] Earlier in June, the Soviet government unilaterally cancelled a series of agreements signed in 1957 to help the PRC develop nuclear weapons. The Chinese interpretation was plain and simple: the Soviets attempted to deny the Chinese nuclear technology in order to please the Americans.[168]

What was to follow in 1960 was not the cause but the effect and the expression of the fundamental differences between the world views of the two powers and the contentions between the two for power and status. At both the Bucharest and the Moscow conferences of the Communist Parties in June and November, the CCP and the CPSU accused each other of 'revisionism' and 'dogmatism'. The CCP's efforts to assert its position in and the CPSU's attempt to ostracise the CCP from the international Communist movement only accelerated the process of mutual alienation. The abrupt withdrawal of all Soviet experts and technicians from the PRC starting in July 1960 did irreparable damage to the relations between the two states. The Sino–Soviet alliance, to all its purposes and intents, was reduced to a piece of paper. The mutual estrangement of the PRC and the Soviet Union was next to total. By virtue of the dominant position of the Soviet Union in the Eastern bloc, the PRC was practically alienated from all the Soviet bloc countries.

The last phase of China's alienation was marked by the PRC's revolutionary opposition to the existing international order, particularly during the period of the Cultural Revolution within the Chinese Revolution. It presented itself as a blunt challenge to the international system presided over by the two superpowers, the United States and the former Soviet Union, in three ways. As a revolutionary power, China's rejection of the prevailing international order was *in toto*. At least, rhetorically, China preached a surgical transformation of the international system through various revolutions to make a new world. In the classical sense, however, the PRC acted more like a dissatisfied power. The international system as it was denied the PRC its full legitimacy as an actor, presented it with a hostile external environment, stood in the way of China's unification, and prevented the PRC from realising its full power potential compatible with its influence in world politics. The PRC called for and set out to establish an international united front against both superpowers, urging revolutionary changes to the international system. Even more pertinent to our context, the PRC's behaviour fell squarely into the pattern of an alienated power. The PRC did not share any common interests or the work of common institutions, nor did it endorse the prevalent arrangements, in the society of states in regulating international relations. *Détente* was fiercely denounced as 'utter fraud'. Even Zhou Enlai denounced the United Nations as 'a US tool' in legitimising its global aggression and Marshal Chen Yi called for the establishment of a new and revolutionary United Nations. The PRC also bluntly rejected and unreservedly denounced the Partial Test Ban Treaty (PTBT) of 1963 and the Non-Proliferation Treaty (NPT) of 1968.

Solving the riddle of the China anomaly

There is a curious phenomenon, however. In spite of China's alienation from international society in the 1950s and the 1960s, and contrary to many allegations, China's compliance with international agreements had a good record. A seminal work concluded, for example, that the PRC had, 'on the whole, complied with the Korean Armistice Agreement'; 'there was no report of Chinese violation of economic assistance agreements'; and the PRC had also delineated through negotiations some of its boundaries 'in a manner which is often favourable to its neighbours'.[169] As far as trade agreements were concerned, 'except for difficulties in connection with the Great Leap Forward and the Cultural Revolution, the PRC has enjoyed an excellent reputation for meeting its obligations', and 'while negotiation with Peking is not always an easy matter, once an unambiguous agreement is reached, compliance likely will follow'.[170]

The great anomaly of China's position in the society of states in the 1950s and the 1960s is, therefore, not its relative isolation in but its grim and unqualified alienation from international society. Alienation not only more accurately describes the anomalous position of China (including its relative isolation), but also interprets the reasons why such an anomaly happened and persisted in that particular period. In plain terms, the period was characterised by the exclusion, more than seclusion, of China from the universal international organisations and international institutions.

For two decades, China remained a pariah to that society. While international society as a whole refused to accord legitimacy to the PRC as a normal player in the system of states, Beijing constantly posed itself as a challenge to the existing international system. Beijing could see little reason to share any common responsibility and the work of common institutions in maintaining a world order which continued to deny its existence. Beijing also felt every reason to reject the common values prevalent in the existing system which it tried to 'break up' in the 1960s after failing to 'break in' in the 1950s.[171] The understanding of such an alienation of China provides an essential backdrop for interpreting Chinese foreign policy in years of China's de-alienation and integration into international society.

It must be noted, however, that China's alienation from international society resulted as much from China's international policy as from the China policies of dominant members of the society of states. Nixon latter admitted that China's anomalous position 'distorted the international scene' and was 'partly self-imposed and partly the result of the policies of others'.[172] In particular, the American policies to isolate China and to contain Chinese Communism in the period and the Soviet policy of estranging the Chinese Communists from the international Communist movement in the 1960s must share the responsibility of keeping China an alienated state outside and hostile to the existing international order. The exclusion of the PRC from multilateral diplomacy immobilised any possible initiative to modify the alienation. By the same token, the de-alienation of China in international society would depend as much on the systemic changes as on the changing orientation of China's international policies. It is only natural that the process should have started from the admission of the PRC into the UN.

3 Mutual Legitimation

In his book *The World and China, 1922–72*, published in the early 1970s, John Gittings claimed that 'how the Chinese have managed to extricate themselves from their isolation in the early 1960s to attain a central position in world affairs must be counted the diplomatic success story of the century'.[1] By making this claim, Gittings actually asked, rather than answered, two questions which he must have also marvelled at. First, how could China, a recent pariah in international society, become so significant a player in world politics in such a short time? And second, what was the successful diplomacy that helped the Chinese achieve this? If so, Gittings has asked the right question in the first instance, but misdirected his question in the second. The reason for this is simple. Whatever success story the Chinese diplomacy was, China's changing role and position in international society were determined not only by the diplomacy of the People's Republic of China. They were also predicated on changes in the international system and on interactions between Chinese diplomatic initiatives and responses to them from other members of international society. In other words, the dramatic 'ascendancy' of China in world politics cannot simply be attributed to the success of Chinese diplomacy. As in the case of China's alienation from international society, the systemic factors and responses of members of international society to Chinese initiatives were as important as Chinese diplomacy in China's de-alienation process.

It is not difficult to see today that China's relations with international society in the 1970s was fundamentally different from that of its alienation in the 1950s and the 1960s. Whereas the exclusion of the PRC from the United Nations earmarked 20 years after 1950, the 1970s was characterised by China's return to the international community and to international organisations and by China's participation in global multilateral diplomacy. Whereas in the previous two decades the PRC was largely treated as an international pariah, in the 1970s, China was a universally accepted, legitimate actor in international politics. By the end of the decade, 120 countries had established diplomatic relations with China, compared with 52 in 1970. China was no longer regarded as an alien, an outcast from the international community. The weight of China no longer 'rested outside the international framework'.[2] Instead, the China factor contributed significantly to the emergence of a new pattern of global distribution of power. The resurgence of China as a great power of global significance gave substance to the structural transformation of the post-war bipolar world into a multipolar one. The so-called strategic triangle featuring Washington, Moscow and Beijing became an index of the global balance of power for most of the 1970s.

The de-alienation of China in international society which took place at the beginning of the 1970s, of course, does not mean that contentions and confrontation between China and other dominant powers of the international system vanished overnight. It is hard to imagine that such a revolutionary and dissatisfied power as China would stop immediately and altogether advocating revolutionary changes in the existing international system. The 1970s was also marred by frequent contentions between China and the two superpowers – in particular, the former Soviet Union. Nor does it suggest that China no longer presented a challenge to the existing international order. China in fact continued to pronounce its opposition to the prevailing world order. There is an important difference, however. If China had previously challenged the legitimacy and rationality of the existing international system from the perspective of an outcast, in the 1970s the China challenge was mostly represented from within the existing system. In other words, China, now an acknowledged member of international society, was obliged to function within the framework of the existing system. The incorporation of China into international society therefore immediately modified the nature of China's challenge, which was now related more to reforming, rather than to transforming, the existing international political and economic systems. There is also strong evidence to indicate China's acceptance of those most important common institutions identified by Martin Wight and Hedley Bull as operating in international society; namely, balance of power, the diplomatic system, international law, war and great power concert.[3] China, for example, actively participated in the global balance of power in the 1970s through the so-called strategic triangle. It also, as will be discussed later, swiftly and attentively globalised its diplomacy.

How can we then interpret these dramatic and sometimes perplexing changes in China's position in international society? Was China again integrated into the global international society? There is no doubt that the changing systemic context of China's international relations did substantially increase the inter-communication and interaction between China and other member states and between China and international society as a whole. China's behaviour in the society of states did begin to be significantly affected by the constraints and incentives provided by the new international environment in which China found itself. Furthermore, China's international policy also started to be shaped and guided by commonly accepted rules and norms of international society and by its relations with other members. Nevertheless, this is best seen as the accommodation of China into international society, a process whereby China acquainted itself with norms and values of that society as well as with the work of common institutions and whereby international society gradually took China into its embrace with necessary adjustments, but not undue disruptions. Such is a preliminary process for the socialisation of China into the global international society.

Because of China's alienation from international society in the previous decades, the mutual legitimation between China and the universal international society in the 1970s becomes part of a necessary and preliminary process of China's socialisation into international society. The mutual legitimation refers not only to China's admission into the United Nations, which re-established the universality of that global international organisation, but also to China's participation in global parliamentary politics and its share of the work of UN subsidiaries and many other international institutions. It relates to extensive bilateral relations established between China and other member states and to links with other economies. Equally importantly, the mutual legitimation also refers to a process of China's learning and adopting rules, conventional practices, and norms of the existing international society in conducting international relations. Further, it is concerned with China's modifications of its behaviour and even of some values to comply with the rules of world politics.

As David Armstrong has argued most recently, the socialisation process of a revolutionary state into international society helps mediate that state's 'initial hostility towards ... institutions of international society' and ensures its 'grudging acceptance of their value'. Like other members in international society, revolutionary states also seek to secure the privileges and protection that international society, and its institutions (statehood and sovereignty, for example), can provide for its members.[4] The mutual legitimation as the beginning of socialisation of revolutionary China in the 1970s strongly supports Armstrong's arguments. It also prepared China for its eventual integration into international society politically and economically in the 1980s and the 1990s.

This chapter looks at the mutual legitimation between China and international society in the 1970s as the beginning of China's socialisation into international society. Three aspects are examined. The first part reinterprets the significance of the Sino–American *rapprochement*. It argues in particular that it is the *changing nature* of the international system, rather than the *changing structure* of that system, that is the most important factor in accounting for China's accommodation into international society at that particular moment. The second part looks at Chinese initiatives and the responses from the UN and member states to those initiatives in the mutual process of adjustment in international politics as well as in world economy. The third part suggests limitations of China's socialisation into international society in the 1970s.

THE 'CHINA BREAKTHROUGH' RECONSIDERED

At the beginning of the 1970s, a combination of the passing of the postwar *Pax Americana* and China's emergence from the tribulations of the Cultural Revolution at home brought China back into the mainstream of world politics. The opening up of the 1970s initiated the beginning of an end to China's alienation from international society.

The spectacular American opening to China symbolised by Henry Kissinger's secret visit to China in July 1971 and President Nixon's personal homage to Beijing in February 1972 have been the subject of many studies in the last 20 years. Most of these studies have dwelt on two main themes. One is what prompted the Americans to approach the Chinese or the Chinese to send overtures to the Americans at that particular moment to initiate the so-called China breakthrough, which eventually led to the normalisation of bilateral relations between the United States and China. The other, probably more fascinating to many, is how Sino–American *rapprochement* materially affected the international strategic landscape and the transformation of the international system in the 1970s. There is still another, arguably minor, theme explored mostly by American historians of East Asia: namely, why should the Americans and the Chinese have regarded each other as mortal enemies in the two decades of deadly confrontation with no communication? Barbara Tuchman provocatively asked the question, '[What] if Mao had come to Washington [in 1945]?'[5] John King Fairbank was convinced that historians 'will conclude that our contact with Peking was less surprising than the fact that it was so long delayed'.[6] Well into the 1980s, American historians still tried to grapple with an argument whether Sino–American military and ideological confrontations in the 1950s and the 1960s were a Greek tragedy or a Christian one.[7] A clear line of introspection of American China policy in the two decades of confrontation keeps company with the assessment of the implications and importance of Sino–American *rapprochement* for the changing climate of world politics.

The end of an era

With hindsight, it is not difficult to recapture the momentum of the strategic breakthrough in Sino–American relations in the early 1970s. When

Nixon took his office in the White House in 1969, he inherited an international strategic context hardly favourable to the United States. The Soviet Union had just invaded and occupied Czechoslovakia a few months before. The US–Soviet confrontation in the Middle East seemed deadlocked. With America's self-imposed ceilings on its intercontinental ballistic missiles (ICBMs), sea-launched ballistic missiles (SLBMs) and anti-ballistic missiles (ABMs), the indisputable American superiority in strategic weapons prevailing in the entire post-war period had ended and was replaced by a strategic balance between the United States and the Soviet Union. The number of Soviet missiles which could be used against mainland United States was approaching the number of American missiles available in retaliation against the Soviet Union. Further added to Nixon's heritage was the quagmire of the unpopular and politically divisive shooting war in Vietnam, a war with no victory in sight and with defeat of the United States in the jungles of Vietnam a not too distant possibility. The massive Soviet supply of arms to North Vietnam and its moral support of North Vietnam's intransigent position at the Paris Talks, the Americans believed, hampered their successful negotiations with the North Vietnamese to finish the war and hence their efforts to liquidate the Vietnam War from their political agenda. A new perspective was needed to reactivate the American initiatives in international relations, which had been almost paralysed by the agony of Vietnam in the last years of the Johnson administration.

Other changes in the international system had not gone unnoticed by the American leadership. The paramount position of the United States in the post-war international system was also challenged by its allies. A much invigorated Western Europe was no longer willing to take the American prescriptions for their policies in East–West relations and in the alliance relationship across the Atlantic. De Gaulle's veto of the British applications to join the EEC and Chancellor Brandt's pursuit of *Ostpolitik* were far cries from the desired American line. The dependence on the dollar as a reserve currency in the international monetary and trading system, 'unfair' in the eyes of the Europeans, caused further strains in political relations between the United States and its allies. Further, a much weakened dollar was both the cause and effect of a changing balance sheet of the American trade surplus. Coupled with the rise of the West German and the Japanese economies, it symbolised the beginning of the end of the American predominance in world economy in the post-war period. International society was leaving behind it an era when the United States sat at the apex of the power, politically and economically, of the world. Gone was the time when the Americans could impose their own conceptions and perceptions on its allies and on the international community as a whole. 'By the end of the 1960s, any belief in a Pax Americana was dead.'[8]

More significantly, perhaps, America's two principal adversaries, the Soviet Union and China, were embroiled in armed conflicts along their borders in 1969. If the polemics in the Sino–Soviet split earlier in the 1960s could not convince the hard-headed Americans of the breakdown of a monolithic Communist bloc, the armed clashes did. The Nixon administration was more willing than its predecessors to begin the long-delayed exploitation of the Sino–Soviet adversary relationship, which was now militarised. It saw in it an opportunity to make strategic move not to advance but to retreat from its anti-Communist crusade in open confrontation. The single action of opening talks by Washington with Beijing would, as Nixon put it, 'squeeze the Soviet Union into short term help on Vietnam' for the American disengagement.[9] It would also, as Kissinger rightly predicted, make the Soviets more accommodating in the ongoing Strategic Arms Limitation Talks (SALT). On a higher strategic plane, it would give the United States options previously thought unavailable.

China's perception of the changing international system

For the People's Republic of China, the Soviet factor had always been a principal determinant in its strategic alignment. In its early years, the PRC decided to 'lean to one side' not so much because of its ideological commitment to Communism as because the Soviet Union was seen as the only state capable of defending New China against any perceived prospective armed intervention by imperialists in the Chinese Revolution.[10] Equally, the Sino–Soviet split was a mobilising force behind China's search for a united front in its international strategy in the early 1960s. By the late 1960s, the People's Republic increasingly felt that it was being encircled by the Soviet Union and its clients in the North, the Northeast and the Northwest. The Soviet Union was replacing the United States as the principal and more immediate military threat to the security of China. The armed conflicts along the border in 1969 only exacerbated this perception.

China's reading of the changes in the international system was necessarily different from that of the United States and reflected its own national experience and its own security concerns. There were some convergent points, none the less. Like the Americans, the Chinese concluded that the decisive strategic superiority of the United States was replaced by a strategic balance between the two superpowers. Like the Americans, the Chinese saw the clear-cut bipolarity in the post-war international relations blurred with the emergence of an assertive Western Europe and the rise of Japan as the third largest industrial economy. Like the Americans, the Chinese believed that the disappearance of the American predominance in the post-war international political and economic system was among the most fundamental changes in the system, which would entail radical adjustments to international policies by all powers of any international significance.[11]

The Chinese, however, had their own distinct perspective. Mao Zedong in 1967 already perceived possible prospective changes in American policy towards China. Mao was particularly impressed by Nixon's 1967 article in *Foreign Affairs* and by his dropping of the 'domino theory' and his emphasis on the need for 'patience born of realism' in understanding the importance of China's future role in world affairs. It was left to Zhou Enlai to reveal this to the world only in December 1974 by means of a talk with US Senator Mike Mansfield.[12] While Nixon declared that his one-week visit to China in February 1972 changed the world, Mao was convinced that it was the world that had changed Nixon.[13]

Furthermore, the Chinese were probably among the first to perceive and pronounce the American retrenchment and the Soviet advancement in the global confrontation of the late 1960s. They had good reasons. The United States was overstretched in its world-wide commitments and was immobilised by the unpopular Vietnam War and domestic political difficulties. The Soviet Union, on the other hand, embarked on world-wide adventurism, taking advantage of the American immobilisation. It was making net gains in the Middle East and Africa.[14] In terms of strategic forces, the United States no longer retained its absolute superiority *vis-à-vis* the Soviet Union. More ominously to the Chinese, the announcement of the Brezhnev doctrine of limited sovereignty following the Soviet invasion of Czechoslovakia in 1968 foreshadowed a possible Soviet military intervention in China. The massive build-up of the Soviet military forces along the Sino–Soviet borders both preceding and following the border clashes in 1969 was, in the eyes of the Chinese, a prelude to such an intervention. The Soviet threat to use its strategic weapons to 'neutralise' the Chinese nuclear forces in the Northwest desert not far from the Sino–Soviet borders gave more substance to a conceivable Sino–Soviet war. The Soviet Union, the more aggressive, was emerging as the more palpable enemy. The worst scenario, which had been always on the mind of the Chinese leadership, was of course a US–Soviet condominium to destroy China. In their very first encounters during Kissinger's secret visit to Beijing in July 1971, Zhou Enlai confided to Kissinger the Chinese concerns that Europe, Japan, the United States and the Soviet Union might decide in collusion to carve up China again.[15] The Chinese concluded that their strategic position *vis-à-vis* the Soviet Union could be improved only by a spectacular opening to the United States. Contacts with the United

States would also help to prevent the unfolding of a US–Soviet condominium against China.

Already in May 1969, after the outbreak of fighting along the Ussuri River, four Chinese marshals – Chen Yi, Nie Rongzhen, Xu Xiangqian and Ye Jianying – under heavy 'bombardment' in the chaotic Cultural Revolution were summoned, with the consent of Mao, to hold special discussion sessions on the new developments in China's international relations. It was at these sessions that the former Foreign Minister Chen Yi, probably the first among the Chinese strategists, made a proposal to reopen the Sino–American Warsaw talks as the first step to a *rapprochement* with the United States so as to counter the Soviet military threat to China. The four marshals adopted this proposal and recommended it to Mao and Zhou. It was this proposal that eventually led to China's strategic realignment with the United States in the 1970s.[16] By late 1970, Mao was finally persuaded by this view.

Memoirs by Nixon and Kissinger have detailed how the Nixon administration made subtle manoeuvres to prepare the Americans and the American public opinion for contacts with the PRC. Kissinger's memoirs also gave us a rare glimpse into how Mao told Nixon that Lin Biao and his 'reactionary group' opposed Sino–American contacts.[17] In 1970, with the Cultural Revolution reaching a stalemate at home after the Ninth National Congress of the CCP, the Chinese reactivated their foreign policy initiatives. Ambassadors were returned to their posts. Perceiving the changes in the international system, China was determined to come back to the international scene, but in a different capacity. For the Chinese, the opening to America could serve to balance the Soviet threat, to prevent the resurgence of Japanese militarism, and to facilitate the emergence of a new international order, inclusive of China as a major player active in shaping and maintaining such an order. The Chinese and the American strategic interests therefore converged on their common adversary relationship with the Soviet Union and a common perception of an international system in transition and transformation. The China breakthrough thus served the broad strategic interests of China as well as those of the United States.

Reinterpreting the 'China breakthrough'

The Sino–American *rapprochement* was a masterpiece of *realpolitik*. There is no doubt that it further signalled the end of *Pax Americana* and that it changed the structure of the post-war international relations in that it gave more substance to the transition from a bipolar to a multipolar world. Neither is there any question that a geopolitical revolution was sparked by this singular opening. The introduction of the China factor into the global balance of power gave both China and the United States much-needed edge *vis-à-vis* the Soviet Union. The international strategic contour was radically changed. The so-called 'strategic triangle' featuring the United States, the Soviet Union and China emerged. The strategic triangle, as was commonly recognised, did have disparities and discrepancies in the triangular politics and strategic balance. However, it not only guided China and the two superpowers in making their strategic decisions, but also heavily influenced the allies and clients of the superpowers in making their policy choices.

The actual benefits derived by both China and the United States from the 'China breakthrough' were exactly what its architects intended to reap. By a single stroke, Mao and Zhou neutralised the greatest threat posed to China's national security by 'Soviet Social Imperialism'.[18] The perception of China as a geopolitical trump card, the weight of which, when added to whichever superpower, would decide the outcome of an overall global confrontation between Washington and Moscow, gained China considerable manoeuvrability in East–West relations. This so-called 'swing value' also gave China much leverage in pursuing its policies towards the United States in bilateral matters. For the United States, the introduction of the China factor in the strategic calculus of the Soviet Union complicated the Soviet strategic planning in the event of a global military conflict and tied down one-third of its active divisions along the Sino–Soviet borders. With the 'China card' in hand, the United States also strengthened its position in dealing with Soviet Union on other strategic issues, such as the arms control and disarmament. Furthermore, a cooperative relationship with China helped to contain the expansion of the Soviet interests in East Asia at minimum cost to the United States.

In the last 20 years or so, Sino–American *rapprochement* has been largely assessed in this light. Structural changes in the international system initiated by the *rapprochement* have been vigorously examined.[19] With the vantage point of today, it is not difficult to see that the international strategic landscape created with the help of the China breakthrough has had its day. The so-called strategic triangle has completely disappeared. Even the normalisation of bilateral relations between the United States and China *per se* which culminated in the establishment of full diplomatic relations in 1979 had its limitations. The violent crackdown against the democracy movement in Beijing in June 1989 and the disappearance of the common adversary with the disintegration of the former Soviet Union in 1991 have again thrown Sino–American relations into disarray.

The hindsight and the perspective which history endows us frequently dictate reassessment of historical events. In the light of post-Cold War international relations, what is the lasting significance of changes of the international system signalled by the China breakthrough in the 1970s?

It is often neglected that the changing *structure* in the 1970s actually reflected the changing *nature* of the international system, which in turn sets the parameters of structural changes. As a multipolar world with plurality emerged, the international system became more accommodative of the adversary relationship between ideologically hostile power blocs, and of various challenges, including the emerging collective nationalism of the Third World, as seen in the formation of OPEC (Organisation of Petroleum Exporting Countries), and of revolutionary China. Gone was not only the rigid structure of bipolarity but also the prohibitive nature of the international system as manifested most clearly in the preceding years. This point needs some elaboration.

The most important factor that dictated the fundamental change in the nature of the international system from a prohibitive to an accommodative one is the same as that which prompted the American initiatives to reconstitute a global balance of power. That is the end of *Pax Americana*, and the collapse of the absolute American hegemony in the international system. The end of an era, as discussed above, has made a deep imprint on changing world politics.

It is also often overlooked that structural changes of the international order such as those symbolised by the China breakthrough were underlined by a radical change in the philosophy of American foreign policy. The new philosophy was that the United States would regard other ideologically opposing great powers, in Kissinger's words, 'in geopolitical rather than ideological terms'.[20] The overall American foreign policy objective derived from this new philosophy was therefore to transform fundamentally US relations with both its allies and its adversaries. Such transformation necessitated radically restructuring the international system into such an inclusive one that it would accommodate, not exclude, opposing interests. Raymond Aron, in a perceptive study of the American foreign policy objective of the first Nixon administration, stated in 1972 that

> The urgent task – which was to finish with Vietnam – was now joined by a poorly defined task of a long-term nature, the restoration of an international system in which the United States would have an important, though not dominant, place, and which would not exclude the continued opposition of interests, even of more or less violent conflict; a system that would entail the establishment of an equilibrium of sorts and of more traditional relations among all the great powers, even the revolutionary ones.[21]

In other words, the American foreign policy of the first Nixon administration strove now to create in the contemporary international order a traditional model of balance of power in the global system. Power, not ideology, was made the watchword for restructuring the international system. It was only within such a paradigm that China and the United States, the two arch ideological enemies of the recent past, could reconcile themselves in 1972. It was only within such paradigm that it was conceivable that the two were now talking about their shared common interests in reducing tensions in East Asia in particular and in the whole world in general, while they were adamantly uncompromising in their ideological principles.

To support the arguments above, it must be contended that in the early 1970s, 'the actions and reactions' of the United States can still probably affect the nature of world politics',[22] in spite of the diminishing ability of the United States to dominate world politics. It must also be noted that such a change in the philosophy of American foreign policy took place in response to other systemic changes already present in world politics. The decline of American hegemony in international politics and the world economy expedited the birth of a more plural world. Those conventionally noted systemic changes in the 1970s – the collapse of the Bretton Woods system, the emergence of European Economic Community as a major force to be reckoned with, the challenges of the West German and Japanese economies, the assertion of medium powers such as Romania and Australia, the rise of the Third World and its collective nationalism and the increasing inter-dependence of the world economy – all indicated that a world of diverse interests and values, and of complexity in power calculation and alignment, was in the making. Together, these systemic changes also fulfilled at least three functions. They emphasised the pressing need to restructure the international system. They set limits to the capability of the United States, the hegemon, to change that system. They influenced the direction of change in the nature of the new international system.

To reiterate, the 'China breakthrough' no doubt signals a turning point in post-war international relations. It is however a turning point marked not so much by the changing *structure* as by the changing *nature* of the system of states. In other words, the emergence of multipolarity is but an expression of the emerging international system which is more accommodating of diverse interests and more inclusive of opposing values. The restructuring of the international order, however significant it was, was but a side-show. It is an epic transformation of the nature of the international system that is the central achievement of 'change without war'. The accommodation of China into the international system, the emerging *détente* in the expression of 'adversary partnership' between the two superpowers in the 1970s, and the resilience of the system to take up challenges such as the New International Economic Order (NIEO) are standing testimonies to the accommodating nature of the emerging order.

The changing nature of the international system itself provides only a necessary condition for the accommodation of revolutionary China into the system in the 1970s. The Chinese perspective is the sufficient change to realise the accommodation. As previously argued, China's perception of changes in the international system towards the end of the 1960s also led China to reconsider its international strategy. It is interesting to note that the Chinese leadership had reached the conclusion that even as a revolutionary power, China had to compromise some of its revolutionary principles in order to compensate itself for its vulnerability to the Soviet threat in the world of power politics. That was the rationale behind China's approach to the American initiatives. In other words, the Chinese leadership at least partially acknowledged Kissinger's wisdom; namely, ideological considerations should be subject to geopolitical considerations in foreign policy making and implementation, in particular with regard to great power relations. Based on that principle, China and the United States reciprocated each other's initiatives in realising the breakthrough in bilateral relations.

Symbolically, the China breakthrough represented more than just the beginning of a new relationship between the two powers. It signalled the acceptance by both the hegemonic United States and revolutionary China of the geopolitical factor as the most important element in the institutionalised system of the global balance of power. On that basis, the more accommodating system of states was now willing to incorporate China, and China was certainly receptive to the idea of being embraced by the international system. The China breakthrough, rather than just elevating China's strategic importance in the global balance of power, opened a totally new prospect for China in the society of states. It started inexorably the accommodation of China into the international system. Looking back from the perspective of the early 1990s, Jonathan Pollack concluded that, 'Without the explicit sanction provided by the American accommodation with Peking ... it seems highly unlikely that China's incorporation within the international economic system would have been nearly as complete'.[23]

Before 1972, China was treated as an international outlaw, quarantined by the American-led containment. China was shuttered from normal diplomatic intercourse, particularly at the multilateral level. The estranged PRC was living, in Nixon's words, 'in angry isolation'.[24] The 'China breakthrough', underlined by a change of philosophy in American foreign policy, served to bring down barriers to China's rejoining international society. The last 25 years have seen China's steady and progressive integration into the international political and economic systems. Whereas before 1972 'the weight of China rested outside the international framework',[25] today, China's integration into international society is clearly registered. Whereas the exclusion of the PRC before 1972 from the United Nations and all other international organisations severely dented the universality of international society, China's active participation and cooperative behaviour in the global multilateral diplomacy in the 1990s has certainly strengthened the efforts of this universal world organisation in its search for a new international order and given added vitality to international society. The degree and the extent of China's integration today are both unprecedented in its history and unimaginable at the time of the China breakthrough. Herein lies probably the most significant and lasting contribution which the American opening to China has made to the durable peace of the world.

As has been argued in the previous chapter, alienation was the hallmark of China's relations with international society in the two decades previous to the China breakthrough. China's relative isolation was merely an expression of its alienation. It has been further argued that for more than two decades after the Korean War, the United States followed a multipronged strategy of diplomatic non-recognition, economic embargo and military containment against China. Such policies had a wide range of ramifications in alienating China from the American-dominated international system. For Beijing, therefore, the Sino–American *rapprochement* was a breakthrough in their protracted battle to gain international legitimacy for the PRC. What Nixon claimed to be a change in the philosophy of American foreign policy was seen by the Chinese leadership in Beijing as the abandonment of the American policies against the PRC. While the Americans envisaged a new international order which would accommodate rather than exclude opposing interests, the Chinese believed that such a change of policy was a tacit admission of the bankruptcy of American policies of isolating China in the previous two decades.[26]

Whether the Americans or the Chinese have better arguments is a matter of different opinion and perspective. The important fact is that contact between Washington and Beijing was officially re-established with Nixon's visit to Mao's residence in the Forbidden City. The China breakthrough is therefore revolutionary in the sense that it was an acknowledgement by the American government of the legitimacy of the PRC. By the same token, it brought down the last barrier against the PRC taking China's seat at the United Nations and the Security Council. As the United States quietly dropped its opposition to seating the PRC, many of its NATO allies rebelled against its proposal for dual representation of both Taiwan and the PRC at the United Nations. Between Kissinger's secret journey to China in July 1971 and Nixon's visit to

Beijing in February 1972, the 26th General Assembly of the United Nations voted overwhelmingly, on 25 October 1971, to accept the PRC as the sole legitimate representative of China in the United Nations. China's entry into the United Nations marked both symbolically and practically the end of its anomalous position in the international community and the beginning of its return to international society. China's entry also fulfilled 'the imperative need for the United Nations to achieve universality of membership', called for by Secretary-General U Thant in 1965.[27] The PRC's entry into the UN in 1971 therefore started a process of a long overdue mutual legitimation between China and this global international organisation.

The China breakthrough therefore opened a new vista for China in world politics, not only because it had significantly changed its international strategic context by neutralising the Soviet threat and not only because it gradually put Sino–American relations on the right track. There should not be any doubt that these are two remarkable achievements of the China breakthrough. The most important, however, is that by knocking down the last barrier to the recognition of the PRC's legitimacy in the society of states, it started the irresistible process of China's engagement with the international political and economic systems and with the other member states of the international community within the existing framework of international society. That process led to wider and deeper involvement of China into the contemporary society of states in later years.

The 1970s saw a comprehensive process of mutual adjustment and mutual engagement between the PRC and the international system. The simple inclusion of China in international society is partly accountable for China's 'ascendancy in world politics' and its attaining 'a central position in world affairs' in the 1970s. Indeed, the single most important heritage in China's foreign relations which Mao Zedong and Zhou Enlai had bequeathed to Deng Xiaoping is probably the China breakthrough and its ramifications. It is shrewdly remarked that,

> From the earliest hints of Sino–American accommodation in 1968, Mao was vital to this process. Yet even as the Chairman understood that closer relations with the West were a strategic imperative, he remained to the last highly ambivalent about the long-term implications of incorporating China within the existing international system.[28]

It is now up to Deng Xiaoping to cultivate this legacy, created in the first place by strategic imperatives, in opening China to the outside world at the end of the 1970s and in making China's second revolution in the

Mutual Legitimation

1980s. Deng would also have to deal with the ambivalent relations between China and international society as his reforms have further incorporated China into the international system. For both China and the world, therefore, the China breakthrough is of broader and more profound strategic importance. It marks the beginning of a new era, an era of China's socialisation and its integration into the society of states.

THE PROCESS OF MUTUAL ENGAGEMENT

As argued above, it was a combination of forces of circumstance – the systemic changes in world politics, the change of American philosophy in foreign policy, the PRC's new security concerns, and the PRC's emergence from the tribulations of the Cultural Revolution – that gathered momentum for the historic breakthrough in Sino–American relations. The PRC's entry into the United Nations in 1971, which many in Beijing had viewed as *déjà vu*, became both the inauguration and the focal point of the mutual engagement between the PRC and international society. Throughout the 1970s, this mutual engagement was both extensive and intensive, so much so that it can hardly do justice to it to sum it up in the next few pages. On three levels of analysis, however, the PRC began its meaningful participation in and interaction with the international political and economic systems. On the bilateral level, the PRC had established full diplomatic relations with 120 countries by the end of September 1979, compared with 50 about ten years before.[29] On the multilateral level, the PRC socialised itself in the United Nations and its specialised agencies and went through a period of apprenticeship to master the rules of the game of parliamentary politics at the General Assembly and other institutions. Finally, the PRC's participation in the international economy saw a 'Great Leap Outward' in the late 1970s. The positive and indeed successful mutual engagement put the PRC – an alien in the recent past – on its way to becoming a part of the whole of the existing international order at the end of the 1970s. Our discussion of China's engagement with international society in the 1970s starts with a brief examination of China's entry into the United Nations in 1971.

Mutual legitimation at the UN

In commemorating the fiftieth anniversary of the United Nations, *Time* listed the seating of the PRC in the UN and its Security Council as one of the most important events in the UN's 50 years' history. Let us now first recapture the euphoria with which members of the United Nations greeted the return of China to this global organisation. When the Important Question resolution proposed by the United States regarding China's representation at the United Nations was defeated on 25 October 1971, the *New York Times* reported:

> The Tanzanians, who were among the floor managers for Peking, jumped from their seats in the front row and did a little victory dance. The Algerians, fellow cosponsors, embraced one another. The Albanians sedately shook hands. Others stood up, applauded, cheered. Rhythmic clapping beat against the walls. The vote on the Albanian resolution 90 minutes later was anticlimatic. The result was 76-35, with 17 abstentions (and without a single NATO ally on the American side).[30]

The PRC's first appearance in the General Assembly on 15 November was marked by statements of welcome. To quote Witunski at some length:

> Almost as a group of sinners publicly renouncing their transgressions, representative after representative took the rostrum to wish the Chinese delegation success and to assure their co-operation. The representative of India recalled that his country was the first to propose that the Chinese seat in the UN be occupied by the PRC after its establishment in 1949. The representative of France said that the injustice and absurdity had ended now that China was finally seated. The representative of Burundi, speaking on behalf of the majority of African countries, said that China had become one of the main actors on the international scene. The Minister for Foreign Affairs of Denmark, on behalf of Denmark, Finland, Iceland, Norway, and Sweden, said that this was a day of great satisfaction for those who never failed to support the right of the PRC to take its seat.[31]

Although the PRC had made sustained efforts to gain China's seat at the United Nations since 1950, the actual invitation for it to join the United Nations in 1971 both represented a victory to be celebrated and presented a sticky business to be dealt with. As was recently revealed, the resolution of the 26th General Assembly of the UN to seat the PRC and to expel Taiwan came as a pleasant surprise even to Zhou Enlai and the foreign policy community of the PRC. The Chinese had anticipated that the earliest date for its entry into the United Nations would be 1972 or 1973. When the Foreign Ministry received an invitation from Secretary-General

U Thant to attend the 26th General Assembly of the UN, the Chinese were ill prepared, to say the least.

The invitation presented the PRC with an exciting prospect, but also a trying job at hand. For one thing, the prevailing image in China of the United Nations was invariably heavily tainted by the politics of the Cultural Revolution, by China's experience of being condemned by and excluded from the UN, and by its history of dealing with dominant powers of the West. For the other, the PRC had little knowledge of the inside working of the United Nations and had, if any, only limited human resources capable of dealing with international organisations such as the United Nations and its affiliated organs. Besides, China had only recently advocated surgical revolution to transform the United Nations. What should be its role in such a world organisation controlled by the two superpowers? Which part should it play in such an 'undemocratic and bourgeois forum' of an international nature? How could it stand for the exploited and oppressed of the world within such an organisation? The PRC would barely have time to sort out all these questions should it wish to accept the invitation. However, the invitation was an acknowledgement by international society of the PRC's legitimacy. To accept that would immensely strengthen the PRC's prestige and status in the society of states and open up countless opportunities for China in multilateral diplomacy. Should the PRC accept the invitation? The initial decision was to decline the invitation for 1971.

On the afternoon of 26 October 1971, shortly after Kissinger left Beijing after his second visit, Zhou Enlai gathered a group of people central in Chinese foreign policy making to discuss whether China should attend the 26h General Assembly. In the heat of discussion, Mao Zedong personally intervened. When he was told by Zhou Enlai over the phone that they were considering sending an informal group, not a formal delegation, to the UN for the purpose of familiarising themselves with the working of the United Nations, Mao simply asked,

> Why shouldn't we go? We must go. We must organise a delegation [to the United Nations]. It is our black brothers in Africa who have managed to get us in. If we don't go, we'll cut ourselves from the masses. ... We must send a delegation to the UN and Qiao Guanhua can be the head of the delegation.

Zhou Enlai was then made personally responsible for the organisation of the delegation. Mao Zedong reserved the final approval of its personnel.[32] This little story is not only indicative of a revolutionary power's dilemma, but also the ambivalence of a recently alienated state, eager to become an insider of the system, but apprehensive of the possible consequences and implications resulting from its incorporation.

The importance of the PRC's incorporation into the global multilateral diplomacy at the UN can hardly be overemphasised. At the time when 'the Third World states have enlarged multilateral diplomacy to an extent never previously achieved',[33] the UN provided invaluable opportunities for China to express itself in the international forums. More importantly, it provided channels of information and communication between China and other member states, which were essential for mediating China's alienation and facilitating its socialisation. It not only remedied the China anomaly in the international relations. In ten years' time, it would also transform China from a revolutionary state into a more 'normal' power in international society. The inclusion of the PRC into the United Nations legitimised the UN as a truly universal world organisation. Seating the PRC in the Security Council as one of the permanent members, on the other hand, made the Security Council more representative of the political and geographical realities of the existing international system and reflected more accurately the changing contours of the international strategic landscape. The legitimation was, of course, mutual. By admitting the PRC into the UN family, the General Assembly virtually made China a genuinely legitimate actor in the UN system.

Globalising Chinese diplomacy

The PRC's entry into the United Nations was partly preceded and partly accompanied by another breakthrough in its external relations. From 1970 to the end of 1972, China established full diplomatic relations with 32 countries, including Japan, Australia and all the NATO member states except the United States, Spain and Portugal.[34] By the beginning of 1979, the United States and Portugal also joined the contingent of 120 countries which had established diplomatic relations with China. The global network of diplomatic relations for China not only reaffirmed its international legitimacy; it also enabled China to share, with little hindrance for the first time since 1949, this most basic institution, the diplomatic system, which underlies the very existence of the global international society. Sharing in this very basic institution is the foundation without which China's socialisation and integration into international society would never have been possible.

Under normal circumstances, the recognition of one state by another and the establishment of full diplomatic relations between the two would only have limited, and indeed in some cases, symbolic significance. For China, which had been denied international legitimacy for almost a quarter of a century and which had been cut off from any official links with many parts of the world, it was altogether a different story. The news of China's establishment of diplomatic relations with a foreign nation was always announced with great enthusiasm and in a victorious tone. Almost without exception, the occasion was celebrated by an editorial from the *People's Daily*. There was manifestly what Miller calls 'a whole-hearted, perhaps over-zealous, adoption of the existing diplomatic system in its bilateral aspects'.[35] Deng Xiaoping personally hailed in 1978 the establishment of diplomatic relations with the United States as 'a historic turning point' in Sino–American relations.[36] The normalisation of Sino–Japanese relations was also saluted as the beginning of 'a new chapter in the annals of China–Japan relations'.[37] To all intents and purposes, the opening up of normal diplomacy with the majority of member states in the international community effectively marked the other distinctive aspect of the PRC's return to international society. One official Chinese diplomatic history claims that the 1970s were a decade in which 'China made big strides on the diplomatic front. Thus China further enhanced its role as a force to be reckoned with on the world stage.'[38]

The establishment of diplomatic relations was only the beginning of mutual engagement on the bilateral level. Throughout the 1970s, Beijing had acted as host to a stream of visiting heads of state and government, government ministers and political figures from all continents, who flocked to China. Another index of the development of Sino–foreign bilateral relations in the 1970s can therefore be found in the number of visits to China by the heads of state and of government from all over the world. From 1970 to the end of 1979, more than 100 official visits to China were paid by the heads of state and of government from more than 70 countries. Among them were the Presidents of the United States, Richard Nixon and Gerald Ford, the French President Georges Pompidou, the German Chancellor Helmut Schmidt, King Juan Carlos of Spain, and the Japanese Prime Ministers Tanaka Kakuei and Ohira Masayoshi. On top of that were leaders of Third World countries, from the Algerian President Boumedienne to the Zambian President Kaunda. The intensity of such visits to Beijing from such widely spread geographical areas is an indication of the upsurge of China's contact with the international community and the globalisation of China's day-to-day diplomacy. It is also indicative of the extent to which sustained relations had been developed between China and other members of the international community. China and a majority of member states of the international community were not only getting to know each other; they had also been mutually engaged with each other through the network of bilateral relations thus created.

It must be noted that all these visits were accompanied or followed by the signing of a spate of bilateral treaties and agreements on economic and technical co-operation, cultural exchange and trade protocols between China and the foreign countries concerned. For example, in 1972 alone, China signed either a civil air transport or a maritime transport agreement with Romania, Afghanistan, Ethiopia, Japan, Italy and Iran. The Maltese Prime Minister Dom Mintoff's visit to China in April 1972 ended with the signing of an agreement of an interest-free loan that China would provide Malta.[39] In fact, many Third World countries, while negotiating with China to establish diplomatic relations, had asked China for economic aid and technical assistance. China responded positively to their demands. From 1971 to 1978, 36 more countries were added to the list of recipient countries of Chinese aid. Altogether, 66 countries received Chinese aid in the 1970s. In the official assessment of the development of China's foreign economic aid programmes, this period is dubbed 'the period of rapid expansion'.[40] A network of bilateral economic relations was carefully woven.

More significantly, this diplomatic breakthrough was not only engineered by Mao Zedong and Zhou Enlai but also directly supervised by Mao himself. In the last few years of Mao's life, he indeed assumed 'disproportionate responsibility' for Chinese foreign policy.[41] From September 1973 to June 1976, Mao Zedong, almost on his death bed, went out of his way to see almost all visiting heads of state and government and engaged them in talks on a broad range of international issues.[42] In May 1974 alone, Mao was reported to have made four such public appearances. He met Senegalese President Léopold Senghor, Pakistani President Z. A. Bhutto, Cypriot President Archbishop Makarios and Malaysian Prime Minister Tun Abdul Razak.[43] Even in the twilight months of his life, Mao did not stop seeing foreign dignitaries until after 15 May 1976, less than four months before his death.[44] The establishment of diplomatic relations as such was therefore not just a process of mutual legitimation between China and other members of international society. It also led to personal contacts between the Chinese and other national leaders. Such personal contacts both complemented and reinforced the official dialogue through diplomatic channels. Interaction between China and other members of international society was becoming now 'sufficient to make the behaviour of each a necessary element in the calculation of the other'.[45]

What about the other side of the coin? How about the reciprocal visits by the Chinese leaders to foreign nations? By 1972, when such visits to many parts of the world were made possible by China's diplomatic breakthroughs, both Mao Zedong and Zhou Enlai were dying, one from general ill health and the other from cancer. It remains open to question whether they would have made any such visit if they had been able to. For Mao, to be sure, it would have been more compatible with the Chinese tradition for the foreign dignitaries to come to Beijing to see him anyway. However, China did reach out to the world. Before Mao's death, Deng Xiaoping, in his capacity as the first Vice-Premier, travelled to New York and delivered his forceful speech at the 6th Special Session of the UN General Assembly in 1974. Deng also visited both France and Japan in 1975. Hua Guofeng, as the head of the Chinese government, visited France, Great Britain, West Germany and Italy in 1979. Deng Xiaoping, rehabilitated as Vice-Premier after a period of disgrace, visited Burma, Nepal, Thailand, Malaysia, Singapore and Japan in 1978, and the United States in 1979. Vice-Premier Li Xiannian visited the Philippines and Bangladesh in 1978 and Tanzania, Mozambique, Zambia, Zaïre and Pakistan in 1979.

China and multilateral diplomacy

Parallel to China's diplomatic breakthrough in its bilateral relations was China's participation in the United Nations system. Bilateral engagement and multilateral diplomacy were therefore mutually reinforced to engage China irreversibly in the international political and economic processes. The record of China's participation in global parliamentary politics at the UN and its engagement in the work of UN subsidiaries and other related international organisations in the 1970s was another indicator of successful accommodation of China into the society of states.

The UN system furnished China with opportunities and occasions to get acquainted with the work of international institutions and the rules of the game. At the same time, it also provided China with the forums and platforms to project its images of the world order and to pronounce its global policies. Hundreds of speeches were made by the Chinese delegates in policy statements and in debate not only in the UN headquarters in New York, but also in other locations like Geneva and Paris where some UN specialised agencies were located. It was in the corridors and the committee rooms in New York as well as in Geneva, Paris and Rome that Chinese delegates mingled with thousands of UN representatives from more than 100 countries and regions. It was through public debate as well as private consultation that China familiarised itself with international norms and conventions and learned to adapt itself to fit in not only with the UN system but also with the existing international system at large.

A seminal work based on extensive empirical data by Samuel Kim on China's initial participation in the UN system from 1971 to 1976 has three very important findings particularly relevant to the present study.[47] First, China's participation in the UN in general – either in the General Assembly, or in the Security Council or in UN specialised agencies – was extensive and supportive. From the 26th Session to the 31st Session, the Chinese delegations were the third largest. China's permanent resident mission in New York was also the third largest. China moved swiftly in 1972, the second year of its admission, to take its full part in the work of the General Assembly, with Chinese representatives at all seven main committees. China also opted to participate selectively in the General Assembly subsidiary organs with limited membership such as the Credentials Committee. China, however, only played a 'modest and self-effacing role' in the Security Council as one of the decision makers.[48] 'Instead of defying and ignoring the rules of the game in the Security Council, she has attempted to master them in the pursuit of her principles and/or her interests.'[49] On the other hand, China's participation in UN functional bodies, according to Kim, was 'at a slow but methodical pace'.[50] Two official Chinese accounts of China's participation in UN specialised agencies published in the late 1980s substantiate this finding.[51]

It is worth noting here that this extensive participation took place against a background of near non-participation by the PRC in any international organisations in the previous decades. During the period of its exclusion from the United Nations, China's participation in the functional inter-governmental organisations (IGOs) and non-governmental organisations (NGOs) was minimal. According to one study, in 1966, the PRC was member of only 1 IGO which was outside the UN family, and its membership to NGOs was restricted to only 58 out of a total of several thousands.[52] After China's admission to the General Assembly, most UN specialised agencies followed the guideline provided by the General Assembly as to the Chinese representation. By 1977, China's participation in IGOs had risen sharply to 21.[53] Eight of them were specialised agencies in the UN family.

Second, China's participation in this period was more symbolic than substantive and more reactive than pro-active. It assumed and kept a low profile in both the General Assembly and the Security Council and most other organs of the UN system. It adopted cautious approaches to international issues debated and discussed at the UN and selectively concentrated on issues related to its national interest on certain committees. It never sponsored a draft resolution on its own initiative, except the draft resolution to adopt Chinese among the working languages at the General Assembly. Most interestingly, and probably also importantly, China took an apprentice-like posture in its first years of UN membership. Zhou Enlai readily acknowledged in public in October 1971, before sending the first Chinese delegation to the UN, that

> We do not have much knowledge about the United Nations and are not too conversant with the new situation which has arisen in the United Nations. We must be very cautious. This does not mean, however, that we do not have self-confidence; it means that caution is required and that we must not be indiscreet and haphazard.[54]

Upon arrival in New York, Qiao Guanhua, head of the Chinese delegation, told Adam Malik, the Assembly President, that the Chinese delegation could not participate immediately in all activities of the General Assembly, because UN affairs 'were new to its members'. Indeed, upon joining various main committees of the General Assembly, the Chinese delegates all expressed their willingness to learn the procedures and actual workings of the UN and to listen to and to note the opinions and viewpoints of other delegations. At the Security Council, the Chinese delegates, most notably Huang Hua and Chen Chu,

> sat back and said little on the subjects with which they were not yet familiar or for which they lacked experts. And they took a rather low profile and modest approach, which is not the usual approach for newcomers at the Security Council'.[55]

A similar attitude was adopted by Chinese delegates in its participation in the UN specialised agencies. Even in private consultation process behind the scenes at the UN, the Chinese delegates would usually only 'seek information, ask questions and solicit advice in a manner of a novice student'.[56] Kim concluded that during its first years of participation, China in general 'assumed the low profile posture of a diligent apprentice who was preoccupied in learning a new trade, rather than the high-profile posture of a revolutionary challenger attempting to impose her own concept of how the United Nations should be operated'.[57]

At the same time, the Chinese delegates made befriends with delegates from other member states at all social occasions. There are two prime examples. Ambassador Huang Hua and his colleagues were noted to have gone out of their way to stroll into the delegates' lounge at the UN – the preserve of delegates from the smaller states of Asia, Africa, Latin

America and Europe – for coffee or for a chat, which representatives from great powers rarely did, and still less for delegates from the two superpowers. The Chinese delegation was also remembered for their 'banquet diplomacy', when almost everyone was invited and befriended. It is important to note, however, that passive and cautious though the Chinese participation might be, it involved China closely and inexorably in a global communication network at the UN. It is through this communication network, either officially in the committee rooms and the Assembly Hall during formal debates and discussions, or privately in the corridors of the UN and at the Chinese permanent mission for consultation and during banquets, that modifications of differing perceptions of reality in world politics between China and other members of the UN were taking place. Thus China's participation in the UN provided policy makers in Beijing with a handy and original means of communicating with the world at large.

Third, China's participation in the UN system in general was a success story. It was a success because in just a few years, the UN had successfully accommodated revolutionary China into its system with the necessary adjustment but no major shake-up. The UN 'bent' its rules only occasionally and to a limited extent. It was a success also because China had managed to fit into the structure of the UN without excessive disturbance to the system. China readily fulfilled most of its financial obligations to the UN. It also contributed duly to the Food and Agriculture Organisation (FAO) and the International Civil Aviation Organisation (ICAO) budgets. In order to be accepted into the ICAO, from 1972 to 1974 China recognised or adhered to more protocols of the Chicago Convention which codifies the customary principles of international civil aviation. China's participation, on the other hand, helped in the process of creating and developing new norms in areas previously ungoverned by any agreed rules.

Indeed, the mutual engagement between China and international society in this unique world organisation was, to many, a surprisingly smooth journey. Contrary to many wild predictions before China's entry into the United Nations, throughout the 1970s, China did not conduct itself as a disruptive force in the normal procedures of the UN, either at the General Assembly, or at the Security Council, or in other specialised agencies, as some had worried. Nor did it move in a messianic way to restructure the world in its own image, as some others had feared. China used the UN as an international forum to project its outlook of the world, to pronounce its principles in international relations, and sometimes to pose as the spokesman of the Third World. In this process, China modified its perception of the world, learned the rules of the game in UN politics and began to participate in the work of many common international institutions in the UN family.

The way in which China participated in the 1970s in the UN system is then perhaps not atypical of the socialisation of any newcomer to the United Nations. It was characterised by a process of learning and adaptation, a process in which a low-profile posture and cautious approaches were adopted first as a matter of necessity and later as a matter of design. It was a process through which modifications of China's international behaviour and values were acquired. The important difference here of course is the extraordinary background of China's alienation from international society in the previous 20-odd years. China had been a militant and revolutionary state. The preconceived image of China before its entry had been that of a reckless bull entering the ordered house of the United Nations, destroying everything. No other words therefore summarise better the success story of China's socialisation into the UN system than the following:

> Once settled in the world organisation, China has proved to be neither a revolutionary challenger attempting to impose her own conception of how the Organisation should be operated, nor an institutional reformer. For most of the time, on most of the issues, she has been acting as a cautious and self-effacing newcomer, mastering her new trade and adjusting her ideological preconceptions to the rules and norms of the Organisation. In short, China has played the diplomatic game by the established rules, rather than attempting to replace or repudiate them.[58]

At the end of the 1970s, William Feeney conducted a detailed study of the changes and continuities in China's UN policy after Mao Zedong's death in 1976, and concluded that 'At present, China's UN policies, with the exception of disarmament, conform to those of the current UN majority. Any pronounced alteration is unlikely in the near future.'[59]

China and the world economy

Another striking aspect of the mutual engagement between China and international society was China's increased involvement in the world economy in the 1970s. Systematic description of this involvement is beyond the scope of this study and has already been done almost exhaustively elsewhere.[60] It is a story, one may argue, of limited success, but of unlimited significance. Let us look briefly at three areas of the engagement: namely, China's foreign trade, its changing development strategy and its changing attitude towards international borrowing. These three indices are most illustrative of how China forged closer association with the international economic system in the 1970s.

The first index is China's foreign trade. Two-way trade increased from $4.586 billion in 1970 to $29.333 billion in 1979, more than six times that of the 1970 figure. That is on average approximately to 22 per cent annual increase in trade value.[61] This is particularly significant because it was achieved in spite of the turbulence and upheavals in China's domestic politics immediately before and after the deaths of both Zhou Enlai and Mao Zedong in 1976 and in spite of subsequent trade fluctuations in 1975 and 1976 (see Figure 3.1) By the end of the 1970s, China was seeking long-term stability in its trade relations with its main trading partners. China and Japan signed the Long-term Trade Agreement (1978–85) in Beijing on 16 February 1978, which stipulated that each side was to export to the other about $10 billion during the entire period. It was subsequently revised to target at a total of bilateral trade at between $40 to $60 billion in a 13-year period from 1978 to 1990.[62] In April of the same year, China and the European Community initialled a five-year trade pact in Brussels.[63] In 1978 and 1979, long-term trade or economic cooperation agreements were signed between China and some European countries individually, including Britain, France and Yugoslavia. A formal trade agreement was struck between China and the United States in July 1979 in

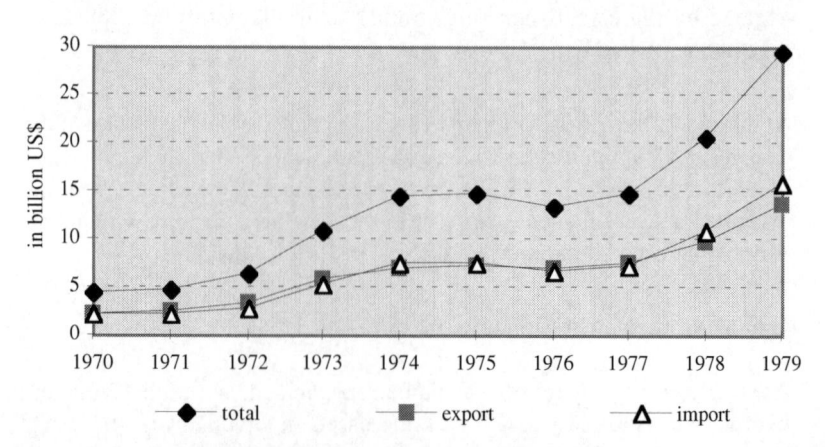

Source: *Zhongguo Duinai Jingji Maoyi Nianjiang, 1989*, p. 299.

Figure 3.1   China's foreign trade, 1970–79

Beijing, an important step towards regularising Sino–American economic relations.[64]

This overall picture can be substantiated most instructively by two cases in bilateral trade: Sino–Japanese trade and Sino–American trade. Before the normalisation of mutual relations between the PRC and Japan in 1972, Sino–Japanese bilateral trade was mostly facilitated by non-governmental organisations. Sino–Japanese trade acquired a new momentum after the establishment of full diplomatic relations between the two countries in September 1972. After 1972 both the Chinese and the Japanese governments moved quickly to construct a legal framework for normal economic relations. A ten-article trade agreement between China and Japan was signed on 5 January 1974 in Beijing, which reduced tariff barriers by one-third on average. It was followed by the signing of a number of bilateral agreements, including a civil aviation agreement on 20 April 1974, a maritime transport agreement on 13 November 1974, and later a shipping agreement and a trademark agreement.[65] There is no doubt that these intergovernmental agreements greatly facilitated the bilateral trade. It must be noted, however, that other factors such as cultural ties, geographic proximity, complementary economies, and institutional connections in trade which pre-dated the normalisation were all brought into full play in developing Sino–Japanese trade. From 1972 to 1979, Sino–Japanese trade increased dramatically at an average of 29 per cent per annum. In seven years, two-way trade was sextupled in volume (see Figure 3.2).

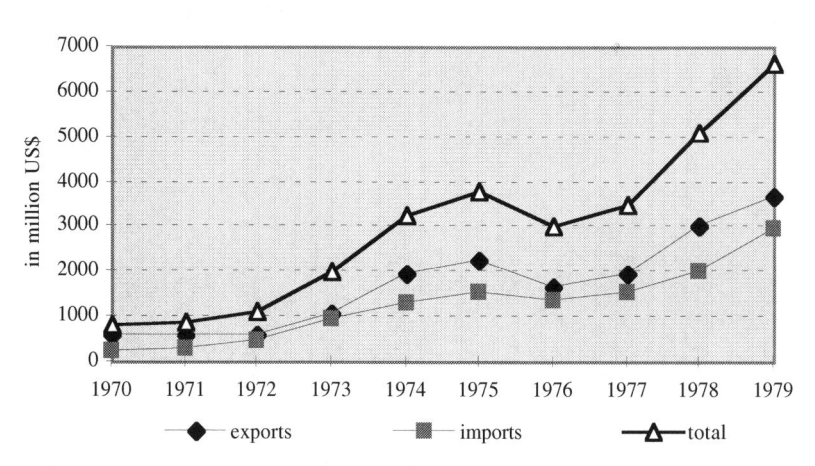

Source: Tomozo Morino, 'China–Japan Trade and Investment Relations', in F. J. Macchiarola and R. B. Oxnam (eds), *The China Challenge: American Policies in East Asia*, p. 88.

Figure 3.2 Sino–Japanese trade, 1970–79

In 1979, Japan was the first developed country to offer China a substantial governmental credit when China declared its willingness to accept economic and financial assistance from other countries. In May 1979, the Japanese government announced that it would provide China with an energy development loan of 420 billion yen. In December of the same year, while visiting China, the Japanese Prime Minister Ohira Masayoshi stated that Japan would provide China with an Overseas Development Cooperation Fund credit of 330 billion yen for the construction of two port projects and two railway projects.[66]

Sino–American trade in the 1970s was more dramatic both in terms of its rise and its fluctuations. Prior to Nixon's China breakthrough in 1972, there was virtually no trade between the two countries. By 1974, two-way trade soared to around $1 billion. The United States suddenly became the second largest trading partner of China, after Japan. Sino–American trade was, however, extremely vulnerable because it was dominated by China's imports from the United States, about 80 per cent of which were agricultural commodities, including wheat, corn, soybeans and cotton, and were particularly susceptible to any policy changes in and by China. In 1975, for example, China suddenly cut off its purchase of grain from the United States, partly because of its improved grain supply due to a good harvest in the previous year and partly out of its consideration of the growing foreign trade deficit. By the same token, the big jump in Sino–American trade in 1978 and 1979 owed much to the start of China's modernisation programme and its outward-ooking foreign economic

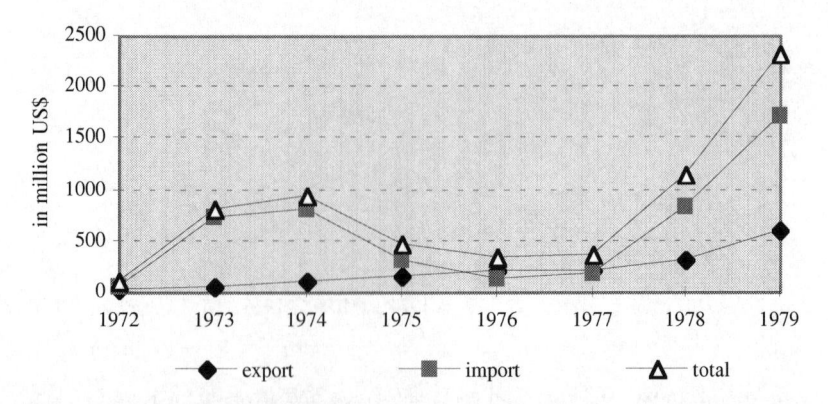

Source: A. Doak Barnett, *China's Economy in Global Perspective*, p. 507.

Figure 3.3   Sino–American trade, 1972–79

policy. Only the normalisation of Sino–American relations in 1979 provided impetus and prospect for the rapid and stable expansion of bilateral economic relations.

It must be noted that Sino–American trade in the 1970s developed in a substantially different context from that of Sino–Japanese trade. Sino–American trade started from scratch in 1972. Unlike the Japanese, the Americans had no commercial contacts whatsoever in China and there were no institutional connections between the trading communities of the two countries. American businessmen had little real knowledge of the China market and had no experience in handling trade with the PRC before 1972. Unlike the Japanese, the Americans could not boast of any common culture and history with China. There was no geographic proximity between the two countries, either. Unlike Sino–Japanese trade, Sino–American trade during most of the 1970s were conducted without an adequate legal framework and institutional arrangements provided by government agreements. More importantly, Sino–American trade was more susceptible to ideological considerations and political changes in China than Sino–Japanese trade. The assessment of the achievement and fluctuations of Sino–American trade in the 1970s must take into consideration all these factors.

The second index is China's outward-looking development strategy. In the 1970s, self-reliance as a fundamental principle for China's economic development was subject to reinterpretation in theory and was seriously challenged in practice.[67] Even before the open debate over self-reliance in early 1974, official policies on the import of technology and capital goods from non-Communist countries had already undergone subtle changes. With the deterioration of Sino–Soviet relations in the early 1960s, China had already begun to turn to non-Communist countries for the import of technology and equipment. China's trade with Western Europe in 1960, for example, was $651.5 million. In 1966, it was $897 million.[68] The process was interrupted by the Cultural Revolution.

Two major changes in China in 1972, some eminent Chinese economists argued, made it possible to restore such a policy. One was that substantial improvement of China's foreign relations 'provided favourable conditions for the expansion of its economic and technical interflow with other countries and its foreign trade as well'. The other was that with Lin Biao's removal, the 'interference' of the extreme 'Leftists' was temporarily diminishing.[69] The year 1973 saw the prelude of what was later called China's 'Great Leap Outward'. It was estimated that the value of contracts signed in the year for importation of whole plants and technology from the West jumped to a total of $1,259 million, which was followed by a total of

$831 million in 1974.[70] Those contracts included the importation of 13 giant chemical fertiliser plants, 4 giant chemical fibre mills, 3 petroleum chemical industrial works, 43 sets of coal combines, 3 giant power stations, and a 1.7 metre rolling machine. This huge wave of importation was personally sanctioned by Mao Zedong and Zhou Enlai.[71] Accordingly, there was a great increase in the value of China's imports of machinery and equipment in 1974 and 1975. The figure jumped from $797 million in 1973 to $1,605 million in 1974, and again to $2,160 million in 1975.[72]

The second upsurge of China's importing machinery and technology in the 1970s occurred during the so-called 'Great Leap Outward' period from 1977 to 1979. Both CCP's Eleventh National Congress in August 1977 and the Fifth National People's Congress in February 1978 called for high-speed socialist economic development so as to complete the mission of modernising China by the end of the century. The extremely ambitious Ten-Year Plan for the Development of the National Economy (1976–85) was adopted in February 1978 with an emphasis on large-scale investment and on importing modern capital goods and modern technology.[73] 'Under the impetus of this ambitious plan, $40 billion in foreign contracts for complete industrial plants were discussed, and $7 billion in contracts were actually signed in 1978 alone, with contracts totalling $3 billion signed in ten frantic days at the end of December.'[74] Many Japanese businessmen were succumbed to 'China fever'.[75] As was confirmed by the State Planning Commission in 1980, China signed in this short period contracts for imports of 'complete sets of equipment and separate units of machinery totalling $7.8 billion'.[76]

Huge import of capital goods and modern technology apart, towards the end of the 1970s China also went out of its way to explore various forms of co-operation and coproduction with foreign companies. Here was another 'leap' in China's outward-looking strategy for development. Standard international commercial practices, such as processing, assembling and compensation trade, were quickly accepted and agreements to process and to assemble for foreign companies were signed. Xinhua (New China) News Agency reported in November 1978 that 'Peking factories produce goods for foreign companies'. By July 1979, more than 300 agreements on processing and assembling for foreign companies had been signed in Guangdong province alone.[77] These were the early prototypes of Sino–foreign 'joint ventures' in China. In December 1978, Minister of Foreign Trade Li Qiang publicly announced in Hong Kong that 'China welcomes joint investments with foreign firms whose equity shares in such ventures may run up to a maximum of anywhere near 49 per cent with the length of such ownership up to negotiation'.[78] This marked a turning point in China's participation in the international economy. In July 1979, China's first joint venture law was passed in the National People's Congress.

The third index, probably the most significant, is China's changing attitude towards international borrowing. History and ideology had heavily influenced China's perception of international debt. Modern Chinese history is full of bitter experience in paying indemnities incurred by the lost wars China fought with Britain, France, Japan and other Western nations in the nineteenth century. The Boxer indemnities were particularly traumatic and freshly remembered by many. Moreover, for the Communists, foreign capital, especially from a capitalist country, was regarded as the spearhead of the capitalist invasion and exploitation of China. On top of that, in the 1950s and early 1960s, the PRC's acceptance and repayment of the Soviet credits ended up on a very bitter note. The common perception was that foreign debt would undermine China's sovereignty and independence. The PRC's trade with non-Communist countries was mostly conducted on a cash-and-carry basis. In January 1973, on the eve of China's first upsurge of importing complete sets of plants and technology from the West, Bai Xiangguo, the Minister of Foreign Trade, did raise the question of deferred payment with his British host in London while discussing China's purchase of heavy equipment from Britain.[79] Such an instrument, however, was only used sparingly. When the first issue of *Foreign Trade* was published in Beijing in 1974, the idea of foreign loans and credits was categorically rejected by the then Foreign Trade Minister Li Qiang.[80] In fact, the Chinese government had earlier given a negative reply to an offer by Japan of a government loan to China immediately after the normalisation of Sino–Japanese relations in 1972.[81] According to Doak Barnett, however, from 1970 to 1977, China's international borrowing was 'substantial' and 'virtually all from non-Communist countries'.[82] Most of these borrowings were short- and medium-term credits and were mostly for purchase of whole sets of plants. China still prudently avoided any long-term indebtedness to any foreign country.

China's public shopping for credits in the international financial market did not occur until 1978. In his visit to Japan in October 1978 after the signing of the Sino–Japanese Treaty of Peace and Friendship, Deng Xiaoping publicly stated that '[T]here are many fields in which we can make use of Japanese scientific and technological achievements and *even funds*'.[83] He also confirmed that China would study the possibility of the Japanese government loans, though '*up to now* China had not considered obtaining loans from the Japanese government'.[84] This foreshadowed an official pronouncement of Chinese policy towards international borrowing. In December 1978, Foreign Trade Minister Li Qiang publicly announced in Hong Kong that, 'As long as the conditions are appropriate, China will consider accepting loans from foreign governments'.[85] Even before this official pronouncement, Chinese and Japanese officials had already been engaged in negotiations for a Japanese government loan to China.[86] By mid-1979, China had signed major loan and credit agreements with Japanese and Western European banks totalling $22.7 billion.[87]

In late 1978, China also began to seek multilateral aid and technical assistance. In August 1978, the Chinese government decided to initiate a new policy of 'give as well as take' in its economic and technical cooperation with the United Nations and its specialised agencies. That effectively meant that China would now seek and accept economic and technical assistance from the UN and its subsidiaries. In October 1978, the Chinese government formally asked the United Nations Development Programme (UNDP) for technical assistance. In January 1979, a UNDP special meeting decided to provide China $15 million for technical assistance for the period from 1979 to 1981. This was the first multilateral technical assistance China had obtained from the UN subsidiaries. In September 1979, the Representative Office of the UNDP in Beijing was inaugurated.[88] It is claimed officially in China that the China–UNDP deal 'marks the beginning of a new era of multilateral economic and technical co-operation between China and the United Nations'.[89] In 1979, the United Nations Industrial Development Organisation (UNIDO) also began to provide aid to China. So did the United Nations Fund for Population (UNFP) and the United Nations International Children's Emergency Fund (Unicef) in 1980.[90]

There is another equally significant aspect of China's search for closer association with the international economy. At the beginning of 1979, immediately after the normalisation of Sino–American relations, Beijing signalled repeatedly that it would actively seek to resume China's seat at two key international economic organisations: the International Bank of Reconstruction and Development (IBRD) and the International Monetary Fund.[91] Like China's decisions to get into other UN affiliates in the early 1970s, this decision was largely politically motivated. The expulsion of Taiwan from these two organisations would mean a final political victory for Beijing. China's prestige and influence in world politics would be enhanced with its participation in more international organisations.

Unlike many other decisions in the early 1970s, however, this decision was also underwritten by some careful economic considerations. On the one hand, membership in the IBRD and the IMF would assist China's development programme in two ways: it would provide China with direct access to information about the international economy; and it would make China eligible for developmental assistance such as the World Bank loans with a concessional interest rate and the IMF drawing privileges. As will be seen in Chapter 6, the World Bank loans and the IMF drawing rights have since China's participation played a significant role in China's economic development. On the other hand, membership would entail some obligations on China. China would have to submit to the World Bank and the IMF its economic data, many of which were classified 'ultra secret', such as China's gold reserves. China would have to assist in every possible way missions sent to China by the IMF and the World Bank, and possibly their resident missions in Beijing, in their studies of the Chinese economy. As a member, China would also have to make a financial contribution to both organisations. Although the economic benefit of joining these two organisations was certainly not the 'least important' consideration of China's top leaders at the time,[92] it is questionable that the principal interest for China in joining the World Bank group was to 'seek World Bank aid to help its hydroelectric power plant, railway, and other industrial projects'.[93]

To sum up, the globalisation of Chinese diplomacy by establishing formal diplomatic relations with most member states, the mutual legitimation process in the UN through China's participation, and the intensification of interactions between the Chinese economy and the world economy in the 1970s steadily and resolutely engaged China with the international political and economic systems. The process of mutual engagement, however, was a process of mutual adjustment as well. It was a process in which China learned to make necessary changes so as to fit itself and to be accepted into the existing arrangements of the international system. It was also a process in which international society in general and the UN in particular endeavoured to incorporate China into its own framework without unnecessary disruption or reconstruction. Few would deny today that the mutual engagement, politically and economically, between China and international society in the 1970s, though problem-ridden, was a success story. To many, it was probably surprisingly smooth. The important question to be discussed now is: What are the limits of this seemingly striking success story?

THE LIMITS OF THE 1970s

Towards the end of the decade, it was clear that some qualitative changes in the relationship between China and international society were in the making. At the beginning of the decade, China was still regarded as a pariah in international society. By the end of the decade, however, China had been successfully accommodated into and embraced by the international community. What then is the significance of the 1970s in the history of the PRC's international relations? The 1970s was conventionally regarded as a decade of China's 'ascendancy in world politics'.[94] In other words, China featured as more and more important in the international system in the 1970s. This 'ascendancy' was first and foremost marked by the PRC's entry into the United Nations and in particular its assumption of China's seat as a permanent member at the Security Council. Second, it was also emphasised by China's becoming one of the three in the so-called strategic triangle, which dominated the balance of power in the international strategic landscape in the 1970s. Third, it was seen in the fact that the emergence of China as a great power, albeit more nominally than formally, contributed significantly to the structural changes in the post-war international political order from bipolarity to multipolarity. The official evaluation of China's diplomatic breakthrough in the 1970s echoed this wisdom.[95]

There is certain degree of truth in this wisdom. It has, however, missed a fundamental point. China's ascending importance in world politics, if any, came from the single and simple fact that China had been positively drawn into the international system and had been constructively involved in building and sustaining the existing international order. China no longer posed a threat from without as a revolutionary state committed to the destruction, or at least revolutionary transformation, of the international system. Instead, it became a challenge, although hostile from time to time, from within the system. The inclusion of China in the global international system as a legitimate actor in world politics was therefore the most revolutionary change in the 1970s. Over time, even revolutionary China under Mao had developed some stake in the existing order in the society of states, and recognised the privileges and prestige it could gain as a significant power by working along with that society.

The 1970s was, therefore, first and foremost a decade of China's de-alienation and accommodation in international society. Mutual legitimation and mutual engagement between China and international society in the decade were constructive, progressive, yet decisive. The PRC's admission into the United Nations in 1971 put to an end the question of the PRC's international legitimacy, which had haunted both China and the international community in the previous two decades. The American opening to China was in fact also China's long-awaited strategic breakthrough in its international relations. At the end of the decade, China enjoyed full diplomatic relations with more than 120 countries, including the United States. China's involvement in global politics was substantial. Through the UN and other international forums, China voiced its concerns about a wide range of international issues, from arms control to the New International Economic Order (NIEO) and to the Law of the Sea. Its participation in the UN affiliates and its specialised agencies was extensive, though sometimes passive. China was acknowledged by most member states not only as a legitimate, but also as an important and indispensable player in world politics. More importantly, China learned to how to play by the existing rules of the game in the politics among nations.

The political de-alienation led to and helped China's engagement with the international economy. China's foreign trade increased more than six times in the decade, which represents an average increase of 24 per cent per annum.[96] Here is a good contrasting example. Whereas the total volume of China's foreign trade in 1969 was only $4.029 billion,[97] the combined foreign trade deficit of 1979–80 reached nearly $4 billion.[98] Other aspects of changes in China's foreign economic policies were far-reaching. The import of whole plants and advanced technologies experienced two huge waves in 1973 and 1978 respectively. By the end of the decade, this had become an established policy in facilitating the Four Modernisations, though more discreet approaches were still cautioned to avoid a huge deficit in foreign trade. International borrowing was justified. Credits from foreign banks, loans from foreign governments and developmental assistance from international organisations were all actively sought after. Joint ventures with foreign equity, a taboo in the socialist construction in China ever since 1949, was initiated in 1979. In July 1979, the first Chinese law on joint ventures, 'The Law of the People's Republic of China on Joint Ventures Using Chinese and Foreign Investment',[99] was promulgated in Beijing. *Beijing Review* may insist that China did not abandon its principle of self-reliance as strongly as many foreign observers argued that China did. This nevertheless signalled at least the beginning of China's acceptance of the international division of labour and international economic inter-dependence. It was also the beginning of China's adherence to common international practice and norms in its economic development.

Yet the 1970s had its limits. It should not be disputed that China was again incorporated as a member into the 'family of nations'. Neither should it be denied that China's participation in international politics and its involvement with the world economy in the 1970s were unprecedented both in degree and in extent, at least in the history of the PRC. China's behaviour in the strategic triangle between Washington, Moscow and

Beijing did suggest that such important common institutions as balance of power and the great powers' special responsibilities in world politics were not only acceptable but even desirable to China.

Nevertheless, such participation and involvement were not sufficient to bring about China's integration in any substantial degree into international society. For one thing, political socialisation in matters affecting international security between China and other member states was insignificant. China's stand on security issues was both foreshadowed and overshadowed by China's repeated insistence that a world war was inevitable and by its claim that 'countries want independence, nations want liberation and peoples want revolution' and that this was an irresistible historical trend. It is also questionable whether China was committed to make the existing international system 'a workable whole'. The militant and rigid stand of anti-Soviet hegemonism which China took both at the United Nations and in its main thrusts of foreign policy hampered its efforts to reach the minimum value consensus necessary to maintain the international order in the 1970s. Indeed, one may also question how much China shared with other members of international society their common interests in maintaining such an order.

For another thing, the economic integration of China into the international economic system was still minimal. Throughout the 1970s, interaction between the Chinese economy and the world economy had become more and more sustained and broader in scope. China did begin to manifest some 'integrative behaviour' in its foreign economic policies towards the end of the 1970s. The policy to open up China to international economy was initiated, and some common international practices were taken up by the Chinese in their economic reform programme towards the end of the decade. However, even at the beginning of the 1980s, the Chinese economy remained very much a closed one, with its door only just opened. As was observed in 1981, 'Of all the major powers, China until recently has been the least involved in the web of global interdependence that has developed during recent decades.'[100] China's attitude towards international economic inter-dependence was at best ambivalent. More than in the realms of politics, China's share of the work of common institutions in the world economy was limited. China was not yet a member of the key international economic organisations such as the World Bank and the IMF. A big gap existed between China's foreign trade regimes and the requirements of the GATT, universally taken as international norms. Further, there were no signs that China was making efforts to conform to those norms. International finance, 'a major force in integrating the modern world economy',[101] was yet to find its place in the

Mutual Legitimation

Chinese economy. Evidence suggests that only at the end of the 1970s did China begin to make serious efforts towards becoming an integral part of the international economy.

The decade of the 1970s therefore only saw China's rejoining the world in a very limited sense. China had returned to and had been accommodated to certain extent by the international community. However, neither China's political participation in the international system nor the economic interaction between China and the world economy was sufficient to ensure any significant degree of China's integration into international society.

There were various factors which underlay these limits of the 1970s. For example, a shortage of specialised talents to work in the United Nations, as previously remarked, partly dictated China's low-profile stance in many UN affiliates and on many UN-sponsored issues. It was only towards the end of the 1970s that 'this low-profile posture [could] no longer be attributed to China's inexperience ... [and had] to be accepted as a deliberate choice of strategy'.[102] Legally and officially, the Sino–Soviet Treaty of Friendship, Alliance and Mutual Assistance, though long regarded by both sides to have lost its *raison d'être*, was still in effect.[103] This single fact may have severely restricted China's diplomatic options. Three other major factors, however, are more responsible. The first is the international environment China was faced with, particularly uncertainties in Sino–American relations. The second is the unfolding drama of China's internal politics. And the third is the political legacy of Mao's world view.

First although the China breakthrough in 1972 had changed the whole perspective of Sino–American relations, for the Chinese the 1970s were full of 'twists and turns in the course of establishing diplomatic relations' with the United States.[104] For the Americans, on the other hand, Sino–American relations 'progressed erratically for much of the 1970s'.[105] The normalisation of mutual relations between China and the United States did not happen until January 1979, after a seven-year Long March. Unless and until China normalised its relations with the United States, one of the two dominant powers in the international system, there were serious constraints in China's overall international strategy. For example, only after Sino–American relations were normalised in 1979 did China decide to seek membership in the World Bank and the IMF. One simple reason was because with the normalisation, the United States 'was not likely to pose obstacles to the expulsion of Taiwan from the IMF and the World Bank'.[106] Another example was China's approach to international security. In the 1970s, China perceived itself being encircled 'from the north, south and west' by the Soviet Union.[107] The lack of fully normalised relations with the United States undermined China's confidence in stability of whatever strategic alignment it formed with the ...unter the Soviet threat. This certainly compounded its ...urity. This could account at least partially for China's military rigid anti-Soviet hegemonism stance in world politics in general ... at the United Nations in particular throughout the 1970s. China's 'obsessions' with the perceived Soviet threat and its rigid anti-Soviet posture had in particular affected China's arms control and disarmament strategy. In so doing, China had, as has been convincingly argued, alienated itself from a large number of Third World countries which China regarded as natural allies in world politics.[108] It also soured other successes in China's bilateral and multilateral diplomacy.

Second, in the 1970s, intense power struggle and political upheavals dominated the convulsive domestic politics in China. Crises followed in succession. Lin Biao's fall in 1971 was followed by the vigorous campaign to criticise Lin Biao and Confucius, a campaign engineered by the Leftists to be directed, ironically, at Zhou Enlai. Zhou Enlai's death in January 1976 and the drama of Deng Xiaoping's rise and fall in 1975–76 were followed by the death of Mao Zedong and the downfall of the 'Gang of Four' in the autumn of 1976, which certainly stymied China's foreign policy initiatives. Even when Deng Xiaoping re-emerged in Chinese politics in July of 1977, the power struggle between the Reformers with Deng as their leading representative and the so-called Restorationists represented by Hua Guofeng continued well into the 1980s.[109] Meanwhile, Deng had to face a daunting task of dealing with political and economic legacies of the Mao era. The Cultural Revolution, which had caused havoc and devastation to the nation, had to be repudiated. The political confidence of the people and the Party had to be restored. The national economy, which was repeatedly claimed to be 'on the verge of bankruptcy', had first to be rescued before it could be further developed. Only after Deng Xiaoping consolidated his position as the paramount leader in the Party hierarchy in the late 1978 did a set of well coordinated and pragmatic political and economic policies gradually emerge, aimed principally at China's economic development. As was well acknowledged, the watershed was the Third Plenum of the Eleventh Central Committee of the CCP in December 1978. At the beginning of 1979, an era was closed. With the establishment of diplomatic relations with the United States and with the CCP putting its house in order, both China's domestic scene and its international environment offered some promising elements for the country's all-out efforts to engage itself further with international political and economic affairs.

Third, it has been argued that 'Mao was never fully reconciled to the implications of China's enhanced international involvement, viewing relations with American more as a means to escape China's acute security predicament rather than a path to economic and technological advancement'.[110] This is also an accurate description of the state of mind of the entire Chinese leadership in the 1970s. *Renmin Ribao*, for example, pronounced in January 1977, several months after Mao's death and the subsequent of the arrest of the 'Gang of Four', that China would 'never permit the use of foreign capital; never run undertakings in concert with foreigners; never accept foreign loans (and by implication) never join the international capitalist IGOs; and never incur domestic nor external debts'.[111] As we will see later, the process of China's socialisation and integration into international society in the last two decades is also a process in which not only the Chinese leadership but also the Chinese population have been struggling to come to terms with the implications of China's enhanced international involvement.

At the end of 1970s, therefore, the biggest hindrance that inhibited China's integration into international society was the burden of the Maoist world view. China's perception of the international system was inevitably rooted in its national experience and history. The 'century of humiliation' from 1840 to 1949 and more than two decades of exclusion from international society both left a deep mark on this perception. In 1971, when Mao was seeing Qiao Guanhua off to head the first PRC delegation to attend the 26th UN General Assembly in New York, he wrote him a well-known Chinese proverb: 'How can you catch tiger's cubs if you do not enter tiger's lair' (*Buru huxue yande huzi*).[112] The comparison of the UN to the tiger's lair was a glaring reflection of Mao's perception that the existing international system was of a malevolent, not benevolent, nature. On war and peace, throughout most of the 1970s, China consistently preached Mao's theme that world war was inevitable. The dictum was, if you want peace, prepare for war. Further, Mao's theory of the three worlds, first publicly and systematically pronounced by Deng Xiaoping at the UN Special Conference in 1974,[113] guided China's global strategy at least up to 1979, 'linking symbolically and normatively China's own fate with that of the Third World in the unfolding struggle to transform the existing international order'.[114] Economic interdependence, on the other hand, continued to be denounced as neo-colonialistic and exploitative of the poor by the rich. This heavily value-tainted world view predetermined China's resistance to rather than acceptance of the existing international order, although China did not, as it had in the 1960s, vehemently deny the legitimacy of that order. The lack of China's integrative behaviour in both the international political and economic systems was partly attributable to this.

It is therefore important to note that, after 1978, the struggle within the CCP between the 'Restorationists' led by Hua Guofeng and the

'Reformers' headed by Deng Xiaoping centred on the so-called 'two whatevers'.[115] The eventual triumph of 'seeking truth from facts' over the 'two whatevers' in the ideological contest inside the CCP was not only a personal victory for Deng Xiaoping. It also started a 'thought emancipation movement' in China which sought to evaluate Mao Zedong more objectively in the scale of history.[116] Accordingly, it offered the CCP an ever-effective weapon to deal with Mao's legacies in both domestic and foreign policies.

With the launching of China's modernisation programme and its policy of opening up (*Kaifang*) to the international economy at the end of 1978, a new perspective was introduced in China's perception of the world. It was now not only imperative but also possible that modifications of China's perception of the world and the international institutions is realised so that a convergence of views of the contemporary international system, political and economic, could be achieved between China and other members of international society. China's further integration into international society was predicated upon this convergence. China's accommodation into international society in the 1970s, in spite of its limitations, prepared China for moving towards convergent views of the international system. The actual process of convergence, however, took place in the 1980s. To the examination of this we now turn.

4 Changing Perceptions

Studies of China's international relations in the 1980s are dominated by analyses of changes in China's international strategy, particularly by examinations of China's independent foreign policy.[1] There are good reasons for that. The 1980s has been sometimes characterised as an 'unusual decade' for China.[2] China's second revolution – the opening of China to the world economy and economic reforms – had a profound impact on the international outlook of China and consequently the orientation of Chinese foreign policy. The emergence first of China's redefined independent foreign policy in 1982 and later the independent foreign policy of peace in 1986 was, the Chinese themselves claimed, the 'timely adjustment, enrichment and improvement' of Chinese foreign policy. The first official pronouncement of China's independent foreign policy in the 1980s was made by General Secretary Hu Yaobang on 1 September 1982. China would, Hu proclaimed, 'consistently carry out an independent foreign policy'. Chinese foreign policy, he continued, would 'definitely not be swayed by expediency or by anybody's instigation or provocation'.[3] One major aspect of this independent foreign policy, as Deng Xiaoping later explained, was that China 'will not play the "United States card" or the "Soviet Union card". Nor will it allow others to play the "China card".'[4]

Towards the end of 1985, China further qualified its foreign policy as an 'independent foreign policy of peace'. In March 1986, Premier Zhao Ziyang stated that,

> At all times and under all circumstances China will act independently, determining its own attitudes and policies on all world issues on the merits of each case. The criterion by which China judges whether an act is right or wrong is whether it helps to maintain world peace, develop friendly co-operation among nations and promote world economic prosperity.[5]

He reiterated specifically that 'China will never attach itself to any superpower, or enter into alliance or strategic relations with either of them'.[6] The basic objectives of the Chinese foreign policy, as defined by Zhao, were 'to oppose hegemonism, maintain world peace, develop friendly co-operation with other countries, and promote common economic prosperity'.[7]

This line of Chinese foreign policy is clearly a far cry from that in the 1970s and even that in the first two years of the 1980s when China actively campaigned for an international united front and made a tacit alignment with the United States to oppose the Soviet hegemonism, 'the more ferocious, the more reckless, the more treacherous and the more dangerous source of world war'.[8]

To be sure, independence from both superpowers in making and executing its international strategy was not the only thrust of this new line of Chinese foreign policy. It was, however, the principal thrust upon the basis of which a whole spectrum of radical adjustments of Chinese foreign policy was effected. From supporting popular peace movement worldwide[9] to endorsing the superpower *détente* and from calling for an economic diplomacy to acquiescing in international economic interdependence, the faces of Chinese foreign policy changed. Striving for a peaceful international environment conducive to China's economic and political reforms became the onus of the Chinese foreign policy now. To this was added in 1986 another basic objective of Chinese foreign policy: namely, to 'promote common economic prosperity [with other countries]'. This is the first time that to facilitate world economic development was declared to be China's foreign policy goal.[10] Around the same time, peace and development were declared to be the two trends governing international relations in the 1980s. What was behind such a fundamental change? Why should there be such a change at this particular moment? What initiated this 'new direction' in Chinese foreign policy?

Existing studies of Chinese foreign policy in the 1980s mostly follow convention in foreign policy analysis. They have tried to seek answers to the above questions almost exclusively in three directions. They either look at the changing systemic context for China's international relations and contend that it is a combination of three major factors – the deterioration of Sino–American relations during the first Reagan administration, Brezhnev's overture to China for Sino–Soviet reconciliation in 1982, and China's increasing confidence in its own influence in world politics – that produced China's pronounced independent foreign policy. Or they explore the inner chapters of Chinese domestic politics and argue that it is the 'Dengisation' both in terms of the CCP's top leadership changes and of China's domestic policy reorientation that is a more plausible explanation.[11] Or they examine the political economy of China's ambitious economic reforms and argue that it is the imperative need to attract foreign capitals for economic modernisation that initiated the adjustments. Indeed, the Chinese themselves emphatically pointed out in the late 1980s that the adjustment of Chinese foreign policy around 1982 was 'required by the domestic tasks set for the new period and by the latest international developments'.[12]

These arguments do have their merits. It is received wisdom that a country's foreign policy should change in response to either incentives and constraints provided by the changing international environment it is faced with, or to the limitation imposed by domestic politics, or more often to both. In the early 1980s, both the systemic context, especially China's relations with both superpowers, and the domestic political environment in China experienced perceptible and demanding changes. They indeed had a powerful impact on the assumptions and presuppositions of the Chinese leadership in their decision making in foreign policy. They dictated a new orientation for Chinese foreign policy.

The probing question is why the new orientation of Chinese foreign policy should be towards such a declared independent foreign policy fostering peace and common economic prosperity in international society. Given the radical nature of Chinese foreign policy in the previous decade, changes in China's international environment and in Chinese domestic politics are necessary conditions for the new orientation. They are not, however, sufficient in explaining away this question.

Max Weber once argued that 'Interests (material and ideal), not ideas, dominate directly the actions of men. Yet the "images of the world" created by these ideas have often served as switches determining the track on which the dynamism of interests kept the action going.'[13] Pursuing this line of Weber's wisdom further, it could be argued that it was China's national interests that dictated fundamental changes of Chinese foreign policy in the early 1980s. It was, however, China's changing images of the world and the ideas behind such changing images that decided that China should opt for an independent foreign policy of peace and common economic prosperity. A decade of socialisation of China in the international community compelled appreciable changes in China's perceptions of the international system and institutions associated with that system.

That this could happen and should have done so in the 1980s has another explanation in the development of domestic politics in China. Roderick MacFarquhar argues that in the wake of the end of Maoism in China, economic reforms 'allowed more freedom of thought and action'.[14] Richard Baum, on the other hand, identifies three cycles of political liberalisation and rebuff and repression in China in the 1980s.[15] Although political liberalisation in the 1980s had a much chequered record and was ultimately thwarted by the Tiananmen incident in 1989, the more open and liberal political climate it brought to China's domestic politics periodically in the decade was indispensable for initiating such radical perceptual changes. This was helped by the fact that the reform-minded leadership, which went out of its way to encourage changes in such a direction held the reins for most of the decade. As will be discussed in the next chapter, for example, Hu Yaobang and Zhao Ziyang were passionate proponents of transcending ideology in international relations.

It has been noted that in foreign policy making, ideas and perceptions of decision makers are particularly important because they 'structure their environment for choice, inform their consideration of various courses of action, and provide rationalisation for the choices that are made'.[16] The thrust of this chapter is therefore to explore the interaction between ideas and events. It examines ideas and perceptions, rather than events, that instructively informed the 'adjustment, enrichment and improvements' in Chinese foreign policy and conclusively shaped its new orientation. It looks at China's changing perceptions of the international system. It inquires into China's changing attitude towards war and peace, revolution and development, and dependence and inter-dependence – three sets of important institutions in contemporary international relations. It argues that China's preliminary socialisation into international society in the 1970s, combined with fundamental changes in China's domestic politics and in the international system, compel a series of profound perceptual changes by China. It contends that such changes led significantly to a process of convergence between China and other members of the society of states in their perception of the international regimes and institutions current in the 1980s. It is those ideas behind China's profound changing perceptions that underlie and sustain the changes and continuities of Chinese foreign policy in the 1980s and in the 1990s. Perceptual changes, however small they are, constitute an important process of China's socialisation into international society.

THE INTERNATIONAL SYSTEM

It is no more than a truism to state that a nation's perception of the international system is deeply affected by its history and national experience. This received wisdom, however, has significant and probably special application to China. As has been argued previously, China's alienation from international society after 1949 derived partly from its historical experience with the West in 'a century of humiliation and aggression'.[17] The denial of the PRC's legitimacy by the American-dominated international community and China's perception of being surrounded by a hostile world in the 1950s and the 1960s only accentuated China's alienation. The clearly articulated radical ideology and militancy in Chinese foreign policy further underlay China's rejection of the existing international system and its institutions. Not surprisingly, China's perception of the international system was a mirror image of this experience. It is little wonder that from the two-camp view of the world in the 1950s to the outright condemnation of the international system in the 1960s, and then to the 'three worlds theory' in the 1970s, the Chinese view of the contemporary international order was in constant flux.[18] Accordingly, China's international strategy had changed from 'breaking into' the system in the 1950s to 'breaking up' the system in the 1960s.[19] Its unreserved hostility towards the existing international order was little disguised. Indeed, 'Mao found it difficult to render support to the structures, values, and rules of the post-war international system in which China had been prevented from playing her legitimate role'.[20]

Even in the most of the 1970s after China's incorporation into the international system, China's opposition to the existing international order was clearly expressed. The 'three worlds theory', representative of China's outlook of the world order, advocated almost revolutionary changes in the existing international system. It firmly identified the two dominant powers in the international system, the Soviet Union and the United States, as 'the biggest international exploiters and oppressors' and 'the common enemies of the people of the world'.[21] It credited the Third World as being 'the main force in the worldwide struggle against imperialism, colonialism and hegemonism'.[22] It called for 'the broadest international united front to smash superpower hegemonism and war policies'.[23] China's support in the United Nations for the implementation of the New International Economic Order, on the other hand, underlined an operational policy of attempting to remould the international system.[24] The change of China's position *vis-à-vis* the international system from that of an outcast to that of a legitimate player inside the system only mitigated to a very limited extent its intense dissatisfaction with the international system.

It is true that, contrary to many ominous predictions prior to the PRC's entry into the United Nations, China was not a disruptive force in the United Nations in the early years of its participation. It is also true that China in the 1970s stopped challenging outright the legitimacy of the international system at the end of the process of mutual legitimation between China and the United Nations in the early years of the decade. Yet China did not stop altogether advocating a militant approach to, if not the break-up, at least a radical reform of the existing international system. It continued to question the desirability and the acceptability of the prevailing international order. It was undesirable because it was full of political and economic injustice and the whole system was unjustifiable. It was unacceptable because of the hierarchical order in the existing international society which ensured the superpowers' dominance and which lay at the root of the inequalities in that society.

It should be noted, however, that even when China's view of the world was subject to considerable changes and its international strategy was in constant flux in the three decades after 1949, there were at least three sustaining themes in China's perception of the international system. First, the post-war international order was full of injustice and inequalities. The old political order was, in Deng Xiaoping's words, 'based on colonialism, imperialism and hegemonism'.[25] The old international economic order was, on the other hand, characterised by the 'imperialist exploitation and plunder' of developing countries.[26] China, for one, was the victim of both the old international political order and the old international economic order. Second, the existing hierarchical structure of the international system and its dominance by the two superpowers lay at the very root of the unjust and irrational international order of the contemporary world. China's pledge never to be a superpower underlined not only China's opposition to, but also its determination to change, such an order. And third, it follows that sweeping reforms, either radical or gradual, of the international system were not only necessary but also desirable. The Chinese image of world order was therefore 'more decisively oriented toward change than toward order'.[27]

However, China in the 1980s was radically different. It is not to be disputed that China continued to preach its opposition to hegemonism and to injustice and inequalities in the international system.[28] Nevertheless, by the early 1980s, China had readily, if also quietly, abandoned the so-called 'theory of the three worlds' in their conceptual analysis of the changing international system. The existing international system was perceived as less malevolent. In an important document of the Central Committee of the CCP on economic reform issued in 1984, it plainly stated that 'although international relations are complex and ridden with contradictions, international economic and technological ties are, general speaking, very close'.[29] China's continuous advocacy of changes in the international economic system now emphasised common interests for both the North and the South in realising the proposed changes through negotiation and mutual concessions and compromise, not through confrontation and opposition. Moreover, China now preached gradual and orderly changes, neither surgical transformation nor radical reform, of the existing international system.

On top of this, a new dimension was emerging. In their analysis of the trend of history, the Chinese leadership repeatedly stated that peace and development had become the 'two outstanding issues' confronting the world in the 1980s.[30] They further specified that peace 'involves East–West relations', whereas development 'involves North–South relations'.[31] Deng Xiaoping was quoted as saying that 'Peace is an East–West problem, while development is a North–South question. All these problems can be covered by four words: East, West, South and North.'[32] On East–West relations, the Chinese government 'wish to see the United States and the Soviet Union reaching a *détente* rather than sharpening their confrontation, which increases the danger of the war' and 'are in favour of improved relations between Eastern and Western European countries and the removal of acute antagonism between the two military blocs'. All efforts towards easing international and regional tensions and resolving armed conflicts would 'have China's support'.[33]

On North–South relations, China became almost reticent about its support for the implementation of the NIEO. In 1985, Deng Xiaoping told a visiting Japanese delegation that the developed nations would have to seek outlets for their capital and to expand their trade and markets to sustain long-term growth. He continued,

> It is not likely that these developed nations, with a combined population of only 1.1 or 1.2 billion, can continue to grow while the developing countries with a combined population of more than three billion, remain in poverty.... Unless their [the Third World countries'] economic problems are solved, it will be hard for all the Third World countries to develop and for the developed countries to advance further.[34]

This is not a North–South, exploiting-cum-exploited paradigm but a North–South inter-dependent formula. Such inter-dependence, though 'most unequal', 'may be mutually beneficial' to both the South and the North.[35] Accordingly, strengthening South–South cooperation and encouraging North–South dialogue and cooperation would make an important contribution to the general growth and prosperity of the world economy.[36] Proceeding from such a perception, China made it one of its basic foreign policy objectives to 'develop friendly co-operation with [all] other countries and promote common economic prosperity'.[37] China would not only 'support the North–South dialogue', but would also 'take an active part in the South–South co-operation'.[38] The North and the South should 'join hands to develop a world economic order leading to common prosperity'.[39] China's adjustments to its foreign policy, based on its fresh analysis of the existing international order, were made, in Zhao Ziyang's words, 'to meet the challenge of international developments in conformity with the trend of the times'.[40] More than ever before, peace and stability rather than great disorder in the prevailing international system became most desirable for China.

It would be hazardous, however, to conclude that China was a *status quo* power in the 1980s, or that China discontinued promoting changes in the international system. It is very clear, however, that China in the 1980s was more orientated to order than to change in the international system. This was seen as compatible with China's principal foreign policy goal, that is to create a peaceful international environment conducive to the domestic reforms. Chinese leaders vowed explicitly on many occasions that China was striving for the preservation of world peace and stability, not for their destruction.[41] Deng Xiaoping even urged visiting American strategists from the Center for Strategic and International Studies of Georgetown University to 'rack our brains to find ways to stabilise the world situation'.[42]

China's orientation for a stable international order suggested an emerging Chinese perception that the existing international system, though far from desirable, was not unacceptable. In contrast to the previous three decades, China displayed relative satisfaction with the *status quo* of the international order. In so perceiving, China signalled its readiness and willingness to work within the existing framework of the international system, which China found an increasing degree of acceptability. In the actual operation of Chinese foreign policy, such a perception was translated into efforts to shore up the existing order. Hu Yaobang declared unequivocally in September 1982 that 'The future of China is closely bound up with that of the world as a whole'.[43]

Equally illuminating, perhaps, is the fact that in their discourse on the international political economy, Chinese leaders as well as Chinese scholars increasingly used such terms and concepts as 'East–West relations', 'North–South dialogue', and 'South–South cooperations in their commonly accepted sense. Such terms as the 'great disorder under heaven' and such proclamations as 'countries want revolution, nations want independence and peoples want revolution were the irresistible trend of history', frequently used in official Chinese statements in the 1970s, were totally discarded. The adoption of a common vocabulary by China in its political discourse in world politics and the international economy is highly significant, symbolic of China's acceptance, however grudging, of the principal concepts as they were universally defined in international relations.

A degree of convergence of China's view of the United Nations with that of other members was also clear. No longer was the United Nations compared to a 'tiger's lair'. On its fortieth anniversary, Zhao Ziyang told the United Nations General Assembly that the UN was a global organisation 'whose universality and importance grow with the passage of time', an organisation 'irreplaceable in the historical mission it shoulders and the impact it exerts on the world'.[44]

It is argued that the deradicalisation of the foreign policy of a revolutionary state happens only when and if two conditions are fulfilled. One is that it comes to perceive the existing international order as strong and enduring. The other is that it believes that it has acquired a fair stake and a proper place in that order.[45] Whether China in the 1980s perceived that the contemporary international order was strong and enduring is highly debatable. It was also doubtful whether China thought it already had a proper place in that international order. There seems to be little doubt, however, that deradicalisation of Chinese foreign policy had happened. More than at any other time in its short history, the PRC did develop a fair stake in the existing international order and in its continuance. Further, China, though still very much a discontented power, was now more willing and ready than ever before to work within the existing arrangements of the international system to search for and gain its proper place in the international order.

If the deradicalisation of Chinese foreign policy was taking place, China's changing perception of the international system is at best only a partial explanation of that deradicalisation in the 1980s. Underlying the reorientation of Chinese foreign policy in the early 1980s are also profound changes in China's perceptions of other institutions in the existing order, such as war and peace, revolution and development, and dependence and inter-dependence. It is to the discussions of those that we will now turn in search of further explanations of China's radical readjustments to its foreign policy.

WAR AND PEACE

Like the antithesis of war and peace, China's preaching in the 1970s of the inevitability of a world war was almost antithetical to its proclamation of peace as one of the two major trends of history in the 1980s. In an important review of China's changing international policy in the 1980s, it was argued that changes in the perception of war and peace in the contemporary international system is one of the key factors which underlie the radical and important adjustments to Chinese foreign policy in the 1980s. It is asserted further that, during the 1980s, 'through a comprehensive analysis of war and peace [in the contemporary international system], China has changed its view which overemphasised the danger of an imminent [world] war, and has accordingly made a realistic judgement that [world] peace can be safeguarded'.[46]

In 1970, Mao Zedong warned that the 'danger of a new world war still exists, and people of all countries must get prepared'.[47] This theme persisted in all the main statements of Chinese foreign policy throughout the 1970s. In a speech to the UN General Assembly after Mao's death in 1976, Qiao Guanhua, the Chinese Foreign Minister, continued to declare that the global war between the United States and the Soviet Union was 'inevitable' and 'independent of man's will'.[48] In a *Renmin Ribao* editorial in 1977 commemorating Mao's theory of the 'three worlds', it was forcefully stated that the rivalry of the two superpowers 'inevitably leads to war'.[49] Throughout the 1970s, it became axiomatic for the Chinese to claim that 'either the war will bring about the revolution or the revolution will bring war to an end'. From a revolutionary perspective, world war was not only inevitable, but also desirable. This line of thinking on war and peace in the 1970s was the pivotal point around which the Chinese foreign policy of anti-hegemonism was evolved.

That Mao's thinking on war and peace in the contemporary world order dominated China's reading of the international situation in the 1970s is beyond dispute. Running a risk of oversimplification, Mao's conceptualisation of war and peace can be summarised as follows. First, Mao's image of human nature was not Hobbesian. Conflicts and violence were therefore not inherent in the biological or psychic make-up of man but in the social process itself. Second, it follows that modern wars in international society could only be attributed to the imperialist system itself. Given the predatory nature of imperialism, there would be war of one kind or another as long as imperialism persisted in the international system. Whether a war would break out or not was determined by imperialist powers. Third, there were only two kinds of wars, just and unjust. Only by opposing unjust wars with just wars and by resisting the imperialists and colonialists with revolutionary violence could world peace be achieved. Accordingly, all wars of national liberation after the Second World War had contributed to the defence of world peace. In other words, peace could only be the result of struggle, not of compromise. Fourth, an all-out nuclear war would help facilitate the triumph of Communism and speed up the end of capitalism.[50]

Mao's thinking, it should be noted, not only reflected, but was also conditioned by, his own revolutionary experience and China's concerns with its security and its strategic weakness *vis-à-vis* the superpowers. For all his life, from the Autumn Uprising in 1927 he led in Hunan to the Sino–Soviet border clashes in 1969, and to the end of his life, Mao could be said to have fought 'just' wars against his enemies both in China and abroad. On the other hand, even after its entry into the United Nations and its *rapprochement* with the United States, China continued to feel encircled by a hostile superpower, this time the Soviet Union. In such a context, peace therefore remained desirable but impossible for China to achieve. The superpower rivalries around the globe with their expression in incessant regional conflicts made world war a constant possibility.

Mao's theories of war and peace, with particular relevance to China's international environment, constituted one of the most important and imperative legacies in foreign policy formulation that Mao left to his successors. However, to redefine war and peace problems in international society in the 1980s involved more than dealing with Mao's legacy. To be sure, by the end of the 1970s, the Chinese leadership was made aware of the damage to its economy and its foreign relations brought about by China's rigid public overemphasis in its international diplomacy of the inevitability of an immediate world war.[51] China's drive for the realisation of the four modernisations, on the other hand, had changed the perspective of its perception of the international system, as argued earlier in this chapter. Equally importantly, it is this new perspective that heralded the new approach to international peace that China would adopt. Coupled with this was the changing international situation concerning China, including subtle changes in China's strategic relations with the two superpowers and its improved security environment *vis-à-vis* its neighbouring countries. These are, among others, the main factors which first prompted the Chinese leadership to reconsider China's position on the inevitability of war. Speaking at an enlarged meeting of the Military Commission of the Central Committee of the CCP on 4 June 1985, Deng Xiaoping stated:

> The danger of world war still exists. Because of the arms race between the two superpowers, the factors making for war will increase. But the people want peace and oppose war, so the world forces for peace are growing faster than the forces for war. The Chinese government will always stand by its policy of opposing hegemonism and safeguarding world peace, pursue an independent foreign policy and side firmly with the forces of peace. *As long as the forces for peace continue to expand, it is possible that world war will not break out for a fairly long time to come, and there is hope of maintaining world peace.*[52]

This is at least a substantial modification, if not a reversal, of Mao's position. If the world war could not be avoided, it could at least be postponed. It follows that world peace could be maintained even in the shadow of fierce superpower rivalries and of the 'balance of terror'.

Theoretically, Chinese scholars began to question the basic assumption that a state's international behaviour is predetermined by its internal political system and its corollary that a socialist country is by definition peace-loving and a capitalist country is by nature war-prone. As a result, 'the orthodox theory of class struggle as the explanation of war and peace had been seriously challenged'.[53]

What are the forces for world peace? How had the Chinese persuaded themselves that the factors making for peace in the 1980s had outgrown those making for war? Surely, the Chinese maintained that the danger of war still existed as long as the United States and the Soviet Union, the two superpowers capable of launching an all-out war, continued to vie for world hegemony. The Chinese rationale that world peace was achievable runs along the following lines. First, they came to believe that the two superpowers

> 'were roughly balanced in terms of military might. Neither was completely successful in its regional rivalry due to constraints both at home and abroad. Neither came near completing its global strategic deployment and each found it very difficult to accomplish this task.[54]

The Chinese also believed that it was unlikely that the United States would start a world war, because it had the biggest vested interest in the existing international order. The Soviet Union had also, on the other hand, acquired a fair stake in the contemporary world order. It was content to fight limited and regional wars to expand its sphere of influence. The Chinese further argued that there were some discernible signs of the changing concept of national security on the part of the Soviet Union. The economic development was becoming an indispensable element in the Soviet consideration of its national security.[55] The result was that neither was willing or capable of launching a world war which would inevitably destroy the existing international system.

Second, a gradual democratisation was effected in international relations. The rise of the Third World (including China) had brought about structural changes in the post-war international system. The Third World, which virtually consisted of a majority of member states in international society, had now more significant influence in deciding important matters concerning war and peace in world affairs. The democratisation of international relations was also seen in the two superpowers gradually losing control over their allies and clients in the two military blocs, NATO and the Warsaw Pact. More importantly, it was seen in the small and medium-sized countries having more and more say in international affairs, and in the fact that more and more countries were pursuing a foreign policy commensurate with their own national interests and independent of the control and the influence of the superpowers. In particular, the Chinese were at pains to point out that the allies of the United States and the Soviet Union in Europe had initiated and pursued a set of policies aimed at easing tensions between them, very often against the advice and despite the pressure of the superpowers to do otherwise. This had put an end, the Chinese argued, to the times when the superpowers or a few great powers could arbitrarily decide the destiny of the whole world.[56]

The Chinese also came to recognise that in the broad context of democratisation in international relations, the peace movement world-wide, which had been growing very fast, began to exercise considerable constraints on any war efforts by the two superpowers. The peace movement in Western Europe in particular had contributed to bringing countries from both Eastern and Western Europe to a common ground in favour of superpower dialogue and *détente* and against superpower rivalry and confrontation.[57] Because of the centrality of Europe in both superpowers' global strategy, the Chinese further reasoned, the peace movement in European countries as an essential force in checking the superpowers from launching an all-out war.[58] From late 1984, China resumed its contact with international peace organisations.[59]

Third, the Chinese came to acknowledge openly that nuclear weapons 'could inflict untold losses on mankind' in war.[60] Nuclear weapons, therefore, made for peace because in a 'balance of terror' situation, neither superpower dared to start a total war which would not only destroy the opponent but also put its own survival in question. Nuclear weapons made for peace also because their destructive capability kept people all over the world alert to any possibility of a nuclear war and boosted the anti-nuclear peace movement, particularly in the developed capitalist countries in Western Europe.[61] Such an acknowledgement is particularly significant because it signals an acceptance, if only reticent, by the Chinese of the theory of nuclear deterrence, a reverse of their previous position on nuclear weapons and war. This position agrees with that held by many other nuclear and non-nuclear member states in the international system.

Fourth, Chinese scholars argued that developments in the international economy were conducive to world peace. The economic inter-dependence which had developed in the past decade had some effect in modifying ideological confrontation and hostility between countries of different social systems.[62] It also created an economic structure within which, 'when one suffers all the rest will suffer and all will prosper when one prospers'. In such circumstances, war could no longer be regarded a feasible means for resolving contradictions and conflicts between member states in the international community. It is interesting to see how close such a position is to that of neo-liberalism. There were additional arguments from the Chinese scholars. Since national power consisted not only of military might, but increasingly of the economic clout of a state, the fundamental structural changes in the international political economy with the decline of the economic hegemony of the United States and the rise of Japan and Western Europe in the world economy also made for peace.[63]

On a higher theoretical level, the Chinese contended that such fundamental changes in their conceptualisation of war and peace in the international system were effected because a new era (*Shidai*) in world politics had arrived. The old era, which was characterised by what Stalin called 'war and revolution' or 'imperialism and proletarian revolution', had gone. The post-war development of world politics and the international economy demonstrated that the capitalist system was *not* on the verge of bankruptcy. On the contrary, it had made such achievements that the capitalist mode of production and the capitalist relations of production were still dominant in the international system. Moreover, owing to the collapse of the old colonial system, the destructiveness of nuclear weapons and the increasing inter-dependence in the world economy, war between capitalist (and by implication 'imperialist') countries was no longer inevitable. On the other hand, the post-war development of socialist countries had shown that the development of the socialist economy would take a long time to catch up with and eventually overtake that of the capitalist economy. It follows that the process of socialism replacing capitalism world-wide, if ever, would be long, and also tortuous. The new era was therefore marked by peaceful coexistence and competition between socialism and capitalism. Peace and development were the common desire of all peoples of the world, because 'it is impossible for development to continue when there is no peace and it is impossible for peace to last long when there is no development'.[64] After the first Gorbachev–Reagan summit in 1985, Chinese scholars and officials alike further argued that the new era in international politics saw more 'irresistible historical trends': dialogue was replacing confrontation in East–West relations; and policies of *détente*, readjustment, reform and opening up were being pursued by more and more members of the international community.[65]

One may indeed disagree with and even dispute much of the above analysis by the Chinese about war and peace and about the coming of a new era in international relations. However, whether the Chinese reasoning could stand rigorous intellectual challenge is not our concern here. What is of great importance is that there occurred a major shift of China's position on war and peace in the contemporary international system. More importantly, this major shift is in the right direction in concurring with the common perception of war and peace held by other member states as important institutions in maintaining the international order.

REVOLUTION AND DEVELOPMENT

In its period of alienation from international society, China frequently proclaimed that the Chinese Revolution was an integral part of the world revolution. As such, China was duty-bound to support revolutionary movements and organisations world-wide. China as a revolutionary state had endorsed many revolutions in Third World countries, particularly in the 1960s.[66] It had given both moral support and material aid to the armed struggle of many national liberation movements in Asia, Africa and Latin America, the so-called 'rear of imperialism'. It had also projected itself as a model for the success of national liberation for 'the oppressed nations in their struggles against imperialism and its lackeys'. Revolutionary violence was endorsed as legitimate means for the oppressed peoples in their struggles. Support for wars of national liberation was therefore one of the main thrusts of Chinese foreign policy. The diplomacy of the PRC was 'revolutionary' as also seen in its united front strategy in challenging the existing international order, whether pursued from an under-dog perspective in the 1960s or adopted from a top-dog perspective in the 1970s.[67]

It was more than coincidental that China's support of national liberation movements took place in a time characterised by 'the anti-colonial revolution' in the post-war period which finally overthrew the colonial system.[68] National liberation movements were the driving force behind the decolonisation process in Asia, mostly in the late 1940s and the 1950s, and in Africa in the 1960s and early 1970s. In China's evaluation of the international situation, this 'revolt against the West' in Asia and Africa consisted of many revolutions in colonial dependencies on the two continents, and indicated an irresistible historical trend of revolution in establishing a new international order. During his tour of Africa in 1964, the peak year of decolonisation in Africa, Zhou Enlai claimed that 'an excellent revolutionary situation exists in Africa' and that the African people were 'pushing the revolution forward'.[69] Mao Zedong, in a grand statement read on the rostrum of Tiananmen on 20 May 1970, declared to the world that 'The present historical trend is revolution'.[70] As late as 1975, 'countries want independence, nations want liberation and peoples want revolution' was still proclaimed as 'irresistible historical trends' by Zhou Enlai in his Government Work Report to the Fourth National People's Congress. Revolutions were accordingly associated with the decolonisation process and with the Third World. As such, the Third World was credited as a force pushing forward the wheel of history. In line with this argument, China's support for revolutions was not only compatible with its ideology, but also served China's national interests and conformed to the proclaimed historical trend.

It is difficult to dispute that the ideology of sinicised Marxism–Leninism dictated China's moral commitment to overseas revolutions. Nor is it easy to dismiss the fact that official Chinese pronouncements supporting national liberation movements had a central theme of promoting a world revolution. However, as findings of Peter Van Ness's empirical study published in 1970 indicate, in the most radical year (1965) of China's revolutionary strategy, Beijing's selection of targets for revolution in another nation had much more to do with the perceived hostility of that country than with the ideology or military strategy of local revolutionary organisations. He concluded:

> Generally speaking, countries ruled by governments hostile to Peking were most often chosen as targets for revolution; those governed by regimes friendly to Peking were *not* selected as targets for revolution, even when revolutionary movements were led by pro-Peking Communists.[71]

A nation was perceived to be hostile to Beijing, Van Ness's empirical study further contends, mainly because, first, it maintained diplomatic relations with Taiwan; second, it voted against the admission of Beijing to the UN; and third, it was a signatory of a defence treaty with the West on China's periphery.[72] Another study by Melvin Gurtov, published a year later, also concluded that 'China's support for revolution in Southeast Asia becomes perfunctory whenever local governments are willing to demonstrate their friendship toward Peking by avoiding excessive dependence on American (or Soviet) support'.[73]

Beijing's specific endorsement of revolutions in foreign countries, therefore, was probably more dictated by China's strategy to break away from its diplomatic isolation, to make a dent on the hostile encirclement of the PRC led by the United States, and to enhance China's international status. In this sense, China's endorsement of revolutions overseas as part and parcel of its foreign policy served the same purpose as the foreign policy of many other states; namely, to preserve the integrity and security of the state and to advance its power and prestige in the international system.

Van Ness and Gurtov's points were also partly borne out by China's de-emphasis on revolution in international relations beginning in the late 1970s. Several factors contributed to this de-emphasis. First, with its admission into the United Nations in 1971, China had developed a higher stake in the engagement of normal state-to-state diplomacy – that is, dealing with the established governments. Public and radical support of revolution in another nation would no longer serve the useful purposes it had done in the 1960s and would damage state-to-state relations. Second, with the collapse of the Portuguese Empire in 1974–75, post-war decolonisation had by and large ended. Many national liberation movements had become the governments of ex-colonial dependencies. The prospect of a new wave of revolutions in Third World countries was receding. With the classic colonial system removed, the struggle to win independence had been replaced by the struggle to safeguard independence largely through the implementation of a New International Economic Order. Third, the death of Mao in 1976 was accompanied by the removal of the 'Leftist' influence in Chinese foreign policy. Even if China still had moral commitment to revolutions overseas, that commitment did not have to, and indeed should not, be translated into public and material support of those revolutionary movements by China. One of the major adjustments Beijing made to its Southeast Asian policies at the end of the 1970s, as Robert Scalapino observed, was to put emphasis on state-to-state relations, rather than on 'comradely' relations with the revolutionary movements in those countries.[74] Last but not least, domestic stability and in some cases prosperity in some Southeast Asian nations in particular undermined both the traditional and the revolutionary dissidence in those countries which formed the basis of the national liberation movements that China had supported.

Accordingly, China's endorsement of revolutions abroad, if any, became subdued except for a few national liberation movements such as the Palestinian Liberation Organisation (PLO) and the African National Congress (ANC), which, after all, were receiving popular support in the international community. In official pronouncements of Chinese foreign policy there were no longer terms referring to a world revolution. At the

Twelfth Party Congress in 1982, Hu Yaobang, in declaring an independent foreign policy, stated:

> We Marxists-Leninists believe that Communism will in the end succeed in the world. However, revolution cannot be exported. It can only be the result of peoples' choice of each nation.[75]

Decisions were made to drop all terms in the new Constitution of the CCP, and later of the Constitution of the PRC, which might be (mis)understood to be promoting a world revolution. The consensus was that 'Inter-state relations should have nothing to do with the world revolution. It is totally wrong to say that [the] foreign policy [of China] serves the world revolution.'[76] In resuming and establishing relations with political parties and groups in the 1980s, CCP leaders emphasised repeatedly that party-to-party relations were restricted to moral and ideological affairs and should not stand in the way of developing relations between states.

While revolution had been pushed to the sideline in China's policy towards Third World countries, economic development assumed centrality. At the beginning of the 1980s, a new dimension in China's perception of the Third World gradually set in. This new dimension emphasised the realities in the Third World: grinding poverty, prolonged economic stagnation, constant domestic instability, and incessant conflicts within and wars between Third World countries. These problems, the Chinese continued to argue, were attributable to the old international economic order: both a legacy of the ex-colonial system and an expression of neo-colonialism. They equally emphasised, however, that economic mismanagement by Third World governments, widespread corruption and inappropriate adoption of economic development models were also to blame. In such a poor and backward society that was characteristic of most Third World countries, therefore, economic development should be the first priority. The political independence of Third World countries could only be consolidated by achieving economic independence.[77] It was only natural that the Chinese claimed that many Third World countries 'have entered a historical period in which their central task is the development of their national economies'.[78] The Chinese also argued that while changes in the existing international economic order were highly desirable, it was urgent for Third World countries to learn how to speed up their economic development in the existing system, even it meant prolonging the life of that system. In this context, South–South cooperation was essential in such efforts. On the other hand, North–South conflicts notwithstanding, dialogue between the two sides would be beneficial to both. Developing countries, including

China, would have little chance in successfully fulfilling their developmental goals without help from the outside – that is, from the developed countries.[79] A prominent Chinese official/economist was blunter in asserting that, 'in order to realise its modernisation, the South must carry out effective economic co-operation with the North. Capital and technology, which are imperative in economic modernisation, cannot be expected to fall from heaven'.[80]

It was therefore small wonder that from the late 1970s China's one-way economic aid programmes were substantially scaled down.[81] An authoritative article in *Hongqi* (Red Flag) in early 1982 called for a comprehensive review of China's policy of rendering aid to Third World countries.[82] China should only give 'whatever assistance is within our [China's] capability' to Third World countries. '*Liangli Erxing, Shishi Qiushi*' (to give whatever aid is within China's capability practically and realistically) became the watchwords of China's policy in rendering economic aid to Third World countries in the 1980s.[83] China's aid would also go to those Third World countries that 'are in dire difficulty and in particular need of help'.[84] On the other hand, South–South cooperation which China envisaged now emphasised bilateral trade and technical cooperation based on accepted international norms. Four new principles governing China's economic and technical cooperation with developing nations were first proposed in January 1983 by Zhao Ziyang while he was visiting Africa. They were 'equality and mutual benefit, stress on practical results, diversity in form, and common progress'.[85]

While scaling down its aid, China substantially expanded its trade with Third World countries in terms of trading partners and trade forms. Latin American countries – a relatively uncultivated region as regards China's foreign trade up to the 1980s – were targeted in China's new trade 'offensive' in the mid- 1980s. For example, China's trade with Brazil in 1984 reached $818 million.[86] Another example was China's participation in international bidding for construction projects, particularly in the Middle East.[87] By the end of 1988, China had developed trade relations with 118 developing nations, with a total trade value of $10.614 billion, 13.19 per cent of China's total foreign trade for the year.[88]

From endorsing revolutions in Asia and Africa in the turbulent 1960s and most of the 1970s to inaugurating a programme of common economic prosperity with developing nations in the 1980s, China's Third World policy saw some profound changes. It is nevertheless best seen as a process of China's coming to terms with its changing position in the international system. It is also the best indicator as to how China has changed from working for an international order shaped according to its own vision to striving for an international system acceptable to most members of the society of states.

DEPENDENCE AND INTER-DEPENDENCE

The Chinese economy in the first 30 years of the PRC was characterised neither by dependence on nor inter-dependence with the capitalist-dominated international economy. Except for moderate aid from the Soviet Union in the early 1950s, the model of China's economic development was characteristically that of self-reliance. Indeed, with its alienation from international society, China opted not to have, as much as it was forced out of, any close involvement with the international economy. The strategy of self-reliance in economic development was probably the only viable option for China. Limited contact with the international economy, whether by design or by force of circumstances, was the hallmark of China's foreign economic relations. 'Conceptually and operationally, the PRC was outside the post-war international economic order.'[89]

This situation notwithstanding, China's image of the international economic order was close to a dependency model, with the exploitative North dominating the exploited South. This does not mean that the Chinese had accepted the validity of dependencia theory.[90] Nor does it even suggest that the dependencia theorists such as Samir Amin and Immanuel Wallenstein had a strong influence in China.[91] It only means that in some important aspects, there was an identity of outlook regarding the international economic system between the Chinese and the dependency theorists. Both insisted that it was the structure of the international economic system, not the internal conditions of each developing country, which was the key variable determining the underdevelopment of the South. Both emphasised that the development process of the South could only be comprehended correctly if it was placed firmly in the historical context of imperialism today and yesterday. As André Gunder Frank argued, 'underdevelopment was and still is generated by the very same historical process which also generated economic development: the development of capitalism'.[92] A similar argument in different and blunter terms was pronounced as the official Chinese view of the international economic order by Deng Xiaoping at the 6th Special Session of the UN General Assembly in 1974, when he stated:

> As we all know, in the last few centuries colonialism and imperialism unscrupulously enslaved and plundered the people of Asia, Africa and Latin America. Exploiting the cheap labour power of the local people and their rich natural resources and imposing a lopsided and single-product economy, they extorted superprofits by grabbing low-priced farming and mineral products, dumping their industrial goods, stran-

gling national industries and carrying on an exchange of unequal values. The richness of the developed countries and the poverty of the developing countries are the result of the colonialist and imperialist policy of plunder... . Imperialism is the greatest obstacle to the liberation of the developing countries to their progress.[93]

This is no doubt a classical Marxian and Leninist analysis of imperialism and development. It is also, and probably more so, a statement of China's historical experience with the West. The 'opening' of China by the 'British imperialists' in the mid-nineteenth century was closely associated with an influx of opium and an outflow of silver. For almost 100 years, economic exploitation of China by Western and 'imperialist' countries was embodied in a number of 'unequal' treaties which granted excessive political rights and economic privileges to all treaty powers operating in China.

The ambivalent attitude of China towards inter-dependence finds an illuminating example in China's general adoption of two historical resolutions for the establishment of the NIEO at the 6th Special Session of the United Nations and its questioning attitude towards two key concepts it contained: inter-dependence and the international division of labour.[94] Inter-dependence, the Chinese representative Huang Hua pointed out in the plenary, was particularly susceptible to distortion by the two superpowers. Inter-dependence in the contemporary international economic system could, therefore, be easily manipulated into an inter-dependence, in his metaphorical term, 'between a horseman and his mount'. There was also the danger that inter-dependence could lead to erosion of full permanent sovereignty of a state over its natural resources and all its economic activities. International division of labour, on the other hand, was but a means to perpetuate the lopsided and abnormal development of national economies in the Old International Economic Order. In Huang Hua's words, the term 'might be used by the Super-Powers to push under that name their self-seeking "economic division of labour" and "economic integration" and to maintain the most unjust and abnormal state of "industrial Europe and North America, but Asia, Africa and Latin America with their agricultural and mineral produce" [sic]'.[95] Not surprisingly, as late as 1979, at the 5th UNCTAD, China still called for the 'Destroying [of] the Old [International Economic Order] and [the] Establishing [of] the New'.[96]

The launching of the policy to open up China to international economic activities at the Third Plenum of the Eleventh Central Committee of the CCP in December 1978 essentially changed the perspective from which the existing international economic system was to be reassessed. The imperative to open up and to modernise the Chinese economy sparked off theoretical debates in China in the early 1980s on three questions regarding to international economy – namely, the unification of the world market, the pure trade theory, and the nature of the international division of labour in the contemporary world economy.

First and least controversial are the questions as to whether the world market was unified and the world economy was an organic whole. It had been largely accepted by Chinese economists in the 1950s that the universal international capitalist economic system before the Second World War had disintegrated with the emergence of the socialist camp, as Stalin and other Soviet theorists had argued. There were therefore two parallel world markets and world economic systems: capitalist and socialist. This view contributed to shaping China's outlook of the world economy in the 1950s and the 1960s. Chinese economists now acknowledged that this Stalinist analysis of the world economy was rigid and ideologised and was completely wrong. They argued that there had never been a disintegration of the single and universal international market and world economy after 1945. They further argued that the unified world market and world economy had been brought into being with the capitalist-dominated international system and that modern industry and the international division of labour were the basis of this unification. As long as modern industry and its resulting international division of labour continued to exist and develop, there would not and could not be a disintegration of the universal international market and the world economy. This was because the world market was only a world-wide expression of the international division of labour based on modern industry and the international exchange of commodities. Different economic systems could and should be accommodated in the unified world economy. The emergence of socialist countries and international exchanges among them on the world market contributed (and is contributing) not to the disintegration, but to the development, of expansion and reform of the world market.[97] By means of this debate, the Chinese came to terms intellectually with the reality that the Chinese economy was only a part of the universal international economic system. In 1984, Huan Xiang declared more unequivocally at a symposium in Wuhan in central China that, 'From a world perspective, there is one unified market in which capitalism has the superiority'.[98]

Second and more intensively, Chinese economists were engaged in a lively debate on the pure trade theory. It concentrated on a reassessment of David Ricardo's theory of comparative advantage in the general framework of Marxian labour theory of value and on the issues concerning unequal trade.[99] The extent of the debate and Chinese economists' critique of Ricardo's theory are less relevant in the context here. What is of significance is the fact that out of this debate emerged a general consensus among Chinese economists that the theory of comparative advantage was not necessarily incompatible with Marxian economics and that international trade could be mutually beneficial. By the extension of this logic, China should explore to the full its comparative advantage in engaging in international trade. Disagreements did exist among Chinese economists, however, in regard to whether trade between the poor and the rich countries according to world market prices was equal or unequal. Some argued that distortions in world markets were severe, resulting from imperfect competition and the immobility of labour, land and capital, as well as the existence of monopolistic capitalists. Different labour productivity among different trading nations also led to unequal trade. Others suggested, however, that with world markets in operation for decades, it was reasonable and possible to identify an 'average unit of universal labour' which found an adequate proxy in world market prices. The debate was closely related to the sensitive question of whether there was 'exploitation'; that is, either China exploiting or being exploited by the other countries in international trade.[100] The debate continued well into the mid-1980s. It was to all intents and purposes, however, academic. China had not only accepted the validity of the theory of comparative advantage, which had become part of its theoretical foundation to develop its international trade;[101] it had also acquiesced in the 'exploitation', if any, in international exchange by actively seeking participation in the international economy.

Third, and closely linked with the theory of comparative advantage, is the question of the international division of labour. The international division of labour, as has been pointed out previously, had been condemned by the Chinese as a means by which imperialism and neo-colonialism tried to perpetuate the lopsided development of the global economy. Chinese economists now argued that classic Marxism held that the international division of labour had emerged and developed at the dictates of productive forces – that is, with the social production of machinery and the formation of a single world market. It was further argued that a careful distinction must be made between the objective inevitability of an international division of labour which was determined by productive forces and the social nature of this division. Under capitalism, the international division of labour between economically developed and underdeveloped countries was carried out by compulsory and non-economic means as well as economic means and was never based on the principle of equality and mutual benefit. The net result was the ruthless exploitation and plunder of the latter by the former. With the socialist relations of production, the progression of the international division of labour should be fully cultivated by actively participating in the world economy on the basis of equality and mutual benefit. Economically, the international division of labour could save social labour. This was particularly true with the third scientific and technological revolution after the Second World War. That revolution had brought about a qualitative change in the international division of labour – for example, a change from inter-industry specialisation to intra-industry specialisation. As a result, only specialised production was economically feasible on the world market. International specialisation and international cooperation were therefore indispensable in any nation's developmental process. The conclusion was that the necessity for China as a socialist country to participate in and utilise fully the international division of labour was determined by objective economic laws and was in complete accord with the progressive historical tendency towards internationalised production. As early as 1981, some economists had argued that the

> International division of labour is incorporated in the process of contemporary economic development and is independent of man's will. No country can choose whether to participate or not participate in the international division of labour. As long as they are engaged in international trade, they are participating in the international division of labour. No country in the world today can separate itself from the international trade and therefore international division of labour. China is no exception.[102]

The expansion of China's foreign economic relations through the international division of labour was therefore, as Chinese economists reasoned, a powerful lever to accelerate China's modernisation. This effectively called for China's application of the principle of comparative advantage to give full play to its superior natural and economic conditions so as to yield the greatest possible economic results in its foreign economic relations. It follows that even a large-scale sale of natural resources, like coal and petroleum, was justified. It also called for an adaptation by China to the post-war development of ever more internationalised production and to an international market so as to utilise more effectively the international division of labour.[103] Some Chinese economists further suggested that in practice, Japan and the four little 'dragons'[104] in Asia had set good examples for China. Their high-speed economic development owed much to their active participation in and effective cultivation of the international division of labour. More importantly, their successes had demonstrated that a nation could move up the ladder in the existing system of the international division of labour in its developmental process.[105]

It must be pointed out, however, that fundamentally it was not the changes in economic theory that led to the evolution of China's new policy of opening itself to the world economy. It was, rather, the reverse. It was the political and economic imperatives of China emerging out of the Cultural Revolution that dictated the change of orientation in China's foreign economic relations. In other words, the debates among academicians which gradually led to China's acceptance of international economic inter-dependence was preceded by China's strategic opening to the international economy. In fact, it was the launching of the open-door policy by the Chinese leadership that spawned a theoretical debate among academics, many of whom sought to justify the soundness of the new policy.

Nevertheless, these debates were important in the early 1980s to emancipate the Chinese economists from ideological yokes and to provide a sound theoretical basis for the new policy. Moreover, out of these debates emerged a new image of the existing international economic order. The dependency model of the 1970s was largely rejected. The world market was 'closely inter-dependent' and national economies were 'interrelated and supplemented through trade, capital, technology, raw materials and sales'.[106] In the early 1980s, the Chinese stretched Marx to the limit in arguing that,

> As far back as more than 100 years ago, Marx and Engels pointed out that along with the emergence of the international market, *the nations of the world were becoming increasingly economically related and dependent on one another.* ... During the past decades, especially since the Second World War, *this situation has been further developed in an unprecedented manner.* This is a fundamental historical fact as well as an inevitable trend of social development.[107]

China thus acknowledged that the world economy was inter-dependent, and increasingly so with the advancement of science and technology. In 1982, Huang Hua, who had poignantly denounced inter-dependence eight years before in the UN, presented to the same forum a radically different conception of inter-dependence. In his words, 'The economies of all countries are closely interrelated. The developed countries cannot achieve economic growth without the rich resources, vast markets and economic prosperity of the developing countries.'[108] Specifically, the inter-dependent relationship between the Chinese economy and the international economic system, in Huan Xiang's blunt yet accurate description, is that 'We can't leave it, and they won't leave us'.[109] It was, more importantly, an inter-dependent international economy that China could and should fully capitalise on to accelerate its economic development. Inter-dependence was taken as a fact in contemporary international economy, and a conducive one at that to Chinese economic development.

The inter-dependent world economy was not only endorsed by scholars. It also found public endorsement among statesmen. As mentioned earlier, Deng Xiaoping told visiting Japanese businessmen in March 1985 that the problems for the developed nations in finding outlets for their capital and expanding their trade and markets could only be solved if the North helped the South to become more prosperous.[110] If Deng's statement was somewhat crude, other Chinese leaders were more explicit. Li Peng, in his capacity of Acting Premier delivering the Report on the Work of the Government to the Seventh National People's Congress in 1988, stated that the increasing inter-dependence, cooperation and competition in the international economy simply provided 'a good opportunity' for China to 'find more international markets'.[111] Indeed, one of the new understandings of the international economy acquired by the Chinese leadership was, as claimed in one official Chinese diplomatic history book, that

> no country was to be ever found in the modern world that could produce all it needed, nor could there possibly be any country, even one with the highest level of industrial development, that possessed all the resources and sophisticated technologies needed for its own economic development. It followed that countries should help supply each other's needs and make up each other's deficiencies through economic and technological co-operation and trade contacts.[112]

CONCLUSION

From a broader perspective, China's initiation of a so-called independent foreign policy *per se* at the beginning of the 1980s had only limited significance. It was only an outward expression of more fundamental changes, perceptual changes and changes of ideas, that had made China's international behaviour in the 1980s 'more akin and more acceptable to other established nations'.[113] Behind this reorientation of Chinese foreign policy, as has been argued in this chapter, are radical, if not revolutionary, changes in China's perception of international political and economic systems and its changing assessment of the role which important institutions, such as war and peace, revolution and development, and dependence and inter-dependence play in the contemporary society of states. The new directions of Chinese foreign policy in the 1980s are both rooted in and sustained by these sweeping changes.

It should be noted that it is more than a coincidence that such radical changes of perceptions should have happened in the 1980s. The struggle within the CCP around the question of 'seeking truth from facts' at the end of the 1970s and the call to 'emancipate the mind' in the early 1980s laid a foundation for some political openness.[114] Reform-minded leaders were firmly in power in most of the 1980s. Deng Xiaoping, Hu Yaobang and Zhao Ziyang all encouraged these perceptual changes.[115] The general orientation of China's opening and economic reforms guided the direction of changing perceptions. Any back-tracking from late 1989 to 1991 was merely transient.

Through these fundamental changes, a process of convergence was taking place between China and other member states in international society in their perceptions of the nature of the existing international system and the functions of its institutions. If we regard China's de-alienation from international society as a continuous process, China's return to the United Nations and its establishing extensive diplomatic contacts with member states of international society in the 1970s are more or less a physical de-alienation. What has happened in the 1980s amounts then to a conceptual de-alienation, a fundamental and decisive step to facilitate China's further and meaningful integration into the international political and economic system. Changes in China's 'images of the world', it must be argued, are preconditions of China's political socialisation and economic integration into international society.

5 Political Socialisation

China's emerging new conceptions of war and peace, revolution and development, as well as dependence and inter-dependence in the present-day international system are not only significant in themselves. More importantly, these changing 'images of the world' are, to adapt Weber slightly, what have since determined the track on which the dynamism of China's national interests keep Chinese foreign policy performing. The changing perceptions on the part of China of the existing international system and major institutions associated with that system are therefore more satisfactory explanations of China's changing behaviour in international society in the 1980s and the 1990s. This argument does not simply derive from the fact that those changing perceptions have clear expressions in China's operational foreign policies. Rather, it is because of the explanatory power/potential of perceptual changes in unriddling China's often puzzling and erratic international behaviour.

Starting in the early 1980s, Chinese foreign policy, as noted earlier, underwent dramatic and sometimes perplexing changes. Operationally, the onus of Chinese foreign policy since the early 1980s was, in the official Chinese jargon, to 'create a peaceful international environment' conducive to China's pursuit of economic development at the highest speed possible. China then opted for a foreign policy which was orientated more towards order than disorder. For the first time, the PRC committed itself to an international order which was analogous to what was conceived by a majority of member states in international society. It was an order, however, which was grudgingly regarded as acceptable, though not desirable and fully justifiable. Such commitment nevertheless dictated modifications and adjustments, sometimes painful, of China's international policies in many sensitive areas.

This chapter studies adjustments of Chinese foreign policy in the 1980s and the 1990s as a continued process of China's political socialisation into international society. The central argument of this chapter is that many changes in Chinese foreign policy are significant because they signal China's gradual acceptance of and conformity to rules and norms universally accepted in international society and because they also indicate the limits thereof. It contends that pressure for China's political socialisation comes not only from China's aspiration for a normal and full statehood in international society, but also from its desire to become a responsible great power in the international system.[1] Such political socialisation has thus arguably made China more accountable in international society today, for the management of which great powers still assume special responsibility.[2]

The detailed examination concentrates on four issue areas: the CCP's struggle to deal with the legacies of ideology in China's international relations; China's changing attitude towards international peacekeeping; China's policies towards arms control and disarmament and acrimonious controversies associated with them; and human rights contentions between China and other members of international society.

Any selection of areas of Chinese foreign policy for detailed examination is inevitably highly arbitrary. There are, however, good reasons for selecting these four issue areas. As we have examined in the previous chapters, in the three decades from 1949 to 1979, the CCP's relations with other Communist Parties and revolutionary movements, China's denunciation of UN peacekeeping, and China's position on the international arms control were the most controversial. Further, those controversial policies played an essential role in alienating China from international society. Accordingly, changes in Chinese policies in these areas have been more pronounced and more significant. These appreciable changes are probably the best indicators of how and how much China has been politically socialised into international society. The selection of China's contentions over its human rights policies has clear and obvious justification. The subject of human rights remains today most controversial between China and many other members of international society. It is a case that perhaps best illustrates the limits of China in moving towards what Fred Halliday calls the 'homogeneity' of international society.[3]

TRANSCENDING IDEOLOGY IN INTERNATIONAL RELATIONS

The establishment of China's global network of diplomatic relations in the 1970s has been discussed in Chapter 3. However, China's bilateral relations with many states cannot be said to have been fully normalised even at the beginning of the 1980s. The complications come mostly from the CCP's tangled relations with other Communist Parties and with various revolutionary and insurgent movements in other countries. To normalise China's bilateral relations in the 1980s, therefore, required mainly a careful handling of the historical baggage of China's ideologised international relations, especially China's relations with the national liberation movements and insurgent Communists in Southeast Asia. It obliged the CCP to redefine the role of ideology in its inter-party relations. It also dictated that the CCP rethink and readjust its relations with other Communist

Parties so that the inter-party relationship was meticulously separated from inter-state relationship. In Zhao Ziyang's characterisation, international relations must be 'de-ideologised'.[4] For the CCP, therefore, in the broad perspective of the 1980s, normalising inter-party relations became the prerequisite for the normalisation of China's relations with many countries concerned. Ultimately, ideology must be transcended in the CCP's inter-party relations as well as in developing China's international relations.

The 'dual track diplomacy' and its demise

The CCP started to deal with its tangled relations with other Communist Parties and revolutionary movements in the context of its normalised inter-state relations in the early 1970s. The eventual admission of the PRC into the United Nations put China's support of national liberation movements and its wide connections with insurgent Communist Parties into a different perspective. How to conduct normal inter-state relations according to generally accepted rules and norms without renouncing its support for national liberation movements and without cutting off its connections with insurgent Communist Parties was a thorny issue. In Africa, there seemed to be little problem.[5] As the decolonisation process was winding up in the 1970s, many national liberation movements became governments in the newly independent African states. The real problem was in Asia, especially Southeast Asia. The CCP had called for the solidarity of the Communist movements in the area and had given substantial support, both material and moral, to the armed struggle of the insurgents in the 1950s and 1960s. In the 1970s, however, China's security interests and the emerging geopolitical factors affecting China's position in the international system urged China to establish and develop diplomatic relations with the non-Communist governments in Southeast Asia which would help to neutralise a possible superpower threat to China's national security. The conflict of interest here was acute. The insurgent Communist Parties in countries like Burma, Malaysia, Thailand and the Philippines were dedicated to the armed struggle to overthrow the governments as resolutely as those national governments were determined to eliminate the insurgent Communists.

China's initial response to this situation was the so-called 'dual track diplomacy'.[6] While maintaining inter-party ties, China set out either to normalise (in the case of Burma) or to establish (in the case of Malaysia, Thailand and the Philippines) inter-state relations with Southeast Asian nations, giving assurances that China would not interfere in the internal affairs of the nations concerned.[7] More specifically, Zhou Enlai was quoted as having told a visiting Thai delegation in Beijing in February 1974 that the CCP's support for the Communist Party of Thailand (CPT) was now 'a thing of the past'. During his visit of Southeast Asian nations in November 1978, Deng Xiaoping explicitly stated, 'We always hold that the relationship between parties should be separated from that between states so that it does not hinder the development of our friendly relations with other countries.'[8] One of the illuminating examples of this dual track diplomacy was that, while the Burmese President Ne Win was having a 'cordial and friendly talk' with the Chinese ambassador in Rangoon prior to his visit to China in mid-September 1977, the Burmese Communist leader Thakin Ba Thein Tin was among a group of foreign Communist Party leaders paying their respects to Mao Zedong's remains in Beijing on the first anniversary of Mao's death.[9]

China's pursuit of the dual track diplomacy in the 1970s, therefore, indicated that efforts were made to downgrade the inter-party relations. The CCP selectively closed down various clandestine radio stations operated by Communist Parties of Southeast Asian countries but based in China.[10] However, exchanges of messages between the CCP and other Southeast Asian Communist Parties were still mentioned in considerable detail from time to time in the official Chinese media in the late 1970s. They became increasingly brief only in the early 1980s before they were phased out in the mid-1980s. Indeed, judging from China's media accounts, there seemed to be an upsurge of China's support for the Southeast Asian insurgent Communist Parties from 1975 to 1978.[11]

There were several constraints on the changing Chinese policy in the 1970s. First, the problem which the CCP was dealing with, as Deng Xiaoping argued in 1978, 'arose in history' and 'cannot be solved overnight'.[12] As late as August 1981, Zhao Ziyang on his tour of Southeast Asia still sought to assure the host countries that China 'would do its utmost' not to let the problems *left over from the past*' hinder the development of its normal relations with the Southeast Asian countries.[13] The historical legacy mentioned above may well refer to some secret agreements signed between the CCP and insurgent Communist Parties in Southeast Asia. This point was partially borne out when in 1986 Hu Yaobang in his capacity as the CCP's General Secretary announced that as a specific principle, the CCP would not enter into any secret agreements with any other parties.[14] Second, events in the turbulent domestic politics in China in the late 1970s – the downfall of Deng Xiaoping in 1975, the temporary upsurge of the 'Leftists' represented by the 'Gang of Four' in 1976, the death of Zhou and Mao also in 1976 – all had ripple effects on China's policies towards the Southeast Asian Communist Parties. Third,

China might well have wished to keep some connections with the insurgent movements to maintain a leverage so as to be able to orient the governments concerned, if need be, towards a regional strategic alignment which would best serve China's security interests. Last but certainly not least, given the Sino-Soviet rivalry in the region, the CCP would be loath to see any vacuum created by any major cutback of its aid and support to the Communist insurgents filled by the Soviet Union. It was a nightmarish scenario for the CCP to see the Communist insurgents it had abandoned operate along its southern borders with Soviet assistance, especially when Vietnam had already shown its hostility towards China.

Nevertheless, the progressive decline of China's support for Southeast Asian Communists in the 1970s was undeniably clear. After 1978, strategic imperatives centring on Vietnam – Vietnam's invasion of Cambodia, its hostility towards China, and China's perception of a Vietnamese rise to regional hegemony as part of the Soviet threat to China's security – all dictated that China have a closer political and security cooperation with ASEAN (Association of Southeast Asian Nations) countries. Not surprisingly, the CCP had further downgraded its relations with the insurgent parties in the region in favour of further improving inter-state relations.[15] China substantially reduced material support to the insurgent Communists, except perhaps the Burmese Communist Party (BCP).[16] Messages from those Communist Parties to the CCP on its anniversaries were still acknowledged without mentioning the contents in the early 1980s in the Chinese media. There was, however, little from the media about their armed struggles against their governments now regarded as friendly to China. The CCP was striving to convert its 'militant friendship and unity' with those Communist insurgencies into a relationship where support to each other was strictly 'moral and political'. The CCP was believed to be behind the abortive negotiations between the Burmese Communist Party and the Burmese government in 1980–81 for national reconciliation.[17] Paradoxically, domestic economic development and political stability in some ASEAN countries also helped the CCP from disentangling itself from its 'revolutionary friendship and militant unity' with Southeast Asian Communists.

There were further evidence in the 1980s to suggest that the dual track diplomacy a few years before was steadily being replaced by a single track diplomacy – normal diplomacy between states. During a visit to Malaysia to mark the tenth anniversary of the establishment of formal diplomatic relations between China and Malaysia, Foreign Minister Wu Xueqian reportedly claimed that the question of China's relations with the Communist insurgents in Southeast Asian nations had basically been solved 'through consultations' with the governments concerned. Specifically, he affirmed that China believed that the insurgent guerrilla movement in those countries 'is an internal affairs in which China will not interfere' and that the CCP maintained 'only a moral relationship with the Malaysian [sic] Communist Party'.[18] In the diplomatic battle to normalise Sino-Indonesian relations, Wu Xueqian even went public to state in May 1985 that 'In the last eighteen years [since 1967], the CCP has had no official relations with the PKI [the Indonesian Communist Party]'. He also claimed that the CCP's alleged involvement in the failed *coup* in September 1965 in Jakarta 'contradicts historical facts' and that 'it was not until after the 30 September Movement occurred that the CCP learned of it'.[19] Wu's bold assertion probably also 'contradicts historical facts' as flatly as the allegation of the CCP's involvement in the 1965 abortive *coup* in Jakarta, given the fact that the PKI 'delegation' headed by Jusuf Adjitorop had been residing in Beijing since 1965 and was even received by the CCP Chairman Hua Guofeng and other CCP politburo members in 1977. The credibility of Wu's assertion is, however, not the most important issue here. What is of great significance is that Wu went public to disavow emphatically the CCP's historical and current connections with the PKI in order to cultivate the possibility of normalising Sino-Indonesian governmental relations. To meet conditions set out by the Indonesian government for normalising bilateral governmental relations, the CCP announced in late July 1985 that it was no longer giving refuge to PKI 'fugitives'.[20] It was not until 1992, however, that China and Indonesia re-established their full diplomatic relations.

The gradual demise of China's dual track diplomacy towards, in particular, Southeast Asian countries was undoubtedly occasioned by China's strategic imperative in the region. It is the beginning of the CCP's readjustment of its inter-party relations. It must also be seen, however, as evidence that, once incorporated into the international system, China was compelled to accept and play by some commonly accepted rules in conducting inter-state relations.

Redefining inter-party relations

In spite of the CCP's strenuous efforts to detach itself from the insurgent Communist Parties in Southeast Asia in the late 1970s and the early 1980s, fundamental problems remained for the CCP both in theory and in practice as to how it should handle inter-party relations. What should be the CCP's principles guiding inter-party relations? Which pattern of inter-party relations was the normal and generally accepted one between the

CCP and political parties in foreign countries? How could China conduct normal inter-state relations while maintaining proper ties with revolutionary movements without being seen as interfering in the internal affairs of other countries? Until these questions were answered properly and unless the CCP adjusted its policies accordingly, normalisation of China's inter-state relations would remain incomplete and its proclaimed acceptance of the principle of non-interference in internal affairs of other countries would be open to question. Furthermore, China's normal relations with other states would still be subjected to possible spill-over of fluctuations in inter-party relations. Dealing with the historical baggage of China's foreign policy therefore involves redefining the role of ideology in the CCP's relations with other political parties and laying down new principles on the basis of this redefinition.

The CCP set out to tackle this task in a more coordinated manner at its Twelfth National Congress in September 1982, when the reform-minded leadership took full control. Hu Yaobang, then General Secretary of the CCP, went out of his way to address the CCP's relations with other Communist Parties in his work report to the Congress. In proclaiming China's independent foreign policy, Hu made it a point to announce that the CCP would develop its relations 'with *Communist Parties or other working-class Parties* in strict conformity with the principles of independence, complete equality, mutual respect and non-interference in each other's internal affairs'.[21] These principles were to become later the so-called 'four guiding principles' for the CCP in establishing, developing and normalising its relations not only with Communist and working-class parties but also with all other political parties. Hu further stated that

> Communist Parties, of course, should help each other. It is absolutely impermissible, however, for any of them to issue orders or run things for others from outside. ... As for the practice of one Party compelling other Parties to make their policies serve its own Party and state interests, or even resort to armed intervention in other countries, it can only undermine the very foundation of the international communist movement.[22]

Referring to the CCP's experience, Hu claimed that the CCP had suffered from the attempt by a self-elevated paternal Party to keep the CCP under its control. 'It is through resisting such an attempt that we have successfully pursued our independent foreign policy.'[23]

Hu's report was the first systematic enunciation of the CCP's newly formulated principles in forging and developing inter-party relations. It laid the foundation for the CCP's policy making to renovate the old ties with other parties and to establish the new. Several significant points can be summarised from Hu's report. First, the CCP began to deal theoretically with the overall question of its inter-party relations. It envisaged a new-style inter-party relationship wherein compatibility or homogeneity of ideology ensures no more than mutual political and moral support. Second, it acknowledged that inter-party relations should not in any way prejudice inter-state relations. The two relationships should be strictly and carefully separated. Third, the CCP reiterated that revolution could not and should not be exported. The mutual support between the Communist and other 'fraternal' parties should be strictly 'political and moral'. Fourth, in line with this principle, the CCP would never impose its will or policy upon the others. Nor would it let the others force their views and opinions on the CCP.

The forerunner of Hu's enunciation of the four principles was a talk by Deng Xiaoping as early as May 1980 to a strictly restricted circle of high-ranking officials in the Central Committee of the CCP. In that talk, Deng laid down an 'important principle' in dealing with inter-party relations; namely, the CCP 'should never issue orders to the others [fraternal Parties]' and that the CCP 'are resolutely opposed the others ordering us about'. He specifically argued that since the success of the Chinese Revolution was achieved through an appropriate application of Marxist principles to the actual, existing conditions of China, the CCP should not demand nor expect other developing countries to follow the Chinese model in making their revolutions. He pointed out, however, 'if the aim of the foreign policy of one Party and the country it is leading is to interfere in the internal affairs of other nations or to invade or to sabotage other countries, then all the other parties have the right to criticise that Party and its policy'. Speaking of Euro-Communism, Deng explicitly stated that the rights and wrongs of its practice should only be judged by the Communist Parties and the peoples of Europe, not by the outsiders (by implication, the CCP). He acknowledged to the visiting General Secretary of the Italian Communist Party, Enrico Berlinguer, that the CCP had made some unjust criticism of the Italian Communist Party and told him that all those polemics between the CCP and the Italian Communist Party should be 'scattered to the winds'.[24]

After the Twelfth National Congress of the CCP, the leaders of the CCP made special efforts to expound their four principles publicly to visiting Communist leaders and other foreign dignitaries. At a banquet on 18 May 1984 for a delegation of the Yugoslavian Communist League, Hu Yaobang formally declared that the four principles – namely, independence, complete equality, mutual respect and non-interference in each other's internal affairs – were guiding principles for the CCP in handling its relations with other Communist Parties.[25]

Like Deng's admission to Berlinguer about the CCP's unjust criticism of Italian Communist Party in the 1960s, Hu was candid and explicit to his guests in admitting that the CCP

> has also shortcomings and made mistakes in handling our relations with other Parties, especially in judging and assessing the right and wrong of other Parties in the light of our own experience and practice, which caused detrimental consequences to certain Parties.

He went on to claim that the CCP had 'conscientiously corrected these mistakes'.[26]

Indeed, one of the justifications for the CCP to mend and to restructure its relations with other Communist Parties was that it had not only fallen a victim to malpractice in the international Communist movement but also mishandled its relations with other parties. It was claimed that self-criticism had been carried out by the CCP leadership for the mishandling. The leaders of the CCP were, however, not altogether prepared to be specific about what exactly were the mistakes the CCP had made,[27] although towards the mid-1980s, the CCP's international liaison work became less secretive and regular statements began to appear in newspapers and journals about its general development.[28]

Re-evaluating the past

From various speeches and statements made in the 1980s by the CCP leaders and officials of the International Liaison Department of the CCP's Central Committee, it is possible to reconstruct a general picture as to the major areas wherein the CCP considered that it had seriously mishandled inter-party relations. First, and more openly, the CCP acknowledged that within the international Communist movement it had, for example, misjudged the Yugoslavian Communists and directed unjust criticism at Euro-Communism. It had allowed ideological disputes to spill over to sour inter-state relations, in particular between China and the Soviet Union and its East European client states. The CCP was also very critical of its own position in Sino-Soviet polemics. The so-called Nine Commentaries (*Jiuping*), the keynote attacks by the CCP on the 'Soviet revisionism' in the early 1960s, were repudiated, not only because they were prepared under Kang Sheng, an ultra-Leftist later condemned by the Party. More importantly, it was also because the expressed views in those commentaries were lopsided and the harsh criticisms of the CPSU were reckoned to be unfair in many cases. Most interestingly, even the 'Anti-Revisionist

Street' by the Soviet Embassy in Beijing regained its former name in 1980.[29] It was only natural, therefore, that in its attempt to resume suspended normal relations with other Communist Parties after 1977, the CCP always encouraged the 'forward-looking' spirit and counselled against looking backward to 'try to settle old accounts'.[30] Based on its bitter experience in the 1950s, the CCP also declared that it 'does not recognise any so-called leadership or guiding "centre" or any ready-made "model" in the international Communist movement. Neither at present nor in the future will our Party act as a "centre" or create a "model".'[31]

Second, and in a relative low key, was the CCP's sponsoring of revolutions abroad by means of moral and material support for the insurgent Communist Parties, particularly in Southeast Asia. The CCP had never openly admitted that it was a mistake. There was, after all, a strategic imperative for the CCP to do so. However, it became very forceful in emphasising that it was entirely up to the people of the country concerned to choose their own social systems and to make their own revolution. It had declared repeatedly that the CCP would never take advantage of its relations with other parties to meddle in the internal affairs of another country. This is an indication that, more than ever before, the CCP was very careful not to be seen as the sponsor of those revolutions for its foreign policy purposes. Zhao Ziyang emphasised during a visit to Bangkok in 1981 that the CCP's relations with Southeast Asian Communist Parties were 'only political and moral' and that China would see to it that such relationship would not 'affect our [China's] relations with ASEAN countries'.[32] At a press conference in October 1986, the spokesman of the International Liaison Department of the Central Committee of the CCP again clearly stated that 'the relationship between the CCP and Southeast Asian Communist Parties, like its relations with Communist Parties elsewhere, is strictly political and moral'. He carefully pointed out that such a relationship between one political party and another was 'a commonly accepted international phenomenon'.[33] The CCP's reiteration of its principle of non-interference aimed probably also at putting off demands by other parties, especially the insurgent Communist Parties of Southeast Asia, for assistance, other than moral and political support.[34] The CCP gradually terminated its material support to most Southeast Asian Communist Parties from 1979 to 1982.[35] This could be seen as an admission that it was a mistake to have more than political and moral relationship, even with those insurgent Communist Parties in Southeast Asia.

The third mistake, though not explicitly stated, was that the CCP had greatly restricted itself to developing formal relations only with other

Communist Parties, thus highly ideologising inter-party relations. Ideological homogeneity, however, had not ensured harmonious relations even between Communist Parties, as the CCP's own painful experience proved. The CCP was itself a victim of the illusory unity of the international Communist movement. On the other hand, such restrictions severely limited the scope of operation of the CCP in developing contacts with other political parties. The CCP did not begin to establish formal relations with political parties in Third World countries until as late as 1978.[36] It was in February 1981 that for the first time the CCP entered into formal relations with a Western, non-Communist political party. During a visit to China by a political delegation of the French Socialist Party led by François Mitterrand, the CCP and the French Socialist Party agreed to establish formal inter-party relations.[37] The CCP now carefully yet emphatically pointed out that it was a generally accepted practice in the international community that a political party establish formal relations with other political parties beyond its national borders, irrespective of ideological commitments.[38] A new direction in the CCP's international liaison work was now to seek to establish relations with socialist parties, social democratic parties and labour parties in other countries.[39] In May 1984, Hu Yaobang chose the occasion of welcoming a delegation of the German Social Democratic Party headed by Willy Brandt to call publicly for 'transcending ideological differences to seek mutual understanding and cooperation' between political parties.[40]

Transcending ideology in inter-party relations

The CCP's call for the transcending of ideology in developing and expanding its inter-party relations could therefore be seen as an attempt to correct what were believed to be its mistakes in the past. Transcending ideology in the inter-party relations means that ideological polemics or differences between the CCP and other political parties, Communist or non-Communist, should not be allowed to impede the development of normal inter-party relations, least of all inter-state relations. Polemics should be settled, if possible, through friendly exchange between parties. Ideological differences, on the other hand, should be transcended in seeking mutual understanding and cooperation. In his Report on the Seventh Five-Year Plan in March 1986, Zhao Zhiyang proclaimed that on the basis of five principles of peaceful co-existence,[41]

> China strives to establish, resume or expand normal relations with all countries in the world and live in harmony and engage in friendly

co-operation with them. China *does not determine its closeness with or estrangement from other countries on the basis of their social systems and ideologies.*[42]

Transcending ideology also means that mutual support between the CCP and other Communist Parties should be purely moral and political. The CCP explicitly declared that

> By support we mean moral and political support, which of course include in some cases necessary humanitarian aid. We are opposed to the 'export of revolution'. It is entirely up to the people of the country concerned to choose what kind of social system they want.[43]

By implication, no other Communist Party should expect the CCP to go beyond moral and political support in their relations with the CCP. The CCP even argued that Communist Parties world-wide should establish and maintain mutual relations 'just like socialist Parties, nationalist Parties, and *religious organisations* of different countries which also maintain various relations between them'. This was now 'a commonly accepted international practice'.[44] Finally, transcending ideology means that the CCP should establish ties with political parties of every description all over the world as long as those parties are the CCP.[45] In other words, inter-party relations as conceived by the CCP now should by no means be constrained by ideological considerations.

In this spirit, the CCP had by the end of 1986 restored and established various ties with around 200 political parties all over the world.[46] The CCP had by then completed the process of renewing its ties with East European Communist Parties, a process started almost ten years earlier, in 1977. In October 1986, it claimed to have 'established good relations with or contacted more than 80 communist parties and organisations the world over'.[47] The normalisation of relations with the CPSU was not on the agenda only because of the so-called 'three obstacles'.[48] The CCP had also by then forged extensive ties with political parties in Third World countries.[49] In South Asia, for example, relations had been established with the Indian Congress Party, the Pakistani People's Party, and the Sri Lankan Unified Nationalist Party.[50] By October 1987, the CCP claimed to have relations with a total of 230 political parties world-wide. The spokesman from the International Liaison Department of the Central Committee also claimed that the CCP had established or resumed relations with more than 130 foreign political parties in the five years after the Twelfth National Congress of the CCP in 1982.[51] Ironically, the relations between the CCP and the CPSU were almost the last to be normalised in May 1989, when Gorbachev visited Beijing and had a summit meeting with Deng Xiaoping,[52] although Gorbachev had declared as early as 1987 that 'we [the Soviet Union] believe that the period of alienation [in our relations with the People's Republic of China] is past'.[53]

For over ten years after August 1977, when the restoration of normal relations between the CCP and the Yugoslavian Communist League led to normalisation of relations between China and Yugoslavia, the CCP wrestled with the challenging theoretical questions and thorny practical issues of readjusting and realigning its relations with other political parties. In theory, it had to redefine the role of ideology in its inter-party relations. Throughout the 1980s, the readjustment and redefinition of the CCP's inter-party relations took place in the context of China's efforts to normalise its relations with other states and was part and parcel of the normalisation of China's international relations. Our examination of the process suggests that the CCP has come to the conclusion that CCP's external relations, as well as Chinese diplomacy, should be conducted within the broad framework commonly accepted in international society and should abide by the common rules made for the maintenance of an international order acceptable to most members of international society. Not only should state relations be distinguished from party relations, as Deng stated in 1978. They could also be distinguished and separated. The CCP's efforts since 1977 to transform its inter-party relations fundamentally have principally aimed at this distinction and separation. It is fortunate that for most of the 1980s, the reform-minded leadership stayed in control, which ensured the success of the CCP's efforts to sideline ideology in inter-party and inter-state relations in this fashion. Indeed, the CCP's redefinition of the role of ideology in international relations and the adjustment of China's relations with former socialist countries based on this definition may have served to cushion the severe impact on China of the collapse of Communism in Eastern Europe and in the Soviet Union in the early 1990s.

UN PEACEKEEPING: FROM CONDEMNATION TO PARTICIPATION

One of the most controversial issues in China's international relations is its policy towards international peacekeeping. In the last 45 years, China has adopted various positions on the peacekeeping operations of the United Nations, ranging from unreserved condemnation to active participation. In the post-Cold War period, the Chinese policy continues to be a subject of controversy. Samuel Kim, for example, argued that China's abstention from voting on Resolution 678 in the Gulf War period proves that 'China remains part of the global problem in the post-Cold War high politics in the Security Council' and 'for the implementation of the Charter-based collective security system in the post-Cold War era'.[54]

The discussions that follow offer a detailed examination of China's changing position on UN peacekeeping, from antagonism in the 1950s and the 1960s to antipathy in the 1970s, and then to active cooperation and participation in the 1980s and the 1990s. It argues that, in spite of the manifest limitations of Chinese policies on UN peacekeeping today, China has come a long way in appreciating and sharing in the working of this particular common institution of international society.

For analytical purposes, four periods are identified in the evolution of the Chinese policy towards UN peacekeeping in the last 45 years. The period of condemnation dates from 1950 to 1971, when China was excluded from the UN. The period of non-disruption lasts from 1971 to 1981. The period of cooperation spans the years 1981 to 1988. The period of participation starts in 1988 and prevails today.

The beginning of an end

The critical turning point of China's position on UN peacekeeping came in December 1981, ten years after the PRC was admitted into the United Nations. On 18 December 1981, at the Security Council's meeting discussing the extension of the mandate of the United Nations Peacekeeping Forces in Cyprus (UNFICYP), the Chinese delegation voted in favour of UN Resolution 498.[55] For the first time in its history, the PRC adopted a positive approach to UN peacekeeping operations. It was more than a decade after the PRC became a member of the UN that such a radical and significant change towards international peacekeeping was effected by China as a permanent member of the Security Council.

Before the vote was cast, Lin Qing, the Chinese Representative at the Security Council, made a brief statement by way of explaining China's changing position on the general question of UN peacekeeping. 'Owing to historical and political reasons', he stated, 'we have up till now adhered to a well-known position *vis-à-vis* United Nations peacekeeping operations'.[56] He declared, however, that considering 'the changes in the international arena and the evolution of the role of UN peacekeeping operations',

> From now on, the Chinese government will actively consider and support such UN peacekeeping operations as are conducive to the maintenance of international peace and security and to the preservation of

the sovereignty and independence of the states concerned in strict conformity with the purposes and principles of the Charter.[57]

The date 18 December 1981 thus marked a turning point in China's stand towards UN peacekeeping from opposition to adoption. What then, are, those 'historical and political reasons' which decided China's 'well-known position *vis-à-vis* United Nations peacekeeping operations'? What was the 'well-known position' of China? And what prompted China at that particular moment drastically to modify its principled position on international peacekeeping?

Condemnation

It should be noted here that the mutual exclusion of the PRC and the UN in the 1950s and the 1960s contributed to the alienation of the PRC from international society. China's acrimony against the United Nations reached a crescendo in 1965. In the wake of the Indonesian withdrawal from the United Nations at the beginning of 1965, *Peking Review* published a series of articles condemning and criticising the United Nations. In an editorial of *Renmin Ribao* on 10 January 1965, it was alleged that the United Nations was simply 'a pliant tool of US imperialism' and that the UN 'has degenerated into a dirty international political stock exchange in the grip of a few big powers; the sovereignty of other nations, particularly that of small ones, is often bought and sold there by them like shares'.[58] This was probably most characteristic of China's negative image of the United Nations. Zhou Enlai immediately followed this up with a call that the United Nations 'under the manipulation of US imperialism ... must be thoroughly reorganised'.[59] Nine months later, Foreign Minister Chen Yi was more blunt at a press conference, when he stated that

> The United Nations has long been controlled by the United States and has today become a place where two big powers, the United States and the Soviet Union, conduct political transactions. This state of affairs has not changed although dozens of Afro-Asian and peace-loving countries have made no small amount of efforts in the United Nations. China need not take part in such a United Nations.

He proceeded to call for the establishment of a 'revolutionary United Nations'.[60]

With such a negative image of the United Nations, it is perhaps only natural that China's condemnation of UN peacekeeping was sweeping in

1965. The UN peacekeeping operation in Congo was a US-manipulated crime 'to strangle the Congolese national liberation movement'. The establishment of the Special Committee for Peacekeeping Operations in the UN, on the other hand, was merely a plot by the United States, already 'a notorious international gendarme', in 'converting the United Nations into a US-controlled headquarters of international gendarmes to suppress and stamp out the revolutionary struggles of the world's people'.[61] China also subtly endorsed a militant view expressed in *Zeri i Popullit*, organ of the Albanian Labour Party, which accused the United States and the Soviet Union of trying to establish 'an imperialist-revisionist international gendarmerie' in their negotiation in the Special Committee on Peacekeeping Operations. Moreover, UN peacekeeping operations up till then had always 'protected the interests of imperialism and undermined the efforts of the peoples to win freedom and independence'.[62]

It is an astute comment that 'the concept of peacekeeping has been politically controversial throughout the span of 40 years'.[63] It is also true that peacekeeping has been a politically divisive issue and that members of the Security Council have been from time to time delinquent in supporting peacekeeping resolutions and have accused each other of partisanship in certain peacekeeping operations in the Cold War years. Nevertheless, such a sweeping condemnation of UN peacekeeping was rare.

Two cautions must be heeded here. One is that the PRC was effectively excluded from the global organisation at the time. And the 1960s was a time when revolutionary China tried to break up the international system. The other is that in its pre-entry period, the PRC had two images of the UN: namely, the UN of the Charter, and the UN under American control.[64] The PRC always claimed that it was the UN under American control that China denounced and that it was the peacekeeping operations which American imperialism (and later, together with Soviet social-imperialism) manipulated in the name of the UN that China condemned.

The Chinese bore a specific deep and bitter resentment against UN peacekeeping operations as a result of the Korean War. UN operations in Korea were, strictly speaking, peacemaking rather than peacekeeping. To the Chinese, however, the differences between the two were only academic. The crucial matter was that China was condemned, together with North Korea, as aggressors in a UN resolution and was at the receiving end of the largest collective security operation mounted by the UN. It fought a fierce war in Korea with multinational troops under American command dispatched in the name of the UN to enforce peace in Korea. As Chen Yi poignantly reminded the international public at the above-mentioned press conference in 1965, that as a practical step to rectify 'its past mistakes', the United Nations 'should cancel its resolution condemning China and the Democratic Republic of Korea as aggressors and adopt a resolution condemning the United States as the aggressor'.[65]

This resentment still echoed in China as late as 1985, on the fortieth anniversary of the United Nations. In an interview making a general assessment of the work of the UN in the 1950s, Huang Hua indicated allusively that the UN operations in Korea were one of the 'aggressive wars launched by superpowers in the name of the United Nations contrary to the purposes and principles of the Charter of the United Nations'.[66] Indeed, in the 1980s as in the 1970s, 'China still suffers from the trauma of the Korean War and the Organisation's involvement in that war. ... The experiential legacy of the Korean War still influences the Chinese response to UN peacekeeping.'[67]

After the Korean War, China had always looked at UN peacekeeping operations with more than a jaundiced eye. The United Nations Emergency Force (UNEF) in 1956, the Chinese suspected, would 'allow US neo-colonialism to supersede British and French colonialism' in the Middle East. The United Nations Observation Group to Lebanon (UNOGIL) in 1958 was merely 'an instrument of US-British intervention'.[68] The United Nations Operation in the Congo (ONUC), the Chinese claimed, 'was US imperialism operating under the UN flag' and 'would open a convenient door to US imperialist intervention in the Congo and establish an evil of encroachment upon the sovereignty of newly independent nations in the name of the UN'. They further claimed in 1960 that 'Numerical historical facts over the past 15 years have repeatedly testified to the fact that US imperialism uses the UN as its instrument of aggression'.[69]

Non-disruption

Given China's negative view of UN peacekeeping operations prior to its entry into the UN, it was hardly surprising that China pronounced its opposition at the Security Council when the first occasion arose only one month after it was seated. At the Security Council meeting on 13 December 1971, debating the renewal of the mandate of the United Nations Force in Cyprus (UNFICYP), the Chinese representative Chen Chu declared that China's opposition to dispatching UN forces was 'well-known to all representatives'. China therefore opted for non-participation in the vote on the resolution.[70]

It was not until late 1973 that China's position on UN peacekeeping operations was more fully explained. At a Security Council meeting discussing the dispatch of the United Nations Emergence Force II (UNEF II) on 25 October 1973, Huang Hua, China's permanent representative to the UN, proclaimed that

> China has always been opposed to the dispatch of the so-called 'peacekeeping forces'. We maintain the same position with regard to the present situation in the Middle East. Such a practice can only pave the way for further international intervention and control with the superpowers as the behind-the-scenes boss.

Huang Hua nevertheless stated that China was 'not in a position to veto the draft resolution' because of the 'requests repeatedly made by the victims of aggression'. The Chinese delegation had therefore decided not to participate in the voting on the resolution.[71] A few days later, Zhuang Yan, China's deputy permanent representative to the UN, made public at the Security Council another principled position of the Chinese government towards UN peacekeeping. In his words, 'As we are not in favour of the dispatch of the UN forces to the Middle East, we, of course, cannot pay the expenses for that UNEF.'[72]

China's 'principled' stand towards UN peacekeeping was then established. In the next eight years, China adopted and adhered to this well-established stand, which includes three aspects. First, China was rigorously opposed to UN peacekeeping operations and would not participate in any Council debate on the matter. Second, China chose non-participation in voting on all draft resolutions concerning peacekeeping operations out of consideration of the requests from other Third World countries. Third, because of China's opposition to UN peacekeeping, China would not make any financial contribution to those operations. It must be emphasised, however, that with such a chosen policy, China as a permanent member of the Security Council aimed at not disrupting the actual adoption of draft resolutions at the Security Council concerning UN peacekeeping operations. Apart from China's declining to make any financial contribution to those operations which it did not approve, its chosen policy had otherwise little adverse effect on the practical execution of UN peacekeeping operations in the period. This policy is characterised as China's 'cooperation by acquiescence' in international peacekeeping.[73]

Cooperation

What then prompted China to change its position towards international peacekeeping at the end of 1981? And why at that particular moment? The answers lie as much in the internal development within China as in China's re-evaluation of the changing international political context. In 1981, difficulties in Sino-American relations during the first Reagan administration and economic reforms in China compelled the Chinese leadership to conduct a thorough review of Chinese foreign policy. What emerged from this review was China's pronounced 'independent foreign policy', which was articulated publicly at the Twelfth National Congress of the Chinese Communist Party in September 1982. By that time, some readjustments of Chinese foreign policy had already been effected, and modifications of China's international strategy materialised. The emergence of an 'independent foreign policy' as defined at the Twelfth National Congress of the CCP, although seen by some as characterised by 'assertive nationalism',[74] actually signalled China's turning away from the rigidity of its so-called 'anti-Sovietism' in its international policy in the 1970s and from its tacit strategic alignment with the United States in the period from 1979 to 1981. It also indicated China's readiness to adopt a more positive attitude towards international cooperation to achieve a better external environment conducive to China's domestic economic construction. China's changing position on UN peacekeeping operations was but part of the overall modification of its international strategy. The timing in announcing such a change in such an important international forum as the Security Council of the UN contained an element of subtlety.

Further elaboration of China's position on the UN peacekeeping was made by Liang Yufan, deputy permanent representative to the UN, on 15 October 1984 at a UN Special Political Committee meeting. 'In this most turbulent and volatile world', he stated, 'there is a universal demand for strengthening the peacekeeping capability of the United Nations. ... China was determined to make the greatest endeavour possible to strengthen the role of the United Nations.'[75]

Liang went on to expound seven points which constituted the new position of the Chinese government on UN peacekeeping operations.[76] Among other things, Liang reaffirmed China's support for UN peacekeeping operations 'which are in conformity with the principles contained in the UN Charter'. Liang expressed the Chinese government's willingness to share the financial burden of UN peacekeeping based on the principle of fair and rational sharing of expenses and by voluntary contributions.[77] In fact, in one assessment, in the period from 1986 to 1988, China was the nineteenth among the top 30 main contributors to the UN regular budget, but was the seventeenth as measured by its contribution to peacekeeping operations.[78]

Liang further clarified China's position on other two important aspects of UN peacekeeping operations. First, China accepted and stressed the principle of consent from the host country in peacekeeping operations. Second, on the more controversial question of the Security Council's authority on peacekeeping operations,[79] Liang emphasised that while the

Security Council, the General Assembly and the Secretary-General should assume their respective responsibilities for maintaining international peace and security, China firmly believed that 'it is within the competence of the UN Security Council to authorise peacekeeping operations'.[80]

The seven points, in fact, endorsed almost all the important principles commonly accepted by all other member states in the UN regarding international peacekeeping. They could therefore be seen as the evidence of a growing consensus between China and other member states on principles and issues concerning UN peacekeeping. Such a consensus indicated that China had changed its perception of UN peacekeeping. It was viewed now as part of the international community's shared collective obligation to preserve and promote international peace and security. Such a changing perception contributed to creating a political climate in which the renewal of faith in the UN helped to revive the role and utility of UN peacekeeping from the late 1980s onwards, and to enhance the competence of peacekeeping as a viable, more effective and readily available instrument of international conflict management.

The emergence of consensus between China and other member states on UN peacekeeping was accompanied, or rather followed up closely, by a public re-evaluation of the UN. In sharp contrast to the scathing criticism of the UN and a call for establishing a revolutionary United Nations 20 years before, in 1985, China presented an overall positive image of this universal world organisation. The United Nations was now the UN of the Charter, indispensable to international peace and security. In a special speech delivered to the General Assembly on 24 October 1985 celebrating the fortieth anniversary of the UN, Premier Zhao Ziyang praised the UN for having 'done much and has played an active part in safeguarding world peace, opposing armed aggression and occupation of one country by another, encouraging the restructuring of the inequitable international economic order and promoting international economic and technological cooperation'. He went on to pronounce the UN, 'whose universality and importance grows with the passage of time', as 'irreplaceable in the historical mission it shoulders and the impact it exerts on the world'.[81] The Chinese also claimed later that 'History has shown that the role of the United Nations in peacekeeping could not be taken over by any other separate state, state group or organisation'.[82]

Participation

Henry Wiseman asserted that 1988 was the year when the international political climate for peacekeeping was dramatically improved and there appeared an atmosphere of greater appreciation of UN peacekeeping operations as an effective instrument in the peaceful solution of international conflicts.[83] It was in 1988 that China began to seek active participation in peacekeeping decision making and peacekeeping operations. On 22 September 1988, Li Luye, China's permanent representative to the UN, sent a letter to Secretary-General Javier Perez de Cuellar, informing him that the Chinese delegation 'has been instructed by the Chinese government to apply for the membership in the Special Committee on Peacekeeping Operations'. Li Luye pointed out in his letter that

> the UN peacekeeping operations constitute an effective means of maintaining international peace and security and have played a positive role in easing regional conflicts and facilitating peaceful settlement of disputes. ... China wishes to take part in its work and, together with other members of the Special Committee, to endeavour to further enhance the efficiency of the UN peacekeeping operations.[84]

On 2 November, the Special Political Committee of the UN unanimously adopted a draft resolution sponsored by Canada, Egypt, East Germany, Japan and Nigeria, accepting China as the thirty-fourth member of the Special Committee on Peacekeeping Operations.[85] In April 1989, when China first participated in the work of the Special Committee, Ambassador Yu Mengjia urged the international community to give 'powerful political support' to UN peacekeeping, because facts had proved convincingly that peacekeeping had become an 'effective mechanism' in realising the purposes of the UN charter as well as an integral part of its efforts in finding political settlement for regional conflicts'.[86] On 31 October 1989, at the tenth meeting of the Special Committee on Peacekeeping of the General Assembly, Yu affirmed China's support of the Secretary-General's continued efforts regarding peacekeeping operations and China's dedication to the cause of maintaining international peace and security. 'To that end', Yu announced, 'China has decided to send a small contingent to take part in peacekeeping operations.'[87] The 'small contingent' China dispatched in 1989 consists of five military observers who joined the UN Disengagement Observer Group (UNDOF) in the Middle East, and 20 Chinese non-military personnel who became members of the United Nations Transition Assistance Group in Namibia (UNTAG).[88] For the first time, China participated in the actual peacekeeping operations of the UN. In 1992, China sent an engineering battalion to Cambodia.[89] During the 'renaissance of international peacekeeping' in the late 1980s and early 1990s, China has become, among more than 60 other member states of the UN, one of the 'peacekeepers'. In 1993 and 1994, the Chinese blue helmets sustained their first casualties in participating in UN peacekeeping in Cambodia and in Kuwait.[90]

Limitations

China's position on UN peacekeeping operations, as argued before, continues to be a subject of controversy in the post-Cold War era. Samuel Kim argued that China failed 'the first litmus test' on its political and moral support of UN peacekeeping during the Gulf Crisis in 1990–91. He pointed out that China, though having voted in favour of other 11 Security Council resolutions, including the resolution on economic sanctions against Iraq, abstained from voting on Resolution 678, authorising the 'use of all necessary means', including the use of force, to expel the invading Iraqi troops from Kuwait.[91] He further argued that the Chinese had cultivated the Gulf Crisis to divert the world's attention from China's post-Tiananmen domestic politics. China had, in other words, 'managed to extract maximum payoffs from the United States with minimum support'.[92]

Whether the UN authorised military operations in occupied Kuwait in the wake of Resolution 678 is peacekeeping or peacemaking is highly debatable. It must also be noted that China abstained only after its amendment on the use of force was rejected at the Security Council. In the same book where Kim's arguments appear, Shichor offered a different line of explanation for China's abstention. In his words,

> China all along supported efforts to work out a peaceful solution within the Arab world, and following its traditional policies, without external, least of all Western, intervention. It was this attitude that determined China's abstention from voting on UN Security Council Resolution 678, which sanctioned the use of military operations against Iraq.[93]

With the perspective that time has given us and with China's vote on UN peacekeeping operations in the last few years on record, it is now clear that China's abstention from voting on Resolution 678 sets limits to China's support of UN peacekeeping operations rather than signals China's renegation on its political and moral commitment to UN peacekeeping. What China could not support, as was made clear then and there, was the use of force in the name of the United Nations for military intervention, not peacekeeping operations. 'The United Nations as an international organisation', the Chinese representative at the Security Council stated, 'is responsible both to international security and to history.'[94] Foreign Minister Qian Qichen later explained to a domestic audience that 'Chinese people still clearly remember that the Korean War was launched in the name of the United Nations'.[95] China was then speaking as well as acting from its own national experience.

The limits of China's support of UN peacekeeping were further elaborated and delineated in its subsequent votes on Security Council resolutions on peacekeeping. The first line of limits is related to the use of force. Wherever the resolutions authorised the use of force – for example, in Bosnia – China abstained.[96] The Chinese strongly argued that 'the practice of stopping a war by expanding it was unacceptable'.[97] In voting for a Security Council resolution imposing a no-flight zone in Bosnia, the Chinese Ambassador Li Daoyu carefully pointed out that 'the Chinese delegation is not in favour of any use of force on the question of establishing a ban on military flights in the airspace of Bosnia and Herzegovina'.[98] In May 1994, China emphasised similar reservations while voting in favour of the Security Council resolution imposing sanctions against Haiti's military regime.[99]

The second line of limits concerns sovereignty. In the Security Council debate on the Haitian situation in June 1993, the Chinese delegation stated that it 'does not favour the Security Council's handling matters which are essentially internal affairs of a Member State, nor does it approve of resorting lightly to such mandatory measures as sanctions by the Council'.[100] In explaining China's abstention from the UN resolution on Rwanda authorising the French dispatch of troops, the Foreign Ministry spokesman was explicit that China abstained because 'the actions authorised by the UN Security Council resolution at present is not guaranteed of cooperation and consent by the parties to the conflict in Rwanda'.[101] In the comprehensive review of UN peacekeeping operations by the Special Political and Decolonisation Committee in 1993, the Chinese delegate made a strong representation on the issue of sovereignty and the need for obtaining consent and cooperation from the parties concerned in carrying out peacekeeping operations.[102]

Qian Qichen, the Chinese Foreign Minister, was blunter about the Chinese position when speaking to the General Assembly in 1994. Qian asserted that UN peacekeeping 'must be conducted with the consent and cooperation of all the parties concerned in strict accordance with the UN Charter and the norms governing international relations'. A lesson should be drawn from 'the experience of UN peacekeeping troops in Somalia', and 'whether in peacekeeping operations or in humanitarian missions, there should be no interference in other countries' internal affairs, much less military involvement in the conflict between the parties concerned'.[103]

A position such as this, as adopted by China, might be partly an assertive, though not necessarily appropriate, expression of China's 'independent' stance in international affairs. China does seem to stick to the traditional statist line on sovereignty. It cannot be argued, however, that China has foundered on its support of UN peacekeeping. Though there is more than an element of truth in Kim's argument that China would be 'a problem for the revival of American hegemony in the United Nations', his claim that 'China remains part of the global problem in the post-Cold War high politics in the Security Council' and 'for the implementation of the Charter-based collective security system in the Post-Cold War era' can hardly be substantiated by evidence of Chinese policies towards UN peacekeeping in the post-Cold War era.[104]

Conclusion

What, then, is the significance of China's changing position on UN peacekeeping from antagonism in the 1950s and the 1960s to antipathy in the 1970s, and then to adoption and active cooperation in the 1980s and the 1990s? How can we evaluate its limitations?

First, it must be noted that the path by which China has reached general consensus with other permanent members of the Security Council on UN peacekeeping is a long and tortuous one. China's condemnation of peacekeeping in the 1960s was as vehement as its endorsement of the same institution in the 1980s. Its position on international peacekeeping today is still beset with limitations. Significant changes in China's international behaviour towards peacekeeping, however, have taken place. As far as the peacekeeping is concerned, China has become a more acceptable part of the international system.

Second, China's changing position on UN peacekeeping has contributed to what Secretary-General Boutros Boutros -Ghali called the 'great unity' and 'collegiality' of the Security Council members. In spite of all difficulties and 'a crisis of expectations' in UN peacekeeping operations in the post-Cold War era,[105] the consensus and unity of permanent members of the Security Council is still an indispensable condition that gives UN peacekeeping operations a better chance to succeed.

Third, and more specifically, as Brian Urquhart argued somewhere, 'The support of the great powers, political and financial, is a *sine qua non*' for the success of UN peacekeeping operations.[106] Clearly, the political support, financial contribution and active participation of China, a permanent member of the Security Council, has first and foremost reinforced the legitimacy of UN peacekeeping by making it a less divisive issue. Coupled with the renewed interest of the international community in multilateral instruments for security and conflict resolution within the UN framework, it has also helped to find the common will among the Security Council members in effectively containing and resolving international conflicts. It has thus strengthened the capacity of the Security Council and the UN in the maintenance of international peace and security. It has also helped to reverse the antipathy among some UN members towards international peacekeeping and contributed to a renewal of faith in the UN and in the competence and utility of peacekeeping. Since 1988, UN peacekeeping operations have proved to be a more viable instrument effective in managing and ending an impressive list of enduring regional conflicts from Afghanistan to Iran and Iraq and from Cambodia to Namibia. The gruelling experience of the UN in Bosnia, however, does expose the severe limitations of peacekeeping and suggests that peacekeeping is not a panacea for solving regional and local conflicts, even in the post-Cold War period.[107]

Fourth, and probably most importantly, is the symbolic significance of China's change from reluctant non-disruption of international peacekeeping at the beginning of the 1980s to willing cooperation and participation at the end of the decade. It has been well argued that 'peacekeeping has evolved as a function of the "universal" values inherent within regional and/or international organisations, which are thereby meant to take precedence over national allegiance or ideological, political, economic, or strategic interests'.[108] It must be argued, therefore, that although limitations still abound in the Chinese policy towards UN peacekeeping, China has opted for the 'universal' level of values in the case of international peacekeeping, a positive step in China's political socialisation into international society.

ARMS CONTROL: THE LIMITS OF PROGRESS[109]

In recent studies, China is often cast in a villain's mould either as an unscrupulous arms merchant, or as a vicious proliferator of missile and nuclear technologies. In *Strategic Survey, 1988–1989*, published by the International Institute for Strategic Studies, China was depicted as 'a rogue elephant in the arms trade, supplying arms virtually without consideration of political or security implications'.[110] In the last few years, China's arms procurements have also become a nagging concern, particularly for countries in the Asia-Pacific region.[111] No one would deny that

China's behaviour in the international army control and disarmament (ACD) is far from satisfactory. Its cooperation in this field leaves a lot to be desired. An alarming gap exists between China's verbal commitments to arms transfer control and non-proliferation regimes and its practice. It is difficult not to agree that China's policies towards international ACD today are still full of 'inconsistencies and ambiguities'.[112] There is, however, also ample evidence to suggest that China has significantly shifted its position on arms control, especially in view of its stand in the pre-1980 period. More importantly, this shift is towards conforming to the existing conventions and accepting the current regimes.

The discussions that follow look at China's changing arms control policies as another process of China's political socialisation into international society. It is therefore only natural that the major questions to be addressed are quite different from those of strategic studies. What are the major changes in China's position on arms control and disarmament and in which direction? Has China come around to accepting existing rules and norms in arms control, and why? How much has China been involved in the institutional framework defined by John Ruggie as multilateralism and has accordingly adjusted its policies on the basis of 'generalised' principle of conduct, and to what effect?[113] Has the involvement of China in the international ACD regimes exercised sufficient pressures to compel China to behave responsibly and normally, particularly as a nuclear power, and to what extent? And finally, what does the Chinese experience in the 1980s and the 1990s tell us about the limits of China's socialisation in international society?

In order to answer all these questions, we first highlight the most visible and measurable aspect of China's socialisation by looking at China's accession to major arms control treaties since 1981. The significance of this development is evaluated against the background of China's arms control policies before 1980. It then moves on to study how and whether a 'change of heart' by China towards arms control took place. This is followed by an examination of some of the most controversial aspects of China's arms control policies before a brief conclusion.

China's accession to arms control treaties

In what particular aspect, then, has China since 1981 made the most conspicuous efforts in converting its arms control policies to bring them in line with the general consensus among members of international society? In other words, what is the most visible evidence that China has come around to accept the generalised principles of appropriate conduct in the international ACD?

The record of China's ratification of or accession to the major multilateral arms control agreements since 1981 offers an answer to these questions.[114] Regrettably, this has not been given due credit. It is true that, as of 1996, China's commitment to the Comprehensive Test Ban Treaty (CTBT) is still wavering. Its verbal and written assurances to adhere to the guidelines of the Missile Technology Control Regime (MTCR) are not entirely satisfactory. Nevertheless, there is a sharp contrast between 1981 and 1996. As of 31 December 1981, China was party to only one of the eight major multilateral arms control treaties listed in the *SIPRI Yearbook*; namely, the Treaty of Tlatelolco.[115] By the end of 1992, however, China became party to all but two of the original eight. China acceded in 1992 to the controversial Non-Proliferation Treaty (NPT), of which it had been most critical.[116] The NPT, it must be noted, has been claimed to be the 'fundamental cornerstone of arms control', which 'has served the security, trade and nuclear cooperation interests of the global community very well'.[117] More significantly, China has become party to the two new agreements added respectively in 1984 and 1986 to the SIPRI list. China signed and ratified 'Inhumane Weapons' Convention[118] on 14 September 1981 and 8 March 1982 respectively.[119] In 1989, China signed Protocol 2 and Protocol 3 of the Treaty of Rarotonga, which are open to China's signature (see Tables 5.1 and 5.2).[120]

Table 5.1   Status of implementation of the major multilateral arms control agreements by five major nuclear powers, 31 December 1981

	China	France	Russia	UK	USA
Antarctic Treaty		1960	1960	1960	1960
PTBT			1963	1963	1973
Outer Space Treaty		1970	1967	1967	1967
Treaty of Tlatelolco	PII:1974	PII:1974	PII: 1979	PI: 1969 PII: 1969	PI: 1981 PII:1971
NPT			1970	1968	1970
Seabed Treaty			1972	1972	1972
BW Convention			1975	1975	1975
Enmod Convention			1978	1978	1980

Source: *SIPRI Yearbook of International Armaments and Disarmament, 1984*, pp. 654–66.

Table 5.2 Status of implementation of some major multilateral arms control agreements by five major nuclear powers, 31 December 1992

	China	France	Russia	UK	USA
Antarctic Treaty	1983	1960	1960	1960	1960
PTBT			1963	1963	1973
Outer Space Treaty	1983	1970	1967	1967	1967
Treaty of Tlatelolco	PII:1974	PI: 1992 PII:1974	PII: 1979	PI: 1969 PII: 1969	PI: 1981 PII:1971
NPT	1992	1992	1970	1968	1970
Seabed Treaty	1991		1972	1972	1972
BW Convention	1984	1984	1975	1975	1975
Enmod Convention			1978	1978	1980
'Inhuman Weapons' Convention	1982	1988	1982	S*	S
Treaty of Rarotonga	P2:1989 P3: 1989		P2: 1988 P3: 1988		

* S = signed but not ratified
Source: *SIPRI Yearbook of International Armaments and Disarmament, 1993*, pp. 765–81.

The contrast between China's accession to and participation in international arms control and disarmaments regimes and institutions in 1981 and 1992 is then graphically striking. From opting largely to stay outside the framework of the international ACD machinery and not to adhere to most of the existing multilateral agreements until 1981, in a little more than ten years' time, China became party to most of the major multilateral arms control treaties by 1992. In practice, China in 1992 acceded to and signed more major multilateral arms control agreements on the SIPRI list than did France. Further, while China had signed and ratified both the 'Inhumane Weapons' Convention and relevant protocols of Rarotonga Treaty, the United Kingdom and the United States had only signed and were yet to ratify the 'Inhumane Weapons' Convention. Neither of them signed any protocols of the Rarotonga Treaty open to their signature.[121]

These tables are therefore telling of a substantial step that China made between 1981 and 1992 towards implementing 'effective global multilateral agreements drawing on the assent and cooperation of the entire international community', in which lies the long-term control and eventual elimination of both nuclear and conventional weapons.[122]

There is more to what these tables can reveal. Even before China's accession to the NPT in 1992, China had promised to conduct a policy 'in accordance with non-proliferation goals'.[123] When it was admitted to the International Atomic Energy Agency (IAEA) in October 1983, it had consented to 'accept the relevant provisions in the statute of the agency, including the relevant provisions on safeguards' and 'fulfil its obligations to the agency'.[124] On 20 September 1988, China signed a safeguard agreement with the IAEA, thus conforming to 'the most important NPT article in operational terms'.[125] On PTBT issues, Zhao Ziyang chose the occasion to mark the United Nations' International Year of Peace to declare at a rally in the Great Hall of the People in Beijing on 21 March 1986 that China had not conducted atmospheric nuclear tests for many years and would no longer conduct such tests in the future.[126] China remained, nevertheless, critical of what it regarded as the 'discriminatory nature' of the PTBT. Even on matters related to the Missile Technology Control Regime (MTCR), from the negotiations of which China was excluded,[127] China quickly adopted its principles and gave verbal assurances that China would abide by the guidelines of the MTCR. China, however, was very unhappy about the way the negotiations in which on MTCR were conducted.

China and arms control before 1980

The significance of China's converting its arms control policies can only be fully brought home when it is evaluated against the background of China's policies on arms control before 1980.[128] China's alienation from the American-dominated international system in the 1950s, and later from the Soviet-led international Communist movement, exerted a strong impact on China's negative attitude towards major international ACD activities initiated by the two superpowers. Its open hostility towards almost all international ACD initiatives, earmarked by its public denunciation of the PTBT in 1963 and of the NPT in 1968, was characteristic of its approach to international ACD matters prior to its entry into the United Nations in 1971. It is true, though, that China put forward a proposal for a complete prohibition of nuclear weapons and did suggest that, as the first step, all nuclear powers pledge not to be the first to use nuclear weapons against non-nuclear powers, or nuclear-free zones or against each other.[129] At the same time, however, China rejected openly an invitation to take part in the Geneva 18-nation Disarmament Conference on two grounds. One was because China had been deprived of its legitimate right to be a member of the United Nations and would have nothing to do with the UN. The other was that both the UN and the Geneva 18-nation Disarmament Conference were under the manipulation and control of the United States and were 'completely incapable of handling the disarmament questions'.[130] Excluded from the UN, China then opted to pursue its disarmament initiatives outside the general and accepted framework of international ACD activities. Naturally, China's behaviour towards international ACD was neither markedly constrained nor positively affected by multilateralism in those years.

The admission of the PRC into the United Nations and the Security Council in September 1971 did have some impact on the way in which China expressed its disapproval of international ACD initiatives in general and on the UN forum in particular. China's entry did not, however, either have an immediate effect on modifying China's principles on international ACD matters, or significantly influence the formulation of China's arms control policy. The ACD proposals presented to the General Assembly by the two superpowers were, as before, invariably characterised by China as 'frauds'.

What China's membership in the UN did was to provide China with a legitimate forum and to engage it in talks and negotiations on international ACD matters. China had to learn to live now with international ACD efforts in its daily diplomacy at the UN, even if it would not affirm, not to say accept, any positive values of a disarmament process through arms control. It was simply 'caught up' in international ACD activities at the UN. In particular, China has been irretrievably involved, willingly or not, in the international ACD process through its membership in the First Committee ever since its admission to the UN. The intellectual communication within the UN arms control forum and the information-rich international ACD regimes would eventually and inexorably influence and condition China's position on arms control and disarmaments.[131] China was compelled to learn about multilateralism in the international ACD.

Why should China have adopted such an approach to international ACD issues in the pre-1980 period? What are the factors most influential in the formulation of China's arms control policies then? Conventional wisdom points to the direction of China's ideology, strategic and geopolitical concerns and its inferior nuclear arsenal *vis-à-vis* those of the two superpowers. They are, no doubt, among the important determinants of China's arms control policies. One element that has decisively shaped China's basic approach to arms control has largely been neglected: namely, its unique national experience in the post-war years. What are they? Three broad areas of inquiry are suggested below.

First, China is the only power that has been threatened by both the United States and the Soviet Union with nuclear attacks in the post-war years. From 1953 to 1958, at least four times, the American administration under Eisenhower threatened to use nuclear weapons against China.[132] The use of the nuclear threat against China at the beginning of 1953 by the Eisenhower administration was even credited as one of the main factors to have 'compelled the CPR [PRC] to capitulate on the prisoner issue and sign an armistice' on the Korean War.[133] During the first Taiwan Strait crisis, Eisenhower explicitly told a press conference on 17 March 1955 that he saw no reason why the United States could not use tactical nuclear weapons 'just exactly as you would use a bullet or anything else'.[134] Even during the final days of the French débâcle in Dien Bien Phu, the Americans considered it an option to attack China with nuclear weapons, if the Chinese Communists were believed to have intervened.[135] The warnings of nuclear attacks on China from the Soviet Union after the Sino-Soviet border conflicts in 1969 were more explicit.[136] Never was there a country threatened so often by so many nuclear blackmails of both superpowers in such a short period. Never was there a country living so consistently in the shadow of nuclear attacks in the first 25 years of the nuclear age from 1945 to 1970. In one of the first documents China submitted to the UN on ACD issues in 1971, it was stated that 'China develops nuclear weapons because it is compelled to do so under imperialist nuclear threats'.[137] This simple fact radically conditioned China's outlook on and eventually approach to international ACD initiatives.

Second, China was the only power (nuclear since 1964) alienated from both superpowers and more broadly alienated and excluded from the existing international system prior to 1971. The dire consequences of this alienation were threefold. First, with membership in neither blocs and without the protection of the nuclear umbrella of either superpower, China, even with its infant nuclear arsenal after 1964, was especially vulnerable to nuclear attacks by the two superpowers. This was particularly true since China, with its radical stance and confrontational approach in world affairs, was perceived as a deadly challenge to first the American and later the Soviet interests in general and their interests in Asia in particular. Second, as a consequence, China harboured a deep suspicion that all ACD initiatives sponsored by superpower(s) were directed against China, particularly those initiatives enjoying the consent of both superpowers. China's enunciation at the UN of the contention-collusion theme in the superpower relationship and its denunciation of superpower 'disarmament fraud' were expressions of the unique perspective of China's alienation. Third, alienation bred suspicion and misunderstanding, which in turn fed into each other. It was practically impossible to have any confidence-building measures (CBMs) between China and other nuclear powers. This irreparably fouled the fundamental precondition of arms control.

The third aspect of China's unique national experience is that, partly as a consequence of its alienation from international society, it was cut off for every practical purpose from any meaningful intellectual communication with the other nuclear powers on international ACD issues. As was claimed recently in a well-researched essay, 'there is no evidence that any overarching strategic doctrine informed Chairman Mao Zedong's decision to proceed with the strategic missile programme in the mid-1950s'. Until the early 1980s, over 15 years after China had become a nuclear power,

> there were no scenarios, no detailed linkage of the weapons to foreign policy objectives, and no serious strategic research. Neither the Chinese leader nor his senior colleagues on the Central Military Commission considered, communicated, or authorised the investigation of the broader strategic purposes of the program [of ballistic missiles].[138]

A glaring example of this intellectual gap has also been illustrated in a recent publication by Alastair Johnston. Only in the post-Cold War years did the Chinese military gradually develop a nuclear doctrine of 'limited deterrence', the essence of which Johnston catches well in his title: 'China's New "Old Thinking"'.[139] The paucity of expertise on arms control in China today is still acute. Only recently have the expression 'arms control' and the concepts associated with it entered Chinese discourse and they are still controversial within China's strategic studies community.[140]

This, however, should probably not come as a surprise. China had never accepted strategic nuclear deterrence through the so-called 'balance of terror' as the 'keystone of national security', as had the two superpowers.[141] Arms control as a process of disarmament was totally alien to Chinese officials and academics alike. The sophistication of the definition of arms control as any kind of military cooperation between potential enemies with the aim of 'reducing the likelihood of war, its scope and violence if it occurs, and the political and economic costs of being prepared for it' was beyond their comprehension.[142] Arms control as a concept totally different from disarmament had rarely, if at all, entered the discourse of Chinese officials or that of the academic community. The basic concept of arms control, which is not always incompatible with and indeed sometimes requires quantitative increase and qualitative improvement of nuclear arms, was simply incomprehensible to the Chinese.[143] For them, nothing short of arms reductions pure and simple, which could be measured quantitatively, was 'genuine' disarmament.[144] The indiscriminate denunciation of almost all arms control initiatives short of actual reduction, and the indiscriminate use of 'disarmament' in all its addresses on international ACD efforts, are evidence of an alarming gap in the understanding of the intellectual basis of the whole spectrum of international ACD initiatives. As late as 1985, Zhao Ziyang told the General Assembly that 'Neither "deterrent force" nor "balance of terror" could ensure peace, rather they gave rise to an intensification of the arms race'.[145] Even in the early 1990s, some Chinese scholars still resisted using the word 'deterrence' in their discussions of arms control and disarmament.[146]

A 'change of heart'?

The de-alienation of China from international society, as discussed previously, which brought about qualitative improvement in China's security environment and which opened up the intellectual communication between China and international ACD regimes, is therefore probably most decisive in shaping China's new direction of arms control commitments. China's accession to arms control treaties was accompanied by gradual and very often grudging moves towards 'normalising' its behaviour on the international forums on arms control and disarmaments. The process is, however, a lengthy one. One official Chinese diplomatic history, recently published, suggests that the year 1983 was a turning point in China's involvement in the ACD negotiations in the UN. It is stated that, 'to achieve genuine disarmament and safeguard world peace, China has since 1983 taken an even more positive attitude in the UN disarmament negotiations and put forward a series of new proposals against the backdrop of new developments in the arms race'.[147]

The real change in China's 'negative and passive' stance in multilateralism in international ACD started probably a little earlier. China joined the United Nations Disarmament Commission in 1979 and the Committee on Disarmament (later called the Conference on Disarmament) in Geneva in 1980. In these two institutions, the Chinese delegates argued that the two superpowers possessing the largest nuclear arsenals in the world had special responsibility in world-wide disarmament efforts. They should take the lead in substantially reducing their nuclear armaments and in ceasing all tests and manufacture of nuclear weapons so as to narrow the huge gap between them and other nuclear-weapon states. That would create the conditions necessary for the convening of a broadly representative international conference on nuclear disarmament.[148]

China's participation in international ACD before 1982 could be regarded as a prelude to the 'normalisation' of its behaviour in international ACD activities. A Chinese scholar observed recently that Chinese policies towards arms control and disarmaments prior to the 1980s was marked by 'opposition rather than proposition'.[149] The 'normalisation' of China's behaviour could then be said to be marked by 'proposition rather than opposition'. Three steps can be identified. The first step was taken at the second United Nations Special Session on Disarmament (UNSSOD) in 1982, Huang Hua enunciated and elaborated on what became China's six basic principles on international ACD issues. First, disarmament and international security are inseparable. Second, the two superpowers should take the lead in reducing their armaments, nuclear as well as conventional. Third, nuclear and conventional disarmament should go hand in hand. Fourth, small and medium-sized countries have the right to maintain the defence capabilities necessary to resist aggression and defend their independence. Fifth, disarmament agreements should provide strict and effective international verification. And sixth, every state, big or small, should be entitled to participate on an equal footing in the deliberations and negotiations on disarmament questions and in the supervision over the implementation of the agreements reached.[150]

In addition, five 'practical' and more specific measures were also proposed by China. First, an agreement should be reached by all the nuclear-weapon states not to be the first to use nuclear weapons. Second, pending such an agreement, each nuclear-weapon state should, without attaching any condition, undertake not to use or threaten to use nuclear weapons against non-nuclear-weapon states or nuclear-weapon-free zones, and not to be the first to use such weapons against each other at any time and under any circumstances. Third, the Soviet Union and the United States should stop testing, improving or manufacturing nuclear weapons and should reduce by 50 per cent all types of their nuclear weapons and means of delivery. This was later dubbed as *Santing Yijian* (three stops and one reduction). Fourth, after that, all other nuclear-weapon states should also stop testing, improving or manufacturing nuclear weapons and should reduce their respective nuclear arsenals according to an agreed proportion and procedure. And finally, as a first step in conventional disarmament, all states should undertake not to use conventional armaments for intervention or aggression against and military occupation of any country.[151]

This was the first time that China publicly enunciated its principles on the international ACD in a less ambiguous way than just a general commitment to disarmaments and total elimination of nuclear weapons. That China's new stand was more sophisticated is demonstrated first by its explicitly stating that peace was indivisible, second by its acknowledging the obligations in all international ACD activities arising from its membership of international society in general and of a nuclear power in particular, and third by its proposing strict international verification as part of the confidence-building measures so vital in arms control procedures.[152] China also began to emphasise the importance of the feasibility of any proposals.[153] This new stand is significant, therefore, because it signals that a convergence of China's position with those of other nuclear powers on general arms control issues was taking place. China was, as it were, 'coming around'.

China's 'change of heart' on its arms control policies also led to its ratifying the 'Inhumane Weapons' Convention in 1982, acceding to, somewhat belatedly, the Antarctic Treaty in 1983, to the Outer Space Treaty also in 1983, and to the Biological Weapons Convention in 1984.[154] At the same time, China reiterated its pledge that it would not produce, store or use chemical weapons, and called for the early conclusion of an international treaty to prohibit the production and to destroy the existing stock of chemical weapons. It was, however, another seven years before China finally signed the Chemical Weapons Convention in 1994. In 1985, Chinese delegate declared that China had in principle not been opposed to the establishment of a subsidiary body on a nuclear test ban: 'If such a subsidiary body were established in 1985, the Chinese delegation would reconsider its position.'[155]

The second step is marked by China's submission in 1986 to the UN General Assembly of two draft resolutions on nuclear and conventional disarmament respectively. This was the first time that China had ever proposed draft resolutions on arms control and disarmaments with its own initiatives to the UN General Assembly. The Chinese were delighted and excited when the two draft resolutions were adopted almost unanimously by the UN General Assembly in November 1986.[156] An editorial in *Renmin Ribao* hailed China's unprecedented move as a 'positive action to promote disarmament', and claimed that the two draft resolutions 'not only represent China's long-held position on disarmament but have also incorporated some sensible proposals by many other countries'.[157] Foreign Minister Qian Qichen did not try to conceal his contentment that China was moving towards shaping the norms of international ACD when he claimed at the third UNSSOD in 1988 that as a result of the Chinese proposals, 'disarmament has been turned from a good desire of the people of all countries into an action that has a clear starting point and a practical goal'.[158]

In urging the superpowers to 'negotiate in earnest' so as to reach agreements on both nuclear and conventional disarmament, the two Chinese-sponsored draft resolutions actually represented a drastic change in China's attitude towards the initiatives in international arms control. In emphasising the special responsibility of the two superpowers, it acknowledged that the superpowers played the key and leading role in international ACD negotiations. It also acquiesced in the special responsibility of nuclear-weapon states (including China) for international peace and security. Negotiations and agreements, particularly between the superpowers, on arms control and disarmament had therefore some positive values which were conducive to international peace and security. It followed that all negotiations between the two superpowers on international ACD measures were to be encouraged, not encumbered, least of all condemned.

Naturally, the third step could be seen as China's endorsement of the arms control and disarmament talks between the two superpowers after the mid-1980s. In February 1985, the Chinese ambassador to the Conference on Disarmament in Geneva stressed that 'China welcomes the recent agreement by the United States and the Soviet Union for the resumption of their arms control talks'.[159] A similar message was also communicated to the domestic audience. Commenting on the obvious 'failure' of the Reykjavik summit between the United States and the Soviet Union, a *Renmin Ribao* commentary argued, however, 'The Chinese people, like peoples of all other countries, endorse the US–Soviet summit meetings and sincerely hope that they are engaged in serious dialogues in order to reach agreements which are conducive to the maintenance of international peace without being detrimental to the interests of any other countries'.[160] In December 1987, the Chinese government 'joined in world-wide acclaim' of the signing of the Intermediate-range Nuclear Forces (INF) Treaty between the United States and the Soviet Union. It officially 'applauded' this 'historical pact', and was convinced that the signing of the INF Treaty, the first agreement to reduce nuclear armaments, 'will help ease international tensions to some extent'.[161]

It is sometimes argued that China's gradual turn-around on arms control issues in the 1980s was politically motivated rather than out of calculated considerations of its security benefits and needs. It is also argued that China's 'selected activism' in the international ACD followed 'a maxi-mini principle – the maximisation of security benefits and the minimisation of normative costs'.[162] There is a lot of truth in these arguments. From the perspective of China's socialisation, however, what is positive about China's participation is that it began to be involved in – or rather, entangled in – the network of the international ACD regimes. Such entanglement not only obliged China to learn the norms and rules of the international ACD regimes; it also helped it to realise and appreciate the benefits of the international ACD regimes for its security and its special responsibility as a nuclear-weapon state, thus inducing as well as compelling China's deeper involvement in the arms control process and its compliance with the existing international ACD regimes. By the end of the 1980s, arms control and disarmaments multilateral forums such as the United Nations had earned a place in China's foreign policy agenda. Discussions and debates about the US–Soviet strategic arms reduction talks and other broader arms control issues had crept into the intellectual discourse of a nascent strategic studies community in China.[163] An embryonic arms control specialist group was emerging.[164]

From NPT to CTBT

The 1990s has seen what may be regarded as 'deeper' integration of China into the international ACD process. China acceded to the Non-Proliferation Treaty (NPT) in March 1992; it offered written assurances twice in 1992 and 1994 respectively to follow the guidelines of the Missile Technology Control Regime (MTCR); it signed the Chemical Weapons Convention in 1994; and it committed itself to signing the Comprehensive Test Ban Treaty (CTBT) in 1996. Such deeper integration could be seen as another move towards China's behaving 'normally and responsibly' in the international arms control procedures. It is an indication that China has accepted, though with much reluctance, that its nuclear programmes have to develop within the constraints of multilateral arms control regimes. It also shows that China has begun to appreciate, though still hesitantly, security gains and benefits it could derive from signing and acceding to those multilateral treaties. Further, although there is little evidence in the Chinese strategic thinking to suggest that China no longer regards nuclear weapons as critical in enhancing its international status in post-Cold War international relations,[165] it does suggest that China believes now that its commitment to multilateral arms control regimes and treaties, many of which are 'discriminatory' and 'unequal' in nature, also enhances its reputation in international society.

In spite of more than two decades' scathing criticism of the 'discriminatory' nature of the NPT, the Chinese government indicated for the first time during Li Peng's visit to Japan in August 1991 that China was considering acceding to the NPT. In March 1992, China became officially a party to the NPT.[166] China's decision, it has been argued, was influenced by, among other things, its considerations to deflect international criticisms of its nuclear export policy; to avoid international isolation on the NPT matter after France announced its intention to accede to the NPT in June 1991; to enhance the image of China as a responsible nuclear power; to respond to the systemic changes in post-Cold War international relations; and to break China's diplomatic isolation in the aftermath of the Tiananmen incident in June 1989.[167] Domestic discussions and debates about China's security strategy, such as the emergence of a doctrine of 'limited deterrence' as ably analysed by Alastair Johnston in his most recent publications, must have also played its part in the decision making of China's accession to the NPT. It is, however, of particular interest to note how much pressure China's socialisation into international society as well as into the international ACD regimes has generated in compelling China not to do otherwise.

It is not very clear whether and how much China's small but burgeoning arms control community contributed to its decision to accede to the NPT in 1992. However, this community seemed particularly articulate in 1995 when China was preparing to participate in the UN conference for the renewal of the NPT. One substantial piece of a specialist's opinion even found its way into the *Beijing Review*'s Expert Forum at the end of April 1995 under an interesting title, 'NPT at Crossroads'. It claimed:

> This conference has a direct bearing on international security in the remaining few years of the century and even in the next century. Some experts even see it as the 'last chance' to peacefully prevent the proliferation of nuclear weapons... .
>
> If the treaty is renewed uneventfully, then not only will the existing mechanisms for non-proliferation be maintained and strengthened, but the nuclear states, particularly the United States and Russia, will be spurred to further reduce their nuclear stockpiles. Otherwise, the 25-year-old NPT will collapse and the world will be thrown into a nightmare of nuclear proliferation.[168]

It also observed that there 'will be strident wrangles between the nuclear-weapon and non-nuclear weapon states, instead of the old strife between the two superpowers'.[169]

It is safe to assume that if this opinion is not representative of the arms control community in China, it is certainly shared by China's arms control decision makers. It represents two radical changes in China's assessment of arms control. One is the positive affirmation of the security gains for China from the arms control treaties such as the NPT. The other is the changing perception of confrontation in the arms control process from that between the superpowers to that between nuclear 'have-nots' and 'haves'. Such changes prescribed that China behave more like a facilitator than a spoiler in the negotiations for the indefinite extension of the NPT. Both changes would also affect China's behaviour towards and condition its approach to the CTBT.

Although Foreign Minister Qian Qichen made public China's commitment to the CTBT as early as 1993,[170] China's initial hesitant and reluctant participation in the CTBT negotiations in the Conference on Disarmament (CD) in 1994 and 1995 seemed to be largely driven by international criticisms of its continued nuclear testing. Such hesitancy and reluctance should not be a surprise, as the conclusion of the CTBT would have serious implications for the development and improvement of China's nuclear arsenals and by the same token for its national security, especially the role of nuclear weapons in the overall Chinese strategy. It will certainly exercise effective constraints on China's ongoing efforts to modernise its nuclear warheads.

Although more detailed studies of the decision process are yet to be conducted, two recent studies have already provided some important findings on China's preparations for the CTBT. First, China is fully aware of the constraints that the successful conclusion of the CTBT would put on China's nuclear programmes as well as the international pressure for China to commit itself to the CTBT. Second, behind closed doors China's arms control community has debated intensively among themselves about the costs and benefits of China's participation in the CTBT and come up with some very sophisticated arguments. There seems to be a 'difference of opinion' between civilian and military arms control specialists. Third, although there is scepticism about the effectiveness of the CTBT to prevent such countries as Japan and Germany to go nuclear, in general, the arms control community seems positive about political and security gains from China's participation in the CTBT. Fourth, China's decision to participate in the CTBT is made 'at the highest level'. It is strongly influenced by Chinese leaders' careful considerations of costs and benefits for China's national security and its image as a responsible member in international society. It also results from the Chinese leadership's evaluation of China's security environment and the other nuclear powers' strategic intentions in the post-Cold War era as well as its attentive management of different interests in China's security and diplomatic communities.[171]

This may indeed provide some explanations for what Johnston called 'China's somewhat obstructionist bargaining behaviour in the CTBT', as well as for its cooperative behaviour in the final stage of negotiations for the treaty. China initially made three controversial propositions to be included into the CTBT: the right of the declared nuclear-weapon states to conduct peaceful nuclear explosions (PNEs), no-first-use (NFU) commitments by the nuclear-weapon states, and the primacy of national monitoring system (NMS) over the use of national technical means (NTM) of individual states for verification. China eventually dropped all three controversial proposals in order not to block the conclusion of the CTBT. It is particularly interesting to note that, even before the Chinese delegates in Geneva officially dropped these three proposals, Chinese officials and Beijing's arms control community had already indicated to the visiting American analysts that Beijing 'will eventually give up its demands during the negotiations if they are not supported by other countries' and 'China will not use PNE issue to prevent conclusion of a CTBT'.[172] In the end, it was not China but India that blocked the successful conclusion of the CTBT.

It is particularly interesting to note that no matter how reluctant China was initially and no matter what originally motivated China's participation, once involved in negotiations of arms control treaties, China has to respond to the international pressure in its policy choices, and its behaviour has been shaped by the existing norms and rules. China's participation in the NPT and the CTBT represents its 'deeper integration' into the international ACD regimes not only in the sense that it has made unprecedented commitments, but also because, in the negotiations particularly for the extension of the NPT and to a lesser extent for the CTBT, China has been actively participating, rather than passively pushed, for compliance.

Martin Wight, while discussing the transformation of diplomacy by international revolutions, observed that 'Conferences with revolutionary powers tend to be, not meetings where statesmen strike bargains, but forums where positions are asserted, either "for the record" or in a direct appeal to the public opinion on the other side'.[173] The important change in China's behaviour during the negotiations for the renewal of the NPT and for the CTBT could be seen therefore in the fact that China no longer takes the multilateral arms control process as forums to assert its principled positions, but rather as opportunities to strike agreements and bargains, thus behaving more like a normal power than a revolutionary state in international diplomacy.

Controversies over arms transfer control

Most controversies over China's arms control policy, especially in the last few years, have however concentrated on a particular area, the so-called 'arms transfer control'. Increasingly in the 1980s, the attention of those engaged in the multilateral arms control process was brought to the international traffic of modern arms. The Iran–Iraq War in the 1980s and the Gulf War of 1991 highlighted the destabilising effect of some conventional weapons systems in regional security. The demise of the Cold War has increased the possibility of cooperation between all big players and among all nations to regulate and restrain weapons sales on the international market. It has also emphasised the importance of the peaceful solution of regional conflicts in the new context of international peace and security, thus underlining the need for consensual arms trade policies for restricted and discriminate sales of arms. The 'arms transfer control' has now been incorporated into, and has become an increasingly important aspect of, multilateral arms control process. On 9 December 1991, the General Assembly of the UN voted to establish a register of arms transfers by a vote of 150 to 0 with two abstentions.[174] In the resolution the UN declared 'its determination to prevent the excessive and destabilising accumulation of arms, including conventional arms, in order to promote stability and strengthen regional or international peace and security' and decided 'to establish and maintain a universal and non-discriminatory Register of Conventional Arms with effect from 1 January 1992'.[175]

China's arms sales suddenly came into the international spotlight in the summer of 1987, when the United States' escort operations for reflagged Kuwaiti tankers were under potential threat of Chinese HY-2 silkworm antiship missiles sold to Iran.[176] China began to be engaged in the international arms trade in a meaningful way only around 1981, when its sales value shot up to $161 million.[177] With the prolonged Iran–Iraq War, China's arms sales on the international market increased aggressively. According to the Stockholm International Peace Research Institute, in 1987, China was ranked fifth in arms exports to the Third World, whether according to its 1987 export figure or according to the aggregate figure of its arms exports from 1983 to 1987.[178] In 1988, China's arms sales value to the Third World was the third largest after the Soviet Union and the United States. The aggregate value of China's arms sales to the developing world in the period of 1988–92 was also the third largest.[179] Only in 1989 did China's arms sales to developing countries fall sharply, probably owing to the end of the Iran–Iraq War (see Table 5.3).

The phenomenal increase in China's arms sales value was admittedly surprising. To the international community, however, it was not as alarming as the nature of the actual weapon systems which China had sold and was prepared to sell and to whom. China sold from its inventory weapons ranging from AK47 machine guns to fighter aircraft and to Silkworm missiles. In March 1988, it was revealed that China had concluded an

Table 5.3 China's arms sales to the developing world, 1988–92 (in million US dollars at 1990 constant price)

Year	1988	1989	1990	1991	1992	Total
Value	2 097	945	1 249	1 705	1 535	7 531

Source: SIPRI Yearbook of International Armaments and Disarmament, 1993, p. 444.

agreement with Saudi Arabia for the sale of its CSS-2 intermediate range ballistic missiles.[180] China was also alleged to be negotiating with Syria for the sale of its M-9 missiles in 1989. It is also claimed that China has sold medium-range missiles to Pakistan and agreed to export nuclear technology to Pakistan, Iran and Algeria.[181]

Chinese arms sales were therefore controversial, because China was selling weapons to politically sensitive areas where regional conflicts were raging and because the weapons systems which China had sold and was alleged to be contemplating selling, such as the CSS-2 IRBM and M-9 and M-11 missiles, were highly destabilising.[182] China was, however, not the principal, and certainly not the only, arms exporter to those sensitive areas. For example, in terms of agreement values, China's arms sales from 1980 to 1987 to Iran and Iraq amounted only to 13 per cent of the total arms sales to these two countries, whereas the former Soviet Union accounted for 29 per cent and Western Europe, 31 per cent in the same period.[183]

The questions that have been asked and addressed in most literature on China's arms trade are understandably related to how much and what China has sold and is selling to whom and, indeed, why. These are important questions concerning international security and regional stability. A different set of questions which are central to China's arms transfer control policy, however, remain largely unexplored. The core of these questions is closely related to one property of John Ruggie's formulation of multilateralism: policy coordination on the basis of the accepted principles. In other words, has China accepted the general principles of international arms transfer control and coordinated its policy with other major players accordingly? Has such policy coordination affected the behaviour of this 'rogue elephant' in the international arms trade?

A brief examination of three cases that follow shows encouraging signs that China's behaviour in international arms transfer control has begun to be constrained by multilateralism. At the same time, it also highlights the existing problems. China's pronounced policies on arms sales are consistent with the accepted general principles on arms transfer control. But there is an alarming gap between China's rhetoric and practice. The fact that China's defence of its missile sales has been couched in terms acceptable to the MTCR regimes shows that multilateral institutions of arms control do affect China's behaviour in international arms transfer. On the other hand, China's efforts to stretch the boundaries of the MTCR regimes in order to justify its missile technology transfer are worrying. It is more so because China's verbal and written assurances to abide by the MTCR have been used as political bargaining chips in its relations with the United States. And finally, the PERM-5 talks in 1991–92 on arms transfer control, in spite of its difficulties, are a clear example that policy coordination on international arms transfer control among major arms suppliers did begin to take place on the basis of generally accepted principles. Such coordination, however, is extremely fragile, and susceptible to volatility in other arena of international politics.

First, let us look at China's pronounced policies on the international arms trade. As early as 8 September 1988, the Chinese Foreign Ministry spokesman went out of his way in a weekly news briefing to announce China's 'three principles of arms sales'. In his words:

> China is a responsible country. We always assume a serious, prudent, and responsible attitude toward the military products export question. In this regard, we strictly adhere to three principles: first, our military products export should help strengthen the legitimate self-defence capability of the countries concerned; second, it should help safeguard and promote peace, security, and stability in the regions concerned; and third, we do not use the military sale to interfere in the internal affairs of other nations.[184]

This first enunciation of China's principles on arms sales was followed by further elaboration at the Disarmament Commission of the United Nations, on 11 May 1989, of China's position on international arms transfer by Fan Guoxiang, the Chinese ambassador for disarmament. Apart from affirming the three principles mentioned above, the nine points Fan made of China's position on arms transfer demanded 'strict prohibition of all types of arms transfer' to 'those states or regimes which, in violation of the UN Charter and the basic norms governing international relations, subject other countries to aggression, expansion and military occupation and practise racism and colonial domination'. It called for 'rational regulation and limitation of international arms transfer'. It also called on the two biggest arms suppliers, the United States and the Soviet Union, to 'take the lead in adopting concrete and effective self-restraining measures' in reducing their arms export, and urged the arms supplier and recipient countries to 'carry out consultations and negotiations on an equal footing' so as to 'reach agreement on the rational regulation and limitation of international arms transfer'. Finally, it exhorted the UN to play its due part in international arms transfer control initiatives.[185] These nine points were submitted later in a working paper by China to the Disarmament Commission.[186]

Some may dismiss the above as China's rhetoric diplomacy and which no relevance to its actual policy. It is, however, important to note that the broad principles set forth in these statements – such as the need for regulating and limiting the flow of the international traffic of arms and for a specific control regime, conduciveness of arms transfer to regional security and stability, commensurability of arms transfer with the need for national self-defence, and the UN as the main forum for arms transfer control talks – were all later adopted collectively by the five permanent members of the Security Council and were embodied in the Final Communiqué issued in Paris on 9 July 1992.

The Paris Final Communiqué confirmed that 'fully conscious of the special responsibilities that is incumbent upon them', the Five 'confirmed that they would not transfer conventional weapons in circumstances which would undermine stability'. They pledged to develop and maintain 'stringent national and, as far as possible, harmonised controls to ensure that weapons of mass destruction related equipment and materials are transferred for permitted purposes only and are not diverted'. They consented to develop 'agreed guidelines' of 'rules of self-restraint' in conventional weapons sales. To increase the transparency on arms transfer, they 'also agreed to support continued work in the United Nations on an arms transfer register to be established under the aegis of the UN Secretary-General, on a non-discriminatory basis'.[187] On 18 October 1992, at the end of a meeting of on arms transfers and non-proliferation in London, the five permanent members of the Security Council produced, in a spirit of 'collegiality', in Boutros Boutros-Ghali's words,[188] *Guidelines for Conventional Arms Transfer* with more specific undertakings.[189] As mentioned above, on 9 December 1991, the UN General Assembly Resolution 46/36 was adopted to establish a UN register of arms transfer with effect from 1 January 1992. Given the complexities and difficulties of conventional arms transfer control,[190] it is significant that such a broad consensus was achieved in such a short time against so many odds on such a complicated issue among the five permanent members of the Security Council and also among member states of the UN. In 1993, China complied with the UN resolution and voluntarily submitted its arms import and export data to the UN register.[191]

There have been and there still are some inconsistencies and discrepancies between China's policy pronouncement and sales practice on international arms transfer. Is China engaged in double-dealing in its arms exports? There cannot be any simple answer to that. The wisdom that John Lewis and others offered in a study published in *International Security* should be helpful in solving the enigma.[192] In brief, Lewis and others identified six systems in the Chinese defence establishment – namely, the General Staff Department, the General Political Department, the General Logistics Department, the Commission of Science, Technology and Industry for Nations Defence (COSTIND), the National Defence University and the Academy of Military Science. All of these six systems have inputs into the policies and practices of China's arms export. In theory, the locus of China's arms-sale decision making resides in both the Central Military Commission and the State Council, with the final say reserved for Deng Xiaoping.[193] In practice, the General Staff Department and COSTIND have the final say on where and what to sell. They also have affiliated national corporations – prominently, Poly Technologies (*Baoli Gongsi*) and New Era (*Xinshidai*) – to close the deal. The Ministry of Foreign Affairs, on the other hand, has to handle 'house-keeping matters' and to coordinate public statements to protests and criticisms from other nations. It is observed that 'the Ministry, however, has increasingly attempted, with spotty success, to limit the independence of the military in this arena'.[194]

This, of course, could not be the full explanation of the gap between China's policy statement and its practice in arms sale. Some have even questioned the validity of such explanations in a Leninist state like China.[195] It does seem, however, that faced with international criticisms, China has responded by establishing an inter-departmental administrative body directly under the State Council and the Central Military Commission to oversee its arms exports. As the recently published White Paper on arms control and disarmament reveals, the body is called the State Administrative Committee on Military Products Trade (SACMPT) and is responsible for 'centralised control of transfers of military equipment and related technologies'. The Ministry of Foreign Affairs, the Headquarters of the General Staff, COSTIND, and MOFTEC, among others, are closely involved in the SACMPT.[196]

The second case to be examined relates more to China's behaviour than to its pronouncement of policies. China expressed in 1991 its willingness to abide by the guidelines of the MTCR, an arms transfer control regime outside the UN framework, although China had been excluded from the negotiation and was not a party to it.[197] Prior to this verbal assurance, Beijing rejected Washington's probing request in 1988 that China adhere to the MTCR controls. Significantly, this initial Chinese rejection was not based on its questioning principles embodied in the MTCR. According to Kathleen Bailey, the three basic reasons given by Chinese officials for the rejection are

> 1 Politically, China could not afford to be viewed by developing countries as a member of a Western condominium designed to deprive them of technology. 2 The United States has made vast amounts of money from arms exports, including missile exports, and China should be able to do the same without interference from the United States. And 3 China was already showing restraint in its missile exports.[198]

The last reason unwittingly reaffirmed the necessity and desirability for some missile export control mechanisms. It is also interesting to note that even before China issued its verbal assurance that it would abide by the MTCR guidelines before 1991, it had already defended its sale of intermediate-range ballistic missiles to Saudi Arabia by invoking the MTCR regime. The first defence, although feeble, was that China was not a party to the MTCR, and therefore should not be constrained by the regime. The second defence has been acknowledged even by Western arms control experts as legitimate. The MTCR guidelines as they stood in 1991 did not prohibit a country that does not have the capability or intention to possess nuclear warheads from becoming a suitable recipient of missile technology.[199] Chinese officials argued that because Saudi Arabia was such a country, 'China's export of intermediate-range CSS-2 ballistic missiles to Saudi Arabia would have been totally legitimate even if China had been a partner in the MTCR'.[200] The crucial question here is not whether Chinese defence is valid or not. The fact that Chinese officials invoked the MTCR regimes at all in their defence is a significant indication that even before its adherence to the MTCR guidelines, China did not like to be seen to have violated the MTCR regime. In this sense, the MTCR as an arms control institution had already begun to affect Chinese behaviour in the missile technology sales.

China's defence of its sale of missiles to Pakistan further reinforces this point. Chinese officials scrupulously acknowledged in 1991 the sale of 'a very small number of short-range tactical missiles' to Pakistan in 1991. In 1993, Chinese officials protested against the 'unfounded accusation' by the United States of China's violation of the MTCR regimes. In defending China's missile sale to Pakistan, Chinese officials asserted that China had never sold complete missile technology or related components to Pakistan that are restricted by the guidelines and parameters of the MTCR. There is evidence to suggest that China had purposely modified the M-11 missile system before it was transferred to Pakistan so as to comply with 300-mile minimum range limit specified in the MTCR.[201] In 1994, China again offered its written assurance that it would abide by the MTCR guidelines and parameters in transferring missile technology.[202] The point which bears repeating here is that, although China may not have genuinely complied with the MTCR and its defence of missile technology transfer to Pakistan is not satisfactory, it is nevertheless significant that China feels the need to defend the legitimacy of its sale within the framework of MTCR and that it does not wish to be seen as non-compliant to a multilateral regime which has been widely accepted and to which it has pledged its adherence.

Finally, there are the ill-fated PERM-5 talks that started in July 1991. The unprecedented consensus on the need to curb the transfer of advanced conventional weapons systems generated by the Iraqi invasion of Kuwait and the Gulf War of 1990–91 provided momentum for the five permanent members of the UN Security Council, who happened to be five leading arms exporters, to meet for the purpose of developing some restraining mechanisms on destabilising arms transfer. The PERM-5 talks were an unprecedented effort by the leading arms exporters to discuss their policy coordination within the multilateral framework of the UN. In spite of all difficulties encountered, the PERM-5 talks in 1992 did lead to a general agreement among the world five leading arms exporters to restrain their exports of destabilising conventional weapons to states in the Middle East and to share among themselves information on arms transfers to the region. In 1992, the PERM-5 did exchange information with one another on a confidential basis about deliveries of weapon systems and equipment to the region in the previous year.

Other broad consensuses reached in the PERM-5 talks in 1992 were reported in August 1992 by Stephen Hanmer, Jr, Deputy Director of the United States Arms Control and Disarmament Agency, as follows:

> So far the five supplier States have agreed to: common guidelines for the export of conventional weapons; interim guidelines related to weapons of mass destruction; preliminary agreement on information sharing on arms transfer to the Middle East; and developing rules of restrain concerning arms transfer.[203]

Political Socialisation   173

It is particularly important to note here that some sharp disagreements between the United States and China as voiced in what can be called the 'Sino-American duel' in the PERM-5 talks have more to do with technicality than with principles. In the PERM-5 talks, for example, China argued that the PERM-5 should establish guidelines on international arms transfer control for global application, while the United States tried to confine the process to the Middle East. On the other hand, whereas the United States insisted on isolating one particular sub-category weapon delivery system (that is, ballistic missiles), for control and limitations, China contended that there was an inconsistency in the American approach and that other delivery systems, including combat aircraft and naval systems, should also be included for transfer control. Although both the United States and China agreed on the importance of transparency measures on arms transfer, the United States argued for advance information of arms sales to the Middle East, whereas China was unwilling to go beyond its commitment to provide retrospective information.[204]

None of these differences, although substantial, contradicts the basic principles of arms transfer control, such as restricted and discriminate sales. Neither the United States nor China challenged the principle of transparency in international arms transfers, which 'may well be the first step towards applying a wide variety of confidence-building measures ... leading eventually to an international consensus on the regulation of arms control in general'.[205] It must also be noted that China suspended its participation in the process in October 1992, only when the Bush administration announced its sale of 150 F-16 fighter planes to Taiwan.[206] This serves as a painful reminder of the fragility of such policy coordination and its susceptibility to volatile international politics in other arenas.

The fall and rise in military spending

For most of the 1980s, China's defence spending fell sharply. According to Chinese sources, the proportion of military spending in government financial expenditures 'dropped by one-third, from 17.5 per cent in 1979 to 10.5 per cent in 1985'.[207] The *SIPRI Yearbook* of 1990 further recorded that, 'As a share of total Government expenditure, official defence spending has fallen in relative terms, from 10.4 per cent to 8.4 per cent between 1985 and 1989'. Even the increase from 21.8 billion yuan in 1988 to 24.55 billion yuan in 1989, a nominal rise of 12.6 per cent, was in fact a fall of 5–6 per cent in real terms, after adjustment for estimated high inflation.[208] In a detailed analysis by a Chinese economist, China's defence spending is claimed to have steadily declined, from 3.52 per cent of its

GNP in 1981 to 1.56 per cent in 1988. Taking the figure of China's defence spending in 1978 as 100, the index of China's defence spending in 1984–88 would be 91.5, 89.1, 88.1, 85.7 and 75.2 respectively in real terms. It was further argued that whereas the reduction of China's military budget from 1979 to 1983 was 'normal', from 1984 to 1988 China's defence spending 'shrank abnormally'.[209] Looking back at the 1980s in 1993, SIPRI confirmed that 'until 1989, China was a major exception to this trend of rising defence spending in the region'.[210]

The fall in China's defence spending was accompanied, and also probably to some extent complemented, by the so-called 'military-industrial conversions'.[211] The move to integrate production of civilian goods into China's defence industry started in 1980. As the state continuously cut back its military spending, military orders fell significantly in the mid-1980s. The military industry was urged to convert part of its production capacity to offset losses caused by insufficient orders and to contribute to the country's economic modernisation. From 1983 to 1985, the number of civilian items produced in the arms industry rose from a little more than 400 to 9,000. The total value of civilian goods produced by arms factories under the Ordnance Ministry – which was responsible for making conventional weapons for the PLA – reached 2 billion yuan in 1985.[212] In 1986, the total value of civilian goods produced by China's military enterprises was estimated at 6.23 billion yuan.[213] In 1987, civilian goods accounted for 48.9 per cent of the total output value of China's defence industry.[214] In the first half of 1989, that per centage climbed to 67.8 per cent.[215] Increasingly, from 1985 onwards, airfields, naval ports, military railroads, military depots and other military facilities were open to civilian use.[216] According to SIPRI's summary of Chinese sources, from 1980 to 1990, the annual growth rate of civil production in China's aerospace was 30 per cent and that of ordnance, 19.8 per cent. On the other hand, the output value of China's nuclear industry in civilian production reached 48 per cent of its total in 1990, with the annual growth rate of civilian production in 21.3 per cent from 1986 to 1990. The arms industry as a whole claimed to produce about 10,000 civilian products in 1990 and to have a 65 per cent share of civilian production in terms of value in 1991.[217] It is estimated that in 1991 the volume of net output of civilian production by the arms industry was 7 billion yuan and sales revenue 6.6 billion yuan – a 20–25 per cent rise from that in 1990.[218]

Since 1989, however, China's official defence budget has seen real increases in successive years. The military spending in the state budget rose to 32.5 billion yuan in 1991, 37 billion yuan in 1992 and 42.5 billion yuan in 1993.[219] And the defending spending in official budget reached 75 billion yuan in 1996–97.[220] More controversial, however, is the extra-budgetary spending on defence. While some foreign analysts agree that the increase in the official defence budget is moderate in real terms, others claim that China's military spending is as much as six times the official figure.[221] The subject is still controversial even among Western analysts themselves and is likely to remain so as long as the Chinese military is enshrouded in secrecy.[222]

The controversy is increasingly linked to another vexing question, which is more difficult to answer, yet more central to arms control in Asia Pacific: namely, how much China is spending on buying advanced military technologies to modernise the PLA. China's White Paper on arms control and disarmament, recently published, claims that in 1994, only 31.69 per cent of its total defence spending was 'spent on equipment, including research, test, purchase, maintenance, transportation and storage'.[223] The actual figure was 17.452 billion yuan, equivalent to a little more than $2 billion. Such a modest figure would certainly raise the eyebrows of many analysts, particularly when evaluated against the claims of China's ambitious arms acquisition programmes in the post-Cold War period. A recent study has systematically documented China's recent 'quest for "Superb and Secret Weapons"'. China is said to have procured from Russia the Kilo Class submarines, Su-27 fighter-bombers and many other items of military technology. There were allegations that China intended to buy an aircraft carrier, the 67 500-tonne *Varyag* from Ukraine in 1992, and that a Spanish firm offered China of aircraft-carrier design in early 1995. There were also speculations that Israel has transferred to China air-defence technology based on the US Patriot anti-missile system as well as avionics and jet fighter technologies.[224] It is difficult to see how such a modest budget as claimed by the Chinese government could sustain anything close to the alleged Chinese programmes for acquisitions of 'smart weapons'.

This is not the place to argue where the hidden subsidies of China's defence spending come from or how extra-budget resources are pumped into the military procurement programme. What is important to our investigation is that the controversies and allegations highlight the limitations of China's socialisation in international society in general and in multilateral security regimes in particular. First, the lack of transparency of the Chinese military is still acute. This lies at the root of controversies and allegations concerning China's strategic intentions and hampers meaningful military cooperation between China and other member countries in any multilateral regimes. Second, the successive increases of China's military spending in the last few years come at a time when many other countries have cut their defence expenditure as the world moves beyond the Cold War. China seems to be going against the norms. Further, China's increased military spending is seen as a factor in fuelling the arms build-up in Asia-Pacific in the post-Cold War period. Third, China's arms procurement programme, though not as comprehensive as is alleged, is very active. This is particularly regrettable because it is taking place when China's security environment has seen obvious improvement; and as acknowledged by the Chinese themselves, China for the first time after 1949 is not faced with any direct military threat around its periphery in the post-Cold War period. Fourth, China's security behaviour as seen in the rise of its military spending and its arms acquisitions programme reflects China's *realpolitik* thinking about its security. China seems to continue to prefer a unilateral approach to its security; that is, building up its military forces, both conventional and nuclear, as the best guarantees for its national security. It has little faith in and is at least ambivalent towards multilateral security arrangements.

Conclusion

China seems to have come a long way since the early 1980s to socialise itself in the multilateral regimes of arms control and to make its arms control policies more acceptable and more in line with the international consensus. It has now signed and acceded to most major multilateral arms control treaties, including the NPT and the CTBT, which it had unreservedly condemned before the 1980s. Its approach to arms control at the international forums is marked now more by proposition than opposition. It has acquiesced in its special responsibility as a nuclear-weapon state in the process of multilateral arms control. Even where the controversies are raging, such as in arms transfer control, China and other major players have been engaged in consultation in an effort to reach some broad consensus. China's behaviour in arms control has already been constrained by the existing regimes, as in the case of MTCR, and its commitment to CTBT further suggests that it is prepared to work within the constraints imposed by multilateral arms control treaties.

If the above suggests that China has changed its behaviour in international arms control activities, it equally exposes the limitations of China's socialisation in multilateral arms control regimes. China is the last nuclear-weapon state to stop nuclear testing. It seems to be shifting its position on participating in five nuclear-power disarmament talks as the reductions of nuclear weapons of the two superpowers are approaching the 50 per cent benchmark set by China. It is still ambiguous about the prospect of its participation in the START process. The compliance by China to self-restraints in arms transfer control regimes remains at best questionable. The rise in China's military spending and its arms acquisition programmes set the limits of its commitment to multilateral arms control. As the post-Cold War international order challenges the legitimacy of nuclear weapons, China seems to be 'moving in the opposite direction'.[225] China is developing and indeed incorporating a nuclear strategy into its grand design of national security. This should not be a surprise, for China's perception of the post-Cold War international system is still very much Hobbesian. Accordingly, it is self-help, not multilateral and interdependent security arrangements, that China has faith in. This underlines the imperative to socialise China further into the global and regional multilateral arms control and multilateral security regimes.

HUMAN RIGHTS CONTENTIONS

In the last decade, particularly since 1989, human rights questions have become one of the most contentious issues in China's international relations. There are two major reasons for this. For one thing, the excessive use of violence by the Chinese government in Beijing and the bloodshed in and around Tiananmen Square in June 1989 put China's human rights conditions squarely in the international spotlight in an unprecedented way. For the other, as argued by David Armstrong, 'international society has developed a greater sensitivity towards human rights ... to a point where they may be said to have amended the general principles of international legitimacy'.[226] Moreover, there have been different interpretations of the impact that the end of the Cold War has had on the idea of human rights. On the one hand, the end of the Cold War is interpreted in terms of a convergence of beliefs, therefore promoting the emergence of a cohesion of common values, norms and rules in post-Cold War international society. Some believe therefore that, with the end of the Cold War, human rights, together with democracy, has been elevated to be among global common values.[227] On the other, the end of the Cold War, it is claimed, has laid bare the 'suppressed regional conflicts and differences over issues such as human rights' as 'a source of international tension'.[228] Human rights has for this reason become 'a new battle ground' in relations between states, particularly between the developed West and the economically resurgent Asia.[229]

For all these reasons, China has been put on the defensive for its human rights record and human rights policy as never before. Andrew Nathan observed that, after 1989, 'the issue of human rights has turned from a shield of China's sovereignty into a spear pointed against it'.[230] China has to reply to the scathing international criticisms of its human rights conditions in practice. It has to respond to and sometimes contest the arguments of human rights in principle. Li Peng told the UN Security Council in January 1992 that China 'stands ready to engage in discussion and cooperation with other countries on an equal footing on the question of human rights'.[231] International human rights regimes also compel the attention of the Chinese government. Chinese foreign policy has accordingly developed a new strand specifically dealing with human rights questions in China's international relations.[232]

Human rights questions are therefore most interesting as a case study in our examination of China's political socialisation as international society. As new rules and standard of behaviour for states have been evolved as international society has moved beyond the Cold War, an examination of these contentions and controversies will illustrate the limits of China's perception of common values with other members of the society of states. It will indicate the extent to which China is or is not moving towards conforming to the emerging norms and rules of the post-Cold War international society.

Our examination starts with a discussion of political socialisation and human rights questions in the post-Cold War international society. It then takes for an empirical analysis *Human Rights in China*, the official White Paper published by the Chinese government in 1991. This is followed by an examination of the evolution of the idea of human rights in China and China's participation in international human rights regimes. It argues that while there are signs that China has been moving grudgingly towards accepting the idea of human rights and its legitimacy in international relations, human rights remains a rugged battlefield for China's political socialisation into international society.

Political socialisation and human rights questions

Socialisation in international society, as argued before, refers to a process through which a state moves gradually to accept or conform to norms, rules and standards of behaviour of states in international relations universally acknowledged by international society as a collective. It has also been argued that the pressure for a state to socialise comes from that state's aspiration for full and undisputed membership in the society of states. Socialisation, some argue, has another pressing aspect, particularly after the end of the Cold War; that is, for states to move towards 'homogeneity' in the sense that states strive for 'a similarity in domestic values and organisation'.[233] If so, socialisation is imperative for all member states in post-Cold War international society.

Among the consequences of what Fred Halliday calls 'a strategic and intellectual earthquake' in international relations[234] in the last few years are the changing concepts and rules in world politics. From balance of power to cooperative security, and from international order to global governance, international society has been seeking not only to reflect but also to accommodate the exceptional and profound changes in international relations since 1989. More importantly, even values for international society have been undergoing significant changes. Fukuyama's controversial claim of the 'end of history', for example, argues that humanity is no longer in conflict over fundamental values. Capitalism and liberal democracy are here to prevail, leading towards universalisation of the world in political and economic terms.[235]

We may indeed continue to debate what is meant by the 'end of history'. We may also chose to dispute the emergence of a coherent set of common values and norms in post-Cold War international relations. But it is hard not to accept the general proposition that with the end of the Cold War, existing rules, norms, values and even standards governing the behaviour of states in their relations with each other have been modified, and new ones are emerging. Humanitarian intervention, for example, has now been largely accepted as legitimate by the international community.[236] Global governance, on the other hand, calls for acceptance of global values and compliance with the rules of international society.[237] The argument here is that because of these fundamental changes, there is a need for all states to socialise in post-Cold War international society.

What of human rights? How far and whether human rights and democracy have been universally accepted as global common values remains controversial today, though not so much as in the 1980s. What is less disputable is the fact that in the new context of international relations, more and more states are taking rights more seriously. This is partly in response to the changing norms with regard to human rights in international relations. First, observance of human rights has been advocated as one constituent of the normative international order in the post-Cold War era. Compliance by member states with the international standards of human rights is believed to constitute the basis of global governance. Second, more than ever before respect for basic human rights is now universally regarded as a norm in the relations between states which member states in international society expect each other to abide by. Third and consequently, human rights conditions in one member country have become the legitimate concerns of other members of international society. The international legitimacy of human rights, in other words, has seen a fundamental transformation, and is now even more closely bound up with the legitimacy of a state.

If new norms, rules, values and standards have evolved around human rights questions in post-Cold War international society, the elements that cause tensions between political socialisation of a state and human rights issues remain classical in the new context. Domestically, protection of human rights challenges the authority and power of the state and entails its responsibility to its citizens. Internationally, human rights issues internationalise what used to be domestic concerns, thus eroding state sovereignty and challenging the principle of non-intervention in internal affairs. It also contests the legitimacy of the state, the very constituting element of international society. It remains true today, as John Ruggie argued in the early 1980s, that 'human rights struggle is condemned to work within a system that remains fundamentally inhospitable to the kinds of claims and challenges it represents'.[238] For all these reasons, the human rights policy of a state should be viewed as a litmus test of its socialisation into international society in the post-Cold War era.

'Human Rights in China': a whitewash?

Our concern about human rights questions and China's political socialisation in post-Cold War international society is threefold. Is the political socialisation of China in international society taking place with regard to human rights issues? To what extent and in what sense is such political socialisation taking place? What are its limitations?

It is a historical irony that the tragedy of June 1989 in Beijing should mark 'the beginning of the large-scale study of human rights in the People's Republic'. To fend off international condemnations and criticisms of China's violation of human rights in the wake of the June crackdown in China, the Chinese government not only tolerated, but also encouraged, and even organised studies and research on human rights.[239] Since 1989, the Chinese government has also made hundreds of statements in defence of its human rights policy and published numerous documents on human rights conditions in China.[240] This is largely in response to severe international criticisms, particularly those voiced in the United Nations and many other international forums.[241] The simple fact that China has been compelled to take such unprecedented actions in defending human rights in China is significant in itself. The end of China as the 'human rights exception' finds a forceful expression in China's being forced to engage itself in an ongoing discourse with members of international society on its human rights questions.[242] Of equal importance, it is a public recognition on the part of China of the legitimation of international concern regarding human rights conditions in China. The defence itself is a tacit acknowledgement that human rights questions now challenge not only the domestic legitimacy but also the international legitimacy of the Chinese government.

China's engagement with members of international society in discourse and debate on human rights questions in the last few years has many facets. One key document, a white paper entitled *Human Rights in China*, published by the Chinese government in November 1991, merits particular attention. This is so not because of the controversial nature of the Chinese government's claims on human rights conditions in China, which seem to have been the focus of many critiques of the White Paper.[243] It is, rather, because official statements in the White Paper provide us with some interesting empirical evidence for analysis of the question of China's political socialisation on this particular issue.

What needs only the briefest summary here, therefore, is the controversial claims that the Chinese government made in the White Paper about human rights conditions in China. To many critics of China's human rights policy and conditions, such claims as 'the Chinese people have gained extensive political rights' and 'citizens [in China] enjoy economic, cultural and social rights' are merely either spurious or contentious. The claims that there is a 'guarantee of human rights in China's judicial work' and a 'guarantee of the rights of the minority nationalities' and that 'citizens [in China] enjoy freedom of religious belief' can be easily refuted.[244] It is also clear that although the Chinese government has laboured through the White Paper to defend human rights in China, its arguments are crude and unsophisticated. However, to dismiss the White Paper simply as the Chinese government's efforts to whitewash the dire condition of human rights in China overlooks the significance that this document demonstrates in regard to China's changing position on the politics of human rights in post-Cold War international society.

The White Paper is, without doubt, a public defence of human rights conditions in China mounted by the Chinese government. It also serves, however, as an engaging point between China and members of international society in discussing and debating human rights in China. Interestingly, the document is couched in language largely acceptable in the international discourse on human rights questions. What is more revealing is how and on what ground the Chinese government defends its policy and defines its position on human rights. They are worth further examination because they are instructive as to China's political socialisation on human rights issues in international society.

In defending human rights conditions in China, the White Paper concedes that China accepts in principle international norms and rules on human rights, if only rhetorically. First, it affirms that China respects human rights in principle, if not already fully in practice. The opening sentence of the White Paper, for example, states that 'it has been a long-cherished ideal of mankind to enjoy human rights in the full sense of the term'. It argues also that 'securing the full range of human rights the world over' is a 'lofty goal'. China 'appreciates and supports the efforts of the UN in promoting universal respect for human rights and fundamental freedom'.[245] Second, it accepts that it is the responsibility of the government to implement and to improve human rights in China. The basic argument of the White Paper, no matter how crude or spurious, is that Chinese government has been working towards improving conditions of human rights in China. More specifically, the White Paper argues that 'China's law provides definite and strict stipulation to protect and guarantee human rights in an effective way'. Third, it asserts that China acknowledges the universality of human rights in principle. In the 'Preface' of the White Paper, it not only claims that to enjoy human rights 'has been a long-cherished ideal of mankind'; it is also stated explicitly that the Chinese government considers the UN Universal Declaration of Human Rights 'the first international human rights document that has laid the foundation for the practice of human rights in the world arena'. And fourth, it maintains that China is committed to active participation in the international human rights regimes. The White Paper further details China's participation, particularly since the mid-1980s. It reassures China's commitment to 'realise the purpose of the United Nations to uphold and promote human rights and fundamental freedoms'.[246]

The White Paper, on the other hand, outlines China's contentions with regard to its human rights policy. One of what Ann Kent regards as 'important innovations'[247] in the White Paper is the establishment of the hierarchy of human rights in the Chinese arguments. The right to subsistence, the White Paper argues very strongly, 'is the most important of all human rights, without which the other rights are out of the question'.[248] This is particularly so for the Chinese people, the White Paper continues, 'for historical reasons', from gaining national independence in the past to securing economic development in China today. The second contention outlined in the White Paper, which is closely associated with the first one, is that 'the evolution of the situation in regard to human rights is circumscribed by the historical, social, economic and cultural conditions of various nations, and involves a process of historical development'. It is interesting to note that subsequent arguments by Chinese scholars and officials alike on human rights conditions in China have all emphasised not so much 'cultural relativism' as 'economic developmentalism'. Developing countries, it is argued, differ in their understanding and practice of human rights.[249] Third and consequently, the White Paper contends that 'a country's human rights situation should not be judged in total disregard of its history and national conditions, nor can it be evaluated according to a preconceived model or the conditions of another country or region' and that no country should impose its own mode of human rights on others. Finally and most contentiously, the White Paper asserts that 'human rights are essentially matters within the domestic jurisdiction of a country'. As such, no state or group of states has the right to intervene. This is in accordance with two universally recognised principles of international law: namely, respect for sovereignty and non-interference in internal affairs.[250] The White Paper further contends that using the human rights issue for political purpose of imposing one's ideology is 'but a manifestation of power politics' in international relations.[251]

The White Paper therefore provides us with a great deal more than just a superficial and spurious defence of China's human rights conditions by the Chinese government. Significantly, it does not challenge the idea of human rights as historically developed and defined primarily in Western political thought and generally accepted now by members of the global international society. Neither did it contest the principle of the universality of human rights in the contemporary world. The arguments of cultural relativism, which had been prevalent, were largely absent in the White Paper. The contentions concentrate mostly on the priority of rights and on sovereignty and intervention. Such contentions constitute what could be regarded as a curious norm in politics of human rights in international relations. As observed by Louis Henkin in 1989,

> much of the resistance to human rights is resistance not to the idea of human rights but to some of its politics in the United Nations, to external scrutiny rejected as interference, to the imposition of sanctions for human rights violations – for example, by the United States – but not to the idea of human rights.[252]

The White Paper, on the other hand, not only concedes the legitimacy of international concern about human rights in China; it also admits openly that there is much to be desired in China's human rights conditions.[253] Premier Li Peng conceded in his government work report in early 1992 that 'China agrees that questions concerning human rights should be the subject of normal international discussion'.[254]

The idea of human rights in China

The single most revealing element in the White Paper which needs reassertion here is that it does not refute nor even challenge the idea of human rights and its universality in principle. Such rhetorical acceptance of the concept and the idea of universal human rights, of course, does not necessarily underwrite respect for human rights in practice in China and may even be hypocritical. Louis Henkin observed some time ago that, universal political and even legal acceptance does not guarantee universal respect for human rights'.[255] Given China's cultural tradition and its contemporary political system, however, such acceptance of the idea of human rights in China is neither automatic nor historical. The tacit acknowledgement of the legitimation of international concern about the human rights situation in China is as grudging as it is significant.

Cultural relativism, as both Vincent and Donnelly contend, presents powerful arguments which could not and should not be readily dismissed in discussion of the universality of human rights both in theory and in practice.[256] Whatever the arguments for the universality of the concept of human rights are today, the origin of the idea of human rights is undoubtedly Western. The human rights idea, as Henkin maintains, 'was not universal not too long ago', and cultural relativism presents the 'strongest challenge' to the emergence of the universality of the concept of human rights.[257] Whether it is the moral principle behind the idea of human rights that makes it universal and whether cultural differences lead to historical and cultural particularity of the concept of human rights are both still highly debatable.

What is less debatable is that the concept of human rights as is defined today, and indeed the very concept of rights, are largely absent from and alien to traditional Chinese philosophy and political culture. Traditional Chinese culture is as unreceptive to the idea of human rights conceived in the Western political thought as it could be. Etymologically, as has been often pointed out, the word *Quanli* (rights) in Chinese was a new coinage in the nineteenth century and most probably an import from the Japanese.[258] Traditional Confucianism, dominant in the Chinese society for more than two millenniums, emphasised duties to the ruler, responsibility to society and obligations to the family and community as the very basis of the social harmony and order of Chinese society. The individual, if not totally submerged, is at least rarely conceived as an independent entity. The central idea as embodied in the concept of human rights – namely, that every individual has legitimate claims upon their own society for certain freedoms and benefits by virtue of being human – cannot be more alien to the traditional Chinese political philosophy and culture. Moral rules and social institutions in traditional China determined its conception of the relationship between the state, society, the individual and the law, which is decidedly different from that of the Western political tradition.[259]

The idea together with the vocabulary of human rights commanded the attention of leading Chinese intellectuals only at the turn of the twentieth century. The abortive 100-day reform in 1898 advocated the constitutional monarchy and introduced the concept of civil rights. In the first ever version of a constitution in the history of China promulgated in 1908, freedoms of speech, correspondence, press, assembly and association were all constitutionalised.[260] However, as observed by Ann Kent, the new concepts introduced from the West were all 'heavily overlaid with traditional nuances'. Liang Qichao's notion of citizens' rights 'did not correlate with the Western notion of claims against the state'. Even the very doctrine of *minquan* (people's rights) introduced by Dr Sun Yat-sen is ambivalent about the relationship between the state and its citizens/people. It did not mean personal and civil liberties but 'the political power due to the people, their part in determining the destiny of China'.[261] What came closest to the original idea of human rights in the West in its vocabulary and its concept in China is the Human Rights Movement in the late 1920s and early 1930s, carried out by a small group of leading Chinese intellectuals trained in the West, typically Hu Shih and Luo Longji.[262]

The political culture in China post-1949 added another strain in the tension between the original idea of human rights and the Chinese concept. It was not the conspicuous absence but the clear metamorphosis of the idea of human rights that the ideological dominance of Marxism brought to post-1949 China. Although civil and political liberties not entirely refuted, the emphasis was now more on social and economic rights, calling for equal distribution of wealth in society and fair share of benefits, entailing a guarantee of the right to work and the right to universal education. Such priorities regarding rights easily accommodated the traditional notion of what we might call 'subsistence rights' in Chinese political thought; that is, that the state guarantees basic subsistence for its people. The dominance of Marxism in China's ideology also reinforces another argument for the priority of rights; namely, that collective rights take precedence over individual liberties. It follows that China perceives and argues that colonialism, imperialism, racism, apartheid and foreign aggression and occupation are gross violations of human rights and should be resolutely opposed.[263] Individual rights, if any, not only come second by a long distance, but also are expendable. As well-summarised by Kim and Dittmer, such human rights 'conceptualised as more collective than individual, more social and economic than civil and political, more needs-based than rights-entitled, and more duties-oriented than rights centred' are 'consistent with both the dominant tradition of Confucian humanism and Maoist proletarian egalitarianism'.[264]

'Traditional nuances', in other words, persist in China's perception of human rights in the post-1949 period, as is indeed still obvious in the 1991 White Paper. Curiously, many human rights principles about political and civil rights as embodied in the Universal Declaration of Human Rights found their way into the first Constitution of the PRC published in 1954. As argued in the 1991 White Paper, all successive revised constitutions have also guaranteed such human rights as freedoms of speech, correspondence, press, assembly, as well as religious belief.[265] There is an important difference, however. These and other rights are assured for the Chinese people in these constitutions not on the fundamental principle that these rights are inalienable for them simply because they are human beings. They are granted and guaranteed by the socialist state more or less as benefits for its citizens to 'enjoy'. It bears repeating that the idea that each individual has legitimate claims upon their own society and state for certain freedoms has never been accepted in Chinese political philosophy, nor has it been reflected in Chinese legal doctrine. As Vincent observed sharply, the very political and civil rights guaranteed by the Chinese constitutions are immediately nullified by the stipulation in the same constitution that 'the fundamental rights and duties of the citizens are to support the leadership of the Chinese Communist Party, support the socialist system'.[266]

The prevalence of the Marxist interpretation of human rights in the official statements is best seen in *Notes on Human Rights* (hereafter the Notes) published in *Beijing Review* in November 1979, probably the first systematic official articulation of China's position on human rights questions in English, if not in Chinese.[267] This was largely provoked domestically by the discussion of human rights questions sparked off in the 'Democracy Wall' period and internationally by the Carter administration's raising human rights questions in the American policy towards China.[268]

In typical Marxist fashion, the Notes claims that 'the theory of "natural rights of man" was a powerful ideological weapon of the rising bourgeoisie in its revolution against feudalism'. Human rights, with its ideological basis derived from the theory of the 'natural rights of man' therefore 'became their main slogan and the basic content of the bourgeois political programme'. Human rights, the Notes continues, although advocated by the bourgeoisie as universal, cannot be for everyone. They are rights only for the bourgeoisie because, 'in the capitalist society, as the bourgeoisie owns the means of production, it has the right to exploit and enslave the proletariat'. 'The principle of human rights (such as liberty and equality) put forth by the bourgeoisie is, to the proletariat, essentially hypocritical.'

The Notes acknowledges that the question of human rights has become 'an important topic in contemporary international political activities'. It also notes that the Third World countries 'are opposed to the monopolised interpretation of the concept of human rights by anyone' and that the United Nations' activities related to human rights are governed by European standards. Human rights, on the other hand,

> is also a slogan with which imperialism and the bourgeoisie attack our proletarian dictatorship and socialist system ... they attack socialist countries as granting no human rights to its people. They slander measures under the dictatorship of the proletariat (such as the suppression of counter-revolutionaries) as violations of human rights.

The Notes maintains that it was the foreign aggression and imperialism that denied the basic human rights of all Chinese people, and that it was the Chinese Communist Revolution that 'once and for all swept away such disgraceful things from our land and acquired [for the Chinese people] the basic rights to live as decent human beings with heads lifted and backs straight? 'How can the imperialists have the effrontery to prate about the so-called human rights question in China?' the Notes asks.[269]

The Notes as the embodiment and pronouncement of the official Chinese position on human rights questions is a far cry from the 1991 White Paper. It denies the universality of human rights in principle. It bespeaks a totally different conception of human rights based on the division of international society by class. It disputes the legitimacy of human rights questions in international relations and rebukes the international concern about human rights questions in China. Last but certainly not least, the vocabulary and language used in the Notes cannot be more distant from those commonly used in discourse on human rights questions in the international community.

A simple comparison of the Notes with the 1991 White Paper and other official Chinese statements on human rights in the 1980s and after is instructively revealing. What does this comparison tell us? It is obvious that China's position on human rights in international relations has changed. In most of the 1980s, together with its political socialisation in many other areas of its international relations, China was grudgingly but also steadily moving towards convergence to the idea of human rights universally accepted by members of international society. Human rights discussions during the Democracy Wall period and the emerging political dissent in China in the 1980s both contributed to this.[270] It is also argued that in post-Mao China, the cultural meanings of rights and obligations have been transformed.[271] The bloodshed in and around Tiananmen

Square in the summer of 1989 represented a great setback for China's political socialisation in the human rights arena. There was clearly a backsliding in China's position on the human rights question in the immediate aftermath of the bloody military crackdown in June 1989. That did not, however, totally negate the progress made in the 1980s. After the summer of 1989, the Chinese government did concede a lot of ground on its previous position on human rights. It did not retreat to its 1979 position, however, as the White Paper demonstrates.

Also in the 1980s, as will be discussed in more detail later, China began to participate in a number of international human rights regimes under UN auspices. More significantly, perhaps, came the official re-evaluation of the Universal Declaration of Human Rights in 1988. In September 1988, the Chinese Foreign Minister told the General Assembly that the Universal Declaration of Human Rights was 'the first international instrument which systematically sets forth the specific contents regarding respect for and protection of fundamental human rights' and 'has exerted a far-reaching influence on the development of the post-war international human rights activities and played a positive role in this regard'.[272] On the fortieth anniversary of the UN adoption of the Declaration in December 1988, for the first time China commemorated the anniversary of the Universal Declaration of Human Rights.[273]

International criticisms of China's human rights conditions since 1989 have had a powerful impact on the popularisation of the idea of human rights in China. It has provoked lively discussions on human rights questions, although sometimes restrained and sometimes restricted, among Chinese academics. To mobilise the intellectual resources in defence of its human rights policy, the Chinese government has sometimes tolerated and sometimes encouraged these discussions. The publication of hundreds of books on human rights, even those sponsored by the Central Propaganda Department of the CCP, has probably unwittingly led to the dissemination of the idea of human rights throughout China.[274] It can be argued that it was the violence in Tiananmen Square in 1989 that facilitated the taking root of the idea of human rights in China.

Most critics of human rights in China, particularly the non-government organisations (NGOs) such as Asia Watch and Amnesty International, have focused their attention on human rights conditions in China. The imprisonment of Wang Dan and Wang Juntao, and the arrest and re-arrest of Wei Jinsheng are all high-profile cases and ones that grab public attention. Their criticisms and constant vigil on China's human rights conditions have played an important part in China's socialisation in international human rights politics. They have helped to raise the international consciousness of abuses of human rights in China and to put human rights issues firmly on the agenda of China's international relations.

No one would deny either that China's human rights conditions are appalling compared with the international standard or that the abuse of human rights in the country is still widespread. Indeed, the Chinese defence of its human rights conditions as seen in the White Paper as well as hundreds of other official statements have either implicitly or explicitly admitted that human rights abuse in China does exist.[275] The existence of widespread human rights abuses in China today, however, should not belie the fact that the idea of human rights is now more accepted there. Neither should it belie any success of international society in converting China to accepting the emerging values on human rights in the post-Cold War international society.

Admittedly, there is still an obvious tension between China's parsimonious rhetorical acceptance of human rights principles and actual abuses of human rights in China. But any acceptance, even rhetorical, of the human rights idea in principle shows the Chinese government's recognition of the stakes of its international legitimacy on the human rights question. Any rhetorical commitment to human rights principles, even it is hypocritical, makes the Chinese government accountable to members of international society regarding its human rights policy and human rights conditions in China.

China and international human rights regimes

In defending its international human rights policy, the 1991 White Paper claims that China 'takes an active part in UN activities in the human rights field'.[276] China's meaningful participation in UN activities, however, started only in 1980, almost ten years after China's admission into the UN, when its membership made it a party to the UN Charter, and thus to human rights principles in the Charter. Given the official Chinese position on human rights as reflected in the 1979 document, it is hardly surprising that prior to 1979 China had not signed or acceded to any UN sponsored human rights conventions nor had it participated in the work of any UN human rights organs.

China's participation in the international human rights activities under UN auspices can be divided into two streams for the purpose of analysis. One is its participation in the work of UN human rights organs, and the other, its commitment to international human rights conventions. China's participation in the work of UN human rights organs can be deemed to have started in February 1979, when the Chinese delegation attended the sessions of the UN Human Rights Commission (UNHRC).[277] China has subsequently become a member of the UNHRC. Human rights experts recommended by China have been involved in the various sub-commissions of the UNHRC. Chinese delegates have participated in the working groups responsible for drafting UN legal documents on human rights, including the Declaration on the Right and Responsibility of Individuals, Groups and Organs of Society to Promote and Protect Universally Recognised Human Rights and Fundamental Freedoms, and the Declaration on the Protection of Rights of Persons Belonging to National, Ethnic, Religious and Linguistic Minorities. Since 1990 Chinese delegates have become more articulate on human rights issues in such forums as the UNHRC and the UN Third Committee. This is because China has now been placed prominently at the receiving end of international criticisms, particularly articulated in the UNHRC. China has to mobilise all its resources to respond to international criticisms and challenges to its human rights conditions. On the other hand, China has to be assertive on its position on human rights questions in an effort to restore its legitimacy and credibility as a normal state in the eyes of the international community. Whether by default or by design, such engagement of China in human rights discourse in the UN is unprecedented.[278]

In the 1980s, China took slow but steady steps towards selected commitment to international human rights regimes. This is largely because of its recognition that such commitment would enhance the reputation as well as the legitimacy of the Chinese government.[279] It could also be seen as an effort by the Chinese government to make China more like a 'normal' state. From 1980 to 1996, China ratified and acceded to eight UN human rights conventions, seven of them in the 1980s.[280] China's official commitment to the eight conventions put its human rights conditions covered by those conventions squarely under the scrutiny of the international community. By ratifying and acceding to those conventions, the Chinese government acknowledges its responsibility and accountability to the international community for the protection of rights embodied in those conventions in China. It is no longer possible for the Chinese government to take refuge in the argument that any violation of those rights is purely a domestic issue. This is not an insignificant concession to its sovereignty. One of the obligations entailed by those conventions is that all parties to the convention should submit regular reports on the implementation of the conventions in their respective countries. Indeed, one official defence that China takes human rights seriously is that 'China has always submitted reports on the implementation of the related conventions, and seriously and earnestly performed the obligations it has undertaken'.[281] China's signature and ratification of the Convention against Torture and Other Cruel, Inhuman or Degrading Treatment or Punishment have been singled out by Dittmer and Kim as the evidence that 'conceptually and legally, China crossed the Rubicon' in committing itself to the protection of individual rights.[282]

The single most important step that China has taken towards participating in the international human rights regimes is its endorsement of the two key UN covenants on human rights in September 1997, namely the International Covenant on Civil and Political Rights and the International Covenant on Economic, Social and Cultural Rights. It was on the eve of President Jiang Zemin's visit to United States for a summit meeting with President Bill Clinton that the Chinese Ambassador to the UN was quietly instructed to make China's commitment to these two most important international human rights covenants, which China was reported to be preparing itself to ratify as early as 1988.[283]

In view of the above, it can be argued that China's commitment to international human rights regimes today is unprecedented. The proposition that China's greater participation in the work of UN human rights organs and in international human rights regimes indicates an increasing acceptance of international human rights norms and rules by China is not easy to reject. It can also be argued that China has conceded a lot in accepting the legitimacy of human rights issues in contemporary international relations. A brief examination of the process of China's participation, however, also reveals severe limitations with regard to its commitment. First, not only is China's participation grudging, but it is also contingent on politics in wider context. China's further participation in international human rights regimes was largely halted after June 1989. From 1989 to 1996, China ratified only one UN human rights convention, that is the UN Convention on the Rights of Children.[284] China also seems to be using its human rights commitment and policies as bargaining chips in world politics, particularly in its relations with the United States. The timing of its recent endorsement of the two UN human rights covenants and the release of Wei Jinsheng are evidence of China's playing 'human rights card'. It is therefore questionable how sincere China's commitment to the two UN human rights covenants is. One may indeed also question its intention and purpose in complying with and implementing international human rights norms and rules. Second, the conventions China has signed or acceded to have more to do with structural violation of human rights, and are more oriented to collective rights and social and economic rights. Only two has clear bearing on individual political and civil rights. It suggests that China is more prepared to put its social and economic rights situation under the international scrutiny but less willing to subject its political and civil rights conditions to international examination. Third, China still insists on its own version of the hierarchy of rights. As recent as November 1994, the Chinese delegate asserted in the Third Committee of the UN that the first priority of international attention to human rights issues should be to such human rights violations as racism, apartheid and foreign aggression; the second priority, to the rights of development and subsistence of developing countries.[285] By implication, individual political and civil rights only come the third, if at all.

China and human rights: limitations of socialisation

At the same time as fundamental transformation of the international legitimacy of human rights is taking place, China's commitment to human rights as an emerging global common value is at most half-hearted. The rhetorical acceptance of general principles of human rights contradicts the continued practice of blatant denial of human rights in many areas of domestic political, social and economic life in China. China continues to advance its arguments on the priority of rights on various international forums on human rights. On the other hand, its limited and selected commitment to international human rights regimes is almost immediately negated by its preaching of the sacredness of sovereignty and its insistence on the principle of non-interference of the internal affairs of others. What does this inform us of China's socialisation in international society on human rights issues?

In a limited sense, the political socialisation of China is taking place. First and foremost, there has been a broad acceptance of the universality the principles of human rights in China, though mostly rhetorical, which was not present in official statements as recently as 1979. In China's discourse on human rights issues with other members of international society, clearly and increasingly, a shared vocabulary and language is being used. Second, the idea of human rights is more accepted and its international legitimacy increasingly acknowledged, notwithstanding the backsliding in the immediate aftermath of the Tiananmen crackdown in 1989. This is not only seen in China's selected adoption of international human rights instruments, which placed its human rights conditions covered by those conventions under international scrutiny. It is also seen in the official statements and documents in defence of China's human rights conditions and policies and in the fact that the Chinese government has been forced to go out of its way in various international forums to defend China's record and policy. Third, human rights values and institutions have been selectively 'internalised'. Some basic principles of human rights have found their way into the Chinese constitution and in various China's domestic laws. Research centres on human rights and related issues have been established. The dissemination of the idea of human rights and the highlighting of human rights issues in China through international criticism have put human rights questions firmly on the agendas of China's international relations as well as domestic politics.

It can be equally argued, however, that the above points do not highlight the distance that China has travelled from its past towards accepting the idea and general principles of human rights as much as they reveal how much further China has to go in conforming to the emerging international norms and rules governing states' behaviour on human rights issues. Rhetorical conformation to the international norms and rules by no means guarantees that the state would abide by them in practice. While China is certainly no longer 'the human rights exception', it is increasingly like an aberration. China's continual insistence on the sacred inviolability of sovereignty, its arguments about the priority of rights, its playing 'human rights card' in world politics, and, most important of all, its continued practice of abuse of human rights – all make China increasingly behave like a deviant in the international politics of human rights.

Political socialisation of China in the human rights arena differs from China's political socialisation in the other areas we have discussed in this chapter in that it is not primarily socialisation of China as a revolutionary state, but of China as a member of international society that has not adopted a particular societal value which is becoming universal. It is also more demanding because to internalise the norms and values of human rights may entail China in radically reforming its political system and accepting a profound transformation in the cultural meanings of rights and sovereignty. For this very reason, human rights, more than any other contentious issues in China's international relations, is likely to continue to be the battleground for China's socialisation into international society.

6 Economic Integration

Writing in 1992, Larry Summers, chief economist of the World Bank, drew the world's attention to the take-off of the Chinese economy in the 1980s, which, he believed, may prove to be the most important economic development of the decade.[1] The rise of China as an economic power in East Asia has increasingly become a topical subject for many economists concerned with development economics and for political scientists interested in East Asia and the Pacific rim. Both the IMF and the World Bank have revised their wisdom and claimed that the Chinese economy has already become either the second or the third largest in the world, just after the United States, or the United States and Japan. Recent studies identify China as the leading Pacific economy, and a report by PECC (Pacific Economic Cooperation Council) experts in 1994 characterised the Chinese economy as the engine of growth for the Asia-Pacific region in the years leading up to the twenty-first century. China, it is claimed, has become the fourth growth pole of the world economy after the United States, the European Community and Japan.[2]

The growth of the Chinese economy in the last decade is certainly striking. It is, however, the way in which such growth has been realised and sustained that is instrumental in understanding the question of China's integration into the international economy. To a considerable extent, the economic integration of China is a less arguable aspect of China's 'rejoining' the world. This is partly because, both analytically and quantitatively, China's integration into the contemporary international economic system is more clearly definable. China's exports, for example, have grown more than ten times between 1978 and 1995. China in 1992 became the world's eleventh largest trading nation and the tenth largest exporter and has managed to keep that position ever since.[3] On the other hand, foreign direct investment in China, zero-rated in 1978, by the end of 1996 had reached more than $450 billion in contracted value and close to $180 billion in realised value.[4] A State Council circular in late 1994 also claimed that China had by then established about 10000 enterprises abroad with a total assets of around 2000 billion yuan.[5] There have been further mutual market penetrations. In 1990, for example, imports amounted to around 28 per cent of gross value of industrial output in China's machinery and transport equipment sector. In the same year, China's export market structure, after readjustment of re-exports from Hong Kong, was already similar to those of other East Asian economies.[6]

Finally, China's membership in global and regional economic organisations is extensive. China joined the IMF and the World Bank group in 1980. In 1984, China obtained a permanent observer status in the GATT and was affiliated to the Multifibre Arrangement (MFA). Negotiations for China's entry into the GATT have been going on for the last decade, since China's formal application in 1986. China became a member of the Asian Development Bank (ADB) in 1986 and has been active since 1991 in the Asia-Pacific Economic Cooperation (APEC).

If economic integration of China is less controversial, it has certainly not been less challenging for either China or international society in the last 18 years. Consider the following properties of the Chinese economy in the late 1970s: a developing economy of an unusual size, traditionally self-sufficient, and a command economy controlled and closed-off by a Communist regime. The economic principles and practices of China and dominant powers in the world economy cannot be further apart. Their economic standards, norms, purposes and even ethics cannot be more incompatible. On top of that, the Chinese economy was presided over by a recently alienated state.

China's integration into the world economy has special significance in our examination of China in international society, broadly for the following reasons. First, it is a process of modification in which China has changed from a society mobilised by revolution to one motivated by modernisation. Second, the legacy of Western dominance is not only found in diplomacy and international law today. Economic dominance by the West for centuries also ensured that international economic institutions, commercial and financial procedures, norms and standards today are predominantly Western inventions and practices. China's participation and eventual integration into the world economy was predicated upon its acceptance of those practices and rules. And third, economic relations as societal bonds are a less nebulous element of international society. In the post-war years, economic life has assumed increasing importance in the society of states. China's sometimes grudging acceptance of, and gradual incorporation into, the global economic order could therefore be seen as a definitive indication of China's integration into international society.

International economic integration is among the most contested ideas. It has been defined and redefined by economists many times over, with the result that it 'means different things in different countries and at different times'.[7] International economic integration in our discussions here does not mean the existence of a customs union, nor a common market, nor even a free trade zone. For analytical purposes, integration in this context simply means 'combination of integral parts into an organic whole' (Oxford English Dictionary). International economic integration here therefore denotes both the existing conditions and the current development of bringing together the national economies as integral parts into an international economic system by whatever means. By the same token, the integration of a national economy into the international economic system takes place when, first, the interactions between national economies and the world economy have developed to such an extent that the national economy constitutes an essential part of an organic whole of the international economy; second, when the gaps between their economic institutions are so narrowed that an institutional convergence is being achieved; and third, when the systemic impact is sufficient to incur substantial damage or bring considerable benefit to the national economy. Trade is commonly recognised as the quintessence of such economic integration, and the division of labour, its underlying principle.[8] The appraisal of international economic integration, however, must look not only at the actual trade, but increasingly at the capital flows among integrated economies and at a nation's adherence to common institutions of multilateralism in the global economy.

This chapter examines China's less nebulous social bonds with international society by looking at three essential aspects of international economic integration concerning China. First, there is trade. The phenomenal growth of China's foreign trade is seen as a strong index of China's intensive participation in the international division of labour as well as in international production and distribution. Second, there are close interconnections between the Chinese economy and global capital markets. The growing financial bondage between China and international financial markets, it is contended, is creating an inextricable inter-dependence between China and the world economy. And third, there is China's membership and bid for membership in international economic organisations, from the GATT to APEC. It is argued that China's membership and its bid for membership in those international economic organisations have both motivated China's institutional and policy changes with regard to its trading practices. The purpose is to narrow down the gaps between Chinese trading institutions and those of the world economy, and to transform the Chinese economy into a market-orientated one. The economic integration as such therefore has both strengthened and tightened China's social bonds with the society of states, thus fundamentally transforming China in international society.

THE TRADE NEXUS

One of the most striking successes of China's economic reforms since 1978 has been the stunning growth of China's foreign trade. In the period from 1978 to 1995, China's foreign trade grew from $20.64 billion in 1978 to over $280 billion in 1995.[9] In the same period, China's exports, after the adjustment for inflation, grew at 12.5 per cent per annum, twice as much as the growth rate of world trade. The share of trade in China's GDP increased from 10.2 per cent in 1978 to 41 per cent in 1995. In 1978, China's share of the world trade was 0.9 per cent. In 1995, it increased to 2.8 per cent. To all intents and purposes, China was transformed in 16 years from a closed economy to one of the major trading nations in the world.[10]

What is significant in our context is not so much the quantitative growth *per se*. It is the qualitative changes in the relationship between the China and the global economy brought about by such spectacular growth that is of interest and importance. Essentially, such growth has created a trade nexus between the Chinese economy and other economies and has inexorably bound China with the world economy.

Kaifang and trade

China's present policies of economic reforms and opening to the outside world (*Gaige Kaifang*) were commonly relegated to be originated at the Third Plenum of the Eleventh Central Committee of the CCP in December 1978. This conventional wisdom, however, does not tell much about what *Kaifang* (opening to the outside world) actually meant, when it was launched, either as a strategy of economic modernisation or as an actual policy of economic development. Deng Xiaoping has been quoted as saying that China should 'import advanced technology from the capitalist countries selectively, in a planned way, and learn other things useful to us [China]'.[11] The Communiqué of the Third Plenum of the Eleventh Central Committee of the CCP also outlined that decentralisation should be the first step to reform the highly centralised and inefficient existing economic system.[12] Deng further declared in February 1980 that 'China has now adopted a policy of opening its doors to the world in a spirit of international co-operation'.[13] That was at best a broad yet still nebulous vision of China's changing strategy of economic development. The truth is that *Kaifang* at the time was probably a very vague and fuzzy concept. Certainly, it was not a carefully worked-out strategy with detailed plans. It is clear now that none of those who had formulated the policy ever clearly envisaged a scenario as to precisely how and in what way *Kaifang* would commit China to participation in the international economy. There was no clear delimitation of what *Kaifang* would involve with regard to the changes in China's overall economic development policies. It was never clearly defined to what extent the Chinese economy should be open and whither such an 'opening' policy would ultimately lead China. As in the whole process of China's economic reforms, the Chinese leadership who formulated the policy of *Kaifang* was to adopt a tactic of *Mozhe Shitou Guohe* (crossing the river by feeling the stones at the bottom) in unfolding its policy of *Kaifang*.

What is absolutely clear from the launching of such a policy, however, was China's determination to abandon its policy of so-called *Biguan Zishou* (literally, closing the country to international intercourse) in the foreign economic relations it pursued previously. Promoting foreign trade was made an important strategy by which to modernise the Chinese economy. As Deng Xiaoping warned later, 'any country that closes its doors to the outside world cannot achieve its progress'.[14] The general direction was therefore defined in which a new vigour in developing the Chinese economy was to be sought. To expand foreign trade vigorously was put at the top of the agenda of *Kaifang*. Implicitly, and even unwittingly, however, the launching of this policy set China firmly on the road to participation in the international division of labour.

After the promulgation of the first joint-venture law in July 1979, China began actively to solicit foreign contracts for compensation trade and for assembling and processing. In 1980, four Special Economic Zones along the coast – Shenzhen, Zhuhai, Shantou and Xiamen – were initially designated largely for this purpose, while equity share joint ventures were also being sought. As has been argued in Chapter 4, theoretical debate among Chinese economists on the laws of comparative advantage and international division of labour followed, rather than preceded, the beginning of China's policy of *Kaifang*. The debate, however, was an effort to justify China's preliminary participation in the international division of labour. It helped to consolidate the position of those advocates of such a policy in the Chinese leadership.

By late 1981, a clearer orientation of China's policy of *Kaifang* was enunciated by Premier Zhao Ziyang. Promoting foreign trade became the central strategy by which to modernise the Chinese economy. In his government work report, Zhao urged that,

> By linking our country with the world market, expanding foreign trade, importing advanced technology, utilising foreign capital, and entering

into different forms of international economic and technological cooperation, we can use our strong points to make up for our weak points through international exchange on the basis of equality and mutual benefit.[15]

This is certainly a more explicit commitment by China to participating in the international division of labour. Arguably, this is the beginning of China's long march towards integration into the world economy.

The Growth of trade

Even while some economic policy issues remained unresolved and while academic debate on the international division of labour continued unabated, the policy of *Kaifang* was yielding its intended result: the rapid expansion of China's foreign trade. The opening of China to the world economy had an immediate and notable impact on the growth of China's imports and exports. In what could be regarded as the first phase of trade growth – that is, from 1979 to 1985 – China's foreign trade grew at an average of 12.8 per cent per annum.[16] In the same period, the value of China's commodity trade jumped from $29.3 billion to $60.2 billion. As Table 6.1 shows, exports increased from $13.6 billion in 1979 to $25.9 billion in 1985, while imports grew from $15.6 billion to $34.3 billion.[17] The proportion of China's exports to GDP rose from

Table 6.1 China's foreign trade, 1979–85 (in billion current US dollars)

Year	Exports*	Imports**	Total
1979	13.60	15.70	29.30
1980	18.10	20.02	38.14
1981	20.90	19.50	40.40
1982	21.80	17.50	39.30
1983	22.23	21.39	43.62
1984	26.14	27.41	53.55
1985	27.35	42.25	69.60

* Value in FOB (freight on board)
** Value in CIF (including cost, insurance and freight)
Sources: *Zhongguo Duiwai Jingji Maoyi Nianjian, 1989* (Yearbook of China's Economic Relations and Trade, 1989), p. 299; *China Statistical Yearbook, 1992*, p. 627.

Table 6.2 Percentage of exports to GDP of China, Brazil and Australia, 1979–85

	1979	1980	1981	1982	1983	1984	1985
China	6.3	7.4	9.5	10.0	9.5	11.5	13.7
Brazil	na	8.2	8.3	6.9	9.8	12.7	10.6
Australia	na	14.8	12.7	12.9	12.1	13.1	14.5

Sources: *Zhongguo Duiwai Jingji Maoyi Nianjian, 1989*, pp. 790–1; and Harding, *China's Second Revolution*, p. 139.

6.3 per cent in 1979 to 13.7 per cent in 1985. Such a proportion compared favourably with that for Brazil and was close to that for Australia in 1985. By such a standard, China seemed to be approaching the 'normal' level of trade for a large and open continental economy (see Table 6.2).

The vigorous growth of China's exports raised China's share of total world exports from 0.83 per cent in 1979 to 1.32 per cent in 1985.[18] China moved up from being the thirty-second largest exporter in the world market in 1979 to being the seventeenth in 1985.[19] The share of trade in China's GDP increased from 10.2 per cent in 1978 to 23.9 per cent in 1985. As early as in 1986, the World Bank observed in its report on China's external trade that,

> With a total trade at 24 per cent of its GDP in 1985, China is no longer the isolated economy that it once was. In fact, with its significant and rising shares of world trade, it has now become an important member of the world community, and coupled with its concentration in certain products and markets, could have a great impact on world trade, far beyond what its trade volume would suggest.[20]

Paradoxically, the same World Bank report concluded that, compared with other outward-orientated developing countries, China's 'open door' policy as it stood in 1986 would still have to be characterised as an 'inward-looking' strategy, even though China had achieved great success in its export performance since 1979. It went on to suggest that to sustain the growth rate achieved, 'China will probably have to undertake substantial additional reforms of its trade system to maintain these gains'.[21]

In fact, the impressive export performance highlighted the limits of the trade system reforms. It is well to remember that the consensus among what Harry Harding calls 'moderate reformers' and 'radical reformers' as to how far and how fast foreign trade system reform should be carried out was by no means definite and was far more tenuous than that on agricultural reform.[22] Any economic disequilibrium, as seen in particular in the surplus in China's imports over its exports, would immediately trigger the retrenchment measures and policy changes. The reform of the foreign trade system was therefore at the mercy of the politics of reform. The trade fluctuations with their heights and troughs in the 1980s were almost a direct reflection of tidal waves of the advance and setback of the economic reforms in China in general.

It is also well to remember that in the period studied above, China was still essentially a centrally planned economy and that both exports and imports were subject to stringent plans. It is true that the number of planned export commodities fell continuously to 199 in 1982 and to 100 in 1984 and that the share of planned imports was also substantially reduced in the same period.[23] Nevertheless, central control remained paramount. Foreign trade was still at the mercy of those planners and of the politics of economic planning. The negative growth of imports in 1981 and 1982, for example, was largely the result of a three-year austerity programme initiated at the Second Session of the Fifth National People's Congress in 1979, to 'adjust, reform, consolidate and improve the national economy in order to bring it step-by-step into the orbit of sustained, proportionate, and high speed growth'.[24] By the same token, the import 'boom' of 1984 and 1985 owed a great deal to trade liberalisation measures introduced at the beginning of 1984 and to a deliberate central decision to import more consumer goods, such as colour televisions and refrigerators, and production lines to produce them in China. Besides, the entire economy still had a built-in bias against trade, and the Chinese currency, Renminbi (RMB) was greatly overvalued.[25] Other institutions and China's infrastructure for exporting were at best highly inadequate. Foreign trade corporations, for example, still largely acted as buyers and sellers of exported and imported goods, not as agents either for exporters or for end-users. Foreign trade enterprises could not even make decisions independently on their own production and exporting. Interference from the government administrations in the day-to-day operation of those enterprises was endemic.[26]

It should be therefore argued that, in the decade from 1986 to 1995, it was the progressive reforms of China's trade system, of its domestic market and its price structure and of its fiscal system, among other things, that sustained a decade of high export performance of the Chinese economy.[27] It was also a decade when China expanded its international economic relations in all directions and all aspects. In 1994, China claimed to have established trade and economic relations with more than

220 countries and regions around the world.[28] China now has varied relations with its trading partners, from commodity trade to technology trade and to service trade. Table 6.3 and Figure 6.1 describe numerically and graphically the growth of China's trade in the decade from 1986 to 1995.

Two other indicators are equally revealing of the increased openness of the Chinese economy and of the importance of the trade nexus in China's economic development. One is that the growth of trade has outpaced that of GDP in the period. Calculated on the basis of current price in RMB, from 1986 to 1995, trade grew from 258.04 billion yuan to 2,349.87 billion yuan (9.11 times), whereas GDP grew from 1,021.14 billion yuan to 5,765 billion yuan (only 5.65 times). The other is that exports as a proportion of GDP increased steadily, from 10.6 per cent in 1986 to 21.57 per

Table 6.3 China's foreign trade, 1986–95 (in current billion US dollars)

	1986	1987	1988	1989	1990	1991	1992	1993	1994	1995
Total	73.84	82.66	102.80	111.68	115.44	135.63	165.53	195.71	236.70	280.85
Export	30.94	39.44	47.52	52.54	62.09	71.84	84.94	91.76	121.00	148.77
Import	42.90	43.22	55.28	59.14	53.35	63.79	80.59	103.95	115.70	132.08

Sources: *Zhongguo Duiwai Jingji Maoyi Nianjian, 1992*, p. 395; and *Zhongguo Tongji Nianjian, 1994*, p. 506; *Zhongguo Tongji Zhaiyao, 1996* (A Statistical Survey of China, 1996), p. 105, *Beijing Review*, 12 (1995) v; and *Beijing Review*, 8–9 (1996) 6.

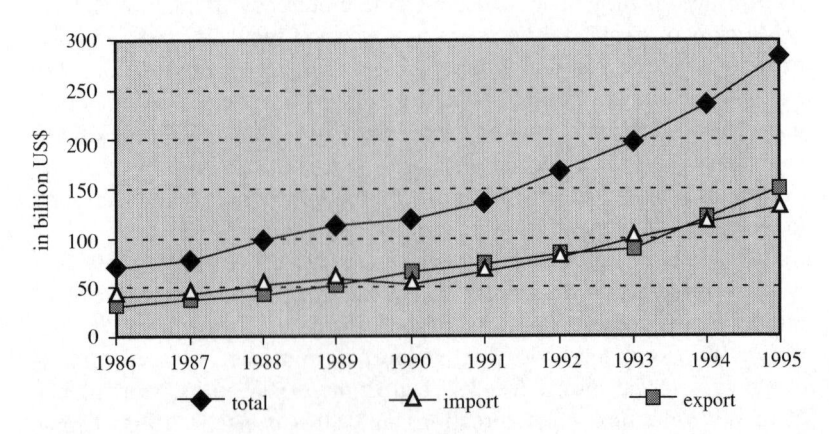

Figure 6.1 China's foreign trade, 1986–95

Table 6.4 China's exports and GDP, 1986–95 (at current billion yuan)

	1986	1987	1988	1989	1990	1991	1992	1993	1994	1995
Exports	108.21	147.00	176.67	195.60	298.58	382.71	467.63	528.48	1 042.18	1 245.10
GDP	1 020.2	1 196.25	1 492.83	1 690.92	1 854.79	2 161.78	2 663.81	3 463.44	4 662.23	5 773.37
Ratio (%)	10.6	12.29	11.83	11.57	16.10	17.7	17.55	15.26	22.35	21.57

Sources: *Zhongguo Tongji Zhaiyao, 1996* (A Statistical Survey of China, 1996), pp. 6, 105.

cent in 1995[29] (see Table 6.4). China's exports 'have grown at twice the rate of the economy as a whole'.[30]

Nicholas Lardy's study in 1992 reveals the same pattern of the increasing openness of Chinese economy, but in a longer historical perspective. The ratio of China's trade to its GDP in dollar terms was 9.7 per cent in 1978, 12.8 per cent in 1980 and 26.8 per cent in 1989. In the decade from 1978 to 1987, the index (with 1978 = 100) of China's trade growth was 320, whereas that of China's GDP was 250.2.[31] In 1990, China's foreign trade constituted about 30 per cent of its GDP, and in 1995, 41 per cent.[32]

It is worth noting that in the decade under discussion, 1989 and 1990 only saw a moderate increase in China's overall foreign trade. Further, in 1990, China suffered a significant decrease in its imports.[33] This owes as much to the austerity programme initiated before and fully implemented after the Tiananmen tragedy of June 1989 as to the subsequent sanctions imposed against China by most Western countries. China's foreign trade picked up its momentum again in 1991 when Chinese politics manifested some degree of stability and when sanctions imposed against China in the aftermath of the Tiananmen tragedy were eventually lifted. This simple fact therefore exposes the vulnerability of China's trade institutions to the politics of reform and political uncertainty and instability in China. The rise and fall of China's foreign trade in this period also demonstrates the significant impact that the world economy could exercise on China's economic development. An inter-dependent relationship between the Chinese economy and the world economy, in other words, is in the making.

Patterns of trade

That trade has become increasingly important in China's overall economy is beyond question. Such a substantial exchange of trade between China and other economies is generally indicative of the openness of the Chinese economy and the increasing inter-dependence between China and the global economy. The pattern of China's exports and imports, on the other hand, is also revealing of the degree of China's integration into the global economy. According to the Chinese statistics, in 1986, over 60 per cent of its trade was with industrialised countries.[34] Only a little over 11 per cent was with centrally planned economies. Imports from developing nations accounted for just 8.9 per cent of China's total.[35] China's economic interests continued to be linked increasingly closely with the market economies and the developed countries.

In what way do the composition and the direction of China's foreign trade add further details to the changing relationship between China and the global economy? In what sense do they reveal the extent of China's actual participation in the international division of labour, thus the degree of China's integration into the global economic order? As has been argued by three IMF economists, 'in assessing the degree of China's integration into the global economy, one must take into account development in its trade and investment flows as well as improvements in its productivity and international competitiveness'.[36] The brief examination of China's trade patterns that is to follow reveals that the total factor productivity has had a very high rate of growth, particularly in the decade from 1986 to 1995. China's international competitiveness has greatly improved, as seen in the increased share of its manufactured exports to the OECD markets.

Let us look first at the commodity composition of China's exports. The share of primary products in its exports (excluding the products of extractive industry, most notably petroleum and coal) continued to fall, from 24.5 per cent in 1985 to 17.2 per cent in 1990. The proportion of petroleum and petroleum products which accounted for 24.8 per cent of China's exports of primary products in 1985 fell sharply to only 7.2 per cent in 1990. Correspondingly, the ratio of manufactured goods in China's exports rose dramatically from 49.4 per cent in 1985 to 80 per cent in 1990.[37] More specifically, the exports of machinery and transport equipment leapt from 2.8 per cent of the total in 1985 to 9 per cent in 1990, of which electronic equipment accounted for 2.8 per cent in 1990 in sharp contrast to a poor 0.3 per cent in 1985.[38] In 1993, this sector accounted for 20.35 per cent of China's export total. The exports of primary goods in the same year stayed at about 18 per cent.[39] In 1994, the export of manufactured goods was valued at $101.3 billion, 83.7 per cent of the total export, whereas that of primary products, only $19.71 billion, less than 17 per cent.[40] In comparison with the period from 1979 to 1985, when China's exports growth was largely motivated by the desire and necessity to finance necessary imports,[41] the period from 1986 to 1995 has seen an increasing shift of China's exports to labour-intensive manufactured goods in order to exploit China's comparative advantage in the international economy. That China's exports structure has become increasingly agreeable to its comparative advantage is an indication of China's harmonious participation in international production and distribution, thus an index of China's growing integration into the existing international economic order.

China's import mix, on the other hand, continues to be dominated by industrial goods, although there was some increase in the import of agricultural products in the latter half of the 1980s.[42] Lardy observed that 'the share of primary commodities in total imports fell from a little over a third in 1980 to about a seventh by 1993'.[43] He also noted that, in the same period, 'the share of industrial products in total imports rose from 63 per cent to 86 per cent'.[44] According to the Chinese statistics, from 1986 to 1994 the share of industrial goods in China's imports hovered between 80 and 86 per cent of the total. In 1993 and 1994, the import of capital goods (machinery and transport equipment) accounted for 43.27 and 44.57 per cent of China's total imports respectively.[45] As China steadily increases the proportion of manufactured goods with improved quality in its exports, it becomes more and more dependent on importing high-tech equipment and high-quality industrial supplies. The changing composition of its commodity imports and exports, in Nicholas Lardy's words, has 'moved China's pattern of trade to one much more congruent with the country's underlying comparative advantage than had been the case in the prereform era'.[46]

An equally telling indication is the direction of China's foreign trade. As it has been observed, more than 90 per cent of China's trade in 1990 was with market economies. Indeed, during the whole decade of the 1980s, China's trade with centrally planned economies remained under 10 per cent, with the exception of 1986, when the proportion reached 11.18 per cent, largely owing to the normalisation of its relations with some Eastern European countries which boosted bilateral trade briefly. It declined in 1987 to 9.22 per cent and further, to 9.19 per cent in 1988.[47] In 1993 and 1994, China's trade with Russia accounted for respectively 3.9 and 2.15 per cent of the total, while trade with Eastern European countries became negligible.[48] The IMF statistics have registered a continued increase in the share of China's exports to industrialised economies, from 36.7 per cent in 1988 to 51.2 per cent in 1994.[49] After adjustment of Hong Kong's re-exports, that per centage in 1994 could jump to as high as 70 per cent.[50] China's overall trade with industrialised economies in 1994 is about 54 per cent of the total, according to the IMF statistics, and would be 64 per cent after adjustment of Hong Kong's re-exports and imports for China.[51]

China's trading relations with the OECD economies is worth examining briefly in this context. China had by the end of the 1980s become the largest non-member trading partner for the OECD states. By 1991, it had become the largest exporter to OECD economies.[52] In the period from 1981 to 1991, China's share of OECD countries' total imports rose from 0.83 per cent to 2.19 per cent. Its share of OECD countries' manufactured imports rose from 0.66 per cent to 2.43 per cent. Of the manufactured imports by OECD countries, machinery and transportation equipment rose from 2.59 per cent in 1981 to 15.49 per cent in 1991. This is particularly significant because it happened in a decade when the commodity prices were weak and the share of non-OECD countries' share of exports had contracted.[53] Underlying this expansion in China's exports to OECD countries is the improved international competitiveness of China in the world economy.

Service trade

Though undoubtedly the most important component of the trade connections between nations, the commodity trade is not the whole trade nexus between the economies. Other forms of trade, such as financial services, labour services and technology trade, are assuming a more and more important place in the trade nexus. In the case of China, what tend to be either totally neglected or inadequately examined in China's foreign trade are its technology trade and engineering and labour services trade. It is true that not long ago the absolute value of China's technology export was so small that it was almost negligible. For example, China's technology export in 1985 was only several million dollars. That has since changed significantly, however. In 1989, China signed 168 contracts (an increase of 26 per cent from that of 1988) for technology export with more than 30 countries in Asia, Africa, Europe and America. The total value of these technology export contracts reached $879 million, more than five times that of the previous year.[54] From 1979 to the end of 1990, China exported, 733 items of technology, with a total transaction value of $2.469 billion. In the first eight months of 1991, 123 items of technology were exported with a total value of $740 million.[55] On the other hand, from 1979 to 1989, China imported some 7000 technology items with a total payment of $27 billion.[56] In 1992 alone, China contracted 504 technology import projects with the contractual value of $6.59 billion. Its technology export in the same year reached a contractual value of $1.51 billion.[57]

China's contracted engineering projects and labour service with other countries constitute at the moment the most prominent part of its service trade. China did not enter the world labour market until the end of 1978,

Table 6.5 China's engineering and labour service contracts with foreign countries, 1979–95 (value in billion US dollars)

	1979–86	1987	1988	1989	1990	1991	1992	1993	1994	1995	Total
Contract	3 952	1 449	2 126	3 100	5 175	8 438	9 405	11 605	17 491	19 321	82 062
Value (a)*	6.53	1.89	2.17	2.21	2.60	3.61	6.59	6.80	7.99	9.67	50.06
Value (b)*	3.39	1.26	1.43	1.69	1.87	2.36	3.05	4.54	5.98	6.59	32.16

* Value (a) is contract value, and value (b) is fulfilled value.
Source: *Zhongguo Tongji Zhaiyao, 1996* (A Statistical Survey of China, 1996), p. 113.

when the State Council first sanctioned the establishment of companies specialising in engineering projects and labour services abroad. It developed rapidly, however, in the following years. By the end of 1986, China had signed 3731 contracts worth a total of $6.37 billion with a fulfilled value of $3.50 billion.[58] In 1990, China had 5175 engineering and labour service contracts with 122 countries and regions in the world.[59] In 1991, more than 5000 contracts worth $3 billion were signed and 89 000 labour service personnel from China were working abroad.[60] At the end of 1992, 130 000 Chinese engineers and labour service personnel were working in foreign countries to fulfil those contracts.[61] From 1979 to 1995, China signed 82 062 labour service and engineering projects contacts worth $50.06 billion, of which $32.16 billion was fulfilled by the end of 1995 (see Table 6.5).

A less prominent, none the less important, service trade is tourism. In the ten years from 1980 to 1990, the number of tourists from foreign countries and from Hong Kong, Macau and Taiwan to China increased almost five times from 5.7 million to 27.5 million. Revenues from tourism in the same period rose from $617 million to $2.218 billion.[62] China's foreign trade deficit in 1985 and 1986, for example, was largely offset by its surplus accounts from the two above-mentioned services.[63] The earnings from tourism increased steadily, from $0.617 billion in 1980 to $1.25 billion in 1985 and to $7.32 billion in 1994 and $8.73 billion in 1995.[64]

Conclusion

As has been argued, 'the ratio of a country's trade to its total output of goods and services is one of the most widely used indicators of international integration: the higher the ratio the greater the country's involvement in international economy'.[65] The development of China's foreign trade in the last decade or so has not only built up but also sustained a trade nexus between China and other economies. Such a trade nexus demonstrates the scale on which and the extent to which China has participated in international economic activities. Trade, the 'oldest and most important economic nexus among nations',[66] has in its turn inextricably linked the Chinese economy with the international economy and made it part of the economic whole.

It is no exaggeration to say that today 'foreign trade has begun to play a greater role in the domestic economy [of China] than at any other period of Chinese history'.[67] The spectacular increase of China's trade in the last decade or so has indeed served as the engine of growth for the Chinese economy, making China one of the fastest-growing economies in the world. Trade has at the same time acted as the most effective means to integrate the Chinese economy into the existing international economic order. China's integration into the global international economic system has been, however, further enhanced by China's engagement with global capital markets. It is to the examination of that engagement that we must now turn.

CHINA AND GLOBAL CAPITAL MARKETS

The growing network of China's international trade has surely already begun to enmesh the Chinese economy into a system of the international division of labour and of global inter-dependence. The expanding trade nexus is, nevertheless, only one aspect of contemporary global inter-dependence, although it remains arguably the most important one. International finance, with the increasing integration of world financial markets which has resulted in the unprecedented flow of capital internationally, has become 'a major force in integrating the modern world economy'.[68] In fact, the volume of the international flow of capital assets has long exceeded the volume of world trade many times over. As early as 1984, for example, total world exports were only $1.8 trillion compared to foreign exchange trading of $35 trillion.[69]

In the 1980s and the 1990s, the expansion of China's trade marched hand in hand with the inflow of foreign capital to China. It is debatable whether the Chinese government, by introducing a large volume of foreign capital into the Chinese economy, has been purposely pursuing a strategy of debt-sustained growth, like many other developing countries. That is probably beside the point. What emerges clearly from this is that China

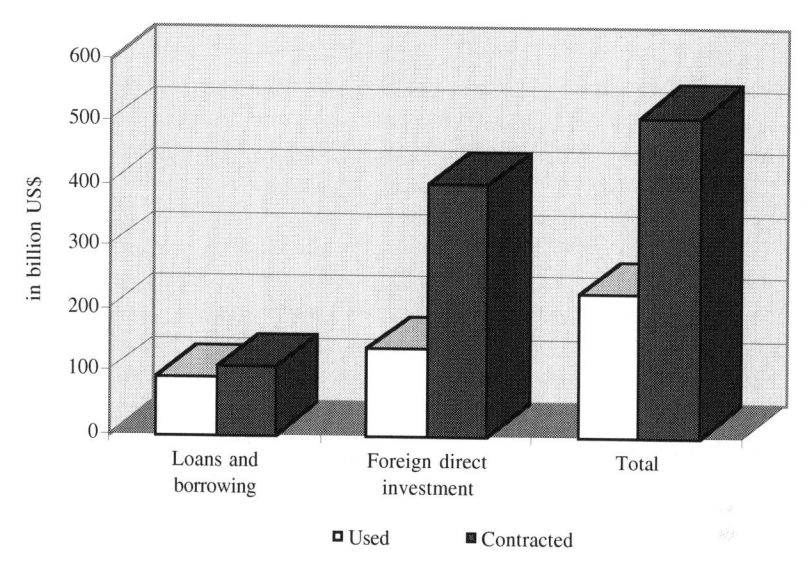

Source: *Zhongguo Tongji Zhaiyao, 1996* (A Statistical Survey of China, 1996), p. 110.

Figure 6.2 International capital inflows into China, 1979–95

has been actively seeking the help of international finance in its programme of economic modernisation. Foreign capital has entered China in the forms of economic aid from governments mostly of developed countries, loans distributed by supranational economic organisations, commercial borrowing on the international financial markets, and foreign direct investment from multinational corporations and from overseas Chinese communities and other sources. The amount of international capital that flowed into China from 1979 to 1995 was already astronomical.

All these inflows of capital, many of which had not been seen in China before the 1980s, have contributed to the dynamic nature of the Chinese economy and to making China an integral part of the world economy. The 1980s, and particularly the 1990s, have also seen capital outflows from China and the emergence of China's multinational corporations. China has therefore 'become a major participant in international capital markets'.[70] The two-way engagement of China with global capital markets has therefore further integrated China economically into the world by strengthening its links with international finance and by increasing its growing interdependence with the global economy.

The initial engagement

With the exception of a few dubious cases, the PRC had little to do with international financial markets before 1970. It is true that the Soviet Union offered a series of credits to China in the 1950s and China did not pay off its debts until 1964. This was not, strictly speaking, an interaction between international finance and the Chinese economy.[71] Neither could China's extensive aid to many newly independent developing countries in the 1960s and early 1970s, some of which involved the export of a large amount of capital, as in the case of Tanzam Railway building, be qualified as international capital flow as conventionally defined and understood.[72] China's insulation from the international economy in the 1950s and the 1960s, which had resulted from China's alienation from the existing international system, had its effective expression in a stricter insulation from international finance than from international commerce. While China engaged selectively, sometimes reluctantly and sometimes enthusiastically, in international trade, its rejection of the penetration of international financial interest was next to total.[73] Even when opportunities arose after the PRC's return to the United Nations in 1971, China's use of international finance in its national economic development was still extremely limited in most of the 1970s. It prudently avoided any long-term or even medium-term indebtedness. One study indicates that in the eight years from 1970 to 1977, China's total borrowing, which was all from non-Communist countries, was $4.86 billion in credits and loans, of which $3.74 billion, or around 77 per cent, 'consisted of short-term commercial loans, generally for periods ranging from six to eighteen months'.[74] Most of these short-term credits and loans were used to facilitate the flow of imports of capital goods and industrial supplies. From 1974 onwards, deferred payments were also regularly used to finance the imports of major capital goods.[75] It was not until September 1979, however, that China formally opened its doors to international finance. On 28 September 1979, Vice-Premier Gu Mu, in his capacity as Chairman of the newly created State Commission for Foreign Investment Control, officially announced at a press conference in Beijing that China was 'ready to accept loans from all friendly countries and financial organisations provided they do not affect China's sovereign rights'.[76] Before that, in July 1979, the Standing Committee of the People's Congress had approved China's first joint-venture law.

The year 1979 also saw intensive institutional changes in China. A series of institutions were created directly under the State Council to deal with the anticipated inflow of international investment. In March, the State General Administration of Foreign Exchange Control was established. Also in March, the Bank of China (BOC) was made China's specialised state bank engaging in foreign exchange business, and it began to expand aggressively its activities abroad. On 7 June, the BOC opened a branch in Luxembourg, its first set-up abroad since 1949.[77] With the approval of the Standing Committee of the Fifth National People's Congress, the State Commission for Foreign Investment Control and the State Commission for Imports and Exports Control were set up on 30 July.[78] In October, China International Trust and Investment Corporation (CITIC) was inaugurated.[79] China was now poised to take the chances as well as the challenges presented by international finance. It is not without good reason that 1979 is officially claimed to mark 'the beginning of a new era of China's making use of foreign capital'.[80]

The timing of this beginning was, however, not at all propitious. By the early 1980s, the international debt crisis loomed threateningly large over the horizon of the global economy. According to *The Economist*, the flow of all forms of capital to non-OPEC developing countries had by then declined dramatically.[81] The reluctance of international banks to continue to finance the strategy of indebted industrialisation was evident, because of the lack of success of such a strategy in Latin America and in Eastern Europe in the 1970s. The natural consequence was a contraction of capital supply in the world financial markets. The success or failure of China's strategy to attract international capital must be evaluated against this background.

International capital transfer into China has largely followed four familiar paths identifiable in other developing economies. Official aid from foreign governments and concessionary loans from supranational economic organisations like the World Bank, the IMF and regional development banks, which became important aspects of international finance only after the Second World War, have played their due part in integrating the Chinese economy with international finance. They are complemented by two more traditional means – commercial borrowing on the world capital markets and foreign direct investment.[82] There is a unique aspect of the foreign direct investment absorbed by China, however. Whereas foreign direct investment in most other developing economies has been made almost exclusively by multinational corporations, the lion's share of foreign direct investment channelled into China to date has been through the overseas Chinese communities, mostly from Hong Kong and Macau, but also increasingly from Taiwan, the United States and the Southeast Asia. In purely statistical terms, this part of foreign investment in China is by far the largest.[83]

For obvious reasons, official development assistance from foreign governments pioneered the way for international capital transfer into China. In December 1979, while on a state visit to China, the Japanese Prime Minister Ohira Masayoshi pledged that the Japanese government would provide long-term low-interest loans for six large projects in China.[84] On 30 April 1980, an official agreement between the Chinese and Japanese governments was signed in Beijing, whereby the Japanese government was to provide a loan of 50 billion yen to China in 1979 alone. This was the first inter-governmental loan that the PRC had ever signed with a capitalist country in its 30 years' history from 1949 to 1979.[85] Also in 1979, the Belgian government undertook to provide an interest-free loan of 900 million Belgian francs to China from 1980 to 1982.[86]

From 1979 to 1985, the Chinese government signed a series of loan agreements with seven developed countries, as well as with Kuwait, for a total of $4.862 billion, which represented about 25 per cent of China's total borrowing for the same period.[87] By 1985, $3.403 billion of the total committed had actually been used. The two sectors which had benefited most from the bilateral aid were the energy industry and transport and telecommunications.[88]

Expanding the engagement

The pioneering action of the government loans in transferring international capital into China was followed very closely by loans from supranational economic organisations, mostly the World Bank group and the IMF. To obtain loans on favourable terms from the two international economic organisations was one strong, though not primary, motive behind China's seeking membership in the two organisations in 1980. It was not to be disappointed. In June 1981, the World Bank and the International Development Agency (IDA) together provided $200 million for their first project in China, the University Development project.[89] Also in 1981, when China's international trade was in serious deficit, China exercised its right to take 759 million special drawing rights (SDRs) from the IMF, which amounted to $931 million, to balance its current account.[90] From 1981 to 1988, a total of $7.4 billion in loans and credits was committed by the World Bank group to China, with the IDA providing an average of $600 million 'soft loans' annually. The Bank quickly became the second largest lender to China, after the Japanese government.[91] In January 1989, the World Bank was prepared to deliver to China over $6 billion in loans and credits in the fiscal years 1989–91. In spite of the temporary suspension of World Bank lending operations to China as a result of the sanctions imposed by the G7 following the Tiananmen tragedy of 4 June 1989, by 30 June 1991 the cumulative borrowing by China from the World Bank had reached $10.79 billion, of which $5.88 billion was IBRD loans and $4.91 billion was IDA credits.[92] By the end of 1995, accumulated World Bank commitments to China has exceeded $23 billion, covering 162 projects. The World Bank 'became China's largest single source of foreign capital and China became the Bank's largest borrower'.[93] In the 1990s, loans from international monetary organisations and from foreign governments have been two major sources of capital inflow into China (see Table 6.6).

More significantly, the World Bank has ceased to be just a lending machine for China. As the head of the World Bank Resident Mission to China recently reported:

> China is beginning to make more active use of new financing instruments offered by the Bank. Three power projects have in recent years

Table 6.6 Net disbursements of World Bank loans to China, 1990–94 (in million US dollars)

	1990	1991	1992	1993	1994
IBRD	375.0	538.0	356.7	731.9	1 065.5
IDA	505.0	610.0	789.9	865.1	671.0
Total	880.0	1 148.0	1 146.6	1 597.0	1 736.5

Source: OECD: *Geographical Distribution of Financial Flows to Aid Recipients*, p. 75.

Table 6.7 Loans to China received from foreign governments and international organisations, 1991–95 (in billion US dollars)

	1991	1992	1993	1994	1995
Loans from foreign governments	1.441	1.501	2.65	3.375	3.465
Loans from Intl organisations	1.311	1.583	2.137	3.298	1.991

Sources: *Zhongguo Tongji Nianjian, 1995*, pp. 578–9; *Zhongguo Tongji Nianjian, 1996*, pp. 620–1.

been co-financed with commercial banks through the ECO financial guarantee facility. The World Bank is assisting China to attract and use efficiently long term private foreign capital for infrastructure development. In this context, it is working with China on BOT (build-operate-transfer) experiments in power and transport.[94]

Other international organisations which have also made loans to China include the International Fund for Agricultural Development (IFAD) and the Asian Development Bank (ADB). China became a member of the IFAD on 1 January 1980. From 1981 to 1985, the Fund provided $83.81 million for agricultural development projects in northern China and Hubei province.[95] From 1986 to 1990, another $49.51 million were committed by the IFAD.[96] On 10 March 1986, China became a member of the Asian Development Bank. From a modest start, a $2.57 million loan in 1988, the total lending by the ADB to China reached $258.62 million in 1991. By the end of 1994, the ADB administered 38 loans to China of a total of $4.076 billion. That amount increased to $5.22 billion by the end of 1995.[97]

Many United Nations agencies – such as the United Nations Development Programme (UNDP), the Food and Agriculture Organisation (FAO), and even the UN Fund for Population Activities (UNFPA), as well as the UN International Children's Emergency Fund (UNICEF) – have all administered multilateral funds into China.[98]

Commercial borrowing

The other two forms of international capital transfer are more traditional, but also more politically sensitive. International finance in general 'creates dependent relationships and is a major source of national power'.[99] Commercial borrowing on international financial markets and foreign direct investment, in particular, involve extensive penetration of the national economy by international capital. They are politically sensitive, not so much because of China's proclaimed ideological values at the time as because of China's experience in the 'century of humiliation', in which it had been indebted to Western capitalist countries and seen the exploitation of the country by foreign capital. Sensitivity is also present because of China's experience in the recent past with the former Soviet Union.

In spite of political difficulties in reconciling its economic practice with the prevailing ideology and with China's historical experience, commercial borrowing and foreign direct investment were incorporated into China's overall strategy of economic modernisation. It is worth remembering that China's short-term borrowing on international financial markets had already become significant by the end of the 1970s.[100] China nevertheless was largely regarded as an nonentity in international capital markets. In the 1980s, China maintained five official government borrowing windows: namely, the Ministry of Foreign Economic Relations and Trade (MOFERT), the Ministry of Finance, the Ministry of Agriculture, the People's Bank of China, and the Bank of China. Each was endowed with authority and responsibility for a portion of China's overall borrowing programme.[101] The Bank of China was designated as the national official window for commercial borrowing. In the actual operation, however, commercial borrowing was substantially decentralised after 1980.

In 1986, eight other entities, in addition to the five official windows mentioned above, were authorised to borrow on international financial markets independently in their own name. Three national-level financial institutions authorised were the Bank of Communications, the China Investment Bank and the CITIC. Two provinces and three municipalities authorised were respectively Guangdong, Fujian, Tianjin, Shanghai and Dalian. In the case of provinces and municipalities, it was mostly the provincial or the municipal international trust and investment companies (ITICs) that acted as the provincial or municipal borrowing windows.[102] The total of China's commercial borrowing from international capital markets rose from $1.137 billion in 1983 to $24.082 billion in 1990. Of this total, $19.291 billion was from commercial banks, whereas $4.791 billion was by the issuing of international bonds.[103]

One example of China's commercial borrowing which probably best exemplifies the mutual engagement between China and international capital, is China's issuing of bonds on world markets to raise funds for its economic modernisation. Bond issuing on international capital markets as an instrument to raise funds was repudiated in China after 1949. Ironically, the insulation of China from international capital markets before the end of the 1970s, by rendering China virtually debt-free, in fact gained China ready access to international capital markets.[104] From 1982 to the end of 1985, 12 issues were made by Chinese institutions on the Japanese, Hong Kong and West German markets.[105] According to IMF statistics, through international bond issues China borrowed $44.5 million in 1982, $20.5 million in 1983, $81.7 million in 1984, and $959.9 million in 1985. In the first three quarters of 1986, China issued international bonds worth $1307.8 million.[106] In absolute terms and considering the size of China's economy, this sum is not at all large. Given China's inexperience in international financial dealings, however, the rapid growth of bond issuing and China's readiness and willingness to explore options and

Table 6.8 China's foreign and Eurobond issues, 1982–85

Date	Borrower	Market	Currency	Amount
1/82	CITIC	Japan	yen	10 billion
8/83	FIEC*	Japan	yen	5 billion
11/84	BOC	Japan	yen	20 billion
1/85	CITIC	Japan	yen	30 billion
4/85	BOC	Japan	yen	20 billion
6/85	BOC	W. Germany	mark	150 million
8/85	CITIC	Hong Kong	HK dollar	300 million
9/85	BOC	Japan	US dollar	150 million
9/85	CITIC	W. Germany	mark	150 million
11/85	FIEC	Japan	yen	10 billion
12/85	CITIC	Japan	US dollar	100 million

* Fujian Investment and Enterprise Corporation.
Sources: Li Cheng, 'China's Foreign and Eurobond Issues', *China Business Review* (January–February 1986) 20; *Beijing Review*, 10 (1986) 29; *Beijing Review*, 24 (1987) 29.

instruments to raise capital on international financial markets are of particular significance. Table 6.8 gives details of those issues.

In 1986 and 1987, China became the most significant borrower among the developing countries through bond issues on international capital markets. In 1986, China issued, in value terms, 32.3 per cent of the total bonds by developing countries and regions. In 1987, the per centage was a higher 38.1 per cent (see Table 6.9).[107] From 1982 to June 1989, China issued altogether more than 40 batches of international bonds.

In June 1991, China resumed its bond issuing in the international financial markets, with the BOC signing a contract in Tokyo for issuing bonds on the Tokyo market worth 20 billion yen.[108] In the last five years, China seems to have returned to the international bond markets with a vengeance. In 1993, the total amount of capital raised by China through 17 issues of bonds was $2.3 billion.[109] Chinese institutions have capitalised on all bond markets world-wide. In September 1993, China returned to the Eurobond market as a sovereign borrower by issuing 30 billion yen bonds.[110] In October 1993, China became the first sovereign borrower on the fledging market for Dragon bonds by launching a $300 million issue in Hong Kong.[111] In 1994, the Chinese government appeared on the American and the Japanese markets as sovereign borrowers for the first time. In February, China placed its first global bonds offering worth of $1 billion in New York.[112] In July, the Chinese government issued two

Table 6.9. International bond issues by selected developing countries, 1985–90 (in million US dollars)

	1985	1986	1987	1988	1989	1990
China	972.8	1 362.1	1 415.2	911.6	150.4	—
India	417.8	323.2	377.0	714.6	668.3	523.0
Indonesia	—	300.0	50.0	221.1	175.0	825.0
Korea	1 730.9	783.0	332.3	130.0	328.2	1 515.4
Thailand	861.7	50.0	—	261.0	231.7	50.0
Algeria	500.0	125.6	49.2	433.3	159.0	—
*Total (developing nations)	8 113.3	4 210.3	3 711.4	6 436.7	5 810.7	6 609.5

* Total international bond issues by all developing countries.
Sources: Goldstein et al, 'Statistical Appendix Table A23: International Bond Issues by Developing Countries and Regions', *International Capital Markets: Developments, Prospects and Policy Issues* (September 1992) 75; IMF, *International Capital Markets: Development and Prospects* (May 1991) 65.

lots of Samurai bonds in Tokyo, with a total value of 60 billion yen.[113] In the space of three years, seven batches of sovereign bonds worth $4 billion were issued by China to test the bonds markets world-wide, including the Dragon bonds for the Asia-Pacific, Yankee bonds in the United States, Samurai bonds in Japan, Japanese yen bonds in Europe and global bonds.[114] Clearly, a two-way intensive engagement between China and international capital is taking place. While China reaches out for capital on the global markets, international capital is keen to embrace China as an emerging market.

Two other portfolio capital inflows – international equity placements and foreign purchase of Chinese stocks – are also worth mentioning in

Table 6.10 China's international bond issues, 1991–94 (in million US dollars)

1991	1992	1993	1994	Total
115	1 359	3 047	4 077	8 598

Source: Folkerts-Landau and Ito, *International Capital Markets: Developments, Prospects and Policy Issues*, p. 42.

this context. According to IMF, from 1990 to 1994, Asian companies' international placements amounted to nearly $25 billion. The leading issuers were Chinese companies, which accounted for more than 20 per cent, at $5.6 billion. It was followed by Indian companies, at $3.6 billion, and Hong Kong and Indonesian companies, each at about $3 billion.[115] On China's domestic stock markets, B shares for floated Chinese companies are priced in Renminbi, but sold in foreign currencies, particularly to foreign investors. Emerging in 1992, B shares are now actively traded on both the Shanghai and Shenzhen Stock Exchanges. In the Chinese statistics, foreign purchases of Chinese stocks and bonds grew from $0.393 billion in 1992 to $3.647 billion in 1993 and $4.493 billion in 1994.[116]

The engagement of international finance with the Chinese market has another indicator. In December 1979, the Export-Import Bank of Japan was the first foreign financial institution to open its agency in Beijing. By early 1986, 40 out of 50 of the world's leading banks had opened more than 150 offices in ten Chinese cities.[117] One year later, it was reported that 110 foreign financial institutions were operating in China, of which 86 were banks, 8 were securities and 16 were insurance companies. They had a total of 179 offices in China, of which 102 were in Beijing, 26 in Shanghai and 20 in Guangzhou.[118] In 1991, *Beijing Review* further reported that, by June 1991, 129 foreign funded financial institutions from 26 countries had established 219 agencies in China's 14 large cities.[119] Although their activities, even in the early 1990s, were restricted by the Chinese government, as Lardy pointed out,[120] their presence itself was significant. The years 1993 and 1994 saw a second march of foreign financial institutions into China, including banks from developing countries such as Pakistan and Thailand. In 1994 alone, Solomon Brothers, Goldman Sachs and Morgan Stanley all opened offices in Beijing, while Merrill Lynch opened its second China office.[121] Securities and accountancy firms such as Nikko Securities and Moore Stephen have both arrived in China.[122] Operations of these foreign financial institutions are no long restricted to coastal areas and three municipalities. They have been extended as far into China's interior as Chengdu.[123] With limited openings for foreign banks to conduct RMB business on a trial basis in Shanghai's Pudong area, these institutional engagements are becoming more significant in integrating China into international finance.[124]

Foreign direct investment

Last but certainly not least, international capital flow into China is taking the form of foreign direct investment (FDI). From 1949 to 1979, China had virtually been closed to any foreign private investment, although it did carry out, fitfully and sometimes in a very limited fashion, other international economic activities. That probably explains why China's open-door policy – in particular, the opening of China to FDI – announced in 1979, immediately caught the world's imagination. FDI in China, however, had a very slow and difficult start.[125] From 1979 to 1982, only around $1.17 billion in foreign capital had actually been invested in China, although the agreements signed by foreign investors for 922 projects amounted to a total of $6.01 billion.[126] Even by the end of 1985, only $4.6 billion had actually been invested,[127] which was only around 1.5 per cent of China's GDP in 1985. From 1985 to 1989, however, the rate of FDI grew rapidly. In the investment boom year of 1988 alone, $5.23 billion had been pledged by foreign investors for a total of 5,945 projects, of which $3.12 billion was realised.[128] By the end of August 1991, the total of the agreement value of FDI in China reached $43.3 billion, with $18.3 billion already realised.[129] At the same time, more than 200 laws and regulations related to foreign investment and economic activities in China were promulgated by the Standing Committee of the National People's Congress and the State Council.[130]

The year 1992 saw an unprecedented boom in FDI in China. In all, 48 857 projects involving foreign investment were approved in the year. The agreement value of FDI was $57.5 billion, more than the accumulated total of the previous 12 years. The realised value of FDI was $11.16 billion.[131] By the end of 1996, the realised value of FDI in China had reached $180 billion and the contract value, $450 billion.

Two characteristics of FDI in China as a form of international capital inflow are worth discussing in some detail. First, in spite of rapid growth in the 1980s, FDI in China, although seemingly large in absolute terms, is in fact still comparatively small in proportion either to the total flow of foreign capital into China, or to the size of the Chinese economy. For example, from 1979 to 1984, FDI actually realised was much smaller than

Table 6.11 Foreign direct investment in China, 1986–96 (in billion US dollars)

	1986	1987	1988	1989	1990	1991	1992	1993	1994	1995	1996
Value[a]	2.834	3.709	5.297	5.60	6.596	11.98	58.12	111.44	81.40	90.29	73.2
Value[b]	1.874	2.314	3.194	3.392	3.487	4.366	11.01	27.52	33.8	37.73	42.3

[a] contracted value and [b], realised value.

220   *China in International Society since 1949*

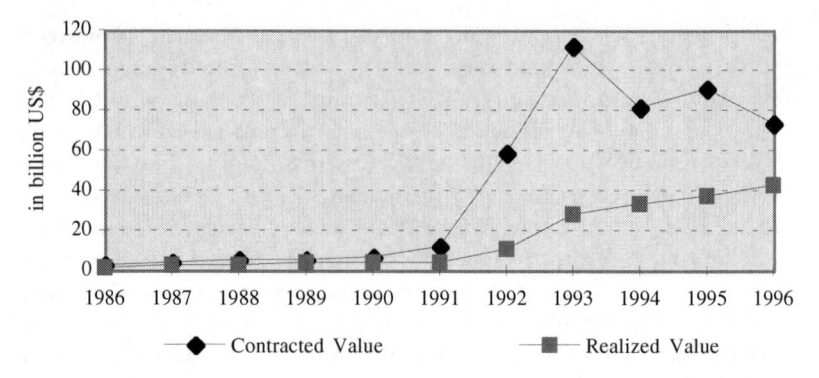

Source: *Zhongguo Tongji Zhaiyao, 1996* (A Statistical Survey of China, 1996), p. 110; and *China Daily*, 26 January 1997.

Figure 6.3   Foreign direct investment in China, 1986–96

loans and credits provided by foreign governments, and was roughly 12.4 per cent of the total foreign capital actually used.[132] Even in the boom year of 1988, FDI accounted for only one-third of China's absorption of foreign capital in that year. Measured against China's GDP over the years, FDI, both the pledged and the realised, is quite small. Its per centage is certainly much lower than those of many other developing countries. According to World Bank statistics, by the end of 1985, a total of foreign investment of $16.2 billion had been pledged, of which only $4.6 billion had been actually invested. They were respectively 5.7 per cent and 1.6 per cent of China's GDP in 1985.[133] In a comparative perspective, the ratio of the realised FDI and GDP of Pakistan and India in 1979 was respectively 4 per cent and 2 per cent.[134] Even at the end of the 1980s, the FDI/GDP ratio for China was still only 3.5 per cent for realised investment and 8.05 per cent for agreed investment. In the overall picture of international capital flow into China up to mid-1991, FDI actually delivered was only a little more than one-quarter of China's external borrowing realised.[135] Only in 1992 did the total FDI actually realised in China ($11.16 billion) for the first time exceed the country's total borrowing from abroad ($10.37 billion).[136]

Second, as has been briefly mentioned earlier in this chapter, international capital flow in the form of FDI in the post-war years has been dominated and almost monopolised by multinational corporations. When China opened its economy, the multinationals lost no time in getting into the Chinese market. For example, by the end of 1978, Coca-Cola had already secured an agreement to open a bottling plant in Shanghai and to sell Coca-Cola in China.[137] However, multinationals started up large-scale investment schemes in China only in 1993. Although Chinese statistics show that so far more than 200 of the world's top 500 multinationals have invested in China,[138] foreign private investment in China to date has not been dominated, even less monopolised, by the multinationals. Chinese overseas entrepreneurs, in particular in Hong Kong, have dominated the picture. World Bank statistics showed that as of June 1985, 'fully 85 per cent of the total value of FDI came from Hong Kong. Japan accounted for another 5 per cent, the United States for 4 per cent, and all other countries combined had only 6 per cent.'[139] In 1991, the realised value of FDI from Hong Kong and Macau was $2.468 billion, 57 per cent of the total.[140] Even at the beginning of 1993, Chinese entrepreneurs in Hong Kong are still accountable for over 60 per cent of FDI in China.[141] In 1994 and 1995, however, the share of contracted foreign investment in China by multinationals increased significantly to over 50 per cent of the total.

While these two features of foreign private investment in China must have contributed to the alleviation of problems and complications associated with China's management of FDI, and in particular the politics of the multinationals' operations in China, they by no means modify the significance of foreign investment as a form of international capital flow in knitting China into international economic inter-dependence. They have certainly played their part in shaping Chinese economic development. In particular, FDI has spearheaded the globalization of the Chinese market, and helped set China firmly on the ladder of the international division of labour through the internationalisation of its industrial production. It has taken China's economic inter-dependence with the global economy beyond the realm of trade into the area of industrial production. In so doing, it has integrated the Chinese economy more extensively and more intimately into the international economic system. Nicholas Lardy even suggests that, given such a high level of FDI in China today, China is more fully integrated with the rest of the world than is Japan.[142]

Capital outflows from China

There is yet another aspect of China's relations with international finance after 1979 which has often been neglected. For China, international capital flow in the 1980s and the 1990s has not been just a one-way traffic.[143] According to a brief by the State Administration for the Management of State-owned Assets reported in *Renmin Ribao* in November 1994, China had established by then more than 10,000 enterprises in more than 120 countries and regions. China's overseas investment amounted to dozens of

Table 6.12 Long-term capital outflows from China, 1991–95
(in billion US dollars)

	1991	1992	1993	1994	1995
Long-term capital outflow	5.157	26.99	22.94	25.03	27.82
Amortisation of debt	2.658	9.757	4.793	9.625	10.12
FDI from China	0.83	4.0	4.4	2.0	2.0
China's investment in foreign bonds & stocks	0.241	0.45	0.59	0.38	0.079

Sources: *Zhongguo Tongji Nianjian, 1995*, pp. 578–9; *Zhongguo Tongji Nianjian, 1996*, pp. 620–1.

billion US dollars. The state-owned assets overseas were close to 2000 billion yuan.[144] According to one report in *Hong Kong Business* in September 1996, China's average annual FDI outflow from 1990 to 1994 was at $2.429 billion, close to that of Taiwan at $2.64 billion.[145] It was further claimed that more than 5,500 affiliates of Chinese corporations held total foreign assets of about $200 billion.[146] China's long-term capital outflow and its direct investment overseas from 1991 to 1995 as recorded in *China Statistical Yearbook, 1995* and *1996* are set in Table 6.12 and Figure 6.4. Although the above groups of statistics are crude and do not agree with each other, the underlying message is clear. Capital outflows from China are becoming increasingly significant.

Part of the long-term capital outflow from China can obviously be accounted for by China's international debt service. In the 1990s, this part of the outflow has become more and more significant, as China's international debt grows. In 1994 and 1995 respectively, for example, China paid $9.625 billion and $10.12 billion for the amortisation of its debt.[147] However, significant as it seems, that only accounts for a little more than one-third of the total capital outflow from China in those two years.

Official Chinese statistics record two categories of China's outward investment as long-term capital outflow. One is China's FDI, and the other, Chinese purchases of foreign bonds and stocks as seen in Table 6.12 and Figure 6.4. That, however, still leaves a significant portion of capital outflow unaccounted for, in both 1993 and 1994, for example, close to $10 billion.[148] In the official Chinese statistics, this is recorded as 'errors and losses'. It may in fact be the unrecorded capital outflow.[149] There is strong evidence to suggest that the official Chinese statistics have significantly understated China's FDI in other economies. Various studies

Economic Integration 223

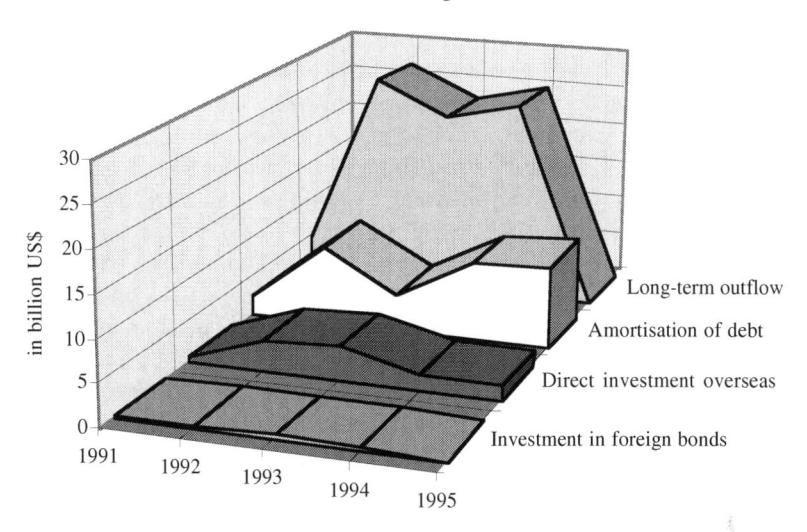

[Figure: 3D area chart showing capital outflows 1991-1995, y-axis "in billion US$" from 0 to 30, with series labeled "Long-term outflow", "Amortisation of debt", "Direct investment overseas", "Investment in foreign bonds"]

Sources: *Zhongguo Tongji Nianjian, 1995*, p. 578; and *Zhongguo Tongji Nianjian, 1996*, pp. 620–1.

Figure 6.4 Long-term capital outflows from China, 1991–95

put China's cumulative investment in Hong Kong alone, for example, at between $20 and $25 billion by 1995.[150]

China's FDI started as early as 1979 and grew very slowly but steadily in the 1980s.[151] Since the late 1980s, the growth of China's FDI has been accompanied by the emergence of China's multinationals. The 1995 *Fortune* Global 500 listed three Chinese multinationals.[152] One of them is Sinochem. As early as 1987, the State Council sanctioned the proposal by the China National Chemicals Import and Export Corporation (CCIEC), more popularly known as Sinochem, in experimenting with transnational operations. Sinochem was also to widen the scope of its business to include financing, transport, insurance, leasing, advertising, real estate and other services.[153] In 1988, the deals in oil futures already accounted for more than 10 per cent of the total business of Sinochem. Also in 1988, Sinochem bought half of the shares of the Pacific Oil Refining Company of the US Coast Company. In 1989, it purchased a phosphate fertiliser factory and a phosphorus mine in the United States and organised the US Agricultural Chemical Company. Sinochem also invested in oil fuelling companies in the form of joint ventures and cooperatives in Singapore, Hong Kong, the Netherlands and New Zealand. The shipping companies jointly and wholly owned overseas by Sinochem controlled ships which exceeded 1 million tons. Sinochem was also involved in financial dealings, making and guaranteeing loans, and handling foreign exchange transactions in support of large and medium-sized domestic projects. By 1990, there was considerable substance in Sinochem's claim to be a transnational corporation.[154] Its total turnover grew from $11.43 billion in 1990 to $15 billion in 1994, of which $7.8 billion was from its international operations.[155] In 1995, when Sinochem celebrated its forty-fifth anniversary, it had organised four overseas group companies – namely, Sinochem Hong Kong Group, Sinochem American Group, Sinochem Asian Group and Sinochem Australian and New Zealand Lief Group – and had more than 40 overseas subsidiaries.[156]

Two other examples of China's multinationals are worth mentioning as well. In early 1988, China International Trust and Investment Corporation (CITIC) extended its operations to Australia. Together with China Non-ferrous Metal Industrial Company, it invested over $100 million in the establishment of the Portland Aluminium Plant in Australia.[157] Before that, in 1986, CITIC had already bought 50 per cent of Celgar Pulpmill in Canada.[158] Today, CITIC has significant investment in most Asia-Pacific economies from Alaska to Australia.

The transnational operation of a Chinese manufacturing conglomerate through FDI finds its best example in Shougang (sometimes translated as Capital Steel). In 1988, Shougang bought 70 per cent of Masta Engineering, an American designer and maker of metallurgical equipment. By early 1992, Shougang already had 18 joint ventures overseas with total assets of more than $120 million.[159] In December 1992, Shougang outbid a Japanese-Mexican-Chilean consortium and bought Peru's leading iron-and-steel complex, Hierroperu. With the $312 million purchase, Shougang became the second largest investor in Peru.[160] Earlier, in November 1992, it had bought the Second California Steel Plant lock, stock and barrel.[161] At the same time, it significantly expanded its operations in Hong Kong.[162]

The growth of China's multinationals and investment associated with such growth may account for part of the unrecorded capital outflow. However, it is perhaps China's purchase of foreign bonds and stocks that are most significantly under-represented in the official statistics. By the end of 1992, for example, China's total investment in US bonds had risen to a gross value of $3.4 billion. China reportedly bought $490 million US treasury bonds and $700 million enterprise bonds in 1992 alone.[163] In early 1997, China's *Guoji Jingrong Xinxi Bao* (International Financial News) reported that according to the statistics published by the Treasury of the United States, from September 1995 to September 1996, China's purchase of American stocks, bonds and other securities reached

$12.1 billion, more than Japan's purchase of $11.6 billion.[164] A significant portion of China's unrecorded capital outflow could have been channelled through into such investment overseas. Regardless of how and how much we can account for China's unrecorded capital outflow, billions of dollars of Chinese capital are wandering in the global capital markets, which is in itself significant in impacting on and integrating Chinese economy.

FROM IMF TO GATT AND APEC

The third aspect of our examination, and arguably the most crucial in China's integration into the international economic order, is China's participation in the common economic institutions of the society of states. This is principally for two reasons. One is that China's share of the work of common economic institutions discussed below involves China deeply in multilateralism. The other is that China's participation in these institutions not only tests the willingness of China to comply with norms and accepted standards; it also contests the will of international society to embrace China. Therefore, China's participation in international economic institutions, global as well as regional, is not only a matter of China's integration into the world economy but also an issue of China's socialisation in international society.

China's participation in the key international economic institutions was only recent. It first took place in 1980, after almost a decade of the PRC's membership in the UN. In the short period of China's participation in the 1980s and the 1990s, there was some degree of success in the mutual embrace between China and the international economic institutions and, at the same time, the gruelling experience of a certain amount of mutual ambivalence and frustration. The conspicuous and curious paradox is that China, one of the major trading nations in the world today, is yet to be granted full membership in the global trading organisation, the newly established World Trade Organisation (WTO), which has now incorporated the General Agreement on Tariffs and Trade (GATT). Beijing has been, as it were, kept at bay.[165] In other words, Beijing has got just one foot in what we may call international economic society, thus being granted only partial membership in that society.

As discussed previously in this chapter, the trade nexus and China's engagement with global capital markets have created an economically binding relationship between China and other members of international society. The sustained growth of China's foreign trade in the last 18 years, on the other hand, owes a great deal to China's unprecedented and increasingly intensive participation in the three principal multilateral economic institutions: the International Monetary Fund, the International Bank for Reconstruction and Development (IBRD, or the World Bank) and the GATT. Although these three institutions were created and designed to provide 'coherence and stability to the international monetary, financial and commercial systems',[166] China's participation in them has, by and large, helped to maintain the outward orientation of China's economic development and provided necessary, albeit still limited, institutions for China's continuous policy coordination with other economies. Sustained contacts with international economic institutions through this participation have also modified China's outlook of the existing international economic order and altered the Chinese perception of their own economic performance. A constant and steady flow of information about the world economy through these contacts has fed into China's economic decision-making process. China's international political and economic policies have clearly indicated, and increasingly so, a preference of evolutionary to revolutionary changes in the existing international economic system. China's share of these common international economic institutions in the last 18 years, therefore, not only contributes to but also itself constitutes a process in China's integration into the international economy.

Participation in and the evolving relationship with the international economic institutions, however, entails compliance with the requirements and regulations of these institutions, which in turn dictates changes, sometimes fundamental, in domestic economic structures, policy processes, and commercial practices in order to ensure that compliance. This is particularly true in the case of China in view of the nature of its economy prior to its participation. Reforms of China's domestic economic institutions have been partly designed and carried out in response to this requirement. These reforms, no less than China's participation *per se* in the international economic organisations, have contributed to making China an integral part of the international economy.

Participation in the IMF and the World Bank

Until the late 1970s, China had shunned any official connections with the principal international economic organisations. The first official Chinese initiative in approaching an international organisation for economic assistance took place only in 1978, when China formally applied for some technical assistance from the United Nations Development Programme.[167] It was not until 1980, after the normalisation of Sino–American relations, that China applied for and resumed its membership in the IMF and the World Bank. This was the beginning of China's participation in the international economic organisations. China's preparations for the membership of these two organisations and its participation in the first few years have been well studied elsewhere.[168] Suffice it here briefly to make two main points relevant to our inquiry.

First, Chinese participation is significant because it was the first time that China was involved with the post-war international economic organisations. While the participation entailed very few preconditions, it yielded for China valuable political and economic benefits. In the political battle, the expulsion of Taiwan from the IMF and the World Bank was a victory in the zero-sum game for the PRC. Its membership in these organisations enhanced the PRC's claim to be the only legitimate government of China. Economically, it made readily available to China facilities such as World Bank loans and IMF Special Drawing Rights to assist China's economic development. Although Chinese officials claimed that China's principal and primary consideration for joining the IMF and the World Bank in 1980 was political, Deng was said to have told Robert McNamara in April 1980 that 'We are very poor. We have lost touch with the world. We need the World Bank to catch up.'[169] Certainly, after joining the World Bank and the IMF, China did not hesitate to cultivate the use of these facilities as much as it could. World Bank loans and credits have played a very important and complementary role in developing, in particular, China's transport, telecommunications and energy industries.[170] As mentioned earlier, by the end of 1995, World Bank commitments to China exceeded $23 billion, with about 63 per cent of loans and 37 per cent of International Development Agency credits.[171] China has also frequently used its SDR and other IMF facilities to balance its current account trade deficit.[172]

This is by no means to say that mutual accommodation in the participation process between China and these two international economic organisations has been easy. China's grudging and reluctant release of data related to its economic performance even to the IMF and the World Bank is a good example of the difficulties. The opposition voiced by the US Secretary of the Treasury in 1980 against incorporating China into the IMF and the World Bank underscored the other dimension of the problem. The success of China's incorporation into these two organisations, as argued by Jacobson and Oksenberg, is due as much to the 'foresight, maturity, and sensitivity' of both China and the two organisations in approaching each other as to the 'alacrity' with which the leadership of both the IMF and the World Bank responded to the opportunity to work with China.[173]

Second, China's membership opened the Chinese economy for evaluation by Western economists. To comply with the requirements of the IMF and the World Bank for member states, China released, though sometimes grudgingly and sometimes reluctantly, more and more economic statistics. More important, perhaps, is the fact that China has been 'converted' to compiling its economic data according to international practices. Partly to comply with the requirements of the IMF and the World Bank and partly to facilitate the comparison of its economy with other developing economies, China has gradually adopted the universal standard of measurements to evaluate itself and describe itself to the outside world. The Chinese economic system has been therefore made more transparent. Membership also opened the possibility of the IMF and the World Bank's involvement in China's economic policy making and implementation. The World Bank reports about the Chinese economy, for example, have been not only circulated widely among the Chinese leadership but also actively sought after by Chinese economists. It has been claimed even that the second World Bank comprehensive report on the Chinese economy, entitled *China: Long Term Development Issues and Options* (1985), affected the direction and pace of China's development strategy in its Seventh Five-Year Plan. While this claim has never been substantiated, it can hardly be denied that policy recommendations contained in this report did have some influence in formulating China's economic development programme in the Seventh Five-Year Plan period. The fact that opinions expressed in the World Bank report converged with China's proposed reform programme certainly reinforced the position of the Chinese leadership committed to reforms.[174] On the other hand, as a member of the IMF, China had certain commitments to fulfil in formulating its exchange-rate policies under Articles VIII and XIV of the IMF Articles of Agreement. As it is accepted that the IMF exercises a general role in the surveillance of its members' exchange-rate policies, it was sought out by the Chinese government for consultations and technical advice on the devaluation of the RMB, for example, in 1986 and for further adjustments to the exchange rate.[175] The IMF's involvement could also be seen in its encouraging China's increases in the domestic interest rate and its management of financial data. Top officials in the World Bank Resident Mission in China also enjoyed special access to the Chinese leadership in the 1980s.

It is beyond doubt that in the process of China's integration into the world economy, China's membership in both the IMF and the World Bank is as essential as the two agencies' involvement in China's development process. China's commitment to participating in these two economic institutions was as important and indispensable a factor as the two organisations' determination to embrace China in their mutual engagement. It should also be made clear, however, that the success story of China's engagement with these two international economic organisations owes a great deal to the fact that China's participation entailed only very limited, although sometimes important, immediate changes in China's existing economic institutional landscape. It is true that new divisions and departments were created in three ministerial level bodies – the MOFERT, the Ministry of Finance, and the People's Bank of China – in dealing in particular with the IMF and the World Bank and its affiliated agencies, notably the International Development Agency and the International Finance Corporation (IFC).[176] It is also true that many other commissions and ministries – for example, the State Education Commission and the Ministry of Commerce as chief beneficiaries of the World Bank loans – also created within their departments of international cooperation a special section to handle the liaison and communication with the World Bank on project planning, allocation of loans and other matters. Nevertheless, these changes were only additional to, not destructive of, the existing institutional landscape. None of these changes touched the essence of China's foreign trade regimes and institutions, which were totally incompatible with accepted international practices at the beginning of the 1980s. It was only when China began to bid for its membership of the GATT that sweeping and very often revolutionary changes in its foreign trade system were dictated.

The bid for GATT/WTO membership

China's membership of the IMF and the World Bank and its bid for its membership of the GATT presented China with similar questions yet different requirements in the process of integration into the international economy. The questions posed were similar because they were all related to how and how much China should participate in the working of these common international economic institutions. The requirements were different in the sense that China's membership in the IMF and the World Bank entailed only comparatively minor institutional changes, not as a precondition for, but as a possible sequence of, China's participation. China's bid for GATT membership, on the other hand, was predicated upon the compatibility of China's trade regimes with those of GATT norms and standards. That is to say, given the nature of China's existing economic institutions, wide-ranging and radical reforms, in particular of China's foreign trade system, were a precondition for China's full participation in the GATT. In other words, China must make its foreign trade system conform to standard international practices before it can be fully accepted into the GATT system. It must be remembered that 'the underlying rules of international economic conduct grow out of the European and American experience'.[177] Therefore, China's reforms to foreign trade system have in fact been conducted to comply with those rules, made, interpreted and implemented in the first instance by the West. It is in this process that partial institutional convergence of China's trade regimes with those of the wider world has been realised.

It is often overlooked that the reform to China's foreign trade system was one of the first reforms initiated after the formulation of the *Kaifang* policy at the end of 1978. It was certainly as early as, if not earlier than, the agricultural reform. The first series of reforms were started in 1979. The promulgation of the Law of the PRC on Joint Ventures with Chinese and Foreign Investment on 8 July 1979 by the State Council amounted to the first assault on the traditional trade system. Joint ventures were to open new channels of import and export for China. Structural changes in China's foreign trade were also to be effected with the introduction of export processing and compensation trade.

No less important, however, was the relinquishment of the monopoly of foreign trade by the central government. China's traditional foreign trade system, established after 1949 and consolidated in the mid-1950s, was highly centralised. Some 12 national import and export corporations monopolised all foreign trade transactions under a central plan. Naturally, the reform of such a system in 1979 started with the decentralisation of foreign trade authorities. The proliferation of foreign trade agencies followed. In just a little over a year, around 800 foreign trade corporations had been created by mid-1981. Many ministries, and almost all provinces, autonomous regions and municipalities rushed to set up their own foreign trade companies.[178] About a hundred large-scale enterprises were also permitted to set up their own foreign trade companies.[179] Special policies had been formulated to grant two provinces, Guangdong and Fujian, extensive authority to conduct their foreign economic relations.[180] The establishment in 1980 of four Special Economic Zones along the coast – Shenzhen, Zhuhai, Xiamen and Shantou – further battered the traditional trade system. By the end of August 1984, all the 29 provinces, municipalities and autonomous regions had been granted authority to conduct foreign trade on their own.[181]

Another reform measure – the implementation of the agency system in export and import, which was launched in 1984 – however, achieved mixed results. Largely because of the domestic price distortions and the overvaluation of the RMB, most procurement for export continued to be made by foreign trade corporations on their own account at domestic prices, as had been done before. The World Bank study of China's reformed trade system in 1986 concluded that, 'despite the apparently wide-ranging reforms that have been announced and implemented in the trade sector, we find an export system that retains many of the features of the pre-1978 system, albeit at a much less centralised level'.[182] The same study found, however, that the agency system was 'well established in the import sector' and '90 per cent of imports have been done on the agency basis'.[183] As part of the reform of China's trade regimes, in April 1985 the State Council approved in principle a system of tax rebates to manufacturers and producers for exported goods.[184]

Reform of the foreign trade system was accompanied by a number of adjustments of macro-economic policies affecting foreign trade. In January 1981, an internal settlement rate of 2.8 yuan to $1 was introduced for all foreign trade transactions.[185] In 1982, the State Council reshaped the foreign exchange retention system first introduced in 1979.[186] A new tariff system was put into effect in 1985, when, on 15 March, two regulations on tariff were approved by the State Council and were published. 'Regulations for Import and Export Tariffs of the PRC' laid down the rules and regulations governing the formulation of tax policy and tax rates as well as the administration of the tariff system. 'Import and Export Customs Tariff of the PRC' established the new schedule for reduced import tariffs and export taxes. In July 1985, the Chinese government also introduced the 'regulatory tariff' as a temporary surcharge on imports.[187] The World Bank study in 1986 concluded that in comparison with 12 other developing countries, 'China's structure of import duties is not unusual'. With a mean duty rate of the whole economy at 38.4 per cent in 1986, China's rate was 'comparable to that in lower middle-income countries such as Ecuador, Thailand, and Turkey'.[188]

These reforms had significantly modified, if not yet totally transformed, the old foreign trade system in China. Trade – in particular, export – expanded quickly; efficiency in foreign trade was improved; centralised control was drastically reduced; and trade channels were diversified. The success was, nevertheless, limited. The reforms of China's foreign trade system so far were piecemeal, haphazard, and of an experimental nature. Wide-ranged decentralisation of foreign trade authorities was effective. But there were no other fundamental structural reforms of the trade system. Macro-economic policies – particularly the foreign exchange system and the pricing mechanisms – remained unchanged, apart from some minor adjustments. The state continued to subsidise the losses of a large number of exported products. The foreign trade plan remained central to China's trade regime. Centralised control was still in place. For example, trade in what were classified as Category One goods was still monopolised by national foreign trade corporations under central control, and that of Category Two by these corporations and their provincial subsidiaries. In a word, the old system of state trading persisted. Zheng

Tuobin, Minister of the MOFERT, admitted in 1987 that in spite of reforms, the 'main maladies of the old system are still largely intact'.[189]

The trade system reforms up to 1986, it is right to argue, were not geared to obtain China's membership in the GATT. As one important component of China's economic reform, the main purpose of the trade system reform, like that of the other reforms of the whole economic system in China, was to 'invigorate the enterprises', to 'increase the efficiency of the system', 'to establish a dynamic economic structure' and 'to promote China's participation in the international division of labour', as clearly specified in the CCP Central Committee's decision in September 1984 on reforming China's economic structure.[190] The goals of reforming China's foreign trade administration, Susan Shirk argues, 'were to increase the volume of trade, particularly exports, while reducing the government's financial burden from trade'.[191] Even China's application in 1983 for membership in the Multifibre Agreement (MFA) of the GATT was aimed principally at protecting China's interests in exporting its textile products.[192] None of these reforms, it was true, was explicitly aimed at fulfilling any requirements stipulated by the GATT. Neither should there be any doubt that the Chinese trade regimes and institutions as they stood at the time were grossly incompatible with the GATT code.

Nevertheless, these reforms did begin to transform the structure of the trade system and were to change the nature of China's trade regimes. The decentralisation of trade authorities, the diminution of the role of the trade plan and the implementation of the import and export agency system had begun to dismantle China's traditional trade system. They also started to convert China's trade regimes and institutions to becoming more conformable to international norms. Moreover, the emphasis on the function of tariffs, the introduction of domestic tax rebates for exported goods, and the new exchange rate policy – all signalled China's intention to use increasingly economic levers to replace administrative means in guiding China's foreign trade.[193] These are compatible with GATT practices. As China's memorandum for its application for GATT membership in 1986 would eventually argue, with the economic reform since 1978, 'China has been witnessing a transition from the traditional system of a central planning economy to a new system of the planned commodity economy', and a convergence of China's trade regimes and institutions with those of the GATT stipulations was already taking place.[194]

China's application to resume its membership in the GATT submitted in July 1986 was claimed to be 'a significant step towards further opening China to the outside world' and to signal 'China's willingness to enter into

Economic Integration 233

the international market and participate in international division of labour and international competition in a more positive and more active manner'.[195] The submission of the application, at the same time, made it imperative for China to orientate its trade system reforms towards meeting the GATT norms. If, prior to 1986, the reforms of China's trade system and the adjustments of its macro-economic policies were not geared to meet the GATT requirements, after July 1986, to comply with the GATT norms became one of the explicitly stated goals of the trade system reforms. China's trade regimes and institutions were now frequently evaluated against the GATT code and regulations. For example, it was argued that China's existing import licensing system must be so reformed as to make it compatible with the GATT norms. That would eliminate one of the main obstacles to China's full participation in the GATT.[196]

The pace and momentum of China's economic reforms in the late 1980s were particularly conducive to the reforms of China's foreign trade system. The domestic political climate meanwhile encouraged lively discussions about China's trade reforms and its bid for GATT membership. It was argued not only that China should 'deepen the reform of the foreign trade system in accordance with the GATT requirements',[197] but also that the basic principles of the GATT should 'guide the reform of China's foreign trade system' and that China's trade system should be reshaped and readjusted as much as possible to conform to the GATT standard'.[198] To overcome the obstacles of China's admission to the GATT should become the motivation for all reform activities. In negotiating China's 'ticket of admission', China should 'strengthen the role of tariffs in regulating export and import and be prepared to reduce the tariffs'. China's tax system should be 'totally overhauled' and 'a single system of value added tax should be introduced and implemented' in conformity with the accepted international practices. Export subsidies, if any, should be rationalised within the framework of GATT provisions allowing export subsidies by developing countries for their economic development. The administration of the subsidies should be reformed. The transparency of China's trade regimes and trade system should be enhanced. Even the export and import licensing systems should be so modified as to be explicable within the framework of the GATT. Any protection measures, such as the non-tariff barriers, should only be employed on the condition that they were not in violation of GATT rules.[199] In a word, any regulatory instruments in China's foreign trade must be as consistent with GATT norms as possible. This amounts to a public call for the sweeping and substantial reform of China's trade regimes so as to achieve a higher degree of GATT compatibility, which would, the Chinese were convinced, ensure China's re-entry into the multilateral trade system. GATT norms and standards began guiding the foreign trade reforms in China.

Accordingly, in the late 1980s, the foreign trade plan continued to undergo changes. It was estimated that, in 1986, 70 to 80 per cent of exports were covered by the export plan, 70 per cent of which was command planning.[200] By 1988, the share of planned exports fell to 45 per cent.[201] The import plan went through more radical reforms. In 1986, only seven key raw materials considered essential to national economic development were still within the command plan.[202] Like the domestic economy as a whole, foreign trade was also, to quote Barry Naughton, 'growing out of the plan'.[203] Moreover, the call for the deep structural reform of China's trade system led to the experiment of a contract system in foreign trade, notably in light industry, arts and crafts, and the garments industries in 1988. The contract system was aimed at making the foreign trade enterprises more responsive to market forces by making them responsible for their own losses and profits.[204] This was the beginning of the end of state subsidies of foreign trade, thus the retreat of the state from trade. The system of contractual responsibility for trade was eventually implemented nation-wide in 1991. State subsidies for exports were abolished in 1993.

At the same time, foreign exchange control was further relaxed and rationalised. The RMB was devalued in 1986 (by 15.6 per cent) and in 1988 (by 9.5 per cent), although the RMB was not brought entirely in line with its real value on the international market. As a complementary measure to the experiment of the contract responsibility system, foreign exchange retention rights were allowed now be both sold and bought in the Foreign Exchange Swap Centres around the country, the first of which was established in Shenzhen in 1985, followed by that in Shanghai in 1986.[205] As early as 1988, there were 39 Foreign Exchange Swap Centres across China. The annual transaction volume of the year was $6.264 billion.[206]

After the submission of a memorandum of its foreign trade system to the GATT, China moved quickly to provide answers to more than 2000 probing questions raised by the contracting parties of the GATT with regard to China's trade practices. In the18 months from October 1987 to April 1989, all the questions were answered. The fact-finding phase was almost completed, and China was prepared to enter into actual negotiations on the terms of its protocol of resumption when the negotiations were suspended following the Tiananmen tragedy in June 1989 in Beijing.[207]

The political setback in China in 1989 held the momentum but did not altogether stop economic reforms in China. Nicholas Lardy observed that

'China's foreign trade reforms by no means floundered after mid-1989'.[208] For example, the RMB was devalued twice within the space of a year. On 15 December 1989 and on 17 November 1990, it was devalued 21.2 per cent and 9.6 per cent respectively. This was partly an attempt to abolish export subsidies by making the exchange rate approach the real value of the RMB. As one study speculated, 'One main consideration in the decision to axe the subsidies must be China's determination to become a contracting party to the General Agreement on Tariffs and Trade.'[209]

In 1991 'the second round and deeper structural reform of the foreign trade system' came into full force. A system of foreign trade contractual responsibility, which had been experimented with since 1988, was implemented nation-wide in China. Trading of foreign exchange on the swap markets was further liberalised. By the end of 1991, reforms resulted in the elimination of state-granted export subsidies.[210] Wu Yi, Vice-Minister of the MOFERT, claimed in a ministerial bulletin:

> The current reform marks a very important turning point in China's foreign trade system .... Reliance on the use of macro-economic leverages such as tariff rate, foreign exchange rate, etc., to regulate foreign trade has been emphasised, enhancing the role of market regulation and making China's foreign trade system more compatible with the international trade norms and rules, thus facilitating China's participation in international cooperation and labour division.[211]

Li Lanqing, Minister of MOFERT, also claimed that reforms in 1991 'brought China's trade institutions further in line with the accepted international regimes'.[212]

Even before the Working Party on China's Status at the GATT resumed its deliberations on China's application on 13 February 1992,[213] China took further steps to reduce both tariff and non-tariff barriers in its trade regimes. At the end of 1991, China announced unilateral reductions of tariffs for 225 commodities, which came into effect from 1 January 1992.[214] From October 1991 to February 1992, the Chinese government annulled 122 internally circulated (*Neibu*) documents regulating China's foreign trade and published another 48 which were to remain valid.[215] By February 1992, China has provided to the GATT Secretariat the English version of 21 of those valid, internally circulated documents. At the tenth meeting of the China Working Party on 13 February 1992, Tong Zhiguang, head of the Chinese delegation, promised to submit to the GATT in six months' time the English version of the other 17 which had already been published in *Guoji Shangbao* (International Business

Journal) in China.²¹⁶ The import regulatory tax, on the other hand, was abolished on 1 April 1992. While streamlining the import licensing system, China promised to revoke two-thirds of its import licences in two years' time. China also indicated its willingness to sign some individual GATT codes formulated during the Tokyo Round.²¹⁷ At the end of 1992, China again reduced the import tariffs for 3 371 products.²¹⁸ China also reached an agreement with the United States on market access in 1992.

Further trade liberalisation and transparency measures have been taken with the promulgation of China's first Foreign Trade Law in 1994 and the unified exchange rate of the RMB, also in 1994. China at the same time pledged to realise RMB convertibility in its current account as soon as feasible. Such liberalisation of China's trade regimes are undoubtedly guided by requests of GATT contracting parties and aimed specifically at complying with what Arthur Dunkel called 'the rules of the game of international trade'.²¹⁹

Given that 'in broad terms, the Chinese trade regime is as open as that of some GATT members', what then are the obstacles standing in the way of China's bid for GATT/WTO membership?²²⁰ Although the Tiananmen incident in 1989 did not completely stop China's economic reforms, it nevertheless represented a great setback to China's socialisation into international society. It affected China's bid for membership not only because it led to the suspension of the negotiations; equally importantly, it dented irreparably the goodwill of the international community in considering sympathetically China's application to resume its membership in the GATT. Many members, for example, would no longer be prepared to give the benefit of the doubt to many areas of China's commercial practices which were serious concerns for them.²²¹ The onset of the post-Cold War era also brought with it changing expectations and demands regarding China's behaviour in international economic organisations. Unlike in the 1980s, few key member countries would be prepared to accept trajectory projection of China's economic reforms. Most GATT members of the West, particularly the United States, now insist that China fulfil its GATT obligations before joining. Such 'deeper integration' issues as the protection of intellectual property rights, introduced only after the Uruguay Round, further complicated the negotiations between Chinese and GATT contracting parties.²²²

It is increasingly clear in the 1990s that the question of China's GATT membership is no longer just a matter of complying with GATT norms. It has been argued that 'the more significant problems of [China's] admission to GATT are political, not economic, in nature.'²²³ The Chinese themselves also pointed out that the GATT is not only a multilateral trading system. It is also the locus of international political and diplomatic battles. The GATT activities are accordingly not only governed by the economic and trade elements. The negotiations for China's entry is no exception.'[224]

The politicisation of China's application to enter the GATT/WTO can be seen principally in the following two respects. First, the consideration of China's membership in the global trading system, either in the GATT or the WTO, is increasingly associated with China's future role in the post-Cold War international order. In the 1980s, political and strategic imperatives seemed to have overshadowed considerations of possible economic disruption of the global trading system resulting from China's entry. That had resulted in a generally sympathetic and favourable attitude towards China's application. In the 1990s, however, there are a completely different set of perceptions. China's strategic importance seems to have declined in the post-Cold War era. The reformist Communist China of the 1980s becomes the last Leninist state in the 1990s. China's existing political system stands against world-wide democratisation. It is therefore not surprising that speculations and calculation of economic consequences of China's joining the global trading system have been associated with the assumptions of China's growing power and China's intentions regarding the use of that power. Lardy subtly alluded to the political problem of China's entry into GATT when he remarked that

> It is likely that if China were an average-size, low-income developing country with modest exports to market economies, comparable to, say, Polish exports of just under $1 billion at the time of its accession in 1967, it would have been admitted to the GATT some years ago.

Second, from the Chinese perspective, China's entry into the GATT/WTO has also become a political battle. Taiwan's application to enter the GATT in 1990 introduced an element of cross-strait rivalry into the politics of the global trading system. Although China is not adamantly against Taiwan's entry, it does insist that China, as the original contracting party of the GATT, should rejoin the GATT first. Further, as the drama of the renewal of China's Most Favoured Nation (MFN) status evolves in American politics, China increasingly sees its membership in the GATT as a possible permanent solution to the perennial problem, although as Shirk argues, this may not be the case.[225] China's efforts to enter the GATT/WTO have also been perceived as a 'scramble for status'. For China, membership in the so-called 'Economic United Nations', either the

GATT or the WTO, is a matter of prestige for a increasingly powerful nation. The waxing and waning of Sino–US relations has further exacerbated the politicisation of China's bid for GATT/WTO membership. While the United States negotiators manifested recalcitrance to compromise, a popular perception in China is that the United States is constantly moving the goal posts so as to block China's entry, and that such recalcitrance is a component of American containment strategy against China.[226]

More than a decade of negotiations for China's admission to the GATT/WTO has already come down in the history of the GATT as the longest saga of negotiations of any member states seeking GATT membership. Yet China's return to the GATT and its joining the WTO seem not to be substantially closer than they were ten years ago. The negotiations for China's joining the GATT/WTO have long gone beyond trade diplomacy. The rich empirical evidence of the period does suggest, however, that China, a revolutionary state committed to economic reforms, has come to accept and adopt common institutions in the international economy. Furthermore, it provides some possible explanations as to why and how China has been motivated to reform its economic institutions to conform to the international norms and standards. It also clearly demonstrates that China's participation in multilateralism is more than just a matter of its integration into international economic institutions. The experience of China's participation in the IMF and the World Bank and of its bid for GATT/WTO membership reflects the crucial role that the political will of other member states plays in socialising China into any system of multilateral cooperation.

China and APEC

In contrast to China's bid for GATT/WTO membership, its participation in Asia Pacific Economic Cooperation (APEC) tells a different story. APEC is today the most prominent regional international economic institution in Asia Pacific. As a multilateral forum on regional economic cooperation and trade liberalisation, it is still an infant. Formally launched in November 1989 in Canberra, Australia, APEC has, however, grown from an informal dialogue between 12 Pacific economies to a major regional institution for promoting open trade and practical economic cooperation. Its current 18 economies are committed to maintaining an open multilateral trading system, facilitating economic liberalisation and to the eventual realisation of free trade and investment in the region.

China was among the first group of countries in Asia Pacific which Australia had approached to establish APEC in early 1989. In a recent study, Chinese scholars claim that, 'as early as when the idea of founding an APEC was being considered, China showed a positive attitude and supported ex-Prime Minister Bob Hawke of Australia in his initiative to establish an inter-governmental cooperative mechanism for the Asia-Pacific region'.[227] Indeed, when Richard Woolcott visited Beijing in May 1989 to broach Bob Hawke's idea of APEC with the Chinese leaders, these leaders, including Li Peng, 'expressed sincere interest in the concept' in the midst of the boiling political crisis in Beijing. China's support, as in many other international forums, was however dogged by the problem of Taiwan's participation. Li Peng is reportedly said to have told Woolcott that 'only sovereign states had ministers, therefore by definition Hong Kong and Taiwan should be excluded'.[228]

China was conspicuously absent from the launch of APEC in Canberra in November 1989 for a number of reasons. First, in the aftermath of the Tiananmen tragedy of June 1989, Australia, the host country of the first APEC ministerial meeting, suspended its high-level contract with China.[229] Second, the problems of Taiwan's representation were not resolved during Woolcott's visit to Beijing in May 1989; and China would not participate before a satisfactory formula was found. Third, the ASEAN nations, the United States and Japan all had reservations as to how and when to include all three economies of Greater China, although Bob Hawke argued that leaving China out of APEC was 'like getting married without having a bride'.[230] It was not until November 1991 that the 'bride', together with Taiwan and Hong Kong, was accepted at the third APEC ministerial meeting in Seoul, Korea.

China's initial participation in APEC in 1991 was probably more motivated by political and diplomatic considerations than by economic calculations. In 1991, the sanctions imposed on China by most Western countries in the wake of the Tiananmen tragedy were still largely in place. The suspension of high-level contacts with most Western countries, particularly the United States, was still in effect. China was anxious to break its political and economic isolation. Participation at the APEC ministerial meeting provided an opportunity for China to restore and establish ministerial-level contacts with in particular, the United States, Australia and Japan. It was at Seoul that Vice-Premier and Foreign Minister Qian Qichen met the American Secretary of State, James Baker, re-establishing official ministerial contact between China and the United States absent since June 1989. Diplomatically, a formula acceptable to both China and Taiwan was hammered out through diligent diplomacy in the months leading to the Seoul meeting.[231] Three economies of Greater China were welcomed to APEC in November 1991, with Taiwan joining as Chinese Taipei.[232] China's attendance of APEC in Seoul also opened a new channel for direct contact between the foreign ministers of China and Korea, which facilitated negotiations between the two countries for mutual recognition and for establishing the formal diplomatic relations already under discussion. Less than one year later, China established diplomatic relations with South Korea.

That China's participation in APEC clearly fulfils a political function could also be seen in the Chinese President Jiang Zemin's meeting with President Bill Clinton at the first informal meeting of APEC leaders in Seattle in November 1993. The United States was the host country of the fifth APEC ministerial meeting in 1993. As president of the host country, Bill Clinton called for an informal meeting of leaders of APEC members. Clinton's initiative created the first opportunity since 1989, and certainly an unanticipated one, for Jiang Zemin to go to the United States and meet Clinton in a more cooperative and less confrontational atmosphere. The Jiang-Clinton meeting, one Chinese scholar observed, 'broke the deadlock in the relations [between China and the United States] since 1989, and ended a dangerous period of possible confrontation of national interests between the two countries'.[233] The Chinese press reports of the Jiang-Clinton summit meeting clearly, probably also naturally, overshadowed the importance of the first APEC leaders' meeting on their commitment to free trade and open economies.[234]

It is equally clear that China's participation in APEC has been frequently looked upon as a vehicle to propel China's entry into the GATT/WTO. China's active participation in APEC has, it is argued, 'created favourable conditions and environments for her attempt to join the WTO'.[235]

However, APEC is first and foremost a regional economic institution committed to trade and investment liberalisation and economic and technical cooperation in the region. China's involvement and participation in such an international economic institution in the last five years have therefore integrated China into the APEC process and induced it to make a firmer commitment to APEC principles and basic objectives. China has also been made fully aware of the benefits and difficulties of its participation in APEC.

China's involvement and participation in APEC process is comprehensive. President Jiang Zemin himself has attended all four APEC leaders' meetings since 1993. China has not only participated in but also hosted some APEC ministerial meetings and Senior Official Meetings (SOM) in the last few years. Equally importantly, Chinese entrepreneurs and economists have participated in the Eminent Persons Group (EPG) as well as the newly created APEC Business Advisory Council (ABAC). Like other APEC members, China has established its own national APEC Studies Centre at Nankai University and APEC Policy Research Centre at the

Chinese Academy of Social Sciences in Beijing to conduct intellectual networking for the purpose of consultations and research on APEC. China also hosted the 11th Congress of the Pacific Economic Cooperation Council (PECC) in Beijing in September 1995.[236]

China's involvement and participation has followed, and probably also helped formulate, the so-called 'APEC approach', which includes recognition of diversity, emphasis on flexibility, gradual progress and openness, mutual respect, equality, mutual benefit, consensus through consultation and voluntarism. This involvement and participation entails China's commitment to the overall principles and objectives of APEC, including open regionalism and free trade and investment. China agreed to the vision of wider economic liberalisation at Seattle. It adopted the Bogor Declaration of Common Resolve in 1994, thus committing China to free trade and investment by the year 2020. In 1995, China embraced the Osaka Action Agenda for trade and investment liberalisation. It was at the Osaka informal leaders' meeting that Jiang Zemin surprised his counterparts in announcing that China would reduce its import tariffs on more than 4000 items by at least 30 per cent, effective from 1996. In its efforts to implement the Osaka Action Agenda, China also announced that it would scrap tariff quotas and import control measures for more than 170 categories of products and committed itself to making its current account of RMB fully convertible in the near future.[237] By 1 April 1996, import duties of more than 4900 tariff items were significantly reduced. China's average tariff level dropped from 35.9 to 23 per cent, equal to a total reduction of a 36 per cent tariff.[238] As was announced by President Jiang Zemin at the Manila meeting of APEC leaders in November 1996, China submitted its Individual Action Plan on Trade and Investment Liberalisation on schedule for the implementation of the Osaka Action Agenda.[239] The APEC process therefore has induced as well as compelled China to make commitments that in another context China would not necessarily be expected to have done. It has thus facilitated the liberalisation of China's trade and investment regimes which otherwise could not have been done so effectively in such a short time.

China seems to have settled in well in APEC. Its participation has neither led to politicisation of APEC nor swamped APEC process, as has been feared. Challenges to APEC, however, should not be underestimated. The APEC process itself is fraught with difficulties. For one thing, coordination of the so-called 'concerted unilateralism' in trade liberalisation, central to attaining APEC goal, is extremely difficult, if not impossible. For another, voluntary implementation of unilateral plan is especially vulnerable to political and economic conditions in individual countries, and any failure in implementation could delay, if not derail, APEC process. In addition, how and to what extent trade and investment liberalisation should be accompanied and complemented by economic and technical cooperation remains a subject of contention among APEC members.

China has participated in APEC not without misgivings. Rhetorical commitment to trade and investment liberalisation is one thing. To fulfil this commitment in so short a period of time as less than 25 years is quite another. Needless to say, China has such a long way to go in fully liberalising its trade and investment regimes that it cannot go too slowly. Going too fast, however, would not be in China's interest. Chinese economists have recently argued, for example, that some non-tariff measures have to be maintained for some time and that 'domestic monetary and insurance industries will be crushed by foreign firms unless there are selective, incremental measures of opening up'.[240] On the other hand, the reform of state-owned enterprises probably presents the single most daunting challenge to China's commitment to economic liberalisation by 2020. Unless and until this state economic institution is transformed so as to be compatible with international norms, liberalisation of the Chinese economy is impossible. However, such reform may result in millions of unemployed and generate such socio-economic disruptions that society itself may not be able to cope with them. The Chinese government does not seem to have a solution to this dilemma. In international forums, some Chinese scholars publicly expressed their concerns, arguing that 'a quicker pace is improper for [China's] trade and investment liberalisation in the latter half of the 1990s'.[241] Finally, although less so than in the fields of politics and security, China is still making a wary approach to multilateralism in international economic cooperation.

Conclusion

China's integration into the world economy today is unmistakable. The contrast between China in the world economy in 1979 and in 1997 cannot be more striking. The expansion of trade, the engagement with international capital and China's participation in international economic organisations discussed above are all unprecedented in Chinese economic history. Susan Shirk, among others, argues that this is China's 'successful shallow integration' with the world economy.[242] But behind this shallow integration is the fundamental transformation of China's domestic economic policies and institutions, and of its international economic behaviour and practice in the last 18 years. One can stress how substantially different some aspects of these remain from those in the developed market economies today as much as how surprisingly compatible and similar most of them have become.

Adam Watson argued recently that the international economic order is 'now more integrated, and more managed by an institutionalised directorate of economic great powers, than anything previously attempted by a society of politically independent states'. This, Watson further suggested, is 'an innovation of post-war international society'.[243] Therefore, it is of significance that since 1980 China has hardly asserted itself, either as a non-European nation, or as a revolutionary state of the recent past, to challenge the nature of that order and the continued dominance of the West in the world economy. Neither does it resemble many Third World countries as characterised by Miller as 'passive members of international society'.[244] What is most characteristic of China in the global economic order is not only its participation in that order, but also the institutional and policy changes it has initiated to adopt and observe rules, practices and principles of that order.

Conclusion: China in the Post-Cold War International Society

The central argument of this study is essentially a simple one. The international relations of the People's Republic of China is a saga of the isolation-alienation-socialisation-integration of China in international society since 1949. This saga is the continuation of a historical search by both China and the wider world for mutual accommodation. It is still unfolding. Hedley Bull once argued that international society is 'one of the basic elements at work in international politics'.[1] David Lampton remarked recently that 'a central difficulty in China's foreign relations has been that of reconciling the seeming imperatives of the international system with the Middle Kingdom's own traditions, self image and desire to modernise.'[2] An understanding of this evolving saga is, therefore, indispensable to our comprehension of China in world politics since 1949, and, more broadly, of what Fairbank calls 'the great Chinese revolution' in the last fifty years.[3]

I started this study by a historical survey of how the Chinese world order collapsed under the assault of the expansion of the European system of states in the second half of the nineteenth century and how China was first brought into the global international society dominated by European powers in the first half of the twentieth. The emergence of Revolutionary China with a Communist regime in 1949 presented a new challenge to an international society now divided by the Cold War.

For more than 20 years after 1949, China occupied an anomalous position in international society. What seemed to be China's relative isolation was in fact underlined by Revolutionary China's unqualified alienation from international society and by the denial of the international legitimacy of the PRC by a majority of the member states of international society. The total exclusion of the PRC from almost all international organisations and the non-recognition of the PRC by many states in the period were the hallmarks of mutual estrangement between the PRC and international society. As a revolutionary state, the PRC also set out to challenge the legitimacy of the international system in its own fashion. The frequent and uncompromising confrontations between China and the United States and, later, also the Soviet Union, were part of that challenge. The behaviour of the PRC in international relations during this period was that of an alienated power more than that of an isolated state.

The major concern of this study is, therefore, whether, how and to what extent China as a revolutionary power and an alienated state has gradually come to accept international society as it is conceptually, politically and economically in the 1980s and the 1990s and how China's foreign policy behaviour in this period has been affected by its alienation from and socialisation into international society. From this perspective, the Sino–American *rapprochement* in the early 1970s has much more profound political and strategic significance than transforming the international strategic milieu at the time. It embodies the changing nature of the international system wherein ideological considerations give way to geopolitical imperatives and which accordingly has become more inclusive of and accommodating to opposing interests of great powers. The mutual accommodation between China and the United States in such a changing international system is the beginning of the end of China's alienation from international society. Symbolically, the admission of the PRC into the United Nations and the UN Security Council marks the commencement of China's socialisation and integration into the society of states. In the mutual legitimation process in the 1970s, China swiftly effected the globalisation of its diplomacy, while the United Nations and many of its subsidiaries accommodated China with necessary adjustments but not major disruption.

Looking from today's perspective, the accommodation and socialisation of China, a revolutionary power and an alienated state, into global international society is surprisingly non-violent, and almost peaceful. The changing behaviour of China in international relations is, however, by no means insignificant. Changes in Chinese politics and society and transformations of its economy are exceptionally profound. Conceptually shaking off the Maoist legacy in its world outlook was the first step in China's changing perception of the nature of the contemporary international system. The emergence of China's independent foreign policy in the early 1980s was underpinned by and in turn reflected profound perceptual changes on the part of China of three sets of important institutions in international relations: war and peace; revolution and development; and dependence and inter-dependence. More significantly, China's perception of these key institutions in international relations is converging with that of other members of international society. China's socialisation into international society is predicated upon such convergence.

How, then, is China's international behaviour affected by its changing perception of and position in international society in the last two decades? This question is examined through the prism of China's political socialisation in international society by detailed studies of four controversial cases. The broad argument here is that China's international behaviour in all four areas have seen significant changes in the last 20 years. Further, for China, a revolutionary power and an alienated state of the recent past, political socialisation is a process whereby it learns to adapt itself and conform to the existing norms and rules universally accepted in international society. China's radical policy changes – from overhauling the CCP's inter-party relations, to participating in UN peacekeeping and to accepting multilateralism in international arms control – are part of the process. The pressures for China's political socialisation come from its aspiration to acquire full membership in international society as well as its desire to become an accountable great power in the contemporary international system. The limitations of China's political socialisation, particularly in the arms control and human rights fields, reflect its entrenched ambivalence towards its full integration into international society.

Finally, the integration of China into the world economy is striking and can be clearly defined and quantified. In spite of the lack of membership in the WTO, China's economic integration is now a less arguable aspect of China's integration into the global international society. As I have argued, this is particularly seen in the spectacular growth of China's foreign trade, its intensified activities on global capital markets as well as its participation in the global and regional economic organisations such as the IMF and APEC. It is clear that China, a society mobilised by revolution in the recent past, is now the one motivated by modernisation. China seems less ambivalent about its economic integration than its political socialisation into international society.

It would be too simplistic to say that this is just a story of China from alienation to integration in international society. Behind this story is China's tumultuous quest for its place in the ever-evolving international society since 1949. It could equally be seen as reactions and responses of international society to the emergence of a revolutionary China and to challenges posed by that revolution to international society. The process of mutual adaptation and accommodation is undoubtedly a lengthy and sometimes an agonising one. The exclusion of the PRC from the United Nations lasted for over 20 years, the bitter legacies of which could still be widely felt, for example, in China's scepticism of multilateral consultation and cooperation and collective diplomacy, particularly on political and security matters. The incorporation of China into international society since 1971, is in fact very recent. The incorporation has, however, created such imperatives and pressures for China to socialise itself in international society that by the early 1980s the revolutionary power of the 1970s became a reformist state. At the same time, China, a have-not nation not long before, acquired substantial stakes in the existing international order. Its confrontational approach to international relations was broadly replaced by its adaptation and conformation to accepted conventions governing international relations in the society of states. China has at the same time developed the widest possible involvement in both political and economic institutions of contemporary international society. International society inclusive of China, on the other hand, has not only obtained its universalism but also strengthened its legitimacy and resilience.

China's socialisation and integration into international society undoubtedly has its limitations, which should not be underestimated. The controversies over human rights questions, as I have argued earlier, reflect China's deeply held ambivalence towards its further integration into international society. Such campaigns as anti-bourgeois liberalisation and anti-spiritual pollution in the 1980s and the call for the building up of socialist spiritual civilisation in the 1990s in China's domestic politics are indications of China's misgivings about the impact on and implications for the Chinese society that further integration into international society might bring about. On the other hand, international society seems to have reciprocated ambivalence about further integrating China. This can be seen in the question of China's membership in the GATT/WTO.[4] It can also be seen in the recent debates, particularly in the United States on how to conduct constructive, conditional, and comprehensive and deep engagement of China and on whether and how to contain or to constrain China in the post-Cold War and the post-Communist international order.[5]

In the final analysis, however, China and international society are more mutually acceptable than ever before. Whatever the China challenge may be today, its nature is radically different from that when China was an alienated state. What is surprising is perhaps not the limitations of China's socialisation and integration but how much China has come to accept international society as is defined and continues to be redefined politically, economically, socially, diplomatically and strategically by the West. Even in post-Cold War international society where the West 'in effect is using international institutions, military power and economic resources to run the world in ways that will maintain Western predominance, protect Western interests and promote Western political and economic values',[6] China is seeking a reconciliation to this fact rather than outright challenge to this predominance.

In analysing China's international relations, the perspective of international society therefore provides compelling explanations for China's otherwise seemingly unstable, erratic, unpredictable and changeable behaviour regarding international and foreign policy. As I have argued in this study, China's major foreign policy shifts and thrusts – from its deadly confrontations with the United States to the Sino-Soviet split in the 1950s and the 1960s, and from the Sino–American *rapprochement* to the emergence of China's independent foreign policy of peace in the 1970s and the 1980s – can in fact find explanations in China's alienation from and socialisation in international society. David Shambaugh asked in a recent seminal work on Chinese foreign policy, 'What have been the principal sources and patterns of foreign policy behaviour of the People's Republic of China (PRC) since 1949?'.[7] To such a central question, the international society perspective provides its own answers, answers sometimes additional and complementary to – and more often challenging – both realist and liberalist explanations of Chinese foreign policy.[8]

The critical insight that the international society perspective casts on China's international relations is particularly valuable in assessing the China problematique in the post-Cold War international society. The historical irony is that, although China has come a long way to give its consent to and accept common rules and norms in conducting relations between states and although its sharing of common institutions in maintaining the existing international order today is unprecedented, its integration into international society, from the post-Cold War perspective, is regarded at best as superficial and insufficient.

The end of the Cold War has had a double impact on China's position in international society. By a single twist of history, China, the reformist model for socialist countries in the 1980s, becomes a reactionary state in the world-wide democratisation of the 1990s. A reforming Communist country is now the last Leninist state. The breathtaking changes in international politics have simply left the Chinese leadership in Beijing in the lurch. China has also resumed, for a few years, its pariah state status in international society in the wake of its bloody crackdown in Beijing in June 1989. The nature of China's political system and the stagnation of political reforms make China increasingly look like an aberration in post-Cold War international society.

New theories in international relations further contest China's position in international society. In 'Clash of Civilisations?', Samuel Huntington contended that 'the fault lines between civilisations are replacing the political and ideological boundaries of the Cold War as the flash points for crisis and bloodshed', and further, that 'a Confucian-Islamic connection has emerged to challenge Western interests, values and power'.[9] The theory of democratic peace posits that because empirical data show that liberal democracies do not wage war against each other, the precondition for peace is the spread and consolidation of democracy world-wide.[10] Theoretical argument about the homogeneity of international society, in Halliday's words, 'explains why deviations from internal norms are so threatening to international relations'.[11] Mirrored against these theoretical propositions, China with its current regime in Beijing is a natural alien in post-Cold War international society, if not a designated enemy for liberal democracies. The recent revival of the 'China threat' is in part underlined by these theoretical arguments.

However, of far-reaching significance are the emerging new principles and changing norms and values of international society in the post-Cold War period. As James Mayall argued, the idea and the original conception of international society has been modified continuously throughout the twentieth century.[12] The latest modification, which stems partly from human rights norms, certainly pre-dates the end of the Cold War. John Vincent observed ten years ago that in the face of human rights arguments, 'the old principles of international society, like sovereignty and non-intervention, no longer have a clear run'.[13] Mayall also observed 'the firm entrenchment of human rights on the international agenda' before the end of the Cold War.[14] However, only in the post-Cold War period is it widely accepted that how a state can and should behave towards its citizens is a legitimate concern of international society as a whole and that the international legitimacy of a state is closely bound with its human rights behaviour both at home and in international forums. Andrew Nathan, in addressing China's human rights problems, argued explicitly that China should 'behave in a way that does not offend the conscience of that [international] community' in return for the benefits of full membership.[15] Granted that this may represent the projection of the culture and values of dominant and influential core members of international society,[16] this enhanced legitimation of human rights norms in international society nevertheless is a further assault on the traditional sovereignty-based normative order. While sovereignty may not be said to be disintegrating, peoples as well as other non-state entities are contending for their membership in post-Cold War international society.

Both in theory and in practice, China's behaviour regarding human rights is at odds with the emerging norms of international society, despite China's limited socialisation in human rights matters. China continues to argue that human rights are the internal affairs of a sovereign state. As such, no other country should interfere in human rights matters in China, since such interference is in contravention of the principle of non-intervention in international relations. China also insists that its cultural tradition and economic conditions predetermine its human rights policies. These arguments look increasingly anachronistic, to say the least. China's untenable defence of its human rights policies, on the other hand, bespeaks how threatened China feels by further acceptance of human rights norms. This, however, may be regarded as a symptom of a larger problem. As post-Cold War international society is going beyond Westphalia in search of a new order, China still insists on the state-centred order with absolute sovereignty. Over a hundred years ago, in the second half of the nineteenth century, the West used guns to force China to accept the Westphalia order and diplomatic practices. It would be an arduous task for the West to persuade China at the turn of the twenty-first century to give up the order that China found so difficult to embrace in the first place.

Challenges to China regarding emerging norms and rules, of course, are not restricted to human rights matters. Even the 'international society of economies', where China's integration is more definite, is presenting norm challenges to China: norms of so-called deeper integration.[17] Susan Shirk most recently observed:

> Having achieved a successful shallow integration with the world economy, China is now becoming the target of international efforts to promote harmonisation of standards for international production process. As a country that is quite late to develop, China is not allowed any breathing room before the issues of deeper integration such as intellectual property rights, environmental protection, and labour treatment confront it.[18]

China thus occupies an uneasy position in post-Cold War international society. It is neither completely in nor entirely out. It is now a target of international efforts not only to promote harmonisation of international economic practices but also to facilitate political changes and democratisation. Further integration of China into international society therefore contests its multiple identities: as a non-European culture, as a civilisational-state, as a Communist regime, as a dynamic economy, as a developing nation and as a rising power. It is small wonder that China's approach to integration issues and to its participation in multilateralism clearly and probably also understandably continues to be marked by enthusiasm as well as apprehension, for fear that its sovereignty, security and identity may be threatened or eroded by any further integration. Post-Cold War international society, on the other hand, is in a very strong position now to dictate the terms for China's social, political and economic integration. It nevertheless hesitates from time to time, for, because of the nature of the China challenge, it does not seem to be confident of its capacity to accommodate it without severe disruptions, and is unsure of the consequences of such an accommodation for global international society. Current debate in such international forums as the WTO and the ASEAN Regional Forum and in the American foreign policy establishment on whether and how to engage China is but an expression of such an attitude. Ambivalence between China and international society on integration issues is reciprocated.

There is no doubt that China has again 'established by dialogue and consent [with other member states] common rules and institutions for the conduct of their relations, and recognise their common interest in maintaining these arrangements'.[19] It remains at the same time, however, undoubtedly in the outer ring of the concentric circles of international society.[20] The evolution of new rules, principles and norms of international society in the post-Cold War years, and intrinsic challenges that 'deep integration' in international society present to China's security and identity have dictated that the relations between China and post-Cold War global international society continue to be ambivalent. China's international behaviour is likely to be continuously shaped by such ambivalence. The challenge to international society is how to deal with and adapt to the rise of China in this ambivalent relationship as we move to the next millennium.

Notes

PREFACE

1. J. Rosenau, 'China in a Bifurcated World: Competing Theoretical Perspectives', T. W. Robinson and D. Shambaugh, (eds), in *Chinese Foreign Policy: Theory and Practice*, pp. 524–5.
2. S. Kim, 'China and the World in Theory and Practice', in S. S. Kim, (ed.), *China and the World: Chinese Foreign Policy in the Post-Cold War Era*, p. 3.
3. Y. Zhang, *China in the International System, 1918–1920: The Middle Kingdom at the Periphery* (Basingstoke: Macmillan, 1991).

INTRODUCTION

1. US Deputy Secretary of State Strobe Talbott's speech to the Japan National Press Club on 25 Jan. 1995 entitled 'US-Japanese Leadership in the New Pacific Community'.
2. For theoretical arguments about democratic peace, See M. Brown, et al, *Debating the Democratic Peace*; for arguments about the homogeneity of international society, see in particular, F. Halliday, *Rethinking International Relations*, chap. 5, 'International Society as Homogeneity', pp. 94–123. For a brief discussion of deep integration in the Brookings Project of Integrating National Economies, see S. Shirk, *How China Opened Its Door: The Political Success of China's Trade and Investment Reforms*, pp. xi–xxiv.
3. See Ssu-yu Teng and J. K. Fairbank, (eds), *China's Response to the West – A Documentary Survey, 1839–1923*; I. Hsu, *China's Entrance into the Family of Nations – The Diplomatic Phase, 1861–1880*; and C. P. Fitzgerald, *The Chinese View of Their Place in the World.*
4. See J. Gittings, *The World and China, 1922–1972*; Wang Gungwu, *China and the World since 1949: The Impact of Independence, Modernity and Revolution*; and S. S. Kim, *China, the United Nations and World Order*, and V. P. Dutt, *China and the World: An Analysis of Communist China's Foreign Policy*; S. Fitzgerald, *China and the World*, and I. Wilson, *China and the World Community.*
5. See J. K. Fairbank, (ed.), *The Chinese World Order: Traditional China's Foreign Relations.*
6. See A. D. Barnett, *China's Economy in Global Perspective*; and S. S. Kim, (ed.), *China and the World: New Directions in Chinese Foreign Relations.*
7. See N. Lardy, *China's Entry into the World Economy: Implications for Northeast Asia and the United States*: J. C. Hsiung, and S. S. Kim, (eds), *China in the Global Community*; and H. Jacobson and M. Oksenberg, *China's Participation in the IMF, the World Bank and GATT: Toward a Global Economic Order.*

8. See, for example, the latest edition of S. S. Kim, (ed.), *China and the World: Chinese Foreign Relations in the Post-Cold War Era.*
9. S. Huntington, 'Clash of Civilisations?' *Foreign Affairs,* 72, 3, (1993) 22–49. For critiques of Samuel Huntington's claim, see 'The Responses to S. P. Huntington's "The Clash of Civilisations"', by Fouad Ajami et al, *Foreign Affairs,* 72, 4, 2–26. See also, S. Huntington, 'If Not Civilisation, What?', *Foreign Affairs,* 72, 5, 196–94.
10. For the international society tradition in the English school, see C. Manning, *The Nature of International Society*; H. Butterfield, and M. Wight, (eds), *Diplomatic Investigations: Essays in the Theory of International Politics*; M. Wight, *International Theory: The Three Traditions,* [ed. by G. Wight and B. Porter]; H. Bull, *The Anarchical Society: A Study of Order in World Politics*; H. Bull and A. Watson (eds), *The Expansion of International Society*; H. Bull, B. Kingsbury and A. Roberts (eds), *Hugo Grotius and International Relations*; A. Watson, *The Evolution of International Society*; and R. Fawn, and R. Larkins, (eds) *International Society after the Cold War: Anarchy and Order Reconsidered.*
11. Bull, *The Anarchical Society,* p. 13. Italics in the original text.
12. For this point, see in particular B. Buzan, 'From International System to International Society: Structural Realism and Regime Theory Meet the English School', *International Organisation,* 47, 3, (Summer 1993), 327–52.

1 THE PAST AS A PROLOGUE

1. Sir Geoffrey Howe, Cyril Foster Memorial Lecture at Oxford University, 27 October 1988.
2. Many historians are at pains to argue that in both Han (206 B.C.–A.D. 220) and Tang (A.D. 618-907) dynasties, there were extensive commercial dealings between the Chinese and the Romans, the Byzantines, and the Arabs and that Buddhism, arriving from India in late Han, was to become an important part of both religious and cultural life of the Chinese. Viewed in the overall long span of Chinese history, however, those events, like Jesuits in the Imperial Palace and Zheng He's fleet to Western Africa during the Ming Dynasty (1368–1644), were more of an exception than norm in China's contacts with the outside world. See J. F. Hudson, *Europe and China: A Survey of Their Relations from the Earliest Times to 1800*; and M. H. Hunt, 'Chinese Foreign Relations in Historical Perspective', in H. Harding, (ed.), *China's Foreign Relations in the 1980s,* pp. 4–10. For a more general survey of China's historical contact with the outside world, see S. A. M. Adshead, *China in World History.*
3. M. Mancall, *China at the Centre – Three Hundred Years of Foreign Policy,* p. xiii.
4. For a revealing account of the British mission to China in 1793, See A. Peyrefitte, [trans. by Jon Rothschild], *The Collision of Two Civilisations: The British Expedition to China in 1792-4.*
5. Teng, Ssu-yu and J. K. Fairbank, (eds), *China's Response to the West,* p. 19.
6. For details, see I. Hsu, *China's Entrance into the Family of Nations,* pp. 132–3.

7. It was followed by dispatches to Germany (1877), the United States and France (1878), Russia and Spain (1879), and Peru (1880).
8. A. Watson, 'Hedley Bull, States Systems and International Society', *Review of International Studies*, vol. 13, No. 2, 1987, p. 151.
9. See G. Gong, *The Standard of 'Civilisation' in International Society*, Part II
10. J. Lorimer, *The Institutes of the Law of Nations*, vol. I, pp. 101–3.
11. T. E. Holland, *Lectures on International Law*, p. 39.
12. G. Wilson, *Handbook of International Law*, 2nd ed., p. 25.
13. For further elaboration of this argument, see Y. Zhang, 'China's Entry into International Society: Beyond the Standard of "Civilisation"', *Review of International Studies*, Spring, 1991, pp. 1–15.
14. Quoted in Gong, *The Standard of 'Civilisation'*, p. 158.
15. For details, see Zhang, *China in the International System, 1918–20: The Middle Kingdom at the Periphery*.
16. See Zhang, *China in the International System, 1918–1920*, cha. 5.
17. J. W. Garner, *Recent Development in International Law*, p. 25.
18. L. Oppenheimer, *International Law*, (4th ed. by A. B. MacNair), p. 40.
19. W. R. Fishel, *The End of Extraterritoriality in China*, p. 1.
20. Quoted in A. Iriye, 'The United States as an Asian-Pacific Power', in G. T. Hsiao, (ed.), *Sino-American Detente and Its Policy Implications*, p. 12.
21. Ibid, p. 11.
22. See ibid.

2 ISOLATION OR ALIENATION?

1. Mao Zedong, *Selected Works of Mao Zedong*, vol. V, pp. 15–18. See also, M. Y. M. Kau and J. K. Leung (eds), *The Writings of Mao Zedong, 1949–1976*, vol. I, pp. 5–6.
2. See for example, P. Calvocoressi, *World Politics since 1945*, 3rd edn, chap. 2, 'The Resurgence and Isolation of China'; H. Kapur, *The End of An Isolation: China after Mao*; M. Yahuda, *Towards the End of Isolationism: Chinese Foreign Policy after Mao*; and J. Gittings, *China and the World, 1922–1972*.
3. Yahuda, *Towards the End of Isolationism*, p. 34.
4. H. Kissinger, *The White House Years*, p. 167.
5. Unless otherwise indicated, $ refers American dollars in this study.
6. C. Riskin, *China's Political Economy: The Quest for Development since 1949*, p. 317. The exchange rate at the time was $1=2.32 yuan.
7. H. Hinton, *Communist China in World Politics*, p. 24.
8. This argument is also advanced and maintained by some Chinese scholars in their publication in English. See Y. Hao and G. Huan (eds), *The Chinese View of the World*, p. xi.
9. D. Geldenhuys, *Isolated States: A Comparative Analysis*, p. 6.
10. For a recent detailed study of American policy towards the PRC in this period, see R. Foot, *The Practice of Power – US Relations with China since 1949*, particularly chaps 2, 3 and 4. See also Chen Jian, *China's Road to the Korean War: The Making of Sino–American Confrontation*; and Zhang Shuguang, *Deterrence and Strategic Culture: Chinese–American Confrontation, 1949–1958*.

11. J. D. Pollack, 'The Opening to America', in R. MacFarquhar and J. K. Fairbank (eds), *Cambridge History of China*, vol. 15, *The People's Republic, Part 2: Revolutions within the Chinese Revolution, 1966–1982*, p. 471.
12. H. Shapiro, *Democracy in America*, p. 345.
13. X, 'The Sources of Soviet Conduct', *Foreign Affairs*, 25, 4 (July 1947) 566–82.
14. See A. Iriye, *The Cold War in Asia: A Historical Introduction*; and Y. Nagai and A. Iriye (eds), *The Origins of the Cold War in Asia*.
15. 'Draft Report by the National Security Council on United States Policy Regarding Trade with China', *Foreign Relations of the United States (FRUS)*, IX (1949), *Far East and China*, p. 828.
16. Ibid.
17. See W. I. Cohen, 'The United States and China since 1945', in D. Borg and W. I. Cohen (eds), *The United States and China since 1945: New Frontiers in American–East Asian Relations*, pp. 136–40. More broadly, see also D. Borg and W. H. Heinrichs (eds), *Uncertain Years: Chinese-American Relations, 1947–1950*.
18. See J. L. Gaddis, 'The American "Wedge Strategy"' in H. Harding and M. Yuan (eds), *Sino–American Relations, 1945–1955 – A Joint Reassessment of a Critical Decade*, pp. 157–83.
19. For a brief and recent account of Mao's visit to Moscow and the signing of the Sino–Soviet treaty, see Pei Jianzhang et al, *Zhonghua Renmin Gongheguo Waijiaoshi, 1949–1956* (A Diplomatic History of China, 1949–1956), pp. 16–28.
20. M. Nakajima, 'Foreign Relations: From the Korean War to the Bandung Line', in R. MacFarquhar and J. K. Fairbank (eds), *Cambridge History of China*, vol. 14, *The People's Republic, Part 1, The Emergence of Revolutionary China, 1949–1965*, p. 259.
21. See S. Ambrose, *Rise to Globalism – American Foreign Policy since 1938*, p. 188.
22. Ibid.
23. Ibid., p. 210.
24. For more details, see Foot, *The Practice of Power*, chap. 2, 'US Hegemony and International Legitimacy: The Chinese Representation Issue at the United Nations'; and chap. 3, 'Trading with the Enemy: The USA and the China Trade Embargo'.
25. R. Blum, *The United States and China in World Affairs*, p. 114.
26. In Richard Falk's words, the American government clearly saw 'the desirability of maintaining the constitutional anomalies created by insisting that the government in Taipei is entitled to continue acting in the United Nations as the state of China'. See Tsou Tang (ed.), *China in Crisis*, vol. 2, *China's Policies in Asia and America's Alternatives*, p. 128.
27. See R. Gilpin, 'The Global Political System', in J. D. B. Miller and R. J. Vincent (eds), *Order and Violence: Hedley Bull and International Relations*, p. 133.
28. All in all, by 1956, the United States had concluded entangling alliances with 42 other states in strategic locations around the globe. See T. H. Von Laue, *The World Revolution of Westernisation: The Twentieth Century in Global Perspective*, p. 178.
29. See Borg and Cohen (eds), *The United States and China since 1945*, pp. 154–7.

30. Blum, *The United States and China in World Affairs*, p. 160.
31. R. Aron, 'Richard Nixon and the Future of American Foreign Policy', *Daedalus*, (Fall 1972) 16.
32. For more details, see Foot, *The Practice of Power*, pp. 52–65.
33. For a detailed exposition of the trade embargo imposed by the United States on China, see J. R. Grason, 'The American Trade Embargo Against China', in A. Eckstein (ed.), *China Trade Prospects and US Policy*, pp. 3–66.
34. H. Kapur, *Distant Neighbours: China and Europe*, p. 73.
35. Ibid., p. 70.
36. See P. Evans and B. M. Frolic (eds), *Reluctant Adversaries: Canada and the People's Republic of China, 1949–1970*.
37. Although the United Kingdom recognised the PRC as early as January 1950, full diplomatic relations between the two countries at the ambassadorial level were not established until 1972. For more details, see Pan Jin, 'Zhong Ying Jianjiao Tanpan de Changqi Fuza Licheng' (The Protracted Negotiation between China and Britain in Establishing Full Diplomatic Relations), *Waijiao Xueyuan Xuebao* (Journal of Foreign Affairs College), 3 (1992) 13–18. For Australia and New Zealand's recognition of China, see E. Fung (ed.), *From Fear to Friendship: Australia's Policies Towards the People's Republic of China, 1965–1982*; and J. Scott, 'Recognising China', in M. McKinnon (ed.), *New Zealand in World Affairs, 1957–1972*.
38. R. Nixon, *US Foreign Policy for the 1970s: Sharping a Durable Peace*, p. 16.
39. John Foster Dulles on a visit to Japan when the American Senate was to ratify the San Francisco Treaty told Prime Minister Yoshida that unless Japan chose to make peace with the KMT government in Taiwan, a majority of senators would not ratify the treaty. See F. C. Langdon, *Japan's Foreign Policy*, p. 94.
40. For details, see Yoko Yasuhara, 'Japan, Communist China and Export Control in Asia, 1948–1952', *Diplomatic History*, 10, 1 (Winter 1986) 75–91.
41. For details, see Xue Mouhong et al, *Dangdai Zhongguo Waijiao* (China Today: Diplomacy) 196–203. The fourth accord was abandoned by the PRC because of the 'anti-PRC policies of the Kishi government'. See also Lee, Chae-lin, *Japan Faces China*, pp. 136–9.
42. Langdon, *Japan's Foreign Policy*, p. 96.
43. Lee, Chae-Jin, *Japan Faces China*, p. 177.
44. K. W. Radtke, *China's Relations with Japan, 1945–1983: The Role of Liao Chengzhi*, p. 98.
45. Lee, Chae-Jin, *Japan Faces China*, p. 1.
46. Rosemary Foot provides an outstanding detailed study of the American manoeuvring at the UN to exclude the PRC in her most recent publication, *The Practice of Power*. See in particular chap. 2, 'US Hegemony and International Legitimacy: The Chinese Representation Issue at the United Nations', pp. 22–51.
47. N. B. Tucker, 'China and America: 1941–1991', *Foreign Affairs*, 70, 5 (Winter 1991/92) 83. See also Borg and Cohen (eds), *The United States and China since 1945*, p. 160.
48. Xue Mouhong et al, *Dangdai Zhongguo Waijiao*, p. 322.
49. Aron, 'Richard Nixon and the Future of American Foreign Policy', *Daedalus*, (Fall 1972) 9.
50. Tucker, 'China and America', *Foreign Affairs*, 70, 5 (Winter 1991/92) 84.

Notes 257

51. R. Nixon, 'Asia after Vietnam', *Foreign Affairs*, 46, 1 (October 1967) 121.
52. Ibid.
53. Nixon, *US Foreign Policy for the 1970s*, p. 2. Italics my own.
54. For a concise examination of this dependent relationship, see L. Dittmer, *Sino–Soviet Normalisation and Its International Implications: 1945–1990*, pp. 17–25.
55. Ibid., p. 100.
56. Xinhua News Agency, *China's Foreign Relations: A Chronology of Events: 1949–1988*, pp. 462–5.
57. Ibid., p. 461.
58. *Renmin Ribao* (People's Daily), 6 Sept. 1963.
59. See in particular Dittmer, *Sino–Soviet Normalisation and Its International Implications*, chap. 6, 'China and the International Communist Movement', pp. 99–120; See also Kapur, *Distant Neighbours*, pp. 41–6.
60. A. Whiting, 'The Sino–Soviet Split', in MacFarquhar and Fairbank (eds), *Cambridge History of China*, vol. 14, p. 478.
61. A. Eckstein, *Communist China's Economic Growth and Foreign Trade*, p. 98.
62. Zhou Enlai, 'Women de Waijiao Fangzheng he Renwu' (Our Foreign Policy and Its Tasks), in *Zhou Enlai Waijiao Wenxuan* (Selected Works of Zhou Enlai on Diplomacy), p. 51.
63. Eckstein, *Communist China's Economic Growth and Foreign Trade*, pp. 94 and 319.
64. Mah, Feng-Hwa, *The Foreign Trade of Mainland China*, p. 16.
65. Eckstein, *Communist China's Economic Growth and Foreign Trade*, p. 93.
66. As an official version of China's foreign trade history shows that in 1959, for example, China imported from Western Europe $450 million, 21.2% of China's total imports of the year. See Shen Jueren (ed.), *Dangdai Zhongguo de Duiwai Maoyi* (Contemporary China's Foreign Trade), p. 419.
67. Eckstein, *Communist China's Economic Growth and Foreign Trade*, p. 216.
68. For details of the direction of China's trade in the 1950s and the 1960s, see ibid., p. 98. Mah, on the other hand, put China's trade with non-Communist countries in 1966 at 73.9%.
69. China even traded with South Africa before 1960.
70. To the 11 socialist-bloc countries were added India, Indonesia, Sweden, Denmark, Burma, Switzerland, Finland, Pakistan, the United Kingdom, Norway, Yugoslavia, Afghanistan and Nepal. In fact, all countries bordering with the PRC, with the exception of Laos, recognised the PRC. The United Kingdom recognised the PRC on 6 Jan. 1950 and exchanged *charges d'affaire* with the PRC in 1954. However, only in 1972 were full diplomatic relations between the two countries at the ambassadorial level established.
71. See Xue Mouhong et al, *Dangdai Zhongguo Waijiao*, pp. 134–7. See also B. D. Larkin, *China and Africa 1949–1970*, pp. 38–46.
72. Apart from the countries mentioned above, the other countries are Cuba (Sept. 1960), Laos (April 1961), Tunis (Jan. 1964), Mauritania (July 1965) and the People's Republic of Yemen (Jan. 1968).
73. See H. Bull, 'The Revolt against the West', in Bull and Watson (eds), *The Expansion of International Society*, pp. 217–28.
74. See Xue Mouhong et al, *Dangdai Zhongguo Waijiao*, p. 131. For more details of China's support of national liberation movements, see P. Van Ness, *Revolution and Chinese Foreign Policy*; J. Taylor, *China and*

Southeast Asia: Peking's Relations with Revolutionary Movements; and M. Gurtov, China and Southeast Asia – The Politics of Survival: A Study of Foreign Policy Interaction. China's moral and material support of Southeast Asian Communists only diminished from late 1970s onwards.

75. R. L. Price, 'International Trade of Communist China, 1960–65', in Joint Economic Committee, An Economic Profile of Mainland China, p. 58.
76. For details of China's foreign aid programme from 1952 to 1970, see Shi Lin et al, Dangdai Zhongguo de Duiwai Jingji Hezuo (China Today: Foreign Economic Cooperation), pp. 23–55. See also W. Bartke, China's Economic Aid.
77. See R. C. Keith, The Diplomacy of Zhou Enlai, p. 68–87. Keith also noted that in the Vietnamese recriminations against China during the 1970s, 'Zhou was charged to have sacrificed the Vietnamese revolutionary movements at Geneva when he agreed to the neutrality of the Laotian and Cambodian royal governments', and China was charged to 'have a hidden agenda of annexation in Southeast Asia'. Ibid., p. 69. See also Zhai Qiang, 'China and the Geneva Conference of 1954', China Quarterly, 129 (March 1992) 103–22.
78. H. Harding, 'The Legacy of the Decade for Later Years: An American Perspective', in Harding and Yuan (eds), Sino–American Relations, p. 322.
79. For China's sweeping condemnation of the UN, in particular following the Indonesian withdrawal from the UN in January 1965, see Peking Review, 3, 5, 10, 17 and 45 (1965).
80. See Yahuda, Towards the End of Isolationism and Kapur, The End of an Isolation and M. Mancall, China at the Centre.
81. G. Craig, 'The Historian and the Study of International Relations', American Historical Review, 88, 1 (Feb. 1983) 7.
82. A. J. P. Taylor, for example, defines Britain's isolation as 'aloofness from the European balance of power'. A. J. P. Taylor, The Struggle for Mastery of Europe, p. 400.
83. See, for example, C. Howard, Splendid Isolation; and M. Jonas, Isolationism in America, 1935–1941. See also E. A. Nordlinger, Isolationism Reconfigured: American Foreign Policy for a New Century.
84. Mao Zedong, 'On the People's Democratic Dictatorship', Selected Works of Mao Zedong, vol. IV, p. 412.
85. M. H. Hunt, 'China's Foreign Relations in Historical Perspective', in Harding (ed.), China's Foreign Relations in the 1980s, pp. 25–9.
86. Italics my own. For an interesting account of the PRC's policy towards foreign interests around 1949, see B. Hooper, China Stands Up: Ending the Western Presence, 1948–1950.
87. For a brief account of the origin of this visit and Liu's talk with Stalin, see Pei Jianzhang et al, Zhonghua Renmin Gongheguo Waijiaoshi, 1949–1956, pp. 9–14.
88. Chi Aiping, 'Mao Zedong dui Xinzhongguo Waijiao Gongzuo de Zhanlue Zhidao' (Mao Zedong's Strategic Guidance to New China's Diplomatic Work), Dang de Wenxian (Documentary Record of the CCP), 1 (1992), 33–4.
89. Mao Zedong, Mao Zedong Waijiao Wenxuan (Selected Works of Mao Zedong on Foreign Affairs), p. 83.
90. Mao Zedong, 'Address to the Preparatory Meeting of the New Political Consultative Conference', Selected Works of Mao Zedong, vol. IV, p. 408.

91. Chi Aiping, 'Mao Zedong dui Xinzhongguo Waijiao Gongzuo de Zhanlue Zhidao', *Dang de Wenxian*, 1 (1992) 34.
92. Xue Mouhong et al, *Dangdai Zhongguo Waijiao*, pp. 5–6.
93. Ibid., p. 6, italics added.
94. Ibid., p. 7.
95. Mao Zedong, *Mao Zedong Waijiao Wenxuan*, p. 122.
96. Bian Yanjun et al, 'Mao Zedong he Xinzhongguo de Qibu' (Mao Zedong and the Early Years of New China), *Hongqi* (Red Flag), 6 (1988) 28.
97. As late as August and September 1950, Zhou Enlai was still communicating with Trygve Lie about the PRC's representation at the UN. For telegrams between Zhou and Lie, see J. Cohen and H. Chiu (eds), *People's China and International Law: A Documentary Study*, pp. 268–72.
98. See Pei Jianzhang et al, *Zhonghua Renmin Gongheguo Waijiaoshi, 1949–1956*, pp. 366–71. According to a chronology of China's foreign relations compiled by Xinhua News Agency, from November 1949 to June 1950 when the Korean War broke out, Zhou Enlai sent altogether 9 telegrams to the UN and Secretary-General Trygve Lie, urging the UN to accept the Chinese ambassador to the UN. See Xinhua News Agency, *China's Foreign Relations: A Chronology 1949–1988*, pp. 3–6.
99. See, for example, Keith, *The Diplomacy of Zhou Enlai*, chap. 3, '"Peaceful Coexistence" v. Containment at Geneva and Bandung', pp. 59–87. See also, J. A. Camilleri, *Chinese Foreign Policy: The Maoist Era and Its Aftermath*, p. 79; and Nakajima, 'Foreign Relations: From the Korean War to the Bandung Line', in MacFarquhar and Fairbank (eds), *Cambridge History of China*, vol. 14, pp. 261 and 283. See also Hinton, *Communist China in World Politics*, pp. 249–54.
100. Xue Mouhong et al, *Dangdai Zhongguo Waijiao*, p. 57.
101. Ibid., pp. 77–8. See also Larkin, *China and Africa*, p. 18.
102. Ibid., pp. 97–100.
103. See J. Mayall, *Nationalism and International Society*, chap. 8, 'The Third World and International Society'.
104. Calvocoressi, *World Politics since 1945*, 3rd edn, p. 71.
105. See Wu, Yuan-li, 'The Weapon of Trade', *Problems of Communism*, IX, 1 (1960), 31–9.
106. See, for example, C. Neuhause, *Third World Politics: China and Afro-Asian People's Solidarity Organisation, 1957–1967*; C. Johnson, *Communist China and Latin America, 1959–1967*; and L. Harris and R. Worden (eds), *China and the Third World: Champion or Challenger?*
107. See D. Armstrong, *Revolutionary Diplomacy – Chinese Foreign Policy and the United Front Doctrine*; and Tang Tsou and M. Helperin, 'Mao Tse-tung's Revolutionary Strategy and China's International Behaviour', *American Political Science Review* (March 1965) 80–99.
108. F. Schumann and O. Schell (eds), *Communist China – China Readings 3*, p. 331.
109. Zhou Enlai, 'Women de Waijiao Fangzheng he Renwu', *Zhou Enlai Wenxuan*, p. 51.
110. R. Nixon, *President Nixon's Foreign Policy Report, 1972*, p. 16.
111. For more details, see Dong Zhikai, *Jishen Guoji Shichang de Jianxin Qibu* (A Difficult Start to Get into the International Market).

112. See *Zhongguo Duiwai Jingji Maoyi Nianjian, 1989* (Yearbook of China's Foreign Economic Relations and Trade, 1989), pp. 299 and 302.
113. Of the total in 1950, China's export was $83.95 million, and its import, $77.09 million. Of the total in 1959, China's export was $201 million, and import, $450 million. See Dong Zhikai, *Jishen Guoji Shichang de Jianxin Qibu*, p. 177.
114. According to Kapur, these 17 countries are Austria, Belgium, Luxembourg, Denmark, Finland, France, Greece, Ireland, Italy, the Netherlands, Norway, Portugal, Spain, Sweden, the Switzerland, the United Kingdom and West Germany, Kapur, *Distant Neighbours*, p. 62.
115. See Pauline Lewin, *The Foreign Trade of Communist China: Its Impact on the Free World*.
116. Bartke, *China's Economic Aid*, pp. 12–13. See also J. F. Cooper, *China's Foreign Aid: An Instrument of Peking's Foreign Policy*.
117. Bull, *The Anarchical Society*, pp. 308–9.
118. See J. Der Derian, *On Diplomacy*, chap. 2, 'Alienation', pp. 8–29.
119. See J. Der Derian, 'Hedley Bull and the Idea of Diplomatic Culture', in Fawn and Larkins (eds), *International Society after the Cold War*, p. 92.
120. Geldenhuys, *Isolated States*, pp. 5–6.
121. D. Armstrong, *Revolution and World Order: The Revolutionary State in International Society*, pp. 1–11.
122. See J. Der Derian, 'Mediating Estrangement: A Theory for Diplomacy', *Review of International Studies*, 13, 2 (Spring 1987), 91–110.
123. Quoted in Der Derian, *On Diplomacy*, pp. 9–10.
124. For a concise but systematic discussion of classicist theories of alienation, see Der Derian, *On Diplomacy*, pp. 8–29.
125. R. Aron, *Peace and War – A Theory of International Relations*, p. 7.
126. J. Cropsey, 'Alienation or Justice?' in J. Cropsey, *Political Philosophy and Issues of Politics*, p. 44.
127. Bull and Watson (eds), *The Expansion of International Society*, p. 1.
128. Armstrong, *Revolution and World Order*, p. 7.
129. Quoted in Der Derian, 'Mediating Estrangement: A Theory for Diplomacy', *Review of International Studies*, 13 (Spring 1987) 2, 92.
130. M. Shaw, 'Global Society and Global Responsibility: The Theoretical, Historical and Political Limits of "International Society"', in Fawn and Larkins (eds), *International Society after the Cold War*, p. 50.
131. David Armstrong argues, however, that only in the late 1980s did the Soviet Union finally socialise itself into international society. See Armstrong, *Revolution and World Order*, chap. 4, 'State and Class: The Russian Revolution', pp. 112–57.
132. Mayall, *Nationalism and International Society,* p. 3.
133. See Der Derian, 'Mediating Estrangement: A Theory for Diplomacy'.
134. Hunt, 'Chinese Foreign Relations in Historical Perspective', in Harding (ed.), *China's Foreign Relations in the 1980s*, p. 1.
135. B. Schwartz, *Reflections on the May Fourth Movement*, p. 13.
136. L. P. Van Slyke (ed.), *China White Paper* (Aug. 1949) xvii.
137. Office of Intelligence Research Report (18 Sept. 1947), in *Foreign Relations of the United States (FRUS)* (1947) VII, *The Far East: China*, p. 287.
138. Shapiro, *Democracy in America*, p. 33.

139.	Acheson's words in a speech delivered on 30 July 1949. Quoted in T. Tsou, *America's Failure in China, 1941–1950*, p. 508.
140.	MacFarquhar, *Sino–American Relations*, pp. 99–100.
141.	Aron, 'Richard Nixon and the Future of American Foreign Policy', *Daedalus*, (Fall 1972) 14.
142.	John L. Gaddis, *The United States and the Origins of the Cold War 1941–1947*, p. 317.
143.	Mao Zedong, *Mao Zedong Waijaio Wenxuan*, p. 76.
144.	Mao Zedong, *Selected Works of Mao Zedong*, vol. IV, p. 420.
147.	Ibid., p. 407.
146.	Xue Mouhong et al, *Dangdai Zhongguo Waijiao*, p. 4.
147.	Shi Yinhong, *Didui yu Chongtu de Yulai, 1949–1950* (The Origins of Sino–American Confrontation and Hostility, 1949–1950), pp. 55–6.
148.	For more details, see Tucker, *Patterns in the Dust: Chinese-American Relations and the Recognition Controversy, 1949–1950*.
149.	H. Hinton, *China's Turbulent Quest: An Analysis of China's Foreign Relations since 1949*, pp. 264–5.
150.	This point was made explicitly clear again by Zhou Enlai in his speech at the inauguration of the Foreign Ministry of the PRC on 8 November 1949. He stated: 'We would not recognise the status of the embassies, consulates and diplomats of those countries which do not recognise our country. We only treat their diplomats as foreign residents in China.' Zhou Enlai, *Zhou Enlai Waijiao Wenxuan* (Selected Works of Zhou Enlai on Diplomacy), p. 5.
151.	Quoted in Yuan, Ming, 'The Failure of Perception: America's China Policy, 1949–1950', in Harding and Yuan (eds), *Sino–American Relations*, p. 145.
152.	Tsou (ed.), *China in Crisis*, vol. 2, p. 118.
153.	H. Truman, *Memoirs*, vol. 2, *Years of Trial and Hope*, p. 397.
154.	Ambassador Warren Austin's speech at the United Nations. See Ambrose, *Rise to Globalism*, p. 206.
155.	Quoted in ibid., p. 207.
156.	See Harding, 'The Legacy of the Decade for Later Years: An American Perspective', in Harding and Yuan (eds), *Sino–American Relations*, pp. 311–12.
157.	Ambrose, *Rise to Globalism*, p. 207.
158.	Xue Mouhong et al, *Dangdai Zhongguo Waijiao*, pp. 74 and 105.
159.	See R. C. North, 'Peking's Drive for Empire: The New Expansionism', *Problems of Communism*, IX, 1 (1960) 23–30.
160.	See K. T. Young, *Negotiating with the Chinese Communists: The United States Experience, 1953–67*, p. 58.
161.	J. W. Fulbright, *The Arrogance of Power*, p. 152.
162.	J. S. Service, *The Amerasia Papers: Some Problems in the History of US–China Relations*, p. 166.
163.	Nixon, *US Foreign Policy for the 1970s*, p. 2.
164.	In Kissinger's words, 'Sino–Soviet conflict transcended ideology and it was primeval'. H. Kissinger, *Years of Upheaval*, p. 47.
165.	See Xue Mouhong et al, *Dangdai Zhongguo Waijiao*, p. 115.
166.	Ibid., pp. 115–16. See also Borg and Cohen (eds), *The United States and China since 1945*, p. 157.
167.	Ibid., p. 116.

168. For a brief but authoritative account of the Sino–Soviet split, see Whiting, 'The Sino–Soviet Split', in MacFarquhar and Fairbank (eds), *Cambridge History of China,* vol. 14, pp. 478–538.
169. L. T. Lee, *China and International Agreements: A Study of Compliance*, pp. 119–20. For a broader survey of China's attitude and practice of international law in the period, see also Cohen and Chiu (eds), *People's China and International Law: A Documentary Survey*; and H. Chiu, *The People's Republic of China and the Law of Treaties.*
170. Ibid., p. 119.
171. Harding, 'China's Changing Role in the Contemporary World', in Harding (ed.), *China's Foreign Relations in the 1980s*, pp. 179–200.
172. Nixon, *US Foreign Policy for the 1970s*, p. 16.

3 MUTUAL LEGITIMATION

1. J. Gittings, *The World and China, 1922–1972*, p. 260.
2. R. Nixon, *US Foreign Policy for the 1970s*, p. 2.
3. For more details, see Bull, *The Anarchical Society*, Part II, Order in the Contemporary International System, pp. 101–229.
4. Armstrong, *Revolution and World Order*, pp. 301–2.
5. B. Tuchman, 'If Mao Had Come to Washington: An Essay in Alternatives', *Foreign Affairs*, 51, 1 (Oct. 1972) 44–64.
6. J. K. Fairbank, *China Watch*, p. 125.
7. S. Goldstein, 'Sino–American Relations, 1948–1950: Lost Chance or No Chance?' in Harding and Yuan (eds), *Sino–American Relations*, pp. 119–42.
8. A. Buchan, *Change without War: The Shifting Structure of World Power*, p. 51.
9. Kissinger, *White House Years*, p. 163.
10. See Xue Mouhong et al, *Dangdai Zhongguo Waijiao*. In this most recent publication of the official history of China's diplomacy from 1949 to 1986, it is forcefully stated that 'It is the possibility of an armed intervention in the Chinese Revolution by the imperialist powers that dictated the necessity [for the PRC] to unite with other socialist countries' (p. 4).
11. Wang Shuzhong, 'The Post-war International System', in H. Kapur, (ed.), *As China Sees the World-Persentions of Chinese Scholars*, pp. 19–20.
12. See Keith, *The Diplomacy of Zhou Enlai*, p. 190.
13. Chen Dunde, *Mao Zedong he Nikesong zai 1972* (Mao Zedong and Nixon in 1972), pp. 333–4.
14. In more specific terms, China's reading of the changing international strategic environment in the early 1970s is described as follows:

> With the opening of the 1970s, China was faced with great changes in the international strategic environment. The balance of military power between the two superpowers, the United States and the Soviet Union, developed in a way favourable to the latter. The Soviet Union stretched its hands everywhere on the strength of its rapidly expanding military might, whereas the United States was first deeply bogged down in the quagmire of the Vietnam War and was later haunted by the aftermath of that war.

There emerged a situation in the Soviet-American rivalry in which the Soviet Union was on the offensive, while the United States, the defensive.

See Xue Mouhong et al, *Dangdai Zhongguo Waijiao*, p. 214.
15. Kissinger, *Years of Upheaval*, p. 49.
16. Chen Dunde, *Mao Zedong he Nikesong zai 1972* , p. 261; Gong Li, 'Mao Zedong yu Zhongmei Guanxi Jiedong' (Mao Zedong and the Breakthrough in Sino–American Relations), *Zhongguo Waijiao* (China's Diplomacy), 3 (1993) 43. For the analysis by Western scholars, see J. Garver, *China's Decision for Rapprochement with the United States, 1968–1971*; and T. Gottllieb, *Chinese Foreign Policy Factionalism and the Origins of the Strategic Triangle*.
17. Kissinger, *White House Years*, p. 1061.
18. The Soviet threat to China's security in the 1970s, it is maintained in an official publication, was paramount.

> In the areas around China, the Soviet Union not only stepped up its military build-up along its border with China and in Mongolia, but also backed and encouraged Viet Nam in its invasion of Kampuchea and its anti-China activities. The Soviet Union also sent its troops to occupy Afghanistan. If shortly after the birth of New China, it was the United States that posed a threat to it from three fronts, namely Korea, Taiwan and Indo-China; towards the end of the 1970s, it was the Soviet Union that encircled China from three directions, the North, the South and the West.

See Xue Mouhong et al, *Dangdai Zhongguo Waijiao*, p. 214.
19. See, for example, Buchan, *Change without War*; R. Ashley, *The Political Economy of War and Peace: The Sino–Soviet–American Triangle and the Modern Security Problematique*; and I. J. Kim, (ed.), *The Sino–Soviet–American Strategic Triangle*.
20. Kissinger, *White House Years*, p. 685.
21. Aron, 'Richard Nixon and the Future of American Foreign Policy', *Daedalus* (Fall 1972) 4
22. Buchan, *Change without War*, p. 49.
23. Pollack, 'The Opening to America', in MacFarquhar and Fairbank, (eds), *Cambridge History of China*, vol. 15, p. 471.
24. R. Nixon, 'Asia after Vietnam', *Foreign Affairs*, 46, 1 (1967), 121.
25. Nixon, *US Foreign Policy for the 1970s*, p. 2.
26. In an internal report on the international situation made by Zhou Enlai in 1971, it is claimed that 'The visit of the head of US imperialism [to China] … renders bankrupt the China policy of the US' See K. C. Chen, (ed.), *China and the Three Worlds: A Foreign Policy Reader*, pp. 137–8.
27. Quoted in L. Bloomfield, 'China, the United States and the United Nations', *International Organisation*, XX, 4 (1966), 654.
28. Pollack, 'The Opening to America', in *Cambridge History of China*, vol. 15, p. 402.
29. *Renmin Ribao*, 27 Sept. 1979.
30. *New York Times*, 31, Oct. 1971.
31. M. Witunski, 'Epilogue', in G. T. Hsiao, (ed.), *Sino–American Détente and Its Policy Implications*, p. 272.

32. See Chen Dunde, *Mao Zedong he Nikesong zai 1972*, pp. 258–61. See also H. Jacobson and M. Oksenberg, *China's Participation in the IMF, the world Bank and GATT*, p. 61.
33. J. D. B. Miller, 'The Third World', in Miller and Vincent (eds.), *Order and Violence*, p. 81.
34. China established full diplomatic relations with Spain on 9 March 1973.
35. Miller, 'The Third World', *Order and Violence*, p. 81.
36. Han Nianlong (ed.), *Diplomacy of Contemporary China*, p. 283.
37. Ibid., p. 357.
38. Ibid., p. 266.
39. C. Mackerras, *Modern China – A Chronology from 1842 to the Present*, p. 565.
40. Shi Lin et al, *Dangdai Zhongguo de Duiwai Jingji Hezuo* (China Today: Economic Cooperation with Foreign Countries), pp. 55–7. Before 1971, 30 countries had received China's aid. For China's aid to Africa from 1976 to 1966, see Larkin, *China and Africa*, pp. 93–103.
41. The phrase from Jonathan Pollack. For a short and interesting discussion of personalities in Sino–American relations, see Pollack, 'The Opening to Amereica', in *Cambridge History of China, vol. 15*, pp. 404–7.
42. From 1970 to 1976, Mao had come out more than 50 times to receive visiting foreign heads of state and government. He was also frequently seen on TV meeting with other visiting foreign dignitaries.
43. See Mackerras, *Modern China*, p. 576.
44. The foreign dignitaries received by Mao in the five months before 15 May 1976 include Mr and Mrs David Eisenhower (31 Dec. 1975), Mr and Mrs Richard Nixon (Feb.), Laotian Party and government leaders and the Vice-President of Egypt (April), and the Prime Ministers of New Zealand, Singapore and Pakistan (May). See *Yearbook on International Communist Affairs*, 1977, p. 278.
45. Bull, *The Anarchical Society*, p. 10.
46. The speech was made at the Sixth Special Session of the UN General Assembly on the problems of raw materials and development. In fact it is in this speech that Deng first expounded Mao's theory of the three worlds. For the full text of Deng's speech, see *Peking Review*, Supplement, 15 (1974).
47. See S. S. Kim, *China, the United Nations and World Order*. Except where specified, the following account is based on this study.
48. Ibid., p. 161.
49. Ibid., p. 196.
50. Ibid., p. 496.
51. See Xue Mouhong et al, *Dangdai Zhongguo Waijiao*, pp. 330–1; and Shi Lin et al, *Dangdai Zhongguo de Duiwai Jingji Hezuo*, pp. 496–534. Shi Lin's book contains sections with detailed descriptions of China's early participation in and cooperation with, in particular, the United Nations Development Programme (UNDP), the United Nations Industrial Development Organisation (UNIDO), the United Nations Fund for Population Activities (UNFPA), the United Nations International Children's Emergency Fund (UNICEF), the United Nations Conference on Trade and Development (UNCTAD), and the United Nations Committee for Transnational Corporations (UNCTC).

Notes 265

52. See G. Chan, *China and International Organisations*, p. 16. A pioneering study on China's participation in international organisations before its entry into the United Nations has a slightly different figure. It claims that the PRC was a member in 2 out of 193 IGOs outside the UN system as of December 1966; and that as of December 1968, the PRC's membership in NGOs was around 60 out of a total of 2188. See also B. S. J. Weng, 'Some Conditions of Peking's Participation in International Organisations', in J. Cohen (ed.), *China's Practice of International Law: Some Case Studies*, p. 322.
53. Ibid.
54. Kim, *China, the United Nations and World Order*, p. 110.
55. Ibid., p. 196.
56. Ibid., p. 134.
57. Ibid., p. 110.
58. Ibid., p. 500.
59. W. R. Fenney, 'China's Global Politics at the United Nations', in J. C. Hsiung, and S. S. Kim (eds), *China in the Global Community*, p. 160.
60. See A. D. Barnett, *China's Economy in Global Perspective*.
61. *Zhongguo Duiwai Jingji Maoyi Nianjian, 1989*, pp. 299–302. The ratio of the basis growth rate per annum is calculated on the current US dollars.
62. S. S. Kim, 'Chinese Global Policy: An Assessment', in Hsiung and Kim (eds), *China in the Global Community*, p. 222.
63. See Kapur, *Distant Neighbours*, pp. 149–50. From December 1978 to October 1980, China signed bilateral trade agreements with all the EEC countries, except Ireland.
64. Mackerras, *Modern China*, pp. 602–16.
65. Xue Mouhong et al, *Dangdai Zhongguo Waijiao*, pp. 295–6.
66. For details of the Chinese proposals and the Japanese replies, see Lee, Chae-Jin, *China and Japan: New Economic Diplomacy*, pp. 113–20. For a brief round-up of Sino–Japanese economic relations by Japanese scholars, see Tomozo Morino, 'China–Japan Trade and Investment Relations', in F. J. Macchiarola and R. B. Oxnam (eds), *The China Challenge: American Policies in East Asia*, pp. 87–94.
67. See Barnett, *China's Economy in Global Perspective*, pp. 122–48.
68. Kapur, *Distant Neighbours*, p. 62.
69. Liu Suinian and Wu Qungan, *China's Socialist Economy: An Outline History 1949–1985*, pp. 383–4.
70. Barnett, *China's Economy in Global Perspective*, p. 193.
71. Liu Suinian and Wu Qungan, *China's Economy in Global Perspective*, p. 384.
72. Barnett, *China's Economy in Global Perspective*, p. 190.
73. According to Harry Harding, total investment envisaged at the time was $300 billion between 1976 and 1985, with $70–80 billion for the import of foreign equipment and technology.
74. Harding, *China's Second Revolution*, p. 149.
75. A. Whiting, *China Eyes Japan*, p. 96.
76. See Foreign Broadcast Information Service (FBIS), *Daily Report – PRC*, 9 April 1980, p. L2.
77. Barnett, *China's Economy in Global Perspective*, p. 636.
78. New China News Agency, *Xinhua News Bulletin*, 19 Dec. 1978.
79. *International Herald Tribune*, 19 Jan. 1973.

80. Li Qiang, *Foreign Trade*, 1(July 1974) 1–5.
81. Lee, Chae-Jin, *China and Japan*, p. 113.
82. Barnett, *China's Economy in Global Perspective*, p. 224.
83. *Peking Review*, 3 Nov. 1978, p. 15. Italics my own.
84. Ibid. Italics my own.
85. *Beijing Review*, 5 Jan. 1979. Li Xiannian, then Vice-Premier, went out of his way twice in December 1978 to enunciate China's new policy on loans from foreign governments. He told Mr Willard C. Bucker, President of the Chase Manhattan Bank, that, 'On the condition that China's sovereignty is not impaired, we are prepared to accept funds and advanced technology from the developed countries, including the United States, Japan and West European countries, to speed up our socialist construction'. Ibid., p. 9. Earlier, in an interview with a Swedish reporter on 8 December, he reportedly said, 'their [Japanese, American, European and Canadian] bankers are providing us with credits to buy their equipment. They are providing investment, and we are forming joint companies, but not in such a way as to harm our sovereignty.' See Barnett, *China's Economy in Global Perspective*, p. 141.
86. Lee, Chae-Jin, *China and Japan*, pp. 113–20.
87. See *Far Eastern Economic Review*, 21 Sept. 1979, p. 62.
88. See Shi Lin et al, *Dangdai Zhongguo de Duiwai Jingji Hezuo*, pp. 498–9, 515
89. Ibid., p. 499.
90. Ibid., pp. 519–31.
91. Deng Xiaoping was reported to have told the President of Kyodo News Service on 26 February 1979 that 'there would be no hitch on China's part in joining the IMF if the Taiwan issue is settled'. *China Business Review* (May–June 1979) 31.
92. Jacobson and Oksenberg, *China's Participation in the IMF, the World Bank and GATT*, p. 70.
93. Kim, 'China's Global Policy', in Hsiung and Kim (eds), *China in the Global Community*, p. 239.
94. See, for example, H. Kapur, *The Awakening Giant: China's Ascension in World Politics*.
95. Han Nianlong (ed.), *Diplomacy of Contemporary China*, p. 266.
96. According to the figures of the Ministry of Foreign Economic Relations and Trade (MOFERT), whereas in 1970 China's import and export total amounted to $4.586 billion, in 1979, it was $29.33 billion. See *Zhongguo Duiwai Jingji Maoyi Nianjian, 1989*, pp. 299–302.
97. Ibid., p. 299.
98. Harding, *China's Second Revolution*, p. 71.
99. See *A Collection of Laws and Regulations of China Concerning Foreign Economic and Trade Relations*.
100. Barnett, *China's Economy in Global Perspective*, p. 1.
101. R. Gilpin, *The Political Economy of International Relations*, p. 306.
102. Kim, 'China's Global Policy', in Hsiung and Kim (eds), *China in the Global Community*, p. 225.
103. At the 7th meeting of the Standing Committee of the 5th National People's Congress on 3 April 1979, China decided not to renew the Treaty. On the same day, Chinese Foreign Minister Huang Hua met with the Soviet Ambassador Sherbakov and notified him this decision. See Han Nianlong (ed.), *Diplomacy of Contemporary China*, p. 301.

Notes 267

104. Ibid., p. 277. For an official Chinese account of those 'twists and turns', see ibid., pp. 277–83. See also H. Harding, *A Fragile Relationship: The United States and China since 1972*, particularly chap. 2, 'Breakthrough', and chap. 3, 'Normalisation', pp. 23–106.
105. Pollack, 'The Opening to China', in MacFarquhar and Fairbank (eds), *The Cambridge History of China*, vol. 15, p. 403.
106. Jacobson and Oksenberg, *China's Participation in the IMF, the World Bank and GATT*, p. 70.
107. Han Nianlong (ed.), *Diplomacy of Contemporary China*, p. 265.
108. Kim, 'China's Global Policy', in Hsiung and Kim (eds), *China in the Global Community*, pp. 218–24.
109. For a panoramic view of power struggles within the Chinese Communist Party from 1975 to 1985, see Harding, *China's Second Revolution*, pp. 49–69, 'The Evolution of the Political Spectrum since the Death of Mao'.
110. Pollack, 'The Opening to China', in MacFarquhar and Fairbank (eds), *The Cambridge History of China*, vol. 15, p. 470.
111. *Renmin Ribao*, 2 Jan. 1977, as quoted in S. S. Kim, 'China's International Organisational Behaviour', in T. Robinson, and D. Shambaugh, (eds), *Chinese Foreign Policy: Theory and Practice*, pp. 426–7.
112. *Guangming Ribao* (Guangming Daily), 25 June 1986.
113. See Deng Xiaoping, 'Speech at Special Session of UN General Assembly', *Peking Review*, 15 Supplement (1974).
114. Hsiung and Kim (eds), *China in the Global Community*, p. 34.
115. That is that the CCP should first resolutely defend whatever policies Chairman Mao has formulated, and second unswervingly adhere to whatever instructions Chairman Mao has issued.
116. For a broad review of changes in China's domestic politics from 1977 to 1981, see Harding, *China's Second Revolution*, pp. 53–66, and R. MacFarquhar, 'The Succession to Mao and the End of Maoism, 1969–1982', in R. MacFarquhar (ed.), *The Politics of China, 1949–1989*, pp. 248–339.

4 CHANGING PERCEPTIONS

1. See in particular, J. C. Hsiung (ed.), *Beyond China's Independent Foreign Policy: Challenge for the US and its Asian Allies*; H. Harding (ed.), *China's Foreign Relations in the 1980s*; S. S. Kim (ed.), *China and the World: New Directions in Chinese Foreign Relations*; L. Dittmer, *Sino–Soviet Normalisation and Its International Implications, 1945–1990*; T. W. Robinson and D. Shambaugh (eds), *Chinese Foreign Policy: Theory and Practice*. See also published works in Chinese: Tian Zengpei (ed.), *Gaige Kaifang Yilai de Zhongguo Waijiao* (China's Diplomacy since the Opening and Reform); and Xue Mouhong et al, *Dangdai Zhongguo Waijiao*.
2. Foot, *The Practice of Power*, p. 47.
3. See Hu Yaobang, 'Report to the Twelfth National Congress of the Chinese Communist Party', *Beijing Review*, 37 (1982) 29. In December 1982, the independent foreign policy was incorporated into the revised Constitution of the PRC. See 'Constitution of the People's Republic of China', *Beijing Review*, 52 (1982) 11.

4. Deng Xiaoping, *Fundamental Issues in Present-day China*, p. 47.
5. Zhao Ziyang, 'Report on the Seventh Five-Year Plan', *Beijing Review*, 16 (1986), Centrefold, xvii–xviii.
6. Ibid.
7. Ibid. Earlier in June 1985, Zhao Ziyang had already outlined to the international community the objectives of the Chinese foreign policy of independence and peace in a speech at the Royal Institute of International Affairs in London on his visit to Britain. See Zhao Ziyang, 'China's Diplomacy: The Objectives of China's Foreign Policy: for Lasting Peace, Increased Friendly Cooperation and Co-Prosperity', *International Affairs*, 4 (Autumn 1985) 577–80.
8. 'Chairman Mao's Theory of the Differentiation of the Three Worlds Is a Major Contribution to Marxism-Leninism', in Chen (ed.), *China and the Three Worlds*, pp. 99–123.
9. At a press conference at the end of 1983, the Chinese Foreign Ministry spokesman expressed publicly the Chinese government's 'understanding and support' of the anti-nuclear campaign and peace movement in Europe; *Renmin Ribao*, 1 Dec. 1983. In 1984, China resumed contacts with the Campaign for Nuclear Disarmament (CND) and other peace organisations. See *China Daily*, 5 Nov. 1984.
10. Xie Yixian claimed that this was the first time that a leader of a Communist country had advocated 'common economic prosperity' between countries of different social and political systems. See Xie Yixian, 'Bashi Niandai Zhongguo Duiwai Zhengce' (China's Foreign Policies in the 1980s), *Qiushi* (Seeking Truth), 1 (1989) 39.
11. See Hsiung (ed.), *Beyond China's Independent Foreign Policy*, especially chap. 10, 'Challenge of China's Independent Foreign Policy'. Allen Whiting's suggestion that this new orientation was an 'assertive nationalism in Chinese foreign policy' is a different voice. See A. S. Whiting, 'Assertive Nationalism in Chinese Foreign Policy', *Asian Survey*, XXIII, 8 (1983) 913–7. See also Robinson and Shambaugh (eds), *Chinese Foreign Policy: Theory and Practice*.
12. Xue Mouhong et al, *Dangdai Zhongguo Waijiao*, p. 411.
13. Quoted in Buchan, *Change without War*, pp. 50–1.
14. MacFarquhar, 'The Succession to Mao and the End of Maoism, 1969–1982', in MacFarquhar (ed.), *The Politics of China, 1949–1989*, p. 335.
15. See R. Baum, 'The Road to Tiananmen: Chinese Politics in the 1980s', in MacFarquhar (ed.), *The Politics of China, 1949–1989*, pp. 340–471.
16. Steven I. Levine, 'Perception and Ideology in Chinese Foreign Policy', in Robinson and Shambaugh (eds), *Chinese Foreign Policy: Theory and Practice*, p. 30.
17. Allen Whiting noted a particular instance of such a theme recurring in China's acrimony against the United States in 1982. See Whiting, 'Assertive Nationalism in Chinese Foreign Policy', *Asian Survey*, XXIII, 8 (1983) 916.
18. For China's two-camps view of the post-war international system, see Mao Zedong, 'On the People's Democratic Dictatorship', in *Selected Works of Mao Zedong*, vol. IV, pp. 411–25. See also Zhou Enlai, 'Jintian Guojishang de Zhuyao Maodun shi Zhanzheng yu Heping Wenti' (The Main Contradiction in the World Today is Bbetween War and Peace), in *Zhou Enlai Waijiao Wenxuan*, pp. 58–62. For China's three worlds theory, see Deng Xiaoping, 'Speech at the Sixth Special Session of the U.N. General Assembly', *Peking Review*, 15, Supplement (1974); and see also People's

Daily Editorial: 'Chairman Mao's Theory of the Differentiation of the Three Worlds is a Major Contribution to Marxism-Leninism', in Chen (ed.), *China and the Three Worlds*, pp. 99–123.
19. Harding, 'China's Changing Roles in the Contemporary World', in Harding (ed.), *China's Foreign Relations in the 1980s*, pp. 206–8. For an example of China's radically advocating the destruction of the international system, see Lin Biao, 'Long Live the Victory of the People's War!' *Peking Review*, 36 (1965) 9–39.
20. Kim, *China, the United Nations and World Order*, pp. 92–3.
21. Deng Xiaoping, 'Speech at the Sixth Session of the UN General Assembly', *Peking Review*, 15, Supplement (1974) iv.
22. Chen (ed.), *China and the Three Worlds*, p. 111.
23. Ibid., p. 118.
24. See Xue Mouhong et al, *Dangdai Zhongguo Waijiao*, pp. 262–7.
25. Deng Xiaoping, 'Speech at the Sixth Session of the UN General Assembly', *Peking Review*, 15, Supplement (1974) i.
26. Ibid., p. iii.
27. Kim, *China, the United Nations and World Order*, p. 501.
28. See, for example, Hu Yaobang, 'Report to the Twelfth National Congress of the CCP', *Beijing Review*, 37 (1982) 29–33; and Zhao Ziyang, 'Report on the Work of the Government', *Beijing Review*, 24 (1984), Centrefold, x–xvi.
29. 'The Decision by the Central Committee of the CCP on Restructuring the Economy', *Beijing Review*, 44 (1984), Enclosure, p. xiii.
30. Deng Xiaoping, 'Peace and Development Are the Two Outstanding Issues in the World Today', in Deng Xiaoping, *Fundamental Issues*, pp. 97–100.
31. Ibid., p. 99.
32. *Beijing Review*, 26 (1985) 18.
33. Zhao Ziyang, 'Report on the Work of the Government', *Beijing Review*, 24 (1984), Centrefold, p. xii.
34. Deng Xiaoping, 'Peace and Development', in Deng Xiaoping, *Fundamental Issues*, pp. 99–100. See also *Financial Times*, 6 March 1985.
35. Huan Xiang, 'International Conflicts and Our Choices', *Beijing Review*, 48 (1984) 16.
36. Zhao Ziyang, 'Premier Zhao Ziyang's Speech at the Special Session of the UN Celebrating the Fortieth Anniversary of the Establishment of the UN, 24 Oct. 1985', *Guowuyuan Gongbao* (State Council Bulletin), 3 (10 Nov. 1985).
37. Zhao Ziyang, 'Report on the Seventh Five-Year Plan', *Beijing Review*, 16 (1986), Centrefold, xvii.
38. Zhao Ziyang, 'Report on the Work of the Government', *Beijing Review*, 24 (1984), Centrefold, xv.
39. *Beijing Review*, 26 (1985) 18. See also Hua Zhanshi, 'Nanbei Maodun de Jihua ji qi Xintedian' (The Intensification of Contradictions Between the South and the North and Their New Features), *Shijie Jingji* (World Economy), 3 (1988) 1–7.
40. Zhao Ziyang, 'Report on the Work of the Government', *Beijing Review*, 24 (1984), Centrefold, xi.
41. See Deng Xiaoping, 'Peace and Development', in Deng Xiaoping, *Fundamental Issues*, p. 100. See also *Renmin Ribao*, 14 Oct.1985.
42. Deng Xiaoping, 'A New Approach towards Stabilising the World Situation', in Deng Xiaoping, *Fundamental Issues*, p. 42.

43. Hu Yaobang, 'Report to the Twelfth National Congress of the Chinese Communist Party', *Beijing Review*, 37 (1982) 29. This was later incorporated into the Constitution of the PRC.
44. Zhao Ziyang, 'Striving for a Better World', *Beijing Review*, 44 (1985) 15.
45. Tang Tsou, 'Statesmanship and Scholarship', *World Politics*, XXVI, 3 (April 1974) 428–50.
46. Zhang Guang, 'Bashi Niandai Zhongguo Waijiao Zhengce de Zhongda Tiaozheng' (The Important Adjustments in China's Foreign Policy in the 1980s), *Waijiao Xueyuan Xuebao* (Journal of Foreign Affairs College), 1 (1992) 10.
47. See *Peking Review*, Special Issue (23 May 1970).
48. See *Yearbook on International Communist Affairs, 1977*, p. 287.
49. 'Chairman Mao's Theory of the Differentiation of the Three Worlds is a Major Contribution to Marxism-Leninism', in Chen (ed.), *China and the Three Worlds*, p. 119.
50. This paragraph is partly based on 'The Maoist Image of Human Nature, War, and Revolution', in Kim, *China, the United Nations, and World Order*, pp. 58–72.
51. See Zhang Guang, 'Bashi Niandai Zhongguo Waijiao Zhengce', *Waijiao Xueyuan Xuebao* 1 (1992) 10.
52. Deng Xiaoping, 'Concrete Actions for the Maintenance of World Peace', in Deng Xiaoping, *Fundamental Issues*, p. 116. Italics my own.
53. Wang Jisi, 'International Relations Theory and the Study of Chinese Foreign Policy: A Chinese Perspective', in Robinson and Shambaugh (eds), *Chinese Foreign Policy: Theory and Practice*, pp. 486–7. See also Wang Jisi, 'Dui Zhanzheng yu Heping Lilun de Zaisikao' (Rethinking the Theory of War and Peace), *Shijie Jingji yu Zhengzhi* (World Economy and Politics), 12 (1988) 56–64.
54. Xue Mouhong et al, *Dangdai Zhongguo Waijiao*, p. 412.
55. Song Yiming, 'Meisu jian de Songdong he Guoji Guanxi de Shenke Bianhua' (The Soviet-American Détente and Profound Changes in International Relations), *Guoji Wenti Yanjiu* (International Studies), 1 (1988) 3.
56. Li Dai and Zhou Yang, 'Luelun Dangdai de Zhanzheng yu Heping Wenti' (On War and Peace in the Contemporary Era), *Guoji Wenti Yanjiu* (International Studies), 3 (1986) 5.
57. Ding Yuanhong, 'Yinren Zhumu de Xiou Heping Yundong' (The Outstanding Development of the Peace Movement in Western Europe), *Guoji Wenti Yanjiu*,2 (1982) 7–11.
58. Chen Qimao, 'War and Peace: A Reappraisal', *Beijing Review*, 23 (1986) 18–25; and Li Shenzhi, 'A Sharp Lookout – The Price of Peace', *Beijing Review*, 23 (1986) 16–8.
59. *China Daily*, 5 Nov. 1984. In early November 1984, Mrs Joan Ruddock, the CND leader, was received in Beijing by senior Chinese officials.
60. Deng Xiaoping, *Fundamental Issues*, p. 46.
61. Li Dai and Zhou Yang, 'Luelun Dangdai de Zhanzheng', *Guoji Wenti Yanjiu* 3 (1986) 1–5.
62. Ibid., p. 5.
63. Some Chinese scholars argue more radically that the development of the contemporary international capitalist economy is gradually removing the

foundation for an all-out war between imperialist countries. On the other hand, the scientific and technological revolution is making a world war prohibitively costly and irrelevant in the future international contest for power and wealth. See Di Chun, 'Dui Zhiyue Shijie Dazhan Jige Yingsu de Fenxi' (An Analysis of Factors that Prevent the Outbreak of Another World War), *Guofang Daxue Xuebao* (Journal of National Defence University of China), 7 (1988,) 8–11.
64. See Wei Lin and Xu Zhixin, 'Guanyu Women de Shidai' (On Our Era), *Xiandai Guoji Guanxi* (Contemporary International Relations), 2 (1988) 8–12; and also Wang Wenxue and Guo Baozhu, 'Dui Jianli Guoji Zhengzhi Xinzhixu Zhanlue Zhuzhang de Sikao' (Our Thought on the Strategy to Establish a New International Political Order), *Xiandai Guoji Guanxi* (Contemporary International Relations), 3 (1989) 12–16.
65. See Qian Qichen, 'Duihua Daiti Duikang Shi Shidai de Yaoqiu' (Dialogue Replacing Confrontation Is the Demand of Our Era), *Qiushi* (Seeking Truth), 4 (1988) 2–5.
66. For details of China's endorsement of revolutions in other countries, see P. Van Ness, *Revolution and Chinese Foreign Policy – Peking's Support for Wars of National Liberation*, pp. 81–200; and J. Taylor, *China and Southeast Asia: Peking's Relations with Revolutionary Movements* (expanded and updated edn, 1976); and M. Gurtov, *China and Southeast Asia – The Politics of Survival: A Study of Foreign Policy Interaction*.
67. See Armstrong, *Revolutionary Diplomacy – Chinese Foreign Policy and the United Front Doctrine*.
68. See Bull, 'The Revolt against the West', in Bull and Watson (eds.), *The Expansion of International Society*, pp. 217–28.
69. Larkin, *China and Africa*, p. 70. See also Armstrong, *Revolutionary Diplomacy*, p. 112, and Van Ness, *Revolution and Chinese Foreign Policy*, p. 139.
70. *Peking Review*, Special Issue, 23 May 1970, p. 8.
71. See Van Ness, *Revolution and Chinese Foreign Policy*.
72. Ibid., p. 171.
73. See Gurtov, *China and Southeast Asia*.
74. See Wang Xi and R. H. Holton (eds), *Zhongmei Jingji Guanxi: Xianzhuang yu Qianjing* (China–US Economic Relations: Present and Future), p. 5.
75. Hu Yaobang, 'Report to the Twelfth National Congress of the CCP', *Beijing Review*, 37 (1982) 31.
76. Xie Yixian, 'Bashi Niandai Zhongguo Duiwai Zhengce', *Qiushi* (Seeking Truth), 1 (1989) 39.
77. 'Qian Qichen Reviews China's Foreign Policy', *Beijing Review*, 1 (1986) 15.
78. Zhao Ziyang, 'Report on the Work of the Government', *Beijing Review*, 24 (1984), Centrefold, xiv.
79. See Zhimin Lin, 'China's Third World Policy', in Hao and Huan (eds), *The Chinese View of the World*, pp. 240–5.
80. Tong Dalin and Liu Ji, 'North–South Co-operation for Mutual Prosperity', *Beijing Review*, 26 (1985) 19.
81. See Chen Qida et al, 'Zhongguo yu Disan Shijie Guojia de Jingmao Guanxi' (China's Economic and Trade Relations with Third World Countries), *Xiandai Guoji Guanxi* (Contemporary International Relations), 2 (1990) 48.

82. Editorial Board of *Red Flag*, 'Guanyu Woguo de Duiwai Jingji Guanxi Wenti' (On Questions Regarding China's Foreign Economic Relations), *Hongqi* (Red Flag), 8 (1982) 2–10. It argues that although most Third World countries are poor,

> there are also quite a few Third World countries that are richer than our country. Owing to this complicated situation, in carrying out our policies of supporting Third World countries, including the policy of giving them economic aid and promoting our economic contacts with them, we should make a clear distinction between their different economic status and act accordingly.

83. Chen Qida et al, 'Zhongguo yu Disan Shijie', *Xiandai Guoji Guanxi* (Contemporary International Relations), 2 (1990) 48.
84. Zhao Ziyang, 'Report on the Work of the Government', *Beijing Review*, 24 (1984), Centrefold, xiv.
85. They were first proposed by Zhao Ziyang during his visit to Africa in January 1983 as principles in promoting economic and technical cooperation between China and African countries. In November 1985, while visiting Latin American countries, Zhao proposed another four principles: peace and friendship, mutual assistance, equality and mutual benefit, and common progress. Later, these were adopted as principles governing China's economic and technical cooperation with all developing nations. For details of China's trade with Latin American countries in 1987 and 1988, see *Zhongguo Duiwai Jingji Maoyi Nianjian, 1989,* 315–6.
86. See 'Brazilians Boost Trade Relations with Chinese', *Financial Times*, 11 Nov. 1985. See also 'Sino–Brazilian Trade Expands', *Beijing Review*, 13 (1986) 28–9.
87. Zhimin Lin, 'China's Third World Policy', in Hao and Huan (eds), *The Chinese View of the World*, pp. 245–7. By 1987, 12 Latin American countries had signed trade agreements with China. By the end of 1988, China had signed about 1500 contracts with over 80 states, most of them Third World countries. The export of labour and other services contributed over $5 billion a year to China's overall balance of payments.
88. Chen Qida et al, 'Zhongguo yu Disan Shijie', *Xiandai Guoji Guanxi* (Contemporary International Relations), 2 (1990) 47–9.
89. Kim, *China, the United Nations and World Order*, p. 255.
90. For a general elaboration of dependencia theory, see, T. Smith, 'The Underdevelopment of Development Literature: The Case of Dependency Theory', *World Politics*, XXXI, 1, (Jan. 1979) 247–88.
91. Amin and other dependencia theorists were belatedly acknowledged in China only in the 1980s.
92. A. G. Frank, 'The Development of Underdevelopment', in J. D. Cockcroft et al, *Dependence and Underdevelopment: Latin America's Political Economy*, p. 9.
93. Deng Xiaoping, 'Speech at the Sixth Session of the UN General Assembly', *Peking Review*, 15, Supplement (1974) iii.
94. The two resolutions are a Declaration on the Establishment of a New International Economic Order and a Programme of Action on the Establishment of a New International Economic Order. Both were adopted

at the Sixth Special Session of the General Assembly of the UN in April–May 1974.
95. Quoted in Kim, *China, the United Nations and World Order*, p. 265.
96. *Beijing Review*, 24 (1979) 18–9.
97. Chen Dezhao, 'Dui Tongyi Shijie Shichang Wajielun de Jidian Kanfa' (Has the Unified World Market Disintegrated?), *Shijie Jingji* (World Economy), 6 (1982) 6–11. Other Chinese economists argued strongly that the Chinese view on 'two parallel world markets' should be abandoned. See Wang Hong, *China's Export since 1979*, pp. 49, 240.
98. *Guardian*, 27 Sept. 1984.
99. For details of the debate, see Ma, Shu-yun, 'Recent Changes in China's Pure Trade Theory', *China Quarterly*, 106 (June 1986) 291–305. For a fuller elaboration, see also Wang Hong, *China's Exports since 1979*, chap. 2, 'Changes in Chinese Trade Theory since 1979', pp. 45–85.
100. For more details of the debate, see also Chen Qiwei, 'Bijiao Liyi Lun de Kexue Neihan' (The Scientific Core of Ricardo's Theory of Comparative Advantage), *Shijie Jingji* (World Economy), 3 (1981) 14–19; Zhu Zhongdi, 'Bijiao Chengbenshuo de Lilun Quexian' (A Critique of the Theory of Comparative Advantage), *Shijie Jingji* (World Economy), 11 (1981) 25–33; Wang Linsheng, 'Guanyu Li Jiatu Bijiao Chengben Shuo de Pingjia Wenti' (On How to Evaluate Ricardo's Theory of Comparative Advantage), *Guoji Maoyi Wenti* (Issues of International Trade), 3 (1981) 23–30; Wu Yongxun, 'Ye Tan Bijiao Chengbenshuo' (My Thought on the Theory of Comparative Advantage), *Guoji Maoyi Wenti* (Issues in International Trade), 4 (1981) 25–6; Li Dacang and Chen Tiejun, 'Ruhe Lijie Guoji Maoyi Zhongde Boxue' (How to Understand 'Exploitation' in International Trade), *Shijie Jingji* (World Economy), 4 (1982) 16–18; Zhang Lizhi and Liao Xianchi, 'Shilun Guoji Jiazhi he Guoji Shenchan Jiage'(On International Value of Labour and the Cost of International Production), *Zhongguo Shehui Kexue* (China Social Sciences), 4 (1987) 91–100.
101. Wang Shaoxi, 'Lun Woguo Fazhan Duiwai Maoyi de Lilun Yiju' (On the Theoretical Foundation for the Development of China's Foreign Trade), *Guoji Maoyi* (Intertrade), 12 (1986) 4–9.
102. Chen Shouqi, 'Fahui Youshi Jiji Canjia Guoji Fengong' (Take Our Full Advantage and Participate Actively in the International Division of Labour), *Guoji Maoyi Wenti* (Issues of International Trade), 3 (1981) 17.
103. The above points are summarised from an authoritative essay published in the highly regarded *China Social Sciences Quarterly* in January 1980. See Yuan Wenqi et al, 'Guoji Fengong yu Woguo Duiwai Jingji Guanxi' (The International Division of Labour and China's Foreign Economic Relations), *Zhongguo Shehui Kexue* (China Social Sciences), 1 (1980) 3–20.
104. They are Hong Kong, Taiwan, Singapore and Korea.
105. Li Jinliang, 'Guoji Fengong Wenti Qianlun' (On International Division of Labour), *Shijie Jingji* (World Economy), 3 (1981) 23–4.
106. Huan Xiang, 'International Conflicts and Our Choices', *Beijing Review*, 48 (1984) 16.
107. Editorial Board of *Red Flag*, 'Guanyu Woguo de Duiwai Jingji Guanxi Wenti' (On Questions of China's Foreign Economic Relations), *Hongqi* (Red Flag), 8 (1982) 2–12. Italics my own.

108. *Beijing Review*, 41 (1982) 18.
109. *Guardian*, 27 Sept. 1984.
110. Deng Xiaoping, 'Peace and Development', in Deng Xiaoping, *Fundamental Issues*, pp. 99–100.
111. Li Peng, 'Report on the Work of the Government to the Seventh National People's Congress', *Beijing Review*, 17 (1988) 31.
112. Xue Mouhong et al, *Dangdai Zhongguo Waijiao*, p. 412.
113. Kapur, *Distant Neighbours*, p. 162.
114. For more details, see MacFarquhar, 'The Succession to Mao and the end of Maoism, 1969–1982', in MacFarquhar, (ed.), *The Politics of China, 1949–1989*, pp. 248–339.
115. For a more general discussions of political changes in China in the 1980s, see M. Goldman, *Sowing the Seeds of Democracy in China: Political Reform in the Deng Xiaoping Era*.

5 POLITICAL SOCIALISATION

1. David Armstrong argues that 'the concept of socialisation implies that pressure to conform operates upon any entity that aspires to statehood' Armstrong, *Revolution and World Order*, p. 10.
2. As Fred Halliday most recently argued, 'An international society created and maintained by the Great Powers may be the best the human race can come up with, but it is far from being a society based upon shared values' Halliday, *Rethinking International Relations*, p. 102.
3. For more details, see Halliday, *Rethinking International Relations*, especially chap. 5, 'International Society as Homogeneity', pp. 94–123.
4. *Renmin Ribao*, 2 Nov. 1985.
5. As stated by Ji Pengfei, Head of the CCP's International Liaison Department from 1979 to 1982, before 1978 there are no formally established relations between the CCP and other political parties in Third World countries, especially in Africa, though friendly exchanges were conducted and mutual support was given between the CCP and those parties. See 'Tong Disan Shijie Guojia Zhengdang Fazhan Youhao Guanxi' (Developing Friendly Relations with Political Parties in Third World Countries – An Interview with Ji Pengfei), *Shijie Zhishi* (World Affairs), 6 (1984) 10–11.
6. See 'Peking's "Dual Track" Policy in Southeast Asia Produces Gains', Foreign Broadcast Information Service (FBIS), Special Report, 25 Aug. 1975. See also W. R. Heaton, 'China and Southeast Asian Communist Movements: The Decline of Dual Track Diplomacy', *Asian Survey*, XXII, 8 (1982) 779–800.
7. U Thein Maung, Burma's new ambassador to China, the first since 1967, arrived in Beijing on 16 November 1970. On 31 May 1974, China established full diplomatic relations with Malaysia, which was followed by those with the Philippines on 9 June 1975 and with Thailand on 1 July 1975.
8. *Xinhua News Bulletin*, 8 November 1978. It is of significance to note that this statement was made in the wake of a visit by Vietnamese Premier Pham Van Dong to Southeast Asian nations, during which he actually pledged that Vietnam would no longer support any insurgent parties in the area.

9. *Yearbook on International Communist Affairs, 1978*, p. 224.
10. For example, in July 1979, the radio station of the Communist Party of Thailand (CPT), Voice of the People of Thailand, based in Kunming in the southwest of China, was closed down by the CCP. The last broadcast of VOPT was on 11 July 1979. Voice of the Malayan Revolution (VOMR), mouthpiece for the Malayan Communist Party, did not go off the air until July 1981. From 1 July 1981 onwards, VOMR was replaced by the Voice of Malayan Democracy (VOMD) broadcast with a much weaker signal and much less frequency, reportedly from southern Thailand (*Yearbook on International Communist Affairs, 1978*, p. 292; and *1982*, p. 212. Robert Ross claimed, however, that VOMD, 'one of China's last ties to the MCP', only ceased its operation in January 1990. R. Ross, 'China and Post-Cambodia Southeast Asia: Coping with Success', in A. Whiting, (ed.), *China's Foreign Relations*, p. 60. Still another clandestine radio, Voice of the People of Burma, believed to be located in the southwest of China, remained operational until the mid-1980s.
11. For example, on 18 May 1977, Hua Guofeng, Chairman of the CCP and other Politburo members went out of their way to have a well-publicised meeting with Jusuf Adjitorop, Secretary of the Indonesian Communist Party (PKI). Although Adjitorop and his 'delegation' were believed to have resided in China since the failed *coup* in Indonesia 1965, it was the first time in many years that the CCP had given such official approbation to this PKI faction. See *Yearbook on International Communist Affairs, 1978*, p. 255; and *Peking Review*, 21 (1977) 3.
12. Quoted in Heaton, 'The Decline of Dual Track Diplomacy', *Asian Survey*, XXII, 8 (1982) 784.
13. *Xinhua News Bulletin*, 12 Aug. 1981. Italics my own.
14. See *Beijing Review*, 22 (1985) 6.
15. See Ross, 'China and Post-Cambodia Southeast Asia', in Whiting, (ed.), *China's Foreign Relations*, pp. 52–66. For China's relations with the ASEAN countries in the 1970s, see J. A. Camilleri, *Chinese Foreign Policy: The Maoist Era and Its Aftermath*, chap. 10, 'Southeast Asia: The Realignment of Power'.
16. It was reported, for example, that despite China's pronounced policy of providing only moral support for the BCP, China continued to provide a considerable amount of weapons, medical facilities and other material aid to the BCP even as late as 1982. See *Far Eastern Economic Review*, 14 April 1983, pp. 23–30.
17. See Heaton, 'The Decline of Dual Track Diplomacy', *Asian Survey*, XXII, 8 (1982) 792.
18. *Financial Times*, 2 March 1984.
19. *Shijie Zhishi* (World Affairs), 11(1985) 2–3.
20. See J. M. van der Kroef, '"Normalising" Relations with China: Indonesia's Policies and Perceptions', *Asian Survey*, XXVI, 8 (1986) 934.
21. Xue Mouhong et al, *Dangdai Zhongguo Waijiao*, p. 456.
22. Ibid., pp. 457–8.
23. Ibid., p. 458.
24. See Deng Xiaoping, 'Chuli Xiongdidang Guanxi de Yitiao Zhongyao Yuanze' (An Important Principle in Dealing with Relations Between Fraternal Parties), in *Deng Xiaoping Wenxuan, 1975–1982* (Selected Works of Deng Xiaoping, 1975–1982), pp. 278–9.

25. *Beijing Review*, 22 (1984) 16–17. In Hu's formulation, independence means that all Communist Parties 'should choose their own road of revolution and construction and decide on their positions on world affairs independently', because application of the fundamental principles of Marxism 'should always fit in with specific historical conditions and be integrated with the revolutionary practice in each country'. Complete equality means that 'no Party has the right to style itself as the top spokesman'. Mutual respect and non-interference dictates that no Party should be allowed to use any excuse to 'deprive other Parties of their right to independence, control their actions, and make them serve the needs of a certain Party's foreign policy'. Non-interference therefore applies not only to inter-party relations. It also means that no party should take advantage of its inter-party relations to interfere in inter-state relations. For more elaboration of the four principles, see Lian Yan, 'Tantan Zhongguo Gongchandang Duiwai Lianluo Gongzuo de Tiaozheng he Fazhan' (On the Adjustment and Development of the CCP's International Liaison Work), *Renmin Ribao*, 29 June 1986.
26. Ibid., p. 17.
27. For example, in an authoritative article on the CCP's relations with other parties published on the sixty-fifth anniversary of the CCP, it is only vaguely stated that the CCP

> has been a persistent champion of sound party-to-party relations. But it has also made mistakes in handling its relations with other parties. These mistakes have negatively affected certain parties. The CPC [CCP] has, however, learnt from its mistakes, and it has been open about acknowledging and correcting them.

See Lian Yan, 'The CPC's Relations with Other Parties', *Beijing Review*, 27 (1986) 24.
28. For example, Lian Yan, a pseudonym for the spokesman of the CCP's International Liaison Department, features regularly in *People's Daily* and in *Beijing Review*.
29. See G. Rozman, *Chinese Debate on Soviet Socialism, 1978–1985*, pp. 85–6. Among other things, the Chinese admitted that their criticism of the Soviet ideas of peaceful coexistence and peaceful competition was mistaken and that it is not entirely wrong for the Communist Party in developed countries to take part in parliamentary elections and to advocate peaceful transition.
30. See 'Foreign Contacts of the Communist Party', *Beijing Review*, 42 (1984) 19.
31. Ibid.
32. Heaton, 'The Decline of Dual Track Diplomacy', *Asian Survey*, XXII, 8 (1982) 781.
33. *Renmin Ribao*, 6 Oct. 1985.
34. See 'Zhonggong Zhongyang Duiwai Lianluobu Fuzeren jiu Zhongguo Gongchandang de Duiwai Jiaowang Huodong da Xinhuashe Jizhe Wen' (An Interview by Xinhua News Agency Reporter with the Head of the International Liaison Department of the CCP on the CCP's International Liaison Work), *Renmin Ribao*, 18 Sept. 1984. See also Lian Yan, 'Tantan Zhongguo Gongchandang', *Renmin Ribao*, 29 June 1986.
35. At the end of 1985, the Malaysian Prime Minister Mahathir relegated the issue of the CCP–CPM ties to a 'minor problem' in Sino-Malaysian rela-

tions during his visit. The Malaysian government also claimed to be satisfied with China's assurance to Mahathir that China would not interfere in the domestic affairs of Malaysia. *Yearbook on International Communist Affairs, 1986*, p. 216.
36. *Shijie Zhishi* 6 (1984) 10–11.
37. Guo Qingshi and Wu Jun, 'Dang de Duiwai Lianluo Gongzuo de Yige Xinfazhan' (A New Development of our Party's International Liaison Work), *Hongqi* (Red Flag), 11 (1986) 30. See also *Beijing Review*, 24 (1984) 8. It is interesting to note that the Japanese Socialist Party established relations as early as the 1950s with the Chinese People's Institute of Foreign Affairs and the Sino-Japanese Association. From 1957 to 1983, the Japanese Socialist Party had sent 11 delegations to China which met with Mao Zedong, Zhou Enlai, Deng Xiaoping and Hu Yaobang. It was not until March 1983, however, that the CCP and the Japanese Socialist Party established formal inter-party relations. See ibid.
38. See Lian Yan, 'The CPC's Relations with Other Parties', *Beijing Review*, 27 (1986) 21–4. See also *Renmin Ribao*, 6 Oct. 1985.
39. Guo Qingshi and Wu Jun, 'Dang de Duiwai Lianluo Gongzuo', *Hongqi* (Red Flag), 11 (1986) 30–1.
40. Ibid., p. 30. See also *Beijing Review*, 24 (1984) 9.
41. They are principles of mutual respect for sovereignty and territorial integrity, mutual non-aggression, non-interference in each other's affairs, equality and mutual benefit, and peaceful co-existence.
42. Zhao Ziyang, 'Persistence in the Independent Foreign Policy of Peace – Excerpts from the Report on the Seventh Five-Year Plan', in Han Nianlong (ed.), *Diplomacy of Contemporary China*, p. 581. Emphasis added.
43. Lian Yan, 'Tantan Zhongguo Gongchandang', *Renmin Ribao*, 29 June 1986.
44. 'The Prospect of Sino-Indonesian Relations – An Interview with Wu Xueqian', *Shijie Zhishi*, 11 (1985) 2–3. Emphasis added.
45. The spokesman of the International Liaison Department of the Central Committee of the CCP publicly declared that the CCP 'wishes to contact all those parties which would like to have contacts and exchanges with the Chinese Communist Party' (*Beijing Review*, 41 (1986) 7).
46. *Renmin Ribao*, 29 June 1986.
47. See 'Chinese, E. European Parties Renew Ties', *Beijing Review*, 41 (1986) 7. The CCP's attempt to renew normal relations with the Japanese Communist Party (JCP) in 1985–86, however, did not succeed. The two Parties broke their relations in 1967. In November 1985, the JCP began secret discussions with the CCP on the normalisation of their relations, in response to a formal request from the latter. In November 1986, the JCP and the CCP ended their secret negotiations after failing to reach an agreement to mend their relations. The JCP claimed that the failure was mainly because the CCP did not satisfy the two preconditions set by the JCP for normalising their relations. Although the CCP admitted to a few mistakes in handling relations between the CCP and the JCP in the past, it would not comply with the JCP request to sever relations with the Japan Labour Party, which was formed first by the JCP members who broke with the JCP in 1966. See *Yearbook on International Communist Affairs, 1986*, pp. 176 and 195; and *Yearbook on International Communist Affairs, 1987*, pp. 190 and 206.

48. The 'three obstacles' are the Soviet support of the Vietnam's invasion of Kampuchea, the Soviet Army stationed along Sino-Soviet borders especially in Mongolia, and the Soviet invasion of Afghanistan.
49. *Shijie Zhishi* (World Affairs), 6 (1984) 10–11.
50. *Renmin Ribao*, 6 Oct. 1986.
51. *Yearbook on International Communist Affairs, 1988*, p. 166.
52. The possible exception is relations between the CCP and the JCP which remain strained.
53. Quoted in Chi Su, 'Sino-Soviet Relations of the 1980s: From Confrontation to Conciliation', in Kim (ed.), *China and the World*, p. 109.
54. S. S. Kim, 'International Organisations in Chinese Foreign Policy', in Whiting (ed.), *China's Foreign Relations*, p. 151.
55. See UN Doc. S/14790. The last Chinese non-participation vote on resolutions concerning UN peacekeeping operations was cast on 23 November 1981 on draft resolution 493 regarding the renewal of the United Nations Disengagement Force (UNDOF). See UN Doc. S/PV.2320, p. 10.
56. China's position *vis-à-vis* UN peacekeeping operations as outlined by Huang Hua at the Security Council in the discussion of the organisation of United Nations Emergency Forces II (UNEF II) on 25 October 1973 was opposition to the dispatch of the peacekeeping forces and non-participation in the voting on the relevant UN draft resolution. China had held this position until 18 December 1981. See UN Doc. S/PV.1750, p. 2.
57. UN Doc. S/PV.2313, p. 6.
58. *Peking Review*, 3 (1965) 7–9.
59. *Peking Review*, 5 (1965) 5–6.
60. *Peking Review*, 41 (1965) 11–12.
61. *Peking Review*, 10 (1965) 15.
62. *Peking Review*, 17 (1965) 27–8.
63. K. Skjelsbaek, 'UN Peacekeeping: Expectations, Limitations and Results: Forty Years of Mixed Experience', in I. J. Rikhye and K. Skjelsbaek (eds), *The United Nations and Peacekeeping*, p. 52.
64. See B. Weng, 'Communist China's Changing Attitude Toward the United Nations', *International Organisation*, XX, 4 (1966) 677–704.
65. *Peking Review*, 41 (1965) 11–12.
66. Huang Shuhai, 'Lianheguo wei Meihao Shijie er Fendou' (The United Nations Is Fighting for a Better World – Interview with Huang Hua), *Shijie Zhishi* 19 (1985) 2. Even in Premier Zhao Ziyang's interview with *Beijing Review* on the eve of the fortieth anniversary of the UN, he pointed out that the UN had made some serious mistakes in its 40-year history. See *Beijing Review*, 44 (1985) 17–18.
67. Kim, *China, the United Nations and World Order*, p. 241.
68. M. H. Halperin and D. H. Perkins, *Communist China and Arms Control*, pp. 149–50.
69. *Renmin Ribao*, 22 Aug. 1960. In China's most recent reassessment of the UN peacekeeping operations, the ONUC remains 'one of the blemishes' in the history of the UN. See 'Lankui Budui – Lianheguo Weichi Heping Budui' (Blue Helmets – The UN Peacekeeping Forces), *Shijie Zhishi* 21 (1988) 26.
70. Kim, *China, the United Nations and World Order*, p. 217.

71. UN Doc. S/PV.1750, p. 2.
72. UN Doc. S/PV.1752, p. 1.
73. Kim, (ed.), *China and the World – Chinese Foreign Policy in the Post-Mao Era*, p. 215.
74. See A. Whiting, 'Assertive Nationalism in Chinese Foreign Policy', *Asian Survey*, XXIII, 8, 1983) 913–33.
75. UN Doc. A/SPC/39/SR5, p. 3. See also *Renmin Ribao*, 17 Oct. 1984, and *Beijing Review*, 46 (1984) 12.
76. Ibid.
77. Ibid.
78. S. R. Mills, 'The Financing of UN Peacekeeping Operations: The Need for a Sound Financial Basis', in Rikhye and Skjelsbaek (eds), *The United Nations and Peacekeeping*, pp. 102–4. China's contribution to the UN regular budget was 0.97%; so was its financial contribution to peacekeeping operations.
79. See H. Wiseman, 'Peacekeeping in the International Political Context: Historical Analysis and Future Directions', in Rikhye and Skjelsbaek (eds), *The United Nations and Peacekeeping*, p. 34.
80. See *Renmin Ribao*, 17 Oct. 1984, and *Beijing Review*, 46 (1984) 12. Emphasis added. The other three points Liang made are as follow. First, countries or parties concerned should cooperate with peacekeeping operations and make use of the time gained and favourable conditions created from such operations to seek political settlements of the issues in question as quickly as possible (point 3). Second, each peacekeeping operation must have a clearly defined mandate, and no country or party should take advantage of peacekeeping operations for selfish interests or to interfere in the internal affairs of other countries (point 4). And third, for the purpose of strengthening UN peacekeeping operations, it is necessary both to formulate guidelines and to take practical measures. The Special Committee on Peacekeeping Operations should improve its work in the above two aspects simultaneously (point 7).
81. See *Beijing Review*, 44 (1985) 15. In another commemoratiue article, Lai Yali, formerly one of China's ambassadors to the UN, remarked that, 'Though it occasionally looked ineffective, the United Nations has developed into the world's most important international organisation and has become an invaluable forum for international dialogue'. See Lai Yali, 'United Nations and the Third World', *Beijing Review*, 42 (1985) 16–19.
82. *Beijing Review*, 39 (1988) 12.
83. Henry Wiseman eloquently described this changed political climate for UN peacekeeping as follows:

> Gone are the cries that peacekeeping is a neo-colonialist imposition, a cry sounded so vehemently during and in the aftermath of the Congo Operation. Gone are the days when peacekeeping was such a divisive issue that it almost wrecked the UN itself. Gone are the days when socialist states were unwilling or unwelcome contributors to peacekeeping operations.

See Wiseman, 'Peacekeeping in the International Political Context', in Rikhye and Skjelsbaek (eds), *The United Nations and Peacekeeping*, p. 38. See also 'The Special Committee's Comprehensive Review of the Whole

Question of Peacekeeping Operations in All Aspects of 1990', UN Doc. A/SPC/45/SR17, 19, 21, 24, and 27 for favourable assessment by member states of UN peacekeeping operations.
84. UN Doc. A/43/645. See also *Renmin Ribao*, 4 Nov. 1988, as well as Li Enzhao, 'Lianheguo Weichi Heping Xingdong de Chengjiu he Zhanwang' (UN Peacekeeping Operations: Achievements and Prospect) *Shijie Zhishi* 8 (1991) 20–1.
85. UN Doc. A/SPC/43/SR16, p. 2.
86. Xinhua in FBIS-Chi, 13 April 1989.
87. UN Doc. A/SPC/44/SR10, pp. 10–11.
88. *Renmin Ribao*, 13 May 1990. For China's participation in UNTAG, see further United Nations, *The Blue Helmets – A Review of United Nations Peacekeeping*, 2nd edn, p. 356.
89. *Renmin Ribao*, March 1992.
90. There have been three casualties among Chinese peacekeepers. Two members of the Chinese engineering detachment were killed in the UN peacekeeping operation in Cambodia. See UN Doc. A/C.4/48/SR.22, p. 15. See also Xu Zhengfeng, *Zhongguo Laikui: Zhongguo Fu Jian Gongchengbin Dadui Weihe Xingdong Jishi* (The Chinese Blue Helmets: Report on Chinese Engineers Battalion's Participation in Peacekeeping in Cambodia), pp. 78–88. Major Lei Runmin was killed when his patrol car overturned on the Kuwaiti side of the Kuwait–Iraq border on 8 May. Captain Kararuddin from Indonesia was wounded in the same accident. Both were serving on the UN Iraq-Kuwait Observers Mission (UNIKOM).
91. Kim, 'International Organisations in Chinese Foreign Policy', in Whiting (ed.), *China's Foreign Relations*, pp. 149–51.
92. Ibid.
93. Y. Shichor, 'China and the Middle East since Tiananmen', in Whiting (ed.), *China's Foreign Relations*, pp. 93–5. According to Shichor, even the Emir of Kuwait expressed his understanding of China's abstention from the vote on Security Council Resolution 678.
94. UN Doc. S/PV.2963.
95. *Renmin Ribao*, 17 Dec. 1990.
96. See in particular UN Doc. S/VP 3114, p. 10–12. China abstained from voting on both Security Council Resolutions 770 and 776.
97. UN Doc. A/C.4/48/SR.22, p. 15.
98. UN Doc. S/PV.3133, p. 8.
99. The Chinese deputy representative Chen Jian went out of his way to state that

> China does not favour the use of sanctions as a means of resolving conflicts. The sanctions regime contained in this resolution is, in the absence of other effective measures, the exceptional step taken under the highly unique circumstances now prevailing in Haiti. ... Sanctions are not a panacea that can be applied whenever and wherever it suits us for want of better solutions (*Reuters News Service*, 6 May 1994).

100. UN Doc. S/PV.3238, p. 21. The Chinese delegation nevertheless voted in favour of the resolution based on the understanding that it was warranted by the 'unique and exceptional situation in Haiti' and 'should not be considered as constituting any precedent for the future'.

Notes 281

101. *Renmin Ribao*, 35 June 1994.
102. UN Doc. A/C.4/48/SR.22, pp. 14–15. In the words of the Chinese delegate,

    Respect for national sovereignty and non-interference in the internal affairs of Member States were important principles of the Charter and should also be the guidelines for peacekeeping activities. China considered that at any time and under any circumstances, the consent and co-operation of the relevant Governments or parties must be obtained in carrying out activities of preventive diplomacy of peacekeeping.

103. *Renmin Ribao*, 29 Sept. 1994.
104. Kim, 'International Organisations in Chinese Foreign Policy', in Whiting (ed.), *China's Foreign Relations*, p. 151.
105. See C. T. Ramesh and C. A. Thayer (eds), *A Crisis of Expectations: UN Peacekeeping in the 1990s*.
106. B. E. Urquhart, 'Reflections by the Chairman', in Rikhye and Skjelsbaek (eds), *The United Nations and Peacekeeping*, p. 17.
107. For some critical rethinking on UN peacekeeping, see S. Trouval, 'Why the UN Fails?' *Foreign Affairs*, 73, 5 (Sept./Oct. 1994) 44–57. See also G. Picco, 'The UN and the Use of Force', *Foreign Affairs*, 73, 5 (Sept./Oct. 1994) 14–18.
108. H. Wiseman, 'Peacekeeping: The Dynamics of Future Development', in H. Wiseman (ed.), *Peacekeeping: Appraisals and Proposals*, pp. 336–7.
109. It must be noted that in China's official and academic thinking and discourse on strategic matters, 'arms control' (Junbei Kongzhi) has rarely been used. Instead, 'disarmament' (Caijun) is the term denoting both the process of what is commonly known as 'arms control' and the reduction *per se* of arms. There are probably two explanations for this. One is that the Chinese officials and even the academicians have not come to grips with the semantic as well as practical differences between the two. Consequently they use 'disarmament' to cover both areas. The other is that there is a fundamentally different philosophy underlying the Chinese approach to the international disarmament process. Accordingly, they refuse to use 'arms control' as a valid term for the disarmament process. There is nevertheless some evidence to suggest that Chinese officials have begun to accept arms control as a valid concept in the international disarmament process. Jiang Zemin, General Secretary of the CCP, for example, used Junbei Kongzhi (arms control) in his Report to the Fourteenth National Congress of the CCP in October 1992.
110. IISS, *Strategic Survey, 1988–1989*, p. 23.
111. See, for example, G. Gill and T. Kim, *China's Arms Acquisitions from Abroad: A Quest for 'Superb and Secret Weapons'*; and D. Ball, 'Arms and Affluence: Military Acquisitions in the Asian-Pacific Region', *International Security* (Winter 1993/94), 18, 3, 78–112.
112. Kim, 'China's International Organisational Behaviour', in Robinson and Shambaugh (eds), *Chinese Foreign Policy: Theory and Practice*, p. 418.
113. See John G. Ruggie, 'Multilateralism: The Anatomy of an Institution', *International Organisations*, 46, 3 (Summer 1992) 561–598.
114. The major multilateral arms control agreements as listed by Stockholm International Peace Research Institute (SIPRI) in 1981 are Antarctic Treaty,

Partial Test Ban Treaty, Outer Space Treaty, Treaty of Tlatelolco, Non-Proliferation Treaty, Sea-Bed Treaty, Biological Weapons (BW) Convention and Environmental Modifications (ENMOD) Convention. See Stockholm International Peace Research Institute, *Arms Control: A Survey and Appraisal of Multilateral Agreements*, p. 151; and J. Goldblat, *Agreements for Arms Control: A Critical Survey*, p. 303.
115. China signed the Additional Protocol II of Tlatelolco Treaty on 21 Aug. 1973 and ratified it on 23 April 1974. China was also a party to the Geneva Protocol. On 13 July 1952, the PRC government issued a statement recognising as binding the accession to the Protocol in the name of China in 1929.
116. See 'China Accedes to Nuclear Non-Proliferation Treaty', *Beijing Review*, 13 (1992) 12.
117. G. Evans, 'Arms Control and Disarmament: A Chance for Progress', in United Nations, *Disarmament Topic Papers 8: Challenges to Multilateral Disarmament in the Post-Cold-War and Post-Gulf-War Period*, p. 22.
118. 'Inhumane Weapons' Convention – a convention on the prohibition on the use of certain conventional weapons which may be deemed to be excessively injurious or to have indiscriminate effects – was signed in New York on 10 April 1981 and entered into force on 2 December 1983. See *SIPRI Yearbook of World Armaments and Disarmament, 1992* p. 598.
119. See Xue Mouhong et al, *Dangdai Zhongguo Waijiao*, p. 493.
120. Treaty of Rarotonga – South Pacific Nuclear Free Zone Treaty – was signed at Rarotonga, Cook Islands, on 6 August 1985 and entered into force on 11 December 1986. It has three protocols. The treaty is open for signature by members of the South Pacific Forum: Protocol 1, by France, the UK and the USA; Protocol 2 and Protocol 3, by China, France, the USSR, the UK and the USA. This convention, together with the 'Inhumane Weapons' Convention, have been added to the list of the SIPRI's major multilateral arms control agreements since they entered into force. See *SIPRI Yearbook 1992*, pp. 598–9 and 603.
121. They eventually signed the Rarotonga Treaty only after France stopped its nuclear test in the South Pacific in 1996.
122. Evans, 'Arms Control and Disarmament', in United Nations, *Disarmament Topic Papers 8*, p. 20.
123. See *SIPRI Yearbook 1990*, p. 554.
124. *Beijing Review*, 34 (1983) 7; and 43 (1983) 13. China actually asked that the IAEA safeguards be a condition for its exports of nuclear materials and facilities when it joined the IAEA. *Beijing Review*, 21 (1985) 19.
125. *SIPRI Yearbook 1990*, pp. 560–3.
126. *Renmin Ribao*, 22 March 1986 and *Beijing Review*, 12 (1986) 14–15.
127. The Missile Technology Control Regime (MTCR) is an informal agreement negotiated and reached among seven Western nations – namely, Britain, Canada, West Germany, Italy, Japan and the United States – in 1987. Its purpose is to prohibit exports of ballistic missiles and related technologies. It has been criticised for, among other things, the inclusion of too few participants, and especially the exclusion of China and the former Soviet Union. See *SIPRI Yearbook 1990*, pp. 372–3.
128. For detailed studies of China's arms control policies before 1980, see C. C. Hu, *Arms Control Policy of the People's Republic of China, 1949–1978* (unpublished D.Phil. thesis, Oxford University); see also

M. H. Halperin and D. H. Perkins, *Communist China and Arms Control*; and R. N. Clough et al, *The United States, China and Arms Control*.
129. See 'Chinese Statement on Arms Control, 22 Nove. 1964', Appendix A in Halperin and Perkins, *Communist China and Arms Control*, pp. 173–8.
130. Ibid., p. 177.
131. An illustrative example of China's being 'caught up' in international ACD efforts is China's participation in the United Nations Special Session on Disarmament (UNSSOD) in May 1978. In voting for the draft resolution on UNSSOD at the First Committee in late 1977, China chose non-participation. In February 1978, China voluntarily excluded itself from the 54-member UNSSOD Preparatory Committee. Nevertheless, China attended the session in May 1978, with Huang Hua, its permanent representative to the UN, as the head of the Chinese delegation. Reluctant through it might be, China was now part of the global ACD efforts. It is an overstatement to claim that such participation made China 'arms control minded'. It did, however, help foster an understanding on the part of China of the values of international ACD efforts conducive to international peace and security, and facilitate mutual appreciation between China and other members of the international community of each other's positions and principles as regards international ACD matters. That proved to be instrumental in the search for consensus among China and other members of international society on the ACD issues and to China's eventually engaging the West in strategic dialogue on arms control and disarmament.
132. See, for example J. H. Kalicki, *The Pattern of Sino-American Crises*, pp. 67, 80 and 150–1. For the US nuclear threat against China during the Korean War, see M. A. Ryan, *China's Attitude Toward Nuclear Weapons: China and the US during the Korean War*.
133. Hinton, *Communist China in World Politics*, pp. 26–7.
134. See R. MacFarquhar, *Sino-American Relations, 1949–1971*, p. 103. See also G. H. Chang, 'To the Nuclear Brink: Eisenhower, Dulles and the Quemoy-Matsu Crisis', *International Security*, 12, 2 (1983) 96–123.
135. See 'How US urged nuclear strike on China', *The Times*, 2 Jan. 1985.
136. According to Dittmer, at the impromptu meeting between Kosygin and Zhou Enlai at Beijing airport on 11 September of 1969, Kosygin explicitly reiterated the Soviet nuclear threat. etc. See Dittmer, *Sino-Soviet Normalisation and Its International Implications, 1945–1990*, pp. 191–2. See also G. Segal, *Defending China*, pp. 180–90.
137. UN DOC. A/8536, p. 3. Quoted in Kim, *China, the United Nations and World Order*, p. 170.
138. J. W. Lewis and Hua Di, 'China's Ballistic Missile Programs: Technologies, Strategies, Goals', *International Security*, 17, 2 (1992) 5–6. They further claimed that China's ballistic missiles programme was 'essentially technology-driven' and 'only in the early 1980s did Beijing develop relevant strategic and tactical doctrines for its deployed and planned missile forces'. Ibid., p. 7. See also Nie Rongzhen, 'How China Develops its Nuclear Weapons', *Beijing Review*, 17 (1985) 15–20.
139. A. I. Johnston, 'China's New "Old Thinking": The Concept of Limited Deterrence', *International Security*, 20, 3 (Winter 1995/96) 5–42.
140. See B. N. Garret and B. S. Glaser, 'Chinese Perspectives on Nuclear Arms Control', *International Security*, 20, 3 (Winter 1995/96) 43–78; and

Kim, 'China's International Organisational Behaviour', in Robinson and Shambaugh (eds), *Chinese Foreign Policy: Theory and Practice*, pp. 416–21. According to Garret and Glaser, the arms control community comprises only about 100 people, mostly on a part-time basis.
141. M. Sheehan, *Arms Control: Theory and Practice*, p. 8.
142. Ibid., p. 6.
143. Johnston, 'China's New "Old Thinking"', *International Security*, 20, 3 (Winter 1995/96) 5–42.
144. That probably explains why China in the 1970s, for example, had condemned all the superpower initiatives in arms control as 'fraud', since only in the 1980s did arms control talks focus for the first time on actual reductions. In a recent publication by a Chinese scholar, it is claimed that, 'In the forty years since 1954, China has been consistently opposed to arms race and has stood for *genuine* disarmament'. Wu Yun, 'China's Policies towards Arms Control and Disarmament: From Passive Responding to Active Leading', *Pacific Review*, 9, 4 (1996) 578.
145. *United Nations Disarmament Yearbook*, 1985, p. 107.
146. Johnston, 'China's New "Old Thinking"', *International Security*, 20, 3 (Winter 1995/96) 11.
147. Xue Mouhong et al, *Dangdai Zhongguo Waijiao*, p. 391.
148. Ibid., pp. 327–9.
149. Wu Yun, 'China's Policies towards Arms Control and Disarmaments', *Pacific Review*, 9, 4 (1996) 581.
150. See *Beijing Review*, 42 (1985) 16–7; and Han Nianlong (ed.), *Diplomacy of Contemporary China*, pp. 403–4.
151. Ibid., p. 404.
152. A systematic elaboration of China's stand on the verification of all disarmament agreements can be found in a letter by the Chinese delegation to the UN Secretary-General Perez de Cuellar on 28 April 1986. See *Renmin Ribao*, 1 May 1986.
153. Han Nianlong (ed.), *Diplomacy of Contemporary China*, p. 477.
154. *Renmin Ribao*, 17 and 20 Nov. 1984.
155. See *Renmin Ribao*, 21 Feb. 1985; and *United Nations Disarmament Yearbook, 1985*, pp. 199 and 201. Many nations welcomed China's announcement. China had opted in 1982 and 1983 for non-participation in the subsidiary body on a test ban.
156. For the texts of China's draft resolutions, see *Renmin Ribao*, 7 Dec. 1986. See also *Xinhua Yuebao* (New China Monthly), 11 (1986) 193.
157. *Renmin Ribao*, 7 Dec. 1986.
158. *Beijing Review*, 24 (1988) 14–15.
159. *Renmin Ribao*, 21 Feb. 1985.
160. Ibid.
161. *Beijing Review*, 51 (1987) 5.
162. See Kim, 'China's International Organisational Behaviour', in Robinson and Shambaugh (eds), *Chinese Foreign Policy: Theory and Practice*, pp. 418–20.
163. Johnston, 'China's New "Old Thinking"', *International Security*, 20, 3 (Winter 1995/96) 5–42. It is clear from Johnston's extensive footnotes that from the late 1980s, there has been a proliferation of literature by Chinese scholars and military officers on strategic studies and on arms control and disarmament.

164. Two American analysts observed recently, after an extensive interview in China, that 'There has been a proliferation of Chinese arms control specialists in the last decade' and 'the number of arms control experts in China has reached approximately 100 people, although most are part-time participants in arms control research'. See Garret and Glaser, 'Chinese Perspectives on Nuclear Arms Control', *International Security*, 20, 3 (Winter 1995/96) 46.
165. For some persuasive arguments about this point, see Johnston, 'Prospects for Chinese Nuclear Force Modernisation: Limited Deterrence Versus Multilateral Arms Control', *China Quarterly*, 146 (June 1996) 548–76.
166. See 'China Accedes to Nuclear Non-Proliferation Treaty', *Beijing Review*, 13 (1992) 12.
167. See Z. S. Davis, 'China's Non-proliferation and Export Control Policies', *Asian Survey*, XXXV, 6 (June 1995) 592–3; Wu Yun, 'China's Policies towards Arms Control and Disarmament', *Pacific Review*, 9, 4 (1996) 593.
168. Du Gengqi, 'NPT at Crossroads', *Beijing Review*, 38, 17 (1995) 19–21.
169. Ibid.
170. *Beijing Review*, 36, 41 (1993) 10.
171. See Garret and Glaser, 'Chinese Perspectives on Nuclear Arms Control', *International Security*, 20, 3 (Winter 1995/96) 43–78; and Johnston, 'Prospects for Chinese Nuclear Force Modernisation', *China Quarterly*, 146 (June 1996) 548–76.
172. Garret and Glaser, 'Chinese Perspectives on Nuclear Arms Control', *International Security*, 20, 3 (Winter 1995/96) 55 and 60.
173. M. Wight, 'International Revolutions', in M. Wight, *Power Politics*, p. 89.
174. The countries abstaining were Cuba and Iraq.
175. See *SIPRI Yearbook 1992*, p. 300.
176. For a general background to China's arms sales in the 1980s, see E. Y. Woon, 'Chinese Arms Sales and US–China Military Relations', *Asian Survey*, XXIX, 6 (1989) 601–18. For information about China's main arms exporting companies, see J. W. Lewis et al, 'Beijing's Defence Establishment: Solving the Arms-Export Enigma', *International Security*, 15, 4 (1990) 87–105.
177. The figure is at the constant price for 1975. See *SIPRI Yearbook 1986*, pp. 324–5.
178. See *SIPRI Yearbook 1988*, pp. 176–7. In 1982, China was only ranked as the eighth largest arms trader to Third World countries. In 1988, however, it became the third largest arms merchant.
179. See *SIPRI Yearbook 1993*, p. 444. In comparison, China's arms sales to all countries in the same period was ranked the fifth after the USA, Russia, France and Germany.
180. According to SIPRI, the deal included a delivery of 50 CSS-2 East Wind missiles to Saudi Arabia by China in the next two years to be deployed at the Al-Kharj Air Base, 50 km south of Riyadh. *SIPRI Yearbook 1989*, p. 213. For more details of the sale, see Y. Shichor, *East Wind over Arabia: Origins and Implications of Sino-Saudi Missile Deal*.
181. See B. R. Gill, 'Curbing Beijing's Arms Sales', *Orbis* (Summer 1992) 380–381. Gill also claims that fourteen countries have installed Chinese missiles.
182. R. Bitzinger, 'Arms to Go: Chinese Arms Sales to the Third World', *International Security*, 17, 2 (Fall 1992) 84–111.

183. Woon, 'Chinese Arms Sales', *Asian Survey*, XXIX, 6 (1989) 604.
184. *Renmin Ribao*, 9 Sept. 1988.
185. *Beijing Review*, 22 (1989) 13–14.
186. See UN Doc. A/CN.10/118.
187. For the full text of the communiqué, see *SIPRI Yearbook 1992*, pp. 302–3.
188. See UN Doc 1/47/27/S/24111, p. 22.
189. For the full text, see *SIPRI Yearbook 1992*, pp. 304–5.
190. As Gareth Evans argued at a UN Conference on Disarmament Issues at Kyoto in May 1991:

    We need to acknowledge openly the difficulties which stand in the way of conventional arms control: compared with weapons of mass destruction, they are relatively readily available; trade is well established and lucrative; and considerations of national sovereignty, and the legitimate responsibility of any government to ensure national security, mean that countries are reluctant to forgo the right to acquire conventional arms.

191. See E. J. Laurance, *Arms Watch: SIPRI Report on the First Year of the UN Register of Conventional Arms,* pp. 16–23.
192. See Lewis et al, 'Beijing's Defence Establishment', *International Security*, 15, 4 (1991) 87–109. See also 'Reforming China's National Defence Science and Technology Organs', *China New Analysis*, 1410 (15 May 1990).
193. There is a particular account in Lewis's article about this. The sale of DF-3 missiles to Saudi Arabia was negotiated by Poly Technologies, an affiliate of the General Staff Department and the COSTIND, but objected to by the Foreign Ministry on political grounds. When the dispute was referred to Deng Xiaoping, he only asked, 'How much money did you make?' When he was told it would be 'two billion dollars', he replied 'bushao' (quite a large sum). That remark closed the matter. The Foreign Ministry lost its argument. Ibid., p. 96.
194. Ibid., p. 95.
195. T. W. Robinson, 'Chinese Foreign Policy from the 1940s to the 1990s', in Robinson and Shambaugh (eds), *Chinese Foreign Policy: Theory and Practice*, p. 585.
196. The White Paper went out of its way to elaborate the function of this body, which is worth quoting in length

    China strictly controls transfers of military equipment and related technologies and has established an appropriate administrative organisation and operating mechanisms to achieve this goal. The State Administrative Committee on Military Products Trade (SACMPT), under the leadership of the State Council and the Central Military Commission, is responsible for the centralised control of transfers of military equipment and related technologies. Its main function is drafting laws and policies governing such transfers. It is mainly comprised of leading personnel of the Ministry of Foreign Affairs, the Headquarters of the General Staff, the Commission of Science, Technology and Industry for National Defence, MOFTEC and other relevant departments. As the administrative arms of the SACMPT, the State Bureau of Military Products Trade is responsible for handling day-to-day affairs. Government departments and companies engaged in transfers of military equipment and technologies must be authorised, registered and approved by the government. Their business activities must remain strictly within the scope of operation approved. Contracts for transfer of military equipment and technologies require approval before gaining effect. Major transfer items and contracts must be examined by the SACMPT and approved by the State Council and the Central Military Commission. Stern legal sanction shall be taken against any company or individual who transfers military equipment and technologies without proper governmental examination and approval.

See Information Office of the State Council, 'China: Arms Control and Disarmament', *Beijing Review*, 38, 48 (1995) 19.

197. Joseph Nye called the MTCR 'an export control understanding between the United States and its six allies' – namely, Great Britain, France, Canada, Germany, Italy and Japan. See J. S. Nye, Jr, 'Arms Control after the Cold War', *Foreign Affairs*, 68, 5 (1989) 59.
198. K. C. Bailey, 'Can Missile Proliferation be Reversed?' *Orbis* (Winter 1991) 11.
199. This loophole was closed in 1992 when parties to the MTCR agreed 'to expand the scope of the regime's guidelines to cover missiles capable of delivering *any* weapon of mass destruction'. S. R. Hanmer, Jr, 'Strengthening Existing Non-proliferation Regimes', *Non-proliferation and Confidence-building Measures in Asia and the Pacific*, Disarmament Topic Papers 10, p. 40.
200. Bailey, 'Can Missile Proliferation be Reversed?', *Orbis* (Winter 1991) 10.
201. The United States claimed, however, that 'the transfer violated the MTCR because the missile could reach the minimum range of threshold if the payload were lighter than maximum capacity'. See R. Mullins, 'The Dynamics of Chinese Missile Proliferation', *Pacific Review*, 8, 1 (1995) 142–3.
202. A Chinese arms control specialist recounted the saga of Chinese adherence to the MTCR briefly as follows:

> China offered written assurances to observe MTCR guidelines and parameters on 22 Feb. 1992. The Chinese government announced its intention to act in accordance with MTCR guidelines and parameters in 1991. But this commitment was predicated upon US removal of its June 1991 sanctions against China, which took effect on 23 March and thereby triggered enactment of China's commitment concerning MTCR. In August 1993, the US government decided to impose new sanctions against China, based on the unfounded accusation that China had made an M-11 missile-related transfer to Pakistan. In strongly protesting against the US decision to resume sanctions, the Chinese government stated that it had no alternative left but to reconsider its commitment to MTCR. In October 1994, China announced it was to follow the MTCR guidelines and parameters again after the US lifted the sanctions imposed in August 1993.

See Wu Yun, 'China's Policies towards Arms Control and Disarmament', *Pacific Review*, 9, 4 (1996) 599.
203. Hanmer, 'Strengthening Existing Non-proliferation Regimes', *Non-proliferation and Confidence-building Measures in Asia and the Pacific*, Disarmament Topic Papers 10, p. 42. For the purpose of comparison, here is what *Yearbook of the United Nations, 1992* reported of the PERM-5 talks:

At the conclusion of a meeting held in Washington DC on 28 and 19 May (1992) the five permanent members of the Security Council adopted interim guidelines related to weapons of mass destruction, by which they undertook not to assist any non-nuclear weapon state in developing or acquiring nuclear weapons; to notify the International Atomic Energy Agency (IAEA) of the export to a non-nuclear-weapon state of any nuclear materials and to place them under IAEA safeguards; to exercise restraint in the transfer of sensitive nuclear facilities, technology and weapons-usable materials, equipment or facilities; not to assist any recipient whatsoever in developing or acquiring chemical weapons; and to observe similar restrictions concerning biological weapons. In addition, they agreed on other restrictions regarding the export of items that might be used in manufacturing weapons of mass destruction.

204. See *SIPRI Yearbook, 1993*, p. 460.
205. Yasushi Akashi, 'An Overview of the Situation', in United Nations, *Disarmament Topical Papers 3, Transparency in International Arms Transfer*, p. 6.
206. *Beijing Review*, 45 (1992) 6.
207. Ibid.
208. *SIPRI Yearbook 1990*, pp. 184–5.
209. Chen Bingfu, 'Jin Shinian Lai Zhongguo Junfei Zhichu Bianhua de Jingji Fenxi' (An Economic Analysis of China's Military Expenditures in the Last Decade), *Jingji Yanjiu* (Economic Research), 6 (1990) 77–8.
210. *SIPRI Yearbook, 1993*, p. 386. The earlier edition of the *SIPRI Yearbook* for 1990 also stated that China was the 'only major power whose military expenditure has consistently declined throughout the decade' (*SIPRI Yearbook 1990*, p. 184).
211. *SIPRI Yearbook 1992*, p. 245. For a comprehensive analysis of the subject, see M. Gurtov, 'Swords into Market Shares: China's Conversion of Military Industry to Civilian Production', *China Quarterly*, 134 (June 1993) 213–41.
212. See 'Chinese arms factories ordered to increase output of civilian goods', *The Times*, 6 Jan. 1986.
213. *Beijing Review*, 31 (1987) 14.
214. General Office of the Standing Committee of the National People's Congress et al, *Gaige yu Fazhan, 1983–1987* (Reform and Development, 1983–1987) p. 106.
215. *Renmin Ribao*, 24 June 1989.
216. For details, see Jiang Zhenxi, 'PLA Priorities: Disarmament and Development', *Beijing Review*, 43 (1986) 16–17.
217. See *SIPRI Yearbook 1992*, pp. 370–7.
218. See *SIPRI Yearbook 1993*, p. 388.
219. *Beijing Review*, 21 (1993) 10.
220. D. Shambaugh, 'China's Military in Transition: Politics, Professionalism, Procurement and Power Projection', *China Quarterly*, 146 (June 1996) 287.
221. For example, David Shambaugh seems to agree with the assessment that, between 1976 and 1994, Chinese defence spending in its official budget increased 159% in nominal terms, but only 4% in real terms annually. He however argued that official budget was 'only a fraction' of China's real spending. For a different assessment, see Shaoguang Wang, 'Estimating

China's Defence Expenditure: Some Evidence from Chinese Sources', *China Quarterly*, 147 (Sept. 1996) 889–911. See also Arthur S. Ding, 'China's Defence Finance: Content, Process and Administration', *China Quarterly*, 146 (June 1996) 428–42.
222. For a defence of China's increased defence spending, see Information Office of the State Council, 'Arms Control and Disarmament', *Beijing Review*, 38, 48 (1995) 14–15.
223. Ibid. According to the White Paper, in 1994, the other two broad categories – living expenses (including salaries, food and uniform) and maintenance activities (including training and construction) – accounted respectively for 34.08% and 34.22% of China's expenditure on national defence.
224. For more details, see Gill and Kim, *China's Arms Acquisitions from Abroad: A Quest for 'Superb and Secret Weapons'*.
225. Johnston, 'China's New "Old Thinking"', *International Security*, 20, 3 (Winter 1995/96) 42.
226. Armstrong, *Revolution and World Order*, p. 78. Armstrong further argues that international legitimacy is ' international society's collective judgment about what it expects from its members for them to qualify for full and undisputed membership'.
227. See, for example, I. Carlsson and S. Ramphal, *Our Global Neighbourhood*, pp. 46–57.
228. J. T. H. Tang, 'Human rights in the Asia-Pacific Region: Competing Perspectives, International Discord, and the Way Ahead', in J. T. H. Tang (ed.), *Human Rights in the Asia-Pacific Region*, pp. 1–5.
229. See 'Vienna Showdown', *Far Eastern Economic Review* (17 June 1993) 16–20; and Tang, (ed.), *Human Rights and International Relations in the Asia-Pacific Region*.
230. A. Nathan, 'Human Rights in Chinese Foreign Policy', *China Quarterly*, 139 (Sept. 1994) 622. Nathan's examination in this essay of human rights in Chinese foreign policy before 1989 is particularly valuable.
231. *Renmin Ribao*, 1 February 1992.
232. See Tian Zengpei, *Gaige Kaifang Yilai de Zhongguo Waijiao* (China's Diplomacy since the Economic Reforms and Opening), pp. 567–74. In *Zhongguo Waijiao Gailan, 1994* (A General Survey of China's Foreign Relations, 1994), an annual publication by the Ministry of Foreign Affairs, there is a special chapter on China's participation in international human rights activities.
233. Halliday, *Rethinking International Relations*, p. 95.
234. Ibid., p. 216.
235. For more details, see F. Fukuyama, *The End of History and the Last Man*.
236. One can immediately think of the cases of UN intervention in Somalia and Bosnia in 1992 and Rwanda and Haiti in 1994. For elaborations on UN humanitarian intervention and its legitimacy, see C. Ero and S. Long, 'Humanitarian Intervention: A New Role for the United Nations?' *International Peacekeeping*, 2, 2 (Summer 1995) 140–56.
237. As argued in *Our Global Neighbourhood*, 'global values must be the corner stone of global governance', and 'the very essence of global governance is the capacity of the international community to ensure compliance with the rules of society'. Carlsson and Ramphal *Our Global Neighbourhood*, pp. 47 and 326.

238. J. Ruggie, 'Human Rights and the Future International Community', *Daedalus* (Fall 1983) 107.
239. For more details of the development of studies of human rights in China in the early 1990s, see Zhou Wei, 'The Study of Human Rights in the People's Republic of China', in Tang (ed.), *Human Rights in the Asia-Pacific Region*, pp. 83–95.
240. A number of White Papers on various aspects of China's human rights conditions have been published by the Information Office of the State Council, including 'Human Rights in China', 'Sovereignty and Human Rights in Tibet', 'Criminal Reformation in China', 'Women in China'. *Renmin Ribao*, 14 Nov. 1994.
241. For international pressure on China's human rights policy after 1989, see Nathan, 'Human Rights in Chinese Foreign Policy', *China Quarterly*, 139 (Sept. 1994) 635–8.
242. For arguments about China as the human rights exception, see R. Cohen, 'People's Republic of China: the Human Rights Exception', *Human Rights Quarterly*, 9, 4 (Nov. 1987) 447–59.
243. Information Office of the State Council, 'Human Rights in China', *Beijing Review*, 44 (1991) 8–45. For its critiques, see 'White Lies on Mainland's Human Rights', *Ming Pao* (13 Nov.1991).
244. Those are actually subtitles for sections of the White Paper. There are ten sections in the White Paper altogether. The others are: I, The Right to Subsistence – the Foremost Human Right the Chinese People Long Fight for; VIII, Family Planning and Protection of Human Rights; IX, Guarantee of Human Rights for the Disabled; and X, Active Participation in International Human Rights Activities.
245. Information Office of the State Council, 'Human Rights in China', *Beijing Review*, 44 (1991) 8 and 42.
246. All quotes in this paragraph are from 'Human Rights in China', *Beijing Review*, 44 (1991) 8–45.
247. A. Kent, *Between Freedom and Subsistence: China and Human Rights*, p. 222.
248. See also John Vincent's arguments for the priority of rights of subsistence in J. Vincent, *Human Rights and International Relations*.
249. For more details along this line of argument, see Liu Nanlai (ed.), *Fazhan Zhong Guojia yu Renquan* (Developing Countries and Human Rights).
250. China has a seemingly contradictory position on intervention by the international community as a whole. In the White Paper, it is argued that

> China has always held that to effect international protection of human rights, the international community should interfere with and stop acts that endanger world peace and security, such as gross human rights violations caused by colonialism, racism, foreign aggression and occupation, as well as apartheid, racial discrimination, genocide, slave trade and serious violation of human rights by international terrorist organisations.

251. See 'Human Rights in China' *Beijing Review*, 44 (1991) 45. Unless otherwise indicated, all quotes in this paragraph are from 'Human Rights in China', *Beijing Review*, 44 (1991) 8–45. This is essentially the position China adopted at the Second World Conference on Human Rights in Vienna in 1993. See Liu Huaqiu, 'Proposals for Human Rights Protection and Promotion', *Beijing Review*, 26 (1993) 9–11.

252. L. Henkin, 'The Universality of the Concept of Human Rights', *ANALS, AAPSS*, 506, 14.
253. The White Paper states that, 'As a developing country, China has suffered from setbacks while safeguarding and developing human rights. Although much has been achieved in this regard, there is still much room for improvement'. 'Human Rights in China', *Beijing Review*, 44 (1991) 9.
254. *Beijing Review*, 15 (1992) xvi.
255. Henkin, 'The Universality of the Concept of Human Rights', *ANALS, AAPSS*, 506, 3.
256. See Vincent, *Human Rights and International Relations*, in particular, chap. 3, 'Human Rights and Cultural Relativism'; and J. Donnelly, *Universal Human Rights in Theory and Practice,* in particular, Part III, 'Human Rights and Cultural Relativism'.
257. Henkin, 'The Universality of the Concept of Human Rights', *ANALS, AAPSS*, 506, 12–13.
258. See A. Bozeman, *The Future of Law in a Multicultural World*, pp. 144–5.
259. See Kent, *China and Human Rights*, chap. 2, 'Human Rights from Imperial to Communist China', pp. 30–50.
260. Zhang Huanwen, 'Zhonghua Chuantong Wenhua yu Renquan' (Traditional Chinese Culture and Human Rights), Xia Xudong et al (eds), *Shijie Renquan Zongheng* (Human Rights: A World Perspective), p. 209.
261. Kent, *China and Human Rights*, pp. 37–8.
262. Ibid., pp. 40–2.
263. Indeed, China has pursued an active foreign policy along this line. See Nathan, 'Human Rights in Chinese Foreign Policy', *China Quarterly*, 139 (Septe. 1994) 622–43.
264. Dittmer and Kim (eds), *China's Quest for National Identity*, p. 260.
265. 'Human Rights in China', *Beijing Review*, 44 (1991) 12–16 and 30–1.
266. Vincent, *Human Rights and International Relations*, p. 42.
267. The Chinese version was published in *Guangming Ribao* (Guangming Daily) earlier in late October, as written by a 'Commentator', usually the synonym of a high-ranking official. In May 1979, *Hongqi* (Red Flag) carried another article by Xiao Weiyun et al entitled, 'How Does Marxism Look at the "Human Rights" Question?' *Hongqi* (Red Flag) (May 1979) 43–8.
268. For more details of human rights discussions in the 'Democracy Wall' period, see D. Goodman, *Beijing Street Voices*; M. Goldman, 'Human Rights in the People's Republic of China', *Daedalus* (Fall 1983) 111–38. For human rights in the Carter administration's China policy, see R. Cohen, 'People's Republic of China: the Human Rights Exception', *Human Rights Quarterly* (Nov. 1987) 9, 4, 447–59. For human rights in American foreign policy in the 1970s and the 1980s, see D. Forsythe, *Human Rights and World Politics*, chap. 5, 'United States Foreign Policy and Human Rights: Rhetoric and Reality', pp. 102–26.
269. Guangming Daily Commentator, 'Notes on Human Rights', *Beijing Review*, 45 (1979) 17–20.
270. See Goldman, 'Human Rights in the People's Republic of China', *Daedalus* (Fall 1983) 111–38.
271. See R. W. Wilson, 'Change and Continuity in Chinese Cultural Identity: The Filial Ideal and the Transformation of an Ethic', Dittmer and Kim (eds), *China's Quest for National Identity*, pp. 104–24.
272. 'Human Rights in China', *Beijing Review*, 44 (1991) 43.

273. At the symposium commemorating the Universal Declaration of Human Rights, the document was applauded as 'a significant international document that reflects the world people's aspiration for equality and freedom, though it has historical limitations'. See 'China Applauds Human Rights', *Beijing Review*, 51 (1988) 5–6.
274. According to one report, between 1991 and 1994, more than 400,000 copies of books on human rights were published in China. One of the series sponsored by the Central Propaganda Department of the CCP is *Renquan Yanjiu Ziliao Congshu* (Selected Materials in Human Rights Studies), which include seven books.
275. It is interesting to note that one central defensive argument of the Chinese government is that better and fuller realisation of human rights ideals in China takes time and depends on the stage of its economic development.
276. 'Human Rights in China', *Beijing Review*, 44 (1991) 42.
277. This initial changing position seems to have been politically motivated. In December 1978, Vietnam invaded Cambodia. In February 1979, China was using the UN Human Rights Commission to condemn the Vietnamese invasion of Cambodia. See Tian Zengpei (ed.), *Gaige Kaifang Yilai de Zhongguo Waijiao* (China's Diplomacy since the Economic Reforms and Opening), pp. 569–70.
278. For more details of China's participation, see ibid., pp. 567–75.
279. L. Dittmer and S. Kim, 'Whither China's Quest for National Identity?', Dittmer and Kim (eds), *China's Quest for National Identity*, pp. 261–2.
280. The eight UN conventions that China has ratified or acceded to are: (1) The International Convention on the Prevention and Punishment of the Crime of Genocide; (2) The International Convention on the Suppression and Punishment of the Crimes of Apartheid; (3) The Convention on the Elimination of All Forms of Discrimination against Women; (4) The International Convention on the Elimination of All Forms of Racial Discrimination; (5) The Convention Relating to the Status of Refugees; (6) The Protocol Relating to the Status of Refugees; (7) The Convention against Torture and Other Cruel, Inhuman or Degrading Treatment or Punishment; and (8) The UN Convention on the Rights of Children. See Tian Zengpei (ed.), *Gaige Kaifang Yilai de Zhongguo Waijiao* (Chinese Diplomacy since the Economic Reforms and Opening), p. 572.
281. 'Human Rights in China', *Beijing Review*, 44 (1991) 43–4.
282. Dittmer and Kim (eds), *China's Quest for National Identity*, p. 262.
283 *Renmin Ribao*, 18 Sept. 1997. For China's preparations in 1988, see 'Beijing ready to sign UN human rights conventions', *South China Morning Post*, 25 September, 1988.
284. China signed the convention on 29 August 1990 and ratified it on 31 January 1992.
285. *Renmin Ribao*, 28 November 1994.

6 ECONOMIC INTEGRATION

1. *The Independent*, 14 Nov. 1992.
2. For example, as early as 1986, Dwight H. Perkins already noticed the emergence of China as an economic power in Asia. See D. H. Perkins, *China:*

Asia's Next Economic Giant? See also N. Lardy, *Foreign Trade and Economic Reform in China, 1978–1990*; World Bank, *The East Asian Miracle: Economic Growth and Public Policy*; and K. Fukasaku, et al, *China's Long March to an Open Economy*, pp. 59–87.

3. *Renmin Ribao* (overseas edn), 6 Oct. 1994. The statistics are from the State Administration for the Management of State-owned Assets (Guowuyuan Guoyou Zichan Guanliju). They must be treated with caution..
4. *Zhongguo Tongji Zhaiyao, 1996* (A Statistical Survey of China, 1996), p. 110; and *China Daily*, 26 Jan. 1997.
5. *Renmin Ribao* (overseas edn), 29 Sept. 1994.
6. World Bank, *China: Foreign Trade Reform*, pp. xvii and 13. According to Nicholas Lardy, already in 1990, 90 per cent of China's trade was with market economies. See Lardy, *Foreign Trade and Economic Reform in China*, p. 1.
7. M. N. Jovanovic, *International Economic Integration*, p. 7. For the origin of the term and different definitions by economists over time, see ibid., pp. 3–7.
8. F. Machlup, *A History of Thought on Economic Integration*, p. 43.
9. If calculated in RMB, the growth is even more spectacular. In 1978, the total foreign trade was 35.5 billion yuan, whereas in 1995 it was 2349.87 billion yuan – *Zhongguo Tongji Zhaiyao, 1996*, p. 105.
9. The ranking of China's position in the world trading nations is an intriguing one. According to the GATT data, China is the eleventh largest trading nation, while Hong Kong is the tenth. Lardy argued, however, that given that a large proportion of Hong Kong's exports are re-exports of goods produced in China, China should be counted as the tenth largest producer of export goods. N. Lardy, *China in the World Economy*, p. 2.
10. Xinhua Tongxunshe Guonei Ziliaozu (Internal News Group, Xinhua News Agency) *Shinian Gaige Dashiji, 1978–1987* (Chronicle of Ten Years of Reform, 1978–1987), p. 334.
11. See 'The Communique of the Third Plenum of the Eleventh Central Committee of the CCP', *Peking Review*, 52 (1978).
12. Quoted in W. R. Feeney, 'Chinese Policy toward Multilateral Economic Institutions', in Kim (ed.) *China and the World: New Directions of Chinese Foreign Relations*, p. 241.
13. *Xinhua News Bulletin*, 31 Dec. 1984.
14. Quoted in Riskin, *China's Political Economy*, p. 316.
15. At the same time, the annual growth rate of China's GDP is about 9%.
16. *Zhongguo Tongji Zhaiyao, 1996* p. 105.
17. The World Bank figure is slightly higher at 1.52%. On the other hand, China's imports in 1985 are 2.25% of the world total. See World Bank, *China: External Trade and Capital*, p. 116.
18. *Zhongguo Duiwai Jingji Maoyi Nianjian, 1989*, p, 304.
19. World Bank, *China: External Trade and Capital*, p. 116.
20. Ibid., p. 9.
21. Harding, *China's Second Revolution*, pp. 83–95.
22. Lardy, *Foreign Trade and Economic Reform in China*, pp. 40–1.
23. See Zheng Derong et al, *Zhongguo Jingji Tizhi Gaige Jishi* (The Chronicle of China's Economic Reform), p. 28.
24. For a brief review of early reform of China's macro-economic policies, see World Bank, *China: External Trade and Capital*, pp. 60–80.
25. See *Beijing Review*, 43 (1984) 4.

26. For details of these reforms, see World Bank, China: *Foreign Trade Reform*; and Lardy, *Foreign Trade and Economic Reform in China*.
27. Li Lanqing, 'Achievements of China's Foreign Trade', *Bulletin of the MOFERT*, 5 (19 Dec. 1991) 8.
28. See *Zhongguo Tongji Zhaiyao, 1996*, pp. 6 and 105. The calculations are my own.
29. B. P. Bosworth, and G. Ofer, *Reforming Planned Economies in an Integrating World Economy.* p. 58.
30. See Lardy, *Foreign Trade and Economic Reform in China*, pp. 150–4.
31. Calculated on the statistics in *Zhongguo Tongji Zhaiyao, 1996*, the exact figures are 29.97% and 40.7% respectively..
32. In the statistics provided by the MOFERT, the decrease was 17.4%, whereas in the Customs statistics, 9.8%.
34. That estimate has taken into account the adjustment of Hong Kong and Macao's re-exports.
35. *Zhongguo Duiwai Jingji Maoyi Nianjian, 1989*, p. 311. It is also important to note that China exported to more than it imported from developing countries. Developing countries took 13.2% of China's total exports in 1986, but only supplied less than 5% of China's imports..
36. M. Bell, et al, *China at the Threshold of a Market Economy*, p. 61.
37. World Bank, *China: Foreign Trade Reform*, p. 5. This has almost completely reversed the export mix of China's foreign trade in 1953, when the ratio was 79.4% primary products and 20.6% industrial finished goods. See also Zhang Songtao, 'Adjustment of Import-Export Mix', *China's Foreign Trade* (April–May 1990) 3.
38. All the above figures are from *Zhongguo Tongji Nianjian,1991* (China Statistical Yearbook, 1991) p. 618.
39. *Zhongguo Tongji Nianjian, 1994* (China Statistical Yearbook, 1994) p. 507.
40. *Zhongguo Tongji Nianjian, 1995*, (China Statistical Yearbook, 1995) p. 538.
41. According to a World Bank study, the share of China's export of manufactured goods in its total exports hardly changed in the two decades between 1965 and 1985. In 1965, it was 46% of the total, whereas in 1985 it was 49%. See World Bank, *China: Foreign Trade Reform*, p. 5.
42. China's import of food increased steadily from $1.553 billion in 1985 to $1.625 billion in 1986, $24.43 billion in 1987, $34.76 billion in 1988, and $41.92 billion in 1989. See ibid., p. 617.
43. Lardy, *China in the World Economy*, p. 32.
44. Ibid.
45. *Zhongguo Tongji Nianjian, 1991*, p. 619, and *Zhongguo Tongji Nianjian, 1995*, p. 539. Similarly, a study by a group of IMF staff concludes that 'the share of capital (machinery and transportation equipment) and intermediate goods rose steadily, from 25 percent of total imports in 1980 to nearly 40% in 1992': W. Tseng, et al., *Economic Reform in China: A New Phase*, p. 60.
46. Lardy, *China in the World Economy*, pp. 32–3.
47. *Zhongguo Duiwai Jingji Maoyi Nianjian, 1989*, p. 311.
48. *Zhongguo Tongji Nianjian, 1994*, pp. 506 and 513–14; IMF, *Direction of Trade Statistics Yearbook*, 1995, p. 154.
49. IMF, *Direction of Trade Statistics Yearbook, 1995*, p. 155.

50. China's trade with Hong Kong and to a lesser extent Macau represents some complication in calculating how much China actually trades with developed countries. This is especially true, as China's trade with Hong Kong and Macau has increased to around 30% of its total. For example, according to Hong Kong government statistics, in 1987 75% of China's imports from Hong Kong came from outside the territory, while 60% of China's exports to Hong Kong were re-exported. The World Bank estimated that in 1990, $29 billion out of $32.9 billion of China's exports to Hong Kong were re-exported. More than 60% of re-exports ended up in the US, Japan and the EU. See Harding, *China's Second Revolution*, pp. 145 and 331; and World Bank, *China: Foreign Trade Reform*, pp. 12–3.
51. IMF, *Direction of Trade Statistics Yearbook*, 1995, pp. 153–5.
52. K. Fukasaku, et al, *China's Long March to an Open Economy*, p. 64.
53. Ibid.
54. Zhang Zuoqian, '1989 Nian Woguo Duiwai Jingmao de Fazhan', (The Development of China's Foreign Economic Relations and Trade in 1989), *Guangzhou Duiwai Maoyi Xueyuan Xuebao* (Journal of Guangzhou College of Foreign Trade), 1 (1990) 22.
55. Li Lanqing, 'Achievements of China's Foreign Trade', *Bulletin of the MOFERT*, 5 (19 Dec. 1991) 10.
56. Xie Yangan, 'China's Import of Technology', *China's Foreign Trade* (Aug. 1990) 4. There are no specific statistics for the import of technology in either the Yearbook of China's Foreign Economic Relations and Trade or China Statistical Yearbook. Part of technology import as that of complete sets of equipment is included in the commodity trade statistics.
57. Ma Hong and Sun Shangqing (eds), *Zhongguo Jingji Xingshi yu Zhanwang*, 1992–1993 (China's Economic Situation and Prospect, 1992–1993) p. 305.
58. Liu Yongqiang, 'Shijie Laowu Shichang ji Zhongguo Laowu Chukou de Qianjin Fenxi' (An Analysis of the World Labour Market and the Prospect of China's Labour Service Export), *Guoji Maoyi* (Intertrade), 3 (1987) 40.
59. *Zhongguo Tongji Nianjian, 1991*, p. 571.
60. *Beijing Review*, 3 (1992) 29.
61. Ma Hong and Sun Shangqing (eds.), *Zhongguo Jingji Xingshi yu Zhanwang*, p. 305.
62. *Zhongguo Tongji Nianjian, 1991*, p. 572.
63. Harding, *China's Second Revolution*, p. 144.
64. *Zhongguo Tongji Zhaiyao, 1996*, p. 115.
65. M. Panic, *National Management of International Economy*, p. 26.
66. Gilpin, *The Political Economy of International Relations*, p. 171.
67. 'Learning the Rules of Foreign Trade', *China News Analysis*, 1464, p. 8.
68. Gilpin, *The Political Economy of International Relations*, p. 306.
69. Ibid., p. 144.
70. N. Lardy, 'The Role of Foreign Trade and Investment in China's Economic Transformation', *China Quarterly*, 144 (Dec. 1995) 1065.
71. For details, see Shi Lin et al, *Dangdai Zhongguo de Duiwai Jingji Hezuo*, pp. 317–19.
72. See ibid., pp. 23–78.
73. China did use deferred payments in the 1960s in procuring 65 items of advanced technologies and equipment from Austria, Belgium, Britain, France,

74. Barnett, *China's Economy in Global Perspective*, pp. 225–6.
75. Ibid., p. 226.
76. Mackerras, *Modern China*, p. 615.
77. Ibid., p. 613.
78. The two commissions were however, shortlived. In further administrative reforms in early 1982, they were merged with the Ministry of Foreign Trade and the Ministry of Foreign Economic Relations to create the mighty Ministry of Foreign Economic Relations and Trade (MOFERT). The State General Administration of Exchange Control, on the other hand, was made part of the People's Bank of China, China's central bank, also in 1982.
79. See Yao Yunfang, 'Guoji Jinrong Xingshi he Zhongguo de Duiwai Jinrong Gongzuo' (The Current International Financial Situation and China's Foreign Finance), *Shijie Jingji* (The World Economy), 8 (1982) 21.
80. Shi Lin et al, *Dangdai Zhongguo de Duiwai Jingji Hezuo*, p. 321.
81. *The Economist* (15 March 1986) 67.
82. See Gilpin, *The Political Economy of International Relations*, chap. 8, 'Politics of International Finance', pp. 308–40.
83. It is very difficult, if not impossible, to determine the exact percentage of this part of foreign direct investment in the total. A rough indication could be found in the statistics of FDI flow from Hong Kong and Macau into China, although this is not all from overseas Chinese communities. In 1993, the utilised FDI from Hong Kong and Macau was respectively $17.44 billion and $587.56 million, and in 1994, $19.82 billion and $509.44 million. *Zhongguo Tongji Nianjian, 1995*, p. 555.
84. For domestic difficulties and international complications for the Ohira government's decision to make the loan to China, see Lee Chae-Jin, *China and Japan: New Economic Diplomacy*, pp. 113–20.
85. Shi Lin et al, *Dangdai Zhongguo de Duiwai Jingji Hezuo*, p. 322.
86. Ibid., p. 350.
87. The total borrowing by China in the period was $20.417 billion. See *Zhongguo Tongji Nianjian, 1991*, p. 567.
88. Shi Lin et al, *Dangdai Zhongguo de Duiwai Jingji Hezuo*, p. 346. Details of inter-government loans China obtained from 1979 to 1985 are recorded in pp. 346–53..
89. P. Botellier, *China's Economic Reforms since 1978 and the Role of the World Bank*, pp. 10–11.
90. Shi Lin et al, *Dangdai Zhongguo de Duiwai Jingji Hezuo*, p. 354.
91. V., Lide, 'The World Bank in China: Getting Back on Track is Slow Going', *China Business Review* (Jan.–Feb., 1991) 44–5.
92. World Bank, *The World Bank Annual Report, 1991*, p. 182.
93. Botellier, *China's Economic Reforms since 1978 and the Role of the World Bank*, p. 10. Botellier further observed that of the World Bank commitments total to China, 67% came from the IBRD, and 33% came from the IDA.
94. Ibid., p. 11.
95. Shi Lin et al, *Dangdai Zhongguo de Duiwai Jingji Hezuo*, p. 354.
96. The breakdown of the sum on a yearly basis is, for 1986, 18.87 million; for 1987, 15.18 million; for 1989, 11.12 million; and for 1990, 4.34 million.

See *Zhongguo Tongji Nianjian, 1987*, p. 532; *Zhongguo Duiwai Jingji Maoyi Nianjian, 1989*, p. 555; and *Zhongguo Tongji Nianjian, 1991*, p. 568.
97. See *Asian Development Bank Annual Report, 1994*, pp. 83–4; and *Beijing Review*, 8–9 (1996) 35.
98. For early activities of these agencies, see Shi Lin et al, *Dangdai Zhongguo de Duiwai Jingji Hezuo*, pp. 510–35. See also D., Denny, 'The Impact of Foreign Aid', *China Business Review* (Jan.–Feb., 1986) 23.
99. Gilpin, *The Political Economy of International Relations*, pp. 306–7.
100. See Barnett, *China's Economy in Global Perspective*, pp. 222–30. The total volume of China's debt in 1980 was $5.4 billion, just a little less than 1.9% of China's GDP. Most of this debt consisted of commercial borrowing. See also World Bank, *China: External Trade and Capital*, p. 292.
101. The MOFERT is responsible for all concessional and other bilateral borrowing from foreign governments and aid agencies, frame agreements and/or guarantees for export credit agencies. The Ministry of Finance is responsible for all borrowing from the World Bank. The Ministry of Agriculture is responsible for all borrowing from the International Fund for Agricultural Development, and some borrowing from the United Nations Development Programme (UNDP). The People's Bank of China is responsible for borrowing from the IMF and later from the Asian Development Bank when China joined it in 1986. Finally, the Bank of China is responsible for undertaking commercial borrowing on behalf of the Chinese government..
102. World Bank, *China: External Trade and Capital*, p. 295.
103. OECD, *Financing and External Debt of Developing Countries, 1991 Survey*, p. 109.
104. Lardy noted that the only other transition economy which now has ready access to international capital markets is the Czech Republic. See Lardy, 'The Role of Foreign Trade and Investment in China's Economic Transformation', *China Quarterly*, 144 (Dec. 1995) 1065.
105. E. Morrison, 'Borrowing on World Bond Markets', *China Business Review* (Jan.–Feb. 1986) 18–20.
106. See M. Watson, et al, *International Capital Markets: Development and Prospects* (Dec. 1986), p. 50.
107. M. Goldstein, et al, *International Capital Markets: Developments, Prospects and Policy Issues* (Sep., 1992), p. 75.
108. 'China Resumes Bond Issuing', *Beijing Review*, 31 (1991), 29. At the same time, the CITIC was also negotiating for the issue of another 20 billion yen on the Tokyo market.
109. *South China Morning Post*, 4 Feb. 1994.
110. *China Daily*, 13 Sept. 1993.
111. *China Daily*, 16 Oct. 1993.
112. *Xinhua News Agency*, 3 Feb. 1994.
113. *China Daily*, 8 July 1994.
114. See *China Daily*, 26 Jan 1997.
115. D. F. I. Folkerts, and Y. Ito, (eds.), *International Capital Markets: Developments, Prospects and Policy Issues*, p. 38. To this it should also be added the purchase by foreign capital of B shares and H shares of Chinese companies floated on China's domestic stock exchanges in Shenzhen and Shanghai.

116. *Zhongguo Tongji Nianjian, 1995*, p. 578. For a different estimate of China's international equity issues in the period, see Lardy, 'The Role of Foreign Trade and Investment in China's Economic Transformation', *China Quarterly*, 144 (Dec. 1995) 1069–71.
117. 'Foreign Banks Active in China', *Beijing Review*, 13 (1986) 28.
118. *Beijing Review*, 15 (1987) 28.
119. *Beijing Review*, 21 (1991) 30.
120. Lardy, *China in the World Economy*, p. 91.
121. See *Beijing Review*, 12, 43; 13 p. 28, 31, 28, and 46, 28 (1994).
122. In October 1994, Moore Stephen became the tenth foreign accountancy firm to open a Chinese office. In November 1994, Nikko Securities founded a joint partnership with a Chinese firm.
123. In October 1994 and January 1995, Standard Chartered and Bank of Tokyo both opened a Chengdu office.
124. At the end of 1996 and in early 1997, the People's Bank of China, China's central bank, approved eight foreign banks to conduct Chinese currency business on a trial basis from Shanghai's Pudong area. The eight foreign banks are Hong Kong and Shanghai Banking Group, Citibank N A, the Bank of Tokyo-Mitsubishi and Industrial Bank of Japan, Dai-Ichi Kangyo Bank, Sanwa Bank, Standard-Chartered Bank and the International Bank of Paris and Shanghai. See *China Daily* 5 Jan. 1997 and 19 Feb. 1997.
125. See Shi Lin et al., *Dangdai Zhongguo de Duiwai Jingji Hezuo*, p. 356.
126. Ibid., p. 326.
127. World Bank, *China: External Trade and Capital*, p. 252. This estimate is based on Nai-Ruenn Chen's study 'Foreign Investment in China: Current Trends'. Official Chinese statistics disagree greatly with this estimate. According to the Chinese estimate, total agreements signed and approved were 6 321, with $16.32 billion as total foreign direct investment committed and $4.72 billion as foreign capital invested. Although this set of Chinese statistics seem not very different from those of Chen's figures, they *exclude* foreign investment in compensation trade, whereas Chen's figures *include* them. If investment in compensation trade is taken away from Chen's estimate or added to the Chinese statistics, the result would be substantially different. See World Bank, *China: External Capital and Trade*, p. 253; and Shi Lin et al, *Dangdai Zhongguo de Duiwai Jingji Hezuo*, p. 326. For a still different estimate, see Harding, *China's Second Revolution*, pp. 154 and 160.
128. *Zhongguo Duiwai Jingji Maoyi Nianjian, 1989*, p. 554.
129. Li Lanqing, 'Achievements of China's Foreign Trade', *Bulletin of the MOFERT*, 5 (19 Dec. 1991), 3 and 10.
130. Ibid., pp. 9–10.
131. Ma Hong and Sun Shangqing (eds.), *Zhongguo Jingji Xingshi yu Zhanwang*, p. 304.
132. Shi Lin et al, *Dangdai Zhongguo de Duiwai Jingji Hezuo*, p. 326.
133. World Bank, *China: External Trade and Capital*, p. 252.
134. Ibid., p. 243.
135. At the end of August 1991, China's contractual value of external borrowing was $61.35 billion, of which $50.51 billion was actually used. The total agreement value of foreign direct investment, on the other hand, was $43.3 billion, of which only $18.3 billion was realised. See Li Lanqing,

Notes

136. 'Achievements, of China's Foreign Trade', *Bulletin of the MOFERT*, 5 (19 Dec. 1991), 3 and 10.
136. Ma Hong and Sun Shangqing (eds), *Zhongguo Jingji Xingshi yu Zhanwang*, p. 304. The agreement value of foreign direct investment in 1992 is $57.5 billion.
137. Mackerras, *Modern China*, p. 607.
138. See *China Daily*, 26 Jan. 1997.
139. World Bank, *China: External Trade and Capital*, p. 257. These statistics exclude FDI in petroleum ventures. Even if petroleum ventures were included, FDI from Hong Kong would still account for 66.5%. It must be pointed out clearly, however, that not all investment from Hong Kong is from Chinese entrepreneurs there. An unknown part of foreign investors that legally are Hong Kong firms are in fact owned and controlled by its parent companies in other countries. In some cases, the investment was made by a subsidiary of a PRC enterprise in Hong Kong.
140. *Zhongguo Duiwai Jingji Maoyi Nianjian, 1992*, p. 611.
141. See *International Herald Tribune*, 11 Jan. 1993.
142. Lardy also suggests that China is now more fully integrated into the world economy than Taiwan and Korea were at the comparable level of their development. See Lardy, *China in the World Economy*, pp. 110–5.
143. In the official account of China's foreign economic cooperation, it was briefly mentioned that from the early 1950s to the 1970s, China had invested abroad and established some joint ventures or wholly-owned companies in foreign countries engaged in shipping, finance and trade. A notable example is a joint venture between China and Poland in shipping. Sino–Polish Shipping Ltd was opened in 1951 and is still in operation today. See Shi Lin et al, *Dangdai Zhongguo de Duiwai Jingji Hezuo*, pp. 319 and 450. It should also be pointed out that government aid from China as a form of international capital flow is not to be included in our discussion.
144. *Renmin Ribao* (overseas edn), 2 Nov. 1994.
145. D. Wilson, 'China Goes Transnational', *Hong Kong Business*, 15, 171 (Sept. 1996), 6–8.
146. Ibid.
147. *Zhongguo Tongji Nianjian, 1995*, pp. 578–9; and *Zhongguo Tongji Nianjian*, 1996, pp. 620–1. In the Chinese statistics, this category includes China's payments of foreign government loans, international organisations' loans, bank loans, and local government and central department loans from abroad.
148. It is $9.8 billion and $9.77 billion respectively; *Zhongguo Tongji Nianjian, 1995*, p. 579. Estimates by the World Bank are much higher, at $24.9 billion in 1992 and $20.9 billion in 1993. See Lardy, 'The Role of Foreign Trade and Investment in China's Economic Transformation', *China Quarterly*, 144 (Dec. 1995), 1071.
149. Some look at this capital outflow as capital flight. See, for example, F. R. Gunter, 'Capital Flight from the People's Republic of China: 1984–1994', *China Economic Review*, 7, 1 (1996), 77–96. My thanks to Wen Jie of the Department of Economics, University of Queensland, for bringing this article to my attention.
150. For example, Xinhua News Agency reported that by the end of 1994, China's investment in Hong Kong was $19.2 billion. Another study by

Hong Kong academics concluded that China's investment by the middle of 1995 in Hong Kong was $25 billion. See Lin Congbiao and Jian Zeyuan, 'Zhongzi Gongsi yu Xianggang Jingji' (China-funded Companies and the Hong Kong Economy), an unpublished paper presented to the International Conference on *China's Opening and Economic Reform*, 24–25 October 1995, City University of Hong Kong, p. 23.
151. For China's early investment activities overseas from 1979 to 1985, see Shi Lin et al, *Dangdai Zhongguo de Duiwai Jingji Hezuo*, pp. 448–71.
152. See *Fortune*, 7 Aug. 1995. The three Chinese multinationals are Bank of China (ranked 207), Sinochem (ranked 209) and COFCO (ranked 342).
153. *Beijing Review*, 4 (1988), 8–9.
154. Zheng Dunxun, 'The Internationalisation of China's Enterprises', *Intertrade* (Jan. 1991), 9–10.
155. These figures are from *Fortune*, 24 Aug. 1992, p. 53; 23 Aug. 1993, p. 137; 22 Aug. 1994, p. 158; and 15 Aug. 1995, p. 155.
156. *Zhonghua Sishiwu Nian, 1950–1995* (Forty-five Years of Sinochem, 1950–1995), pp. 86–7.
157. *Beijing Review*, 7–8 (1988), 31.
158. Xie Kang et al, *Ruhe Chuangban Zhongguo Haiwai Qiye* (How to Set up China's Overseas Enterprises), pp. 164–5.
159. Ibid., p. 171.
160. *Newsweek*, 15 Feb. 1993, p. 24.
161. The whole plant was then shipped back to China. *Beijing Review*, 46 (1992), 30.
162. See 'Shougang on the Road to Transnational Operation', *Beijing Review*, 40 (1993), 17–18.
163. See SWB (Summary of World Broadcasts), Part III, Asia-Pacific, 23 June 1993, FE/W0287 A/6.
164. *Guoji Jingrong Xinxibao* (International Financial News), 19 Feb. 1997.
165. See recent debate in R. Ross, 'Enter the Dragon'; and G. Mastel, 'Beijing at Bay', *Foreign Policy* (Fall 1996), 18–25 and 27–34.
166. Jacobson and Oksenberg, *China's Participation* in the IMF, the World Bank and GATT, p. 1.
167. See Shi Lin et al, *Dangdai Zhongguo de Duiwai Jingji Hezuo*, pp. 498–9.
168. See Jacobson and Oksenberg, *China's Participation* in the IMF, the World Bank and GATT.
169. Botellier, *China's Economic Reform since 1978 and the Role of the World Bank*, p. 10.
170. See World Bank, *World Bank Annual Report, 1992*, pp. 202 and 222. See also Appendix 1 in Jacobson, and Oksenberg, *China's Participation* in the IMF, the World Bank and GATT, pp. 173–5 for details of the World Bank-funded projects in China up to 1989.
171. Botellier, *China's Economic Reform since 1978 and the Role of the World Bank*, p. 10.
172. See Feeney, 'Chinese Policy toward Multilateral Economic Institutions', in Kim, (ed.), *China and the World*, p. 243.
173. Jacobson and Oksenberg, *China's Participation* in the IMF, the World Bank and GATT, pp. 19–20.
174. See ibid., pp. 124–5. Jacobson and Oksenberg also cited another specific example of China's adopting a policy recommended by the World Bank.

Notes 301

They claimed that 'elements of the coal price reform of 1983–84 came at the request of the World Bank as part of its willingness to extend loans for coal mine development'. See ibid., p. 141.
175. Lardy, *Foreign Trade and Economic Reform in China*, p. 166. China devalued the RMB on 5 July 1986 by 15.8% – not, however, 30% as recommended by the IMF..
176. For example, in both the Ministry of Finance and the People's Bank of China, additional bureaux were created to deal with matters related to the World Bank funding and consultation with the IMF. Even in the Ministry of Agriculture, a new division was established in the Department of International Cooperation to handle the loans and credits provided by the Bank.
177. Jacobson and Oksenberg, *China's Participation* in the IMF, the World Bank and GATT, p. 4.
178. C. M. Clarke, 'Decentralisation', *China Business Review* (March–April 1984) 8–10.
179. Yu Guangyuan, (ed.), *China's Socialist Modernization*, p. 355.
180. Shen Jueren, '1981 Nian Zhongguo Duiwai Maoyi Zhanwang he Dangqian de Waimao Tizhi Gaige' (Prospect of China's Foreign Trade in 1981 and the Current Foreign Trade System Reform), *Guoji Maoyi Wenti* (Issues in International Trade), 1 (1981), 16.
181. Wang Hong, *China's Exports since 1979*, p. 113.
182. World Bank, *China: External Trade and Capital*, pp. 108–9.
183. Ibid., p. 113.
184. 'Regulations for Rebate of Taxes on Export Products' were issued by the State Council in April 1985. The scheme was only partially effectively implemented thereafter. It was not until 1988 that MOFERT vowed to implement the scheme *in toto*. See Shen Jueren, 'Shixing yi Difang Weizhu de Waimao Chengbao Jingying Zerenzhi' (Implementing a Local Responsibility System in Foreign Trade), *Guoji Maoyi* (Intertrade), 9 (1988), p. 4.
185. The official exchange rate remained at 1.93 yuan to $1. The RMB was therefore effectively devalued..
186. For more details, see Lardy, *Foreign Trade and Economic Reform in China*, pp. 52–3.
187. Ibid., pp. 144–5.
188. World Bank, *China: External Trade and Capital*, p. 148–9.
189. Zheng Tuobin, 'Gaige Kaifang Tuidongzhe Woguo Duiwai Jingji Maoyi de Fazhan' (Reform and Opening to the Outside World Gives Impetus to the Development of China's Foreign Trade), *Xinhua Yuebao* (New China Monthly), 12 (1987), 38.
190. See 'Decision of the Central Committee of the CCP on Reform of the Economic Structure', Centrefold, *Beijing Review*, 44 (1984).
191. S. Shirk, *How China Opened Its Door: The Political Success of the PRC's Foreign Trade and Investment Reforms*, p. 44.
192. China made its application for membership in the Multifibre Arrangement in December 1983. In January 1984, it signed the Arrangement Regarding International Trade in Textiles. See Jacobson, and Oksenberg, *China's Participation* in the IMF, the World Bank and GATT, p. 84.
193. It is interesting to read that in the Seventh Five-Year Plan adopted on 12 April 1986 by the Fourth Session of the Sixth National People's Congress, it is explicitly stated that

To promote foreign trade we shall continue to reform the system by which it is managed. For some time to come, our most important task will be to strengthen and improve macroeconomic control and management system, and to reasonably regulate import and export by increased use of such economic levers as exchange rates, customs duties, taxation and export credits, to be supplemented with administrative means when necessary.

See *Almanac of China's Foreign Economic Relations and Trade, 1987*, p. 17.

194. See 'Zhongguo Duiwai Maoyi Zhidu Beiwanglu' (The Memorandum on China's Foreign Trade System), in Shen Bonian (ed.), *Huifu Woguo Guanmao Zongxieding Diwei de Yingxiang he Duice* (Resumption of China's GATT status: Impact and Policies), pp. 328–58.
195. Huang Yaoliang, 'Woguo Huifu Guanmao Zongxieding Diyueguo Xiwei', *Guoji Maoyi Wenti* (Issues in International Trade), 5 (1989), 33.
196. Liu Guangxi, 'Guanmao Zongxieding Jinkou Xukezheng Shouxu Xieyi yu Jinkou Xukezheng Guanli Zhidu' (The GATT Procedure on Import Licensing and the Management of China's Current Import Licensing System), *Guoji Maoyi Wenti* (Issues in International Trade), 9, 18–24; and 10, 40–3 (1988).
197. Huang Yaoliang, 'Woguo Huifu Guanmao Zongxieding Diyueguo Xiwei', *Guoji Maoyi Wenti*, 5 (1989), 37.
198. Xue Yongjiu, 'Guanshui ji Maoyi Zongxieding yu Woguo Waimao Tizhi Gaige' (The GATT and China's Foreign Trade System Reform), *Guoji Maoyi Wenti* (Issues in International Trade), 1 (1988), 19–20.
199. Ibid. See also Huang Yaoliang, 'Woguo Huifu Guanmao Zongxieding Diyueguo Xiwei', *Guoji Maoyi Wenti*, 5 (1989), 36–7.
200. The rest is what is called the guidance planning.
201. Lardy, *Foreign Trade and Economic Reform in China*, p. 40.
202. Ibid., 110.
203. See Barry, Naughton, *Growing out of the Plan: Chinese Economic Reform, 1978–1993*.
204. Li Lanqing, *Jiakuai he Shenhua Waimao Tizhi Gaige Cujin Duiwai Maoyi Fazhan* (Speed Up and Deepen the Foreign Trade System Reform and Promote the Expansion of Foreign Trade), *Xinhua Yuebao* (New China Monthly), 9 (1988), 67–8.
205. *Renmin Ribao*, 13 March 1988. See also Lardy, *Foreign Trade and Economic Reform in China*, p. 58.
206. *Jinrong Ribao* (Financial News), 15 Feb. 1989.
207. For a brief description of the negotiations before June 1989, see Jacobson, and Oksenberg *China's Participation* in the IMF, the World Bank and GATT, pp. 94–104. See also P. Hartland-Thunberg, *China, Hong Kong, Taiwan and the World Trading System*, pp. 73–81.
208. Lardy, *Foreign Trade and Economic Reform in China*, p. 3.
209. 'Learning the Rules of Foreign Trade', *China News Analysis*, 1464, 2.
210. The export subsidies were officially abolished on 1 January 1992.
211. Wu Yi, 'China's Achievements in Foreign Trade System Reform and Its Direction', *Bulletin of MOFERT*, 5 (19 Dec. 1991), 18. See also Wang Zhenggang, 'Shixing Waimao Xintizhi de Qidian' (A Start to Implement the New Foreign Trade System), *Liaowang* (Outlook Weekly), 51 (1991), 10.

212. Li Lanqing, 'Shenhua Gaige Yizhi Qusheng' (Deepen the Reforms and Win the Competition Through Improved Quality), *Liaowang* (Outlook Weekly), 3 (1992), 4–5.
213. *Liaowang*, 5 (1992), 38.
214. Shen Bonian (ed.), *Huifu Woguo Guanmao Zongxieding Diwei de Yingxiang he Duice*, p. 4.
215. Zhao Shouguo and Cheng Long, *Da Chongji: Zhongguo Congfan Guanmao Zongxieding* (The Big Assault: China's Return to the GATT), p. 80.
216. 'Zhongguo Shouxi Tanpan Daibiao zai Guanmao Zongxieding Zhongguo Gongzuozu Dishici Huiyi shang de Fayan' (Speech by the Chief Representative of China at the Tenth Meeting of the GATT Working Party on China), in Shen Bonian (ed.), *Huifu Woguo Guanmao Zongxieding Diwei de Yingxiang he Duice* (Resumption of China's GATT Membership: Impact and Policies), p. 324.
217. *Renmin Ribao* (overseas edn) 15 Dec. 1992.
218. *Renmin Ribao*, 23 Dec. 1992.
219. GATT/1538, 12 March 1992, p. 3.
220. Bosworth and Ofer, *Reforming Planned Economies in an Integrating World Economy*, p. 62.
221. In Lardy's formulation, such change in attitude could be seen in the fact that the GATT Working Party on China would 'expect concrete evidence of compatibility rather than simply examine the trajectory of China's reforms'. Lardy, *Foreign Trade and Economic Reform in China*, p. 4.
222. For 'deep integration' issues and the intellectual property rights in China's negotiations with the United States, see Shirk, *How China Opened Its Door*, pp. 76–86.
223. Bosworth and Ofer, *Reforming Planned Economies in an Integrating World Economy*, p. 62.
224. *Renmin Ribao* (Overseas Ed.), 15 Dec. 1992.
225. Shirk, *How China Opened Its Door*, pp. 71–2.
226. See Sun Geqin and Cui Hongjian, *Erzhi Zhongguo: Shenghua yu Xianshi* (Containing China: Myth and Reality), pp. 687–734.
227. Lu Jianren and Zhang Yunling, *Nurturing Asia-Pacific Economic Cooperation – Policies of Japan, China and ASEAN*, p. 20.
228. See Y. Funabashi, *Asia Pacific Fusion: Japan's Role in APEC*, pp. 56–7.
229. In the words of the Chinese scholars, 'because of the aftershocks of the 1989 political turmoil, China was barred from membership at the time of APEC's birth'. Lu and Zhang, *Nurturing Asia-Pacific Economic Cooperation*, p. 20.
230. According to Funabashi, ASEAN was 'reluctant to include China, particularly without Hong Kong and Taiwan, as they feared that ASEAN's collective voice within APEC would be muted and their lives with Beijing would be complicated'. For Japan, a MITI official stated that 'we were afraid that it would easily turn into a politicisation of APEC if we were to discuss China's membership from the start and derail the process before it even got moving'. The American concern, as a State Department official recalled, was that 'the PRC is so big that it would swamp the whole process'. Y. Funabashi, *Asia Pacific Fusion*, p. 65.
231. Political considerations mentioned above may have also prompted China to be more flexible in accepting the terms on which Taiwan could participate in APEC.

232. For a brief but interesting account of APEC diplomacy to include all three economies of Greater China at the same time in 1991, see Funabashi, *Asia-Pacific Fusion*, pp. 73–6.
233. Chu Shulong, 'From Seattle to Jakarta: The Sino–United States Relations', *Beijing Review*, 46, 7.
234. It should be noted that since 1993, the annual APEC leaders' meeting has always been looked upon by the Chinese leaders and senior officials as valuable opportunities to socialise themselves with their counterparts in the Asia-Pacific countries.
235. Lu Jianren and Zhang Yunling, *Nurturing Asia-Pacific Economic Cooperation*, p. 21. Lu and Zhang also report that 'China hopes APEC mechanism can help diminish American pressure, especially by applying the non-discriminatory principle, halt the American review of the MFN trading status for China'. On another APEC forum, Chinese scholars argued that APEC should adopt measures to support early WTO entry for APEC members still outside that world organisation. Chen Dezhao and Kuang Mei, 'APEC vs China's Reform and Opening Up', in I. Yamazawa, and A. Hirata, (eds), *APEC: Cooperation from Diversity*, p. 59.
236. For details, see 'PECC Members Sign Beijing Statement', *Beijing Review*, 50, 19–20.
237. See 'Osaka Summit: A Step Forward for APEC', *Beijing Review*, 50 (1995), 8–9.
238. See 'China and APEC: A Constructive Partnership', *Beijing Review*, 52 (1996), 8–9.
239. 'Jiang Calls for Closer Economic and Technical Cooperation', *Beijing Review*, 52 (1996), 7.
240. Lu Jianren and Zhang Yunling, *Nurturing Asia-Pacific Economic Cooperation*, p. 27.
241. Chen Dezhao and Kuang Mei, 'APEC vs China's Reform and Opening up', in Yamazawa and Hirata, (eds.), *APEC: Cooperation from Diversity*, p. 56.
242. For details, see Shirk, *How China Opened Its Door*, pp. 12–75.
243. A. Watson, *The Evolution of International Society*, p. 304.
244. Miller, 'The Third World', in Miller and Vincent, (eds) *Order and Violence*, p. 74.

CONCLUSION

1. Bull, *The Anarchical Society*, p. 42.
2. See David Lampton's review of Y. Funabashi, et al, *An Emerging China in a World of Interdependence*, in *China Quarterly*, 140 (Dec. 1994), 1198.
3. See J. K. Fairbank, *The Great Chinese Revolution, 1800–1985*.
4. Chas W. Freeman, Jr. argued, for example, that 'The US, however, has ceased to make any effort to integrate China into global institutions. New organisations, like the Missile Technology Control Regime (MTCR), the World Trade Organisation (WTO), and the New Forum (successor to the Coordinating Committee on Multilateral Export Controls) exclude China. *Foreign Policy* (Fall 1996) 5.

5. See, among others, J. Shinn, *Weaving the Net: Conditional Engagement with China*; P. Dibb, *Towards a New Balance of Power in Asia*, Adelphi Papers, 295; G. Segal, 'East Asia and the "Constrainment" of China', *International Security*, 20, 4 (Spring 1996) 107–35; and J. S. Nye, Jr, 'The Case for Deep Engagement', *Foreign Affairs*, 74, 4 (1995) 90–102.
6. S. Huntington, 'Clash of Civilisations?' *Foreign Affairs*, 72, 3 (1993) 40.
7. D. Shambaugh, 'Introduction', in T. W. Robinson, and D. Shambaugh (eds), *Chinese Foreign Policy: Theory and Practice*, p. 1.
8. For a brief discussion of these two approaches in studying China's international behaviour, see R. Foot, 'The Study of China's International Behaviour: International Relations Approaches', in N. Woods, (ed.), *Explaining International Relations since 1945*, pp. 259–79.
9. S. Huntington, 'Clash of Civilisations?' *Foreign Affairs*, 72, 3, (1993) 29 and 46.
10. See, for example, B. Russet, and W. Antholis, *Grasping the Democratic Peace: Principles for a Post-Cold War World*.
11. F. Halliday, 'The End of the Cold War and International Relations: Some Analytical and Theoretical Conclusions', in K. Booth, and S. Smith, (eds), *International Relations Theory Today*, p. 49.
12. See Mayall, *Nationalism and International Society*, in particular, 'Conclusion', pp. 145–52.
13. Vincent, *Human Rights and International Relations*, p. 99.
14. Mayall, *Nationalism and International Society*, in particular, 'Conclusion', p. 147.
15. Andrew Nathan, 'Influencing Human Rights in China', in J. R. Lilly and W. L. Willkie, (eds), *Beyond MFN: Trade with China and American Interests*, p. 80.
16. See Buzan, 'International Society and International Security', in Fawn and Larkin, (eds), *International Society after the Cold War*, pp. 273–5.
17. One Brookings project defines the deeper integration as 'behind-the-border integration', whereas the shallow integration it classes as 'relaxations at-the-border integration'. See S. M. Collins and R. T. Lawrence, 'Preface to the Studies on Integrating National Economies', in Shirk, *How China Opened Its Door*, pp. xi–xxiv.
18. Shirk, *How China Opened Its Door*, pp. 76–7.
19. Bull and Watson, (eds), *The Expansion of International Society*, p. 1.
20. For arguments about the concentric circles in international society, see Buzan, 'From International System to International Society: Structural Realism and Regime Theory Meet the English School', *International Organisation*, 47, 3 (Summer 1993) 327–52; and Buzan, 'International Society and International Security', in Fawn, and Larkins, (eds), *International Society after the Cold War*, pp. 261–87.

Bibliography

PERIODICALS AND NEWSPAPERS PUBLISHED IN CHINA

Beijing Review
China Daily
China's Foreign Trade
Fuyin Baokan Ziliao
   Waimao Jingji Guoji Maoyi (Foreign Trade Economics, International Trade)
   Zhongguo Waijiao (China's Foreign Affairs)
Guoji Maoyi (Intertrade)
Guoji Maoyi Wenti (Issues in International Trade)
Guoji Wenti Yanjiu (International Studies)
Hongqi (Red Flag)
Jingji Yanjiu (Economic Research)
Liaowang (Outlook Weekly)
Qiushi (Seeking Truth)
Renmin Ribao (People's Daily)
Shijie Jingji (World Economy)
Shijie Zhishi (World Affairs)
Xiandai Guoji Guanxi (Contemporary International Relations)
Xinhua Yuebao (New China Monthly)
Zhongguo Shehui Kexue (China Social Sciences)

BOOKS IN ENGLISH

Adshead, S. A. M. *China in World History* (Basingstoke: Macmillan, 1988).
Ambrose, S. *Rise to Globalism – American Foreign Policy since 1938* 3rd rev. edn., (Harmondsworth: Penguin, 1983).
Armstrong, D. *Revolutionary Diplomacy – Chinese Foreign Policy and the United Front Doctrine* (London: University of California Press, 1977).
—— *Revolution and World Order: The Revolutionary State in International Society* (Oxford: Oxford University Press, 1993).
Aron, R. *Peace and War – A Theory of International Relations* (London: Weidenfeld & Nicolson, 1966).
Ashley, R. *The Political Economy of War and Peace: The Sino-Soviet-American Triangle and the Modern Security Problematique* (London: Francis Pinter, 1980).
Asian Development Bank, *The Annual Report of the Asian Development Bank, 1988–1995* (Manila: ADB, 1989–1996).
Banks, M. (ed.) *Conflict in World Society: A New Perspective of International Relations* (London: Wheatsheaf, 1984).
Barnett, A, D. *China's Economy in Global Perspective* (Washington DC: The Brookings Institution, 1981).

Bartke, W. *China's Economic Aid to Developing and Socialist Countries* (New York: Holmes & Meier, 1975).
Bell, M. W., Klor, H. E., and Kochhar, K. *China at the Threshold of a Market Economy* (Washington DC: IMF, 1993).
Booth, K. and Smith, S. (eds.) *International Relations Theory Today* (Cambridge: Polity Press, 1995).
Borg, D. and Cohen, W. I. (eds.) *The United States and China since 1945: New Frontiers in American East Asian Relations* (New York: Columbia University Press, 1983).
Borg, D. and Heinrichs, W. (eds.) *Uncertain Years: Chinese-American Relations, 1947–1950* (New York: Columbia University Press, 1980).
Bosworth, B. P. and Ofer, G. *Reforming Planned Economies in an Integrating World Economy* (Washington DC: The Brookings Institution, 1995).
Boyd, R. G. *Communist China's Foreign Policy* (New York: Frederick A. Praeger, 1962).
Bozeman, A. *The Future of Law in a Multicultural World* (Princeton: Princeton University Press, 1972).
—— *Politics and Culture in International History* (Princeton: Princeton University Press, 1960).
Brown, M. E., Lynn-Jones, S. M. and Miller, S. E. (eds.) *Debating the Democratic Peace* (Cambridge, Mass.: MIT Press, 1996).
Buchan, A. *Change without War: The Shifting Structure of World Power* (London: Chatto & Windus, 1974).
Bull, H. *The Anarchical Society: A Study of Order in World Politics* (London: Macmillan, 1977).
Bull, H. and Watson, A. (eds.) *The Expansion of International Society* (Oxford: Clarendon Press, 1984).
Bull, H., Kingsbury, B., and Roberts, A. (eds.) *Hugo Grotius and International Relations* (Oxford: Clarendon Press, 1990).
Butterfield, H. and Wight, M. (eds.) *Diplomatic Investigations: Essays in the Theory of International Politics* (London: George Allen & Unwin, 1966).
Calvocorressi, P. *World Politics since 1945*, 3rd. edn (London: Longman, 1977).
Camilleri, J. A. *Chinese Foreign Policy: the Maoist Era and Its Aftermath* (Oxford: M. Robertson, 1980).
Carlsson, I. and Ramphal, S. *Our Global Neighbourhood* (Oxford: Oxford University Press, 1995).
Chan, G. *China and International Organisations: Participation in Non-governmental Organisations since 1971* (Hong Kong: Oxford University Press, 1989).
Chen Jian *China's Road to the Korean War: The Making of Sino-American Confrontation* (New York: Columbia University Press, 1994).
Chen, K. C. (ed.) *China and the Three Worlds: A Foreign Policy Reader* (London: Macmillan, 1979).
Clough, R. N. et al *The United States, China and Arms Control* (Washington DC: The Brookings Institution, 1975).
Cobb, R. W. and Elder, C. *International Community: A Regional and Global Study* (New York: Holt, Rinehart & Winston, 1970).
Cockcroft, J. D. et al *Dependence and Underdevelopment: Latin America's Political Economy* (New York: Anchor Books, 1972).

Cohen, J. (ed.) *China's Practice of International Law: Some Case Studies* (Cambridge, Mass.: Harvard University Press, 1972).
Cohen, J. and Hungdah, Chiu (eds.) *People's China and International Law: A Documentary Study* (Princeton: Princeton University Press, 1974).
Cohen, J. A. (ed.) *The Dynamics of Chinese Foreign Relations* (Cambridge, Mass.: East Asian Research Centre, Harvard University, 1970).
Cooper, J. F. *China's Foreign Aid: An Instrument of Peking's Foreign Policy*, (Lexington, Mass.: Lexington Books, 1976).
Cropsey, J. *Political Philosophy and Issues of Politics* (London: University of Chicago Press, 1977).
Deleyne, J. (trans. by Leriche, R.) *The Chinese Economy* (London: Harper & Row Publishers, 1971).
Deng Xiaoping *Fundamental Issues in Present-day China* (Beijing: Foreign Languages Press, 1987).
Der Derian, J. *On Diplomacy* (Oxford: Blackwell, 1987).
Dibb, P. *Towards a New Balance of Power in Asia* (London: Adelphi Papers, no. 295, OUP/IISS, 1995).
Dittmer, L. *Sino-Soviet Normalisation and Its International Implications, 1945–1990* (Seattle: University of Washington Press, 1992).
—— *China under Reform* (Boulder, Col.: Westview Press, 1994).
Dittmer, L. and Kim, S. S. (eds.) *China's Quest for National Identity* (Ithaca, NY: Cornell University Press, 1993).
Donnelly, J. *Universal Human Rights in Theory and Practice* (Ithaca, NY: Cornell University Press, 1989).
Dreyer, J. T. and Kim, I. J. (eds.) *Chinese Defence and Foreign Policy* (New York: Paragon House, 1989).
Eckstein, A. *Communist China's Economic Growth and Foreign Trade: Implications for the U.S. Policy* (New York: McGraw-Hill, 1966).
—— (ed.) *China Trade Prospects and U.S. Policy* (New York: Praeger Publishers, 1971).
Evans, P. M. *John Fairbank and the American Understanding of Modern China* (New York: Blackwell, 1988).
Evans, P. M. and Frolic, B. M. (eds.) *Reluctant Adversaries: Canada and the People's Republic of China, 1949–1970* (London: University of Toronto Press, 1991).
Fairbank, J. K. *China Watch* (Cambridge, Mass.: Harvard University Press, 1987).
—— *The United States and China*, 4th edn (Cambridge, Mass.: Harvard University Press, 1979).
—— *The Great Chinese Revolution, 1800–1985* (New York: Harper & Row, 1986).
—— (ed.) *The Chinese World Order: Traditional China's Foreign Relations* (Cambridge, Mass.: Harvard University Press, 1968).
Fawn, R. and Larkins, J. (eds.) *International Society after the Cold War: Anarchy and Order Reconsidered* (Basingstoke: Macmillan, 1996).
Fishel, W. R. *The End of Extraterritoriality in China* (Berkeley: University of California Press, 1952).
Fitzgerald, C. P. *The Chinese View of Their Place in the World* (Oxford: Oxford University Press, 1969).
Fitzgerald, S. *China and the World* (Canberra: Australian National University Press, 1978).

Folkerts-Landau, D. F. I. and Ito, T. *International Capital Markets: Developments, Prospects and Policy Issues* (Washington DC: IMF, 1995).
Foot, R. *The Practice of Power: U.S. Relations with China since 1949* (Oxford: Oxford University Press, 1995).
Forsythe, D. *Human Rights and World Politics*, 2nd edn (Lincoln, Neb.: University of Nebraska Press, 1989).
Fukasaku, K. et al *China's Long March to an Open Economy* (Paris: OECD, 1994).
Fukuyama, F. The End of History and the Last Man (New York: Free Press, 1992).
Fulbright, J. W. *The Arrogance of Power* (London: Jonathan Cape, 1967).
Funabashi, Y. *The Asia Pacific Fusion: Japan's Role in APEC* (Washington D. C.: Institute of International Economics, 1995)
Fung, E. S. K. *From Fear to Friendship: Australia's Policies Towards the People's Republic of China* (St. Lucia, Qld: University of Queensland Press, 1985).
Gaddis, J. L. *The United States and the Origins of the Cold War, 1941–1947* (New York: Columbia University Press, 1972).
Garth, B. G. and Editors of Journal of Stanford International Studies (eds.) *China's Changing Role in the World Economy* (New York: Praeger, 1976).
Garver, J. *China's Decision for Rapprochement with the United States, 1968–1971* (Boulder, Col.: Westview Press, 1982).
Geldenhuys, D. *Isolated States: A Comparative Analysis* (Cambridge: Cambridge University Press, 1990).
Gilks, A. and Segal, G. *China and the Arms Trade* (London: Croom Helm, 1985).
Gill, B. and Kim, T. *China's Arms Acquisitions from Abroad: A Quest for 'Superb and Secret Weapons'* (Oxford: Oxford University Press, 1995).
Gilpin, R. *The Political Economy of International Relations* (Princeton: Princeton University Press, 1987).
Gittings, J. *The World and China, 1922–72* (London: Eyre Methuen, 1974).
—— *China Changes Faces: The Road from Revolution, 1949–1989* (Oxford: Oxford University Press, 1989).
Goldblat, J. *Agreements for Arms Control: A Critical Survey* (London: Taylor & Francis, 1982).
—— *Arms Control: A Survey and Appraisal of Multilateral Agreements* (London: Taylor & Francis, 1978).
Goldman, M. *Sowing the Seeds of Democracy in China: Political Reform in the Deng Xiaoping Era* (Cambridge, Mass.: Harvard University Press, 1994).
Goldstein, M. et al *International Capital Markets: Developments, Prospects and Policy Issues*, September 1986 (Washington DC: IMF, 1986).
—— *International Capital Markets: Developments, Prospects and Policy Issues*, September 1992 (Washington DC: IMF, 1993).
Gong, G. *The Standard of 'Civilisation' in International Society* (Oxford: Clarendon Press, 1984).
Goodman, D. S. G., *Beijing Street Voices* (London: Marion Boyars, 1981).
Goodman, D. S. G., Lockett, M. and Segal, G. *The China Challenge: Adjustment and Reform* (London: Routledge & Kegan Paul, 1986).
Gottlieb, T. *Chinese Foreign Policy Factionalism and the Origins of the Strategic Triangle* (Santa Monica, Calif.: The Rand Corporation, 1977).
Gurtov, M. *China and Southeast Asia – The Politics of Survival: A Study of Foreign Policy Interaction* (Lexington, Mass.: Lexington Books, 1971).
Halliday, F., *Rethinking International Relations* (Basingstoke: Macmillan, 1994).

Halperin, M. H. and Perkins, D. H., *Communist China and Arms Control* (Cambridge, Mass: East Asian Research Centre, Harvard University, 1965).
Han Nianlong (ed.), *Diplomacy of Contemporary China* (Hong Kong: New Horizon Press, 1990).
Hao, Y. and Huan, G. (eds.), *The Chinese View of the World* (New York: Pantheon Books, 1989).
Harding, H. (ed.) *China's Foreign Relations in the 1980s* (London: Yale University Press, 1984).
—— *China's Second Revolution* (Washington DC: The Brookings Institution, 1987).
—— *A Fragile Relationship: the United States and China since 1972* (Washington DC: The Brookings Institution, 1992).
Harding, H. and Yuan, M. (eds.) *Sino-American Relations, 1945–1955 – A Joint Reassessment of a Critical Decade* (Wilmington, Dela.: Scholarly Resources, 1989).
Harris, L. *China's Foreign Policy Toward the Third World* (New York: Praeger, 1985).
Harris, L. and Worden, R. (eds.) *China and the Third World: Champion or Challenger?* (Dover, Mass.: Auburn House, 1986).
Harris, S. and Klintworth, G. (eds.) *China as a Great Power: Myths, Realities and Challenges in the Asia-Pacific Region* (Melbourne: Longman, 1995).
Hartland-Thunberg, P. *China, Hong Kong, Taiwan and the World Trading System* (Basingstoke: Macmillan, 1990).
Hawke, R. *The Hawke Memoirs* (Sydney: Heinemann, 1994).
Hinton, H. *Communist China in World Politics* (Boston: Houghton Mifflin Co., 1966).
—— *China's Turbulent Quest: An Analysis of China's Foreign Relations since 1949*, Rev. edn (New York: Macmillan, 1972).
Ho, Ping-ti and Tsou, Tang (eds.) *China in Crisis*, 2 vols. (Chicago: University of Chicago Press, 1968).
Hooper, B. *China Stands Up: Ending the Western Presence 1948–1950* (Sydney: Allen & Unwin, 1986)
Howard, C. *Splendid Isolation* (London: Macmillan, 1967).
Howard, M. *The Lessons of History* (Oxford: Oxford University Press, 1993).
Howe, C. (ed.) *China and Japan: History, Trends, and Prospects* (Oxford: Clarendon Press, 1996).
Hsiao, G. T. (ed.) *Sino-American Détente and Its Policy Implications* (New York: Praeger Publishers, 1974).
Hsiung, J. C. *Law and Policy in China's Foreign Relations: A Study of Attitudes and Practice* (New York: Columbia University Press, 1972).
—— (ed.) *Beyond China's Independent Foreign Policy: Challenges for U.S. and its Asian Allies* (New York: Praeger, 1985).
Hsiung, J. C. and Kim, S. S. (eds.) *China in the Global Community* (New York: Praeger, 1980).
Hsu, I. *China's Entrance into the Family of Nations – The Diplomatic Phase, 1861–1880* (Cambridge, Mass.: Harvard University Press, 1960).
Hsu, J. C. *China's Foreign Trade Reforms* (Cambridge: Cambridge University Press, 1989).
Hu, C. C. *Arms Control Policy of the People's Republic of China, 1949–1978* (unpublished D.Phil. thesis, Oxford: Oxford University).

Hudson, G. F. *Europe and China: A Survey of their Relations from the Earliest Times to 1800* (London: Edward Arnold, 1931).
Hunt, M. H. *Ideology and U.S. Foreign Policy* (New Haven, Conn.: Yale University Press, 1987).
Huntington, S. P. *The Third Wave: Democratisation in the Late Twentieth Century* (Norman: University of Oklahoma Press, 1991).
International Institute of Strategic Studies (IISS) *Strategic Survey, 1988–1996* (London: IISS, 1989–1997).
IMF *Direction of Trade Statistics Yearbook, 1988–1995* (Washington DC: IMF, 1989–1996).
Iriye, A. *The Cold War in Asia: A Historical Introduction* (Englewood Cliffs, NJ: Printice-Hall, 1974).
—— *China and Japan in the Global Setting* (Cambridge, Mass.: Harvard University Press, 1992).
Jackson, R. and James, A. *States in a Changing World: A Contemporary Analysis* (Oxford: Clarendon Press, 1993).
Jacobson, H. and Oksenberg, M. *China's Participation in the IMF, the World Bank and GATT: Towards a Global Economic Order* (Ann Arbor: University of Michigan Press, 1990).
James, A. *Peacekeeping in International Politics* (Basingstoke: Macmillan, 1990).
Johnson, C. *Communist China and Latin America, 1959–1967* (New York: Columbia University Press, 1967).
Johnson, C. (ed.) *Ideology and Politics in Contemporary China* (Seattle: University of Washington Press, 1973).
Jonas, M. *Isolationism in America, 1935–1941* (Chicago: Imprint Publications, 1990).
Jovanovic, M. N. *International Economic Integration* (London: Routledge, 1992).
Kalicki, J. H. *The Pattern of Sino-American Crises* (Cambridge: Cambridge University Press, 1975).
Kapur, H. *The Awakening Giant: China's Ascension in World Politics* (Alphen aan de Rijin: Sijthoff & Noordhoff, 1981).
—— (ed.) *The End of an Isolation: China after Mao* (Dordrecht: M. Nijhoff, 1985).
—— (ed.) *As China Sees the World: Perceptions of Chinese Scholars* (London: Pinter, 1987).
—— *Distant Neighbours: China and Europe* (London: Pinter, 1990).
Kau, M. Y. M. and Leung, J. K. (eds.) *The Writings of Mao Zedong, 1949–1976*, 2 vols. (New York: M. E. Sharpe, 1986).
Keith, R. C. *The Diplomacy of Zhou Enlai* (Basingstoke: Macmillan, 1989).
Kent, A. *Between Freedom and Subsistence: China and Human Rights* (New York: Oxford University Press, 1993).
Keohane, R. O. *After Hegemony: Cooperation and Discord in the World Political Economy* (Princeton: Princeton University Press, 1984).
Kim. I. J. (ed.) *The Sino-Soviet-American Strategic Triangle* (New York: Paragon Books, 1987).
Kim, S. S. *China, the United Nations and World Order* (Princeton: Princeton University Press, 1979).
—— (ed.) *China and the World: Chinese Foreign Policy in the Post-Mao Era* (London: Westview Press, 1984).
—— (ed.) *China and the World: New Directions in Chinese Foreign Relations*, 2nd edn (London: Westview Press, 1990).

—— *China and the World: Chinese Foreign Relations in the Post-Cold War Era*, 3rd edn (San Francisco: Westview Press, 1994).
Kissinger, H. *White House Years* (Boston: Little, Brown & Co., 1979).
—— *Years of Upheaval* (London: Weidenfeld & Nicolson, 1982).
Langdon, F. *Japan's Foreign Policy* (Vancouver: University of British Columbia Press, 1973).
Lardy, N. R. *Foreign Trade and Economic Reform in China, 1978–1990* (Cambridge: Cambridge University Press, 1992).
—— *China in the World Economy* (Washington DC: Institute of International Economics, 1994).
—— *China's Entry into the World Economy: Implications for Northeast Asia and the United States* (London: University Press of America, 1987).
Larkin, B. D. *China and Africa, 1949–1970* (Berkeley: University of California Press, 1971).
Laurance, E. J. *Arms Watch: SIPRI Report on the First Year of the UN Register of Conventional Arms* (Oxford: Oxford University Press, 1993).
Lee Chae-Jin *Japan Faces China: Political and Economic Relations in the Postwar Era* (Baltimore: Johns Hopkins University Press, 1976).
—— *China and Japan: New Economic Diplomacy* (Standford, Calif.: Hoover Institution Press, 1984).
Lee, L. T. *China and International Agreements: A Study of Compliance* (Leyden: A. W. Sijthoff, 1969).
Lilly, J. R. and Willkie, W. L. (eds.) *Beyond MFN: Trade with China and American Interests* (Washington DC: AEI Press, 1994).
Liu Suinian and Wu Qungan *China's Socialist Economy: An Outline History, 1949–1985* (Beijing: Foreign Languages Press, 1986).
Lu Jianren and Zhang Yunling *Nurturing Asia-Pacific Economic Cooperation – Policies of Japan, China and ASEAN*, (Beijing: Institute of Asia-Pacific Studies, Chinese Academy of Social Sciences, 1996).
Mah, Feng-hwa *The Foreign Trade of Mainland China* (Edinburgh: Edinburgh University Press, 1972).
Macchiarola, F. J. and Oxnam, R. B. (eds.) *The China Challenge: American Policies in East Asia* (New York: The Academy of Political Science, 1991).
McCormick, B. L. *Political Reform in Post-Mao China: Democracy and Bureaucracy in a Leninist State* (Berkeley: University of California Press, 1990).
MacFarquhar, R. *Sino-American Relations, 1949–1971* (New York: Praeger, 1972).
—— (ed.) *The Politics of China, 1949–1989* (Cambridge: Cambridge University Press, 1993).
MacFarquhar, R. and Fairbank, J. K. (eds.) *The Cambridge History of China, Vol. 14, The People's Republic, Part 1: The Emergence of Revolutionary China, 1949–1965* (Cambridge: Cambridge University Press, 1987).
—— *The Cambridge History of China, Vol. 15, The People's Republic, Part 2: Revolutions within the Chinese Revolution, 1966–1982* (Cambridge: Cambridge University Press, 1991).
Machlup, F. *A History of Thought on Economic Integration* (London: Macmillan, 1977).
McKinnon, M. (ed.) *New Zealand in World Affairs, 1957–1972* (Wellington: Price Milburn, 1977).
Mackerras, C. *Modern China – A Chronology from 1842 to the Present* (London: Thames & Hudson, 1982).

Mancall, M. *China at the Centre: Three Hundred Years of Foreign Policy* (New York: Free Press, 1984).
Manning, C. *The Nature of International Society* (London: Bell, 1962).
Mao Zedong *Selected Works of Mao Zedong*, 4 vols. (Beijing: Foreign Languages Press, 1961).
—— *Selected Works of Mao Zedong*, vol. V (Beijing: Foreign Languages Press, 1977).
Martin, E. W. *Southeast Asia and China: The End of Containment* (Boulder, Col.: Westview Press, 1977).
Martin, W. A. P. *The Siege in Peking: China Against the World* (Wilmington, Dela.: Scholarly Resources Inc., 1901 [reprinted 1972]).
Mayall, J. *Nationalism and International Society* (Cambridge: Cambridge University Press, 1990).
Miller, J. D. B. and Vincent, R. J. (eds.) *Order and Violence: Hedley Bull and International Relations* (Oxford: Clarendon Press, 1990).
Nagai, Y. and Iriye, A. (eds.) *The Origins of the Cold War in Asia* (Tokyo: University of Tokyo Press, 1977).
Nathan, A. *China's Crisis: Dilemmas of Reform and Prospects for Democracy* (New York: Columbia University Press, 1990).
Naughton, B. *Growing Out of the Plan: Chinese Economic Reform, 1978–1993* (Cambridge: Cambridge University Press, 1995).
Neuhause, C. *Third World Politics: China and the Afro-Asian People's Solidarity Organisation, 1957–1967* (Cambridge, Mass.: Harvard University Press, 1968).
Nixon, R. *President Nixon's Foreign Policy Report, 1972* (London: United States Information Service, 1972).
—— *U.S. Foreign Policy for the 1970s: Shaping a Durable Peace* (Washington DC: United States Government Printing Office, 1973).
Nordlinger, E. A. (ed.) *Politics and Society: Studies in Comparative Political Sociology* (Englewood Cliffs, NJ: Prentice-Hall, 1970).
—— *Isolationism Reconfigured: American Foreign Policy for a New Century* (Princeton: Princeton University Press, 1995).
OECD *Financing and External Debt of Developing Countries, 1991 Survey* (Paris: OECD, 1992).
—— *Geographical Distribution of Financial Flows to Aid Recipients* (Paris: OECD, 1995).
—— *International Capital Markets Statistics* (Paris: OECD, 1996).
Overholt, W. *China: The Next Superpower* (London: Weindenfeld & Nicolson, 1993).
Perkins, D. H. *China: Asia's Next Economic Giant?* (University of Washington Press, Seattle, 1986).
Peyrefitte, A. (trans. by Rothschild, J.) *The Collision of Two Civilisations: The British Expedition to Chinese Empire in 1792–94* (London: Harvill, 1993).
Radtke, K. W. *China's Relations with Japan, 1945–1983: The Role of Liao Chengzhi* (Manchester: Manchester University Press, 1990).
Randle, E. R., Henkin, L. and Nathan, A. J. (eds.) *Human Rights in Contemporary China* (New York: Columbia University Press, 1986).
Rikhye, I. J. and Skjelsbaek, K. (eds.) *The United Nations and Peacekeeping – Results, Limitations and Prospects: The Lessons of Forty Years of Experience* (Basingstoke: Macmillan, 1990).

Riskin, C. *China's Political Economy: The Quest for Development since 1949* (New York: Oxford University Press, 1987).
Robinson, T. W. and Shambaugh, D. (eds.) *Chinese Foreign Policy: Theory and Practice* (Oxford: Clarendon Press, 1994).
Rozman, G. *The Chinese Debate about Soviet Socialism, 1978–1985* (Princeton: Princeton University Press, 1987).
Russet, B. and Antholis, W. (eds.) *Grasping the Democratic Peace: Principles for a Post-Cold War World* (Princeton: Princeton University Press, 1993).
Ryan, M. A. *China's Attitude Toward Nuclear Weapons: China and the United States during the Korean War* (Armonk, NY: M. E. Sharpe, 1989).
Schumann, F. and Schell, O. (eds.) *Communist China – China Readings, 3* (London: Penguin Books, 1968).
Schwartz, B. I. (ed.) *Reflections on the May Fourth Movement* (Cambridge, Mass.: East Asian Research Centre, Harvard University Press, 1972).
Segal, G. *Defending China* (Oxford: Oxford University Press, 1985).
—— (ed.) *Chinese Politics and Foreign Policy Reform* (London: Kegan Paul, 1990).
Service, J. S. *The Amerasia Papers: Some Problems in the History of U.S.-China Relations*, (Berkeley: University of California Press, 1971).
Shapiro, H. R. *Democracy in America – A Political History of the United States, 1620–1789/1984* (New York: Manhattan Communications, 1986).
Sheehan, M. *Arms Control: Theory and Practice* (Oxford: Blackwell, 1988).
Shichor, Y. *The Middle East in China's Foreign Policy, 1949–1977* (Cambridge: Cambridge University Press, 1979).
—— *East Wind over Arabia: Origins and Implications of Sino-Saudi Missile Deal* (Berkeley: University of California Press, 1990).
Shinn, J. (ed.) *Weaving the Net: Conditional Engagement with China* (New York: Council on Foreign Relations, 1996).
Shirk, S. *How China Opened its Door: The Political Success of China's Trade and Investment Reforms* (Washington DC: The Brookings Institution, 1994).
—— *The Political Logic of Economic Reform in China* (Berkeley: University of California Press, 1993).
Solomon, R. (ed.) *The China Factor: Sino-American Relations and the Global Scene* (Englewood Cliffs, NJ: Prentice-Hall, 1981).
State Department *Foreign Relations of the United States* (FRUS), vol. vii, 1947, The Far East: China; vol. ix; 1949, Far East and China (Washington DC: United States Government Printing Office, 1972–74).
Stern, G. *The Structure of International Society* (London: Pinter, 1995).
Stockholm International Peace Research Institute *SIPRI Yearbook of World Armaments and Disarmament, 1985–1995* (Oxford: Oxford University Press, 1986–96).
Tang, J. T. H. *Human Rights and International Relations in the Asia-Pacific Region* (London: Pinter, 1995).
Taylor, J. *China and Southeast Asia: Peking's Relations with Revolutionary Movements*, expanded and updated edn (New York: Praeger, 1976).
Teng Ssu-yu and Fairbank, J. K. (eds.) *China's Response to the West: A Documentary Survey, 1839–1923* (Cambridge, Mass.: Harvard University Press, 1954).
Thakur, R. C. and Thayer, C. A. (eds.) *A Crisis of Expectations: UN Peacekeeping in the 1990s* (London: Westview Press, 1995).
Tow, W. T. (ed.) *Building Sino-American Relations: An Analysis for the 1990s* (New York: Paragon House, 1991).

Bibliography

Truman, H. *Memoirs*, vol. 2, *Years of Trial and Hope* (New York: Doubleday, 1956).
Tseng, W. et al. *Economic Reform in China: A New Phase* (Washinton DC: IMF, 1994).
Tsou, T. *America's Failure in China, 1941–1950* (Chicago: University of Chicago Press, 1963).
—— (ed.) *China in Crisis*, vol. 2 *China's Policy in Asia and America's Alternatives* (Chicago: University of Chicago Press, 1970).
Tucker, N. B. *Patterns in the Dust: Chinese-American Relations and the Recognition Controversy, 1949–1950* (New York: Columbia University Press, 1979).
United Nations *United Nations Disarmament Yearbook, 1985–1995* (New York: United Nations, 1986–1996).
—— *The United Nations and Disarmament: A Short History* (New York: United Nations, 1988).
—— *The Blue Helmets: A Review of United Nations Peace-keeping*, 2nd edn (New York: United Nations, 1990).
—— *Disarmament Topic Papers 8: Challenge to Multilateral Disarmament in the Post-Cold-War and Post-Gulf-War Period* (New York: United Nations, 1991).
Van Ness, P. *Revolution and Chinese Foreign Policy – Peking's Support for Wars of National Liberation* (Berkeley: University of California Press, 1970).
Vincent, J. *Human Rights and International Relations* (Cambridge: Cambridge University Press, 1986).
Von Laue, T. H. *The World Revolution of Westernisation: The Twentieth Century in Global Perspective* (New York: Oxford University Press, 1987).
Waltz, K. *Theory of World Politics* (Reading, Mass.: Addison-Wesley, 1979).
Wang Gungwu *China and the World since 1949: The Impact of Independence, Modernity and Revolution* (London: Macmillan, 1977).
Wang Hong *China's Exports since 1979* (Basingstoke: Macmillan, 1992).
Watson, A. *The Evolution of International Society: A Comparative Historical Analysis* (London: Routledge, 1992).
Watson, M. et al *International Capital Markets: Developments and Prospects* (Washington DC: IMF, 1986).
Whiting, A. *China Eyes Japan* (Berkeley: University of California Press, 1989).
—— (ed.), *China's Foreign Relations*, the Annals of ASPSS, no. 519 (Newbury Park, Calif.: Sage, 1992).
Wight, M. *International Theory: The Three Traditions*, edited by Wight, G. and Porter, B. (London: Leicester University Press, 1994).
Wilson, I. (ed.) *China and the World Community* (Sydney: Angus-Robertson, 1973).
Wiseman, H. (ed.) *Peacekeeping: Appraisals and Proposals* (Oxford: Pergamon, 1983).
Wolfgang, M. E. (ed.) *Human Rights around the World*, the Annals of AAPSS, no. 506 (Newbury Park, Calif.: Sage, 1989).
Woolcock, S. *Western Policies on East-West Trade*, Chatham House Papers 15 (London: Routledge & Kegan Paul, 1982).
Woods, N. (ed.) *Explaining International Relations since 1945* (Oxford: Oxford University Press, 1996).
World Bank, *China: External Trade and Capital* (Washington DC: The World Bank, 1988).
—— *China: Between Plan and Market* (Washington DC: The World Bank, 1990).
—— *The World Bank Annual Report, 1988–1995* (Washington DC: The World Bank, 1989–1996).

—— *China: Foreign Trade Reform* (Washington DC: The World Bank, 1994).
—— *The East Asian Miracle: Economic Growth and Public Policy* (Washington DC: The World Bank, 1994).
Xinhua News Agency *China's Foreign Relations – A Chronology of Events, 1949–1988* (Beijing: Foreign Languages Press, 1989).
Yahuda, M. *Towards the End of Isolationism: Chinese Foreign Policy after Mao* (London: Macmillan, 1983).
—— *China's Role in World Affairs* (London: Croom Helm, 1978).
Yamazawa, I. and Hirata, A. (eds.) *APEC: Cooperation From Diversity* (Tokyo: Institute of Developing Economies, 1996).
Yearbook on International Communist Affairs, 1970–1989 (Standford, Calif.: Hoover Institution Press, 1970–1990).
Yochelson, J. (ed.) *Keeping Pace: U.S. Policies and Global Economic Change* (Cambridge, Mass.: Ballinger Publishing Co., 1988).
Young, K. *Negotiating with the Chinese Communists: the United States' Experience, 1953–1967* (New York: McGraw-Hill, 1968).
Yu Guangyuan (ed.) *China's Socialist Modernisation* (Beijing: Foreign Languages Press, 1982).
Zagoria, D. *The Sino-Soviet Conflict, 1950–1961* (Princeton: Princeton University Press, 1962).
Zhang Yongjin, *China in the International System, 1918–1920: The Middle Kingdom at the Periphery* (Basingstoke: Macmillan, 1991).

ARTICLES IN ENGLISH

Ajami, F. et al 'Responses to S. P. Huntington's "The Clash of Civilisations"' *Foreign Affairs*, 72, 4 (1993) 2–26.
Aron, R. 'Richard Nixon and the Future of American Foreign Policy', *Daedalus*, (Fall 1972), 1–24.
Bailey, K. C. 'Can Missile Proliferation be Reversed?', *Orbis*, 35, 1, (Winter 1991), 5–14.
Bert, W. 'Chinese Policy Toward Burma and Indonesia: A Post-Mao Perspective', *Asian Survey*, XXV, 9, (1985), 963–80.
Bitzinger, R. 'Arms to Go: China's Arms Sales to the Third World', *International Security*, 17, 2, (Fall 1992), 84–111.
Bogert, C. R. 'America's Open Door', *China Business Review*, Sept.-Oct., 1984, 38–41.
Bottelier, P. 'China's Economic Reform since 1978 and the Role of the World Bank', (background paper prepared for a talk at Victoria University of Wellington, Wellington, New Zealand, March 1996).
Brotman, D. 'Reforming the Domestic Banking System', *China Business Review*, (March-April, 1985), 17–23.
Brown D. J. 'Sino-Foreign Joint Ventures: Contemporary Developments and Historical Perspective', *Journal of Northeast Asian Studies*, I, 4 (1982), 25–56.
Buzan, B. 'From International System to International Society: Structural Realism and Regime Theory Meet the English School', *International Organisation*, 47, 3 (Summer 1993), 327–52.

Chang, G. H. 'To the Nuclear Brink: Eisenhower, Dulles and the Quemoy-Matsu Crisis', *International Security*, 12, 2 (1983), 96–123.
Chen Qimao 'War and Peace: A Reappraisal', *Beijing Review*, 23 (1986), 18–25.
Clarke, C. M. 'Decentralisation', *China Business Review* (March-April 1984), 8–10.
Cohen, R. 'People's Republic of China: The Human Rights Exception', *Human Rights Quarterly*, 9, 4 (Nov. 1987), 447–59.
Craig, G. 'The Historian and the Study of International Relations', *American Historical Review*, 88, 1 (1983), 1–11.
Davis, V. and Yi, C. 'Balancing Foreign Exchange', *China Business Review* (March-April 1992), 14–16.
Davis, Z. S. 'China's Non-proliferation and Export Control Policies', *Asian Survey*, XXXV, 6 (1995), 587–603.
Denny, D. 'The Impact of Foreign Aid', *China Business Review* (Jan.–Feb. 1986), 23–4.
Der Derian, J. 'Mediating Estrangement: A Theory for Diplomacy', *Review of International Studies*, 13, 2 (1987), 91–110.
Ding, Arthur S. 'China's Defence Finance: Content, Process and Administration', *China Quarterly*, 146 (June 1996), 428–42.
Du Genqi 'NPT at Crossroads', *Beijing Review*, 17 (1995), 19–21.
Ero, C. and Long, S. 'Humanitarian Intervention: A New Role for the United Nations?', *International Peacekeeping*, 2, 2 (Summer 1995), 140–56.
Freeman, C. W. Jr. 'Sino-American Relations: Back to the Basics', *Foreign Policy* (Fall 1996), 2–17.
Garret, B. N. and Glaser, B. S. 'Chinese Perspectives on Nuclear Arms Control', *International Security*, 20, 3 (Winter 1995–96), 43–78.
Gill, B. R. 'Curbing Beijing's Arms Sales', *Orbis*, 36, 3 (Summer 1992), 379–96.
Goldman, M. 'Human Rights in the People's Republic of China', *Daedalus* (Fall 1983), 111–38.
Griffith, S. S. 'China's GATT Bid', *China Business Review* (July-Aug.), 1987, 36–7.
Griffith, W. 'Sino-Soviet Rapprochement?', *Problems of Communism*, XXXII, 2 (March-April 1983), 20–29.
Gunter, F. R. 'Capital Flight from the People's Republic of China: 1984–1994', *China Economic Review*, 7, 1 (1996), 77–96.
Gurtov, M. 'Swords into Market Shares: China's Conversion of Military Industry to Civilian Production', *China Quarterly*, 134 (June 1993), 213–41.
Heaton, W. R. 'China and Southeast Asian Communist Movements: The Decline of Dual Track Diplomacy', *Asian Survey*, XXII, 8 (1982), 779–800.
Henkin, L. 'The Universality of the Concept of Human Rights', *The Annals of American Academy of Political and Social Sciences*, 506 (1989), 7–18.
Hsiung, J. C. 'China's Omnidirectional Diplomacy: Realignment to Cope with the Monopolar US Power', *Asian Survey*, XXXV, 6 (1995), 573–86.
Huan Xiang 'Disarmament for World Development', *Beijing Review*, 14 (1987), 17–20.
Huntington, S. P. 'Clash of Civilisations?', *Foreign Affairs*, 72, 3 (1993), 22–49.
—— 'If Not Civilisation, What?', *Foreign Affairs*, 72, 5 (1993), 186–94.
Huo, H-L 'Patterns of Behaviour in China's Foreign Policy: The Gulf Crisis and Beyond', *Asian Survey*, XXXII, 3 (1992), 274-
Jiang Zhenxi 'PLA Priorities: Disarmament and Development', *Beijing Review*, 43 (1986), 16–7.

Johnston, A. I. 'Prospects for Chinese Nuclear Force Modernisation: Limited Deterrence Versus Multilateral Arms Control', *China Quarterly*, 146 (June 1996), 548–76.
—— 'China's New "Old Thinking": The Concept of Limited Deterrence', *International Security*, 20, 3 (Winter 1995/96), 5–22.
Kennan, G. (as X) 'The Sources of Soviet Conduct', *Foreign Affairs*, 25, 3 (1947), 566–82.
Kim, S. S. 'The People's Republic of China in the United Nations: A Preliminary Analysis', *World Politics*, XXVI, 3 (1974), 299–330.
—— 'Whither Post-Mao Chinese Global Policy?,' *International Organisation*, 35, 3 (1981), 433–65.
Lai Yali 'United Nations and the Third World', *Beijing Review*, 42 (1985), 16–19.
Lardy, N. 'The Role of Foreign Trade and Investment in China's Economic Transformation', *China Quarterly*, 144 (December 1995),
LeBourgeois, A. A. and Chung, S. K. F. 'Commercial Banks in China', *China Business Review*, (Jan./Feb. 1986), 25–8.
Lewis, J. W. and Hua Di 'China's Ballistic Missile Programs: Technologies, Strategies, Goals', *International Security*, 17, 2 (1992), 5–40.
Lewis, J. W., Hua Di and Xue Litai 'Beijing's Defence Establishment: Solving the Arms-Export Enigma,' *International Security*, 15, 4 (1990), 87–109.
Li Lanqing 'Achievements of China's Foreign Trade', *Bulletin of the MOFERT*, 5 (19 December 1991), 8.
Li Shenzhi 'A Sharp Lookout – The Price of Peace', *Beijing Review*, 23, (1986), 16–8.
Li Zhongzhou 'Issues on China's Resumption of Contracting Country Status in GATT', *China's Foreign Trade* (Oct. 1990), 8–9.
Lichtenstein, N. G. 'China's Participation in International Organisations', *China Business Review* (May-June 1979), 28–35.
Lide, V. 'The World Bank in China: Getting Back on Track is Slow Going', *China Business Review* (Jan.-Feb. 1991), 44–9.
Ma, Shu-yun 'Recent Changes in China's Pure Trade Theory', *China Quarterly*, 106 (June 1986), 291–305.
Mao Liben 'Foreign Trade Strategies in the 90s', *Beijing Review*, 34 (1991), 12–15.
Mastel, G. 'Beijing at Bay', *Foreign Policy* (Fall 1996), 27–34.
Morrison, E. 'Borrowing on World Bond Markets', *China Business Review* (Jan.–Feb. 1986), 18–21.
Mullins, R. 'The Dynamics of Chinese Missile Proliferation', *Pacific Review*, 8, 1 (1995), 135–48.
Nathan, A. 'Human Rights in Chinese Foreign Policy', *China Quarterly*, 139 (Sept. 1994), 622–43.
Nie Rongzhen 'How China Develops its Nuclear Weapons', *Beijing Review*, 17 (1985), 15–20.
Nixon, R. 'Asia after Vietnam', *Foreign Affairs*, 46, 1 (1967), 111–25.
North, R. C. 'Peking's Drive for Empire: The New Expansionism', *Problems of Communism*, ix, 1 (1960), 23–30.
Nye, J. S. Jr. 'Arms Control after the Cold War', *Foreign Affairs*, 68, 5 (1989), 42–64.
—— 'The Changing Nature of World Power', *Political Science Quarterly*, 105, 2 (Summer 1990), 177–83.

—— 'The Case for Deep Engagement', *Foreign Affairs*, 74, 4 (1995), 90–102.
Rosecrance, R. et al 'Whither Interdependence?', *International Organisation*, 31, 3 (1977), 425–42.
Ross, R. 'Enter the Dragon', *Foreign Policy* (Fall 1996), 18–25.
Ruggie, J. 'Human Rights and the Future International Community', *Daedalus* (Fall 1983), 95–109.
—— 'Multilateralism: The Anatomy of an Institution', *International Security*, 46, 3 (Summer 1992), 561–98.
Segal, G. 'East Asia and the Constrainment of China', *International Security*, 20, 4 (Spring 1996), 107–35.
Shambaugh, D. 'China's Military in Transition: Politics, Professionalism, Procurement and Power Projection', *China Quarterly*, 146 (June 1996), 265–98.
Shao Wenguang 'China's Relations with the Superpowers: Strategic Shifts and Implications', *Survival*, xxxii, 2 (1990), 157–72.
Shichor, Y. 'China and the Role of the United Nations in the Middle East: Revised Policy', *Asian Survey*, XXXIII, 3 (1991) 255–69.
Smith, T. 'The Underdevelopment of Development Literature: The Case of Dependency Theory', *World Politics*, XXXI, 2 (1978), 247–88.
Sun Weiyan 'China's Transnational Corporations', *Intertrade*, (Jan. 1991), 4–6.
Tong Dalin and Liu Ji 'North-South Cooperation for Mutual Prosperity', *Beijing Review*, 26 (1985), 18–9.
Tsou, T. 'Statesmanship and Scholarship', *World Politics*, XXVI, 3 (April 1974), 428–51.
Tsou, T. and Helperin, M. 'Mao Tse-tung's Revolutionary Strategy and China's International Behaviour', *American Political Science Review* (March 1965), 80–99.
Tuchman, B. 'If Mao Had Come to Washington: An Essay about Alternatives', *Foreign Affairs*, 51, 1 (1972) 44–64.
Tucker, N. B. 'China and America: 1941–1991', *Foreign Affairs*, 70, 5 (1991), 75–92.
Van der Kroef, J. M. 'Normalising' Relations with China: Indonesia's Policies and Perceptions', *Asian Survey*, XXVI, 8 (1986), 909–34.
Wang, R. S. 'China's Evolving Strategic Doctrine', *Asian Survey*, XX, 3 (1980), 1040–55.
Wang Shaoguang 'Estimating China's Defence Expenditure: Some Evidence from Chinese Sources', *China Quarterly*, 147 (September 1996), 899–911.
Wang Xuewen 'China's Overseas Enterprises', *China's Foreign Trade* (Feb. 1987), 5–6.
Watson, A. 'Hedley Bull, States Systems and International Society', *Review of International Studies*, 13, 2 (1987), 149–53.
Weng, B. 'Communist China's Changing Attitude Toward the United Nations', *International Organisation*, XX, 4 (1966), 677–704.
Whiting, A. 'Assertive Nationalism in Chinese Foreign Policy', *Asian Survey*, XXIII, 8 (1983), 913–33.
Wilson, D. 'China Goes Transnational', *Hong Kong Business*, 15, 171 (September 1996), 6–8.
Wirsing, R. G. 'The Arms Race in South Asia: Implications for the United States', *Asian Survey*, XXV, 3 (1985), 265–85.
Woon, E. Y. 'Chinese Arms Sales and U.S.-China Military Relations', *Asian Survey*, XXIX, 6 (1989), 601–18.

Wu, Yuan-li 'The Weapon of Trade', *Problems of Communism*, IX, 1 (1960), 31–9.
Wu Yun 'China's Policies Towards Arms Control and Disarmament: From Passive Responding to Active Leading', *Pacific Review*, 9, 4 (1996), 577–606.
Xu Xianquan and Li Gang 'International Operations of Chinese Enterprises', *Intertrade* (Jan. 1991), 7–8.
Yasuhara, Y. 'Japan, Communist China and Export Control in Asia, 1948–1952', *Diplomatic History*, 10, 1 (Winter 1986), 75–91.
Yu Xiaosong 'Go-Ahead for Foreign Investment', *China's Foreign Trade* (March 1990), 6–7.
Zhai Qiang 'China and the Geneva Conference of 1954', *China Quarterly*, 129 (March 1992), 103–22.
Zhang Songtao 'Adjustment of Import-Export Mix', *China's Foreign Trade* (April–May 1990), 3–4.
Zhang Wenyuan 'China's Overseas Investment', *China's Foreign Trade* (Aug. 1992), p. 3.
Zhang Yongjin 'China's Entry into International Society: Beyond the Standard of "Civilisation"', *Review of International Studies*, 17, 1 (1991), 3–16.
Zhao Ziyang 'The Objectives of China's Foreign Policy: For Lasting Peace, Increased Friendly Cooperation and Co-Prosperity', *International Affairs*, 61, 4 (1985), 577–80.
Zheng Dunxun 'The Internationalization of China's Enterprises', *Intertrade* (Jan. 1991), 9–10.

BOOKS IN CHINESE

Chen Dunde, *Mao Zedong he Nikesong zai 1972* (Mao Zedong and Nixon in 1972) (Beijing: Kunlun Press, 1988).
Chen Zhongjing, *Guoji Zhanlue Wenti* (On the Issues in International Strategy) (Beijing: Current Affairs Press, 1988).
Deng Xiaoping, *Deng Xiaoping Wenxuan, 1975–1982* (Selected Works of Deng Xiaoping, 1975–1982) (Beijing: People's Press, 1984).
Dong Zhikai, *Jishen Guoji Shichang de Jianxin Qibu* (A Difficult Start to Get into the International Market) (Beijing: Economic Management Press, 1993).
General Office of the Standing Committee of National People's Congress et al, *Gaige yu Fazhan, 1983–1987* (Reform and Development, 1983–1987) (Beijing: Gaige Press, 1988).
Guojia Tongjiju (The Statistics Bureau of China), *Zhongguo Tongji Nianjian, 1985–1996* (China Statistical Yearbook, 1989–1996) (Beijing: China Statistics Press, 1986–1996).
—— *Zhongguo Tongji Zhaiyao, 1996* (A Statistical Survey of China, 1996) (Beijing: China Statistics Press, 1996).
Liu Enzhao, *Luelun Duiwai Jingji Kaifang* (On China's Open Economic Policy) (Beijing: Chinese People's University Press, 1985).
Liu Guoguang et al (ed.), *Zhongguo Jingji Fazhan Zhanlue Wenti Yanjiu* (Studies of China's Economic Development Strategy) (Shanghai: Shanghai People's Press, 1984).
Liu Nanlai (ed.), *Fazhan Zhong Guojia yu Renquan* (Developing Countries and Human Rights) (Chengdu: Sichuan People's Publishing House, 1994).

Ma Hong and Sun Shangqing (eds.), *Zhongguo Jingji Xingshi yu Zhanwang, 1992–1993* (China's Economic Situation and Prospect, 1992–1993) (Beijing: China Development Press, 1993).

Mao Zedong, *Mao Zedong Waijiao Wenxuan* (Selected Works of Mao Zedong on Foreign Relations) (Beijing: Central Record Press/World Affairs Press, 1994).

Pei Jianzhang et al, *Zhonghua Renmin Gongheguo Waijiaoshi, 1949–1956* (A Diplomatic History of the People's Republic of China, 1949–1956) (Beijing: World Affairs Press, 1994).

Quanguo Renda Changweihui Bangongting Deng (General Office of the Standing Committee of the National People's Congress et al), *Gaige yu Fazhan, 1983–1987* (Reform and Development, 1983–87) (Beijing: China Planning Press, 1988).

Shen Bonian (ed.), *Huifu Woguo Guanmao Zongxieding Diwei de Yingxiang he Duice* (Resumption of China's GATT Status: Impact and Policies) (Beijing: CCP Central Party School Press, 1992).

Shen Juren (ed.), *Dangdai Zhongguo de Duiwai Maoyi* (Contemproary China's Foreign Trade) (Beijing: China Social Sciences Press, 1991).

Shi Lin et al, *Dangdai Zhongguo de Duiwai Jingji Hezuo* (China Today: Economic Cooperation with Foreign Countries) (Beijing: China Social Sciences Press, 1989).

Shi Yinhong, *Didui yu Chongtu de Youlai, 1949–1950* (The Origins of Sino-American Confrontation and Hostility, 1949–1950) (Nanjing: Nanjing University Press, 1994).

Sun Geqin and Cui Hongjian (ed.), *Erzhi Zhongguo: Shenghua yu Xianshi* (Containing China: Myth and Reality) (Beijing: Yanshi Press, 1996).

Tian Zengpei (ed.), *Gaige Kaifang Yilai de Zhongguo Waijiao* (China's Foreign Relations since the Economic Reforms and Opening) (Beijing: World Affairs Press, 1993).

Wang Jisi (ed.), *Wenmin yu Guoji Zhengzhi: Zhongguo Xuezhe Ping Hentingdun de Wenmin Chongtu Lun* (Civilisation and International Politics: Chinese Scholars' Critiques of Huntington's Clash of Civilisations) (Shanghai: Shanghai People's Press, 1995).

Wang Xi and Holton, R. H. (eds.), *Zhong Mei Jingji Guanxi: Xianzhuang yu Qianjing* (Sino-U.S. Economic Relations: Present and Future) (Shanghai: Fudan University Press, 1989).

Xia Xudong et al (eds.), *Shijie Renquan Zongheng* (Human Rights: A World Perspective) (Chengdu: Sichuan People's Publishing House, 1994).

Xie Kang et al, Ruhe Chuangban Zhongguo de Haiwai Qiye (How to Set up China's Overseas Enterprises) (Shanghai: Shanghai Communications University Press, 1993).

Xin Xiangming et al, *Zai Zhao Zhongguo: Zhongguo Bainian Da Zoushi* (Remaking China: The Evolution of Chinese History in the Last Century) (Beijing: Mass Art and Literature Press, 1993).

Xinhua Tongxunshe Guonei Ziliao Zu (Xinhua News Agency Domestic Data Group), *Zhonghua Renmin Gonghe Guo Dashiji* (Chronology of Major Events of the People's Republic of China), 2 vols. (Beijing: New China Press, 1983–1985).

Xu Zhengfeng, *Zhongguo Laikui: Zhongguo Fu Jian Gongchengbin Dadui Weihe Xingdong Jishi* (The Chinese Blue Helmets: Report on Chinese Engineers Batallion's Participation in Peacekeeping in Cambodia) (Beijing: PLA Publishing House, 1994).

Xue Mouhong et al, *Dangdai Zhongguo Waijiao* (China Today: Diplomacy) (Beijing: China Social Sciences Press, 1990).
Yuan Ming (ed.), *Kua Shiji de Tiaozhan: Zhongguo Guoji Guanxi Xueke de Fazhan* (Facing the 21st Century: International Relations Studies in China) (Chongqing: Chongqing Press, 1993).
Zhao Shouguo and Chen Long (eds.), *Da Chongji: Zhongguo Congfan Guanmao Zongxieding* (A Big Assault: China's Return to the GATT) (Xi'an: Shanxi Tourist Press, 1992).
Zheng Derong, Han Minxi and Zheng Xiaoliang (eds.), *Zhongguo Jingji Tizhi Gaige Jishi* (The Chronicle of Economic Reform in China) (Beijing: Spring-Autumn Press, 1987).
Zhongguo Duiwai Jingji Maoyi Nianjian Bianji Weiyuanhui (Yearbook of China's Foreign Economic Relations and Trade Editorial Committee), *Zhongguo Duiwai Jingji Maoyi Nianjian, 1985-1995* (Yearbook of China's Foreign Economic Relations and Trade, 1985-95) (Beijing: China International Economics and Foreign Trade Press, 1985-96).
Zhonghua Zonggongsi (Sinochem), *Zhonghua Sishiwu Nian* (Forty-five Years of Sinochem) (Beijing: 1995)
Zhou Enlai, *Zhou Enlai Waijiao Wenxuan* (Selected Works of Zhou Enlai on Diplomacy) (Beijing: Central Document Publishing House, 1990).

ARTICLES IN CHINESE

Benkan Bianjibu (Editorial Board of Red Flag), 'Guanyu Woguo Duiwai Jingji Guanxi Wenti' (On Questions Regarding China's Foreign Economic Relations), *Hongqi* (Red Flag), 8 (1982), 2-12.
Bian Yanjun et al, 'Mao Zedong he Xinzhongguo de Qibu (Mao Zedong and the Early Years of New China), *Hongqi* (Red Flag), 6 (1988), 21-30.
Chen Bingfu, 'Jin Shinian lai Zhongguo Junfei Zhichu Bianhua de Jingji Fenxi' (An Economic Analysis of the Changing Chinese Military Budget in the Last Decade), *Jingji Yanjiu* (Economic Research), 6 (1990), 77-81.
Chen Dezhao, 'Dui Tongyi Shijie Shichang Wajielun de Jidian Kanfa' (Has the Unified World Market Disintegrated?), *Shijie Jingji* (World Economy), 6 (1982), 6-11.
Chen Qida, Zhu Chonggui and Fu Qisong, 'Zhongguo yu Disan Shijie Guojia de Jingmao Guanxi' (China's Economic and Trade Relations with Third World Countries), *Xiandai Guoji Guanxi* (Contemporary International Relations), 2 (1990), 46-52.
Chen Qiwei, 'Bijiao Liyi Lun de Kexue Neihan' (The Scientific Core of Ricardo's Theory of Comparative Advantage), *Shijie Jingji* (World Economy), 3 (1981), 14-19.
Chen Xinlian, 'Woguo Gongye dui Jinkou de Yilai Zhuangkuang ji qi Duice' (The Dependence of China's Industries on Imports and How to Deal with It), *Guoji Maoyi* (Intertrade), 1 (1990), 49-52.
Chen Zhihong, 'Jinyibu Fangkai Waihui Tiaoji Shichang de Jidian Sikao' (Some Preliminary Thoughts on Further Liberalising the Foreign Exchange Swap Market), *Guoji Maoyi Wenti* (Issues in International Trade), 12 (1991), 41-4.

Chi Aiping, 'Mao Zedong dui Xinzhongguo Waijiao Gongzuo de Zhanlue Zhidao' (Mao Zedong's Strategic Guidance to New China's Diplomatic Work), *Dang de Wenxian* (Documentary Record of the CCP), 1 (1992), 32–8.

Di Chun, 'Dui Zhiyue Shijie Dazhan de Jige Yingsu de Fenxi' (An Analysis of the Factors that Prevent the Outbreak of Another World War), *Guofang Daxue Xuebao* (Journal of National Defence University of China), 7 (1988), 8–11.

Fang Sheng, 'Congtan Zunzhong Guoji Guanli' (Again Abiding by the International Norms), *Guoji Maoyi* (Intertrade), 10 (1990), 33–5.

Feng Yushu, 'Guanshui Maoyi Zongxieding zhong de Zhongyang Jihua Jingji Guojia' (Central Planning Economies in the GATT), *Shijie Jingji* (World Economy), 12 (1986), 18–21.

Feng Zuowu, Zhang Yuanlong and Wang Fengmei, 'Waimao Tizhi Gaige Shinian Huigu ji Fazhan Quxiang' (Foreign Trade System Reform: Retrospect of the Last Decade and its Prospect), *Waimao Jingji Guoji Maoyi* (Foreign Trade Economics, International Trade), 2 (1990), 41–4.

Fu Bin, 'Luelun Dang he Guojia de Duiwai Zhengce shi Duli Zizhu Yuanze de Yunyong de Fazhan' (The Party and the Nation's Foreign Policy is the Application and the Development of the Principle of Independence and Self-Reliance), *Zhongguo Waijiao* (China's Foreign Affairs), 9 (1986), 12–17.

Ge Xun, 'Woguo yu Guanmao Zongxieding' (China and the GATT), *Waimao Jingji Guoji Maoyi* (Foreign Trade Economics, International Trade), 5 (1990), 5–8.

Gong Li, 'Mao Zedong yu Zhongmei Guanxi Jiedong' (Mao Zedong and the Breakthrough in Sino-American Relations), *Zhongguo Waijiao* (China's Foreign Affairs), 3 (1993), 40–48.

Guo Mao, 'Zhongguo Guoji Maoyi Xuehui Diyijie Xueshu Nianhui Taolun Qingkuang Zongshu' (A Summary of the Discussion at the First Annual Meeting of the Chinese International Trade Studies Association), *Guoji Maoyi Wenti* (Issues in International Trade), 4 (1981), 1–10.

Guo Qingshi and Wu Jun, 'Dang de Duiwai Lianluo Gongzuo de Yige Xinfazhan' (A New Development of our Party's International Liaison Work), *Hongqi* (Red Flag), 11 (1986), 30–2.

Han Fang, 'Junbei Jinsai yu Fazhan Wenti' (Arms Race and Development), *Shijie Zhishi* (World Affairs), 14 (1986), 10.

Huang Gaozhi, 'Lun Caijun he Jingji Shehui de Fazhan' (On the Relationship between Disarmament and Development of Economy and Society), *Zhongguo Shehui Kexue* (China Social Sciences), 4 (1987), 175–83.

Huang Huikang, 'Lun Lianheguo Weichi Heping Budui de Falu Jichu' (On the Legal Basis of the UN Peacekeeping Forces), *Zhongguo Shehui Kexue* (China Social Sciences), 4 (1987), 163–74.

Huang Shuhai, 'Lianheguo wei Meihao Shijie er Fendou' (The United Nations Is Fighting for a Better World), *Shijie Zhishi* (World Affairs), 19 (1985), 2–3.

Huang Yaoliang, 'Woguo Huifu Guanmao Zongxieding Diyueguo Xiwei yu Baozhang Tiaokuan' (The Restoration of China's Status as a Contracting Country of the GATT and its Guarantee Regulations), *Guoji Maoyi Wenti* (Issues in International Trade), 5 (1989), 32–7.

Jin Junhui, 'Luelun Dangqian Meisu de Xinhuanhe' (Preliminary Thought on the New Detente between the Soviet Union and the United States), *Guoji Wenti Yanjiu* (International Studies), 4 (1988), 5–8.

Jin Xudong, 'Zhongguo yu Dongmeng de Guanxi' (China's Relations with the ASEAN), *Zhongguo Waijiao* (China's Foreign Affairs), 9 (1988), 19–25.

Jing Ye, 'Lankui Budui—Lianheguo Weichi Heping Budui' (The Blue Helmets: UN Peacekeeping Forces), *Shijie Zhishi* (World Affairs), 21 (1988), 26–7.

Li Dacang and Chen Tiejun, 'Ruhe Lijie Guoji Maoyi Zhongde Boxue' (How to Understand 'Exploitation' in International Trade), *Shijie Jingji* (World Economy), 4 (1982), 16–18.

Li Dai and Zhou Yang, 'Luelun Dangdai de Zhanzheng yu Heping Wenti' (On War and Peace in the Contemporary Era), *Guoji Wenti Yanjiu* (International Studies), 3 (1986), 1–5.

Li Jinliang, 'Guoji Fengong Wenti Qianlun' (On the International Division of Labour), *Shijie Jingji* (World Economy), 3 (1981), 19–24.

Li Jun, 'Guanyu Waimao Tizhi Jinyibu Gaige de Sikao' (On Further Reforms of the Foreign Trade System), *Waimao Jingji Guoji Maoyi* (Foreign Trade Economics, International Trade), 3 (1987), 19–27.

Li Lanqing, 'Jiakuai he Shenhua Waimao Tizhi Gaige Cujin Duiwai Maoyi Fazhan' (Speed up and Deepen the Foreign Trade System Reform and Promote the Expansion of China's International Trade), *Xinhua Yuebao* (New China Monthly), 9 (1988), 67–8.

—— 'Shenhua Gaige Yizhi Qusheng' (Deepen the Reforms and Win the Competition through Better Quality), *Liaowang* (Outlook Weekly), 3 (1992), 4–5.

Li Zhaoxing, 'Xinzhongguo de Dansheng he Guoji Zhengzhi Geju' (The Birth of New China and the Concurrent Structure of International Politics), *Zhongguo Waijiao* (China's Foreign Affairs), 2 (1986), 6–14.

Lian Ping, 'Dangdai Shijie Jingji Xianghu Yicun de Ruogan Tedian ji qi Xingcheng Yuanyin' (The Emergence of Contemporary International Economic Interdependence and its Characteristics), *Shijie Jingji* (World Economy), 3 (1987), 26–32.

Lian Yan, 'Tantan Zhonguo Gongchandang Duiwai Lianluo Gongzuo de Tiaozheng he Fazhan' (On the Adjustment and Development of the CCP's International Liaison Work), *Renmin Ribao*, 29 June 1986.

Lin Ye 'Zhongguo Kuaguo Gongsi Lilun, Xianzhuang he Qushi' (China's Multinationals: Theory, Current Situation and Future Prospect), *Guoji Maoyi* (Intertrade), 12 (1990), 8–11.

—— 'Lun Zhongguo Kuaguo Gongsi de Longduan yu Jinzheng' (On the Monopoly and Competition of China's Multinationals), *Guoji Maoyi* (Intertrade), 10 (1991), 13–15.

Liu Enzhao, 'Lianheguo Weichi Heping Xingdong de Chengjiu he Zhanwang' (UN Peacekeeping Operations: Achievements and Prospect), *Shijie Zhishi* (World Affairs), 8 (1991), 20–1.

Liu Guangxi 'Guanmao Zongxieding Jinkou Xukezheng Shouxu Xieyi yu Jinkou Xukezheng Guanli Zhidu' (GATT Procedure on Import Licensing and the Management of China's Current Import Licensing System), *Guoji Maoyi Wenti* (Issues in International Trade), 9 (1986), 18–24 and 10 (1986), 40–3.

—— 'Lun Xinyilun Zhishi Chanquan Houqi Tanpan de Jiaodian Wenti' (On the Central Questions at the Second Stage of the Present Round of International Negotiations on Intellectual Property Rights), *Guoji Maoyi*, (Intertrade), 11 (1990), 43–6.

Liu He, 'Gaige Shinian jian Zhongguo Duiwai Maoyi de Shizheng Fenxi' (An Empirical Analysis of China's Foreign Trade in the Last Ten Years of Reform), *Jingji Yanjiu* (Economic Research), 9 (1991), 61–6.

Liu Rongcang 'Woguo Waizi Shiyong Xiaoyi de Huigu he Duice' (China's Utilization of Foreign Capital: A Review and Policy Proposals), *Waimao Jingji Guoji Maoyi* (Foreign Trade Economics, International Trade), 2 (1988), 47–53.

Liu Yongqiang, 'Shijie Laowu Shichang ji Zhongguo Laowu Chukou de Qianjin Fenxi' (An Analysis of the World Labour Market and the Prospect of China's Labour Service Export), *Guoji Maoyi* (Intertrade), 5 (1990), 40–4.

Luo Yuanzeng and Wu Yufeng, 'Shehui Zhuyi Guojia ying Chongfen Liyong Guoji Jingji Lianxi Jiasu Benguo de Jingji Jianshe' (The Socialist Countries should Make Full Use of their International Economic Relations to Speed up their Economic Construction), *Shijie Jingji* (World Economy), 12 (1979), 4–9.

Pan Jin, 'Zhong Ying Jianjiao Tanpan de Changqi Fuza Licheng' (The Protracted Negotiation Between China and Britain for Establishing Full Diplomatic Relations), *Waijiao Xueyuan Xuebao* (Journal of Foreign Affairs College), 3 (1992), 13–18.

Pei Monong, 'Caijun, Anquan yu Fazhan' (Disarmament, Security and Development), *Guoji Wenti Yanjiu* (International Studies), 3 (1986), 17–21.

Pei Yuanlun, 'Guoji Jingji Zhixu: Cong "Erzhanhou" Zouxiang "Lengzhanhou"' (The International Economic Order: From Post-War to Post-Cold-War), *Shijie Jingji* (World Economy), 9 (1991), 7–11.

Qian Qichen, 'Duihua Daiti Duikang Shi Shidai de Yaoqiu' (Dialogue Replacing Confrontation is the Demand of our Era), *Qiushi* (Seeking Truth), 4 (1988), 2–4.

Qiu Jie, 'Waimao Xitong Chengbao yu Waimao Tizhi Gaige' (Responsibility System in Foreign Trade Enterprises and Foreign Trade System Reform), *Guoji Maoyi Wenti* (Issues in Intertrade), 6 (1987), 8–11.

Qiu Jin, 'Mao Zedong yu Sidalin de Huiwu' (Meetings between Mao Zedong and Stalin), *Dang de Wenxian* (Documentary Record of the CCP), 2 (1996), 82–6.

Shao Wangyu, 'Jinyibu Kaifang Waizi Yinghang Cujin Woguo Duiwai Jingji Maoyi de Fazhan' (Further Open China to Foreign Banking Institutions to Promote China's Foreign Economic Relations and Trade), *Guoji Maoyi* (Intertrade), 8 (1990), 48–50.

Shen Jueren, '1981 Nian Zhongguo Duiwai Maoyi Zhanwang he Dangqian de Waimao Tizhi Gaige' (Prospect of China's Foreign Trade in 1981 and the Current Foreign Trade System Reform), *Guoji Maoyi Wenti* (Issues in International Trade), 1 (1981), 15–17.

——, 'Jiji Wenbu Qianjin Jinyibu Gaige Waimao Tizhi' (Progress Steadily and Positively and Further Reform the Foreign Trade System), *Guoji Maoyi* (Intertrade), 9 (1988), 19–20.

——, 'Shixing yi Difang Weizhu de Waimao Chengbao Jingying Zerenzhi' (Implementing a Local Responsibility System in Foreign Trade), *Guoji Maoyi* (Intertrade), 9 (1988), 4.

Si Chu, 'Guoji Caijun Douzheng he Woguo de Lichang' (Struggles for International Disarmament and China's Stand), *Hongqi* (Red Flag), 9 (1983), 37–40.

Song Yiming, 'Meisu jian de Songdong he Guoji Guanxi de Shenke Bianhua' (The Soviet-American Detente and the Profound Changes in International Relations), *Guoji Wenti Yanjiu* (International Studies), 1 (1988), 3–9.

Sun Weiyan, 'Woguo Kuaguo Gongsi Fazhan Gaiguan' (The Development of China's Transnationals: An Overview), *Guoji Maoyi* (Intertrade), 12 (1990), 4–8.

Tang Haiyan, 'Kaifang Waizi Yinghang yu Fazhan Woguo Yinghangye' (Open to Foreign Banks and Develop China's Banking Institutions), 1 (1990), 53–5.

Tang Hualiang, 'Weihu Shijie Heping Shi Woguo Duiwai Zhengce de Zhuyao Mubiao' (To Safeguard the World Peace is the Principal Goal of China's Foreign Policy), *Hongqi* (Red Flag), 11 (1984), 16–24.

Tao Wenzhao, 'You Zhang You Chi: 1954–1958 de Zhongmei Guanxi' (Tensions and Relaxations in Sino-American Relations, 1954–1958), *Shehui Kexue Yanjiu* (Social Sciences Research), 6 (1996), 96–104.

Wang Chenghan, 'Lun Guofang yu Jingji de Xietiao Fazhan' (On Coordinating the Defense and the Economic Development), *Hongqi* (Red Flag), 17 (1987), 19–23.

Wang He, 'Fazhan Zhongguo Tese de Kuaguo Jituan Gongsi' (Develop Transnationals with Chinese Characteristics), *Guoji Maoyi* (Intertrade), 5 (1989), 4–9.

Wang Kezhong, 'Lijie Guoji Guanli Zhangwo Guoji Guanli' (International Norms: What Are They and How to Grasp Them?), *Waimao Jingji Guoji Maoyi* (Foreign Trade Economics, International Trade), 2 (1989), 61–3.

Wang Jisi, 'Dui Zhanzheng yu Heping Lilun de Zai Sikao' (Rethinking the Theory of War and Peace), *Shijie Jingji yu Zhengzhi* (World Economy and Politics), 12 (1988), 54–64.

Wang Lei, 'Woguo Huifu Guanshui ji Maoyi Zongxieding Diyueguo Diwei de Falu Genju Chuyi' (On the Legal Basis of Restoring China's Contracting Party Status of the GATT), *Guoji Maoyi Wenti* (Issues in International Trade), 2 (1989), 38–41.

Wang Lin, 'Xinjishu Geming yu Jingji Waijiao' (New Technology Revolution and Economic Diplomacy), *Guoji Wenti Yanjiu* (International Studies), 4 (1987), 1–2.

Wang Linsheng, 'Guanyu Li Jiatu Bijiao Chengben Shuo de Pingjia Wenti' (On How to Evaluate Ricardo's Theory of Comparative Advantage), *Guoji Maoyi Wenti* (Issues in International Trade), 3 (1981), 23–30.

—— 'Waimao Tizhi Gaige de Huigu yu Fansi' (Review of and Introspection on the Reform of China's Foreign Trade System), *Waimao Jingji Guoji Maoyi* (Foreign Trade Economics, International Trade), 3 (1990), 42–6.

Wang Shaoxi, 'Lun Woguo Fazhan Duiwai Maoyi de Lilun Yiju' (On the Theoretical Foundation for Developing China's Foreign Trade), *Guoji Maoyi* (Intertrade), 12 (1986), 4–9.

——, 'Guanshui Maoyi Zongxieding zai Guoji Maoyi zhong de Jiji Zuoyong' (GATT Plays a Positive Role in Promoting International Trade), *Guoji Maoyi* (Intertrade), 2 (1989), 24–7.

——, 'Shinian Waimao Tizhi Gaige de Pinggu' (An Assessment of Foreign Trade System Reform in the Last Decade), *Guoji Maoyi Wenti* (Issues in International Trade), 12 (1989), 2–7.

Wang Tianyuan, 'Haiguan hezuo Lishihui yu Zhongguo' (The Customs Cooperation Council and China), *Guoji Maoyi* (Intertrade), 3 (1988), 42–5.

Wang Wenxue and Guo Baozhu, 'Dui Jianli Guoji Zhengzhi Xinzhixu Zhanlue Zhuzhang de Sikao' (Our thought on the Strategy to Establish a New International Political Order), *Xiandai Guoji Guanxi* (Contemporary International Relations), 3 (1989), 12–6.

Wang Yaotian, 'Lun Zhongguo yu Guanmao Zongxieding de "Ulagui Huihe"' (China and the Uruguay Round Talks of the GATT), *Guoji Maoyi* (Intertrade), 7 (1989), 4–10.

——, 'Duiwai Maoyi Tizhi Gaige Lilun Chutan' (Exploring the Theory of Foreign Trade System Reform), *Guoji Maoyi* (Intertrade), 3 (1990), 24–8.

Wang Yixuan, 'Shixing Chengbao Jinyin Zerenzhi shi Gaige Waimao Tizhi de Xintaijie' (Implementing the Responsibility System is a New Step in Foreign Trade System Reform), *Guoji Maoyi Wenti* (Issues in International Trade), 1 (1988), 21–5.

Wang Zhenggang, 'Shixing Waimao Xintizhi de Qidian' (A Start to Implement the New Foreign Trade System), *Liaowang* (Outlook Weekly), 51 (1991), 10–11.

Wang Zhenzhong, 'Fei Guosheng Ziben Xing de Guojia Haiwai Zhijie Touzi de Lilun Sisuo' (Some Random Thoughts on the Overseas Direct Investment by Countries without Surplus Capital), *Jingji Yanjiu* (Economic Research), 5 (1991), 61–6.

Wei Lin and Xu Zhixin, 'Guanyu Women de Shidai' (On our Era), *Xiandai Guoji Guanxi* (Contemporary International Relations), 2 (1988), 8–12.

Wen Xin, 'Zhongguo Duiwai Jingji Maoyi Shinian' (China's Foreign Economic Relations and Trade in the Last Decade), *Guoji Maoyi* (Intertrade), 9 (1989), 4–10.

Wu Hongbo and Wang Jiayu, 'Fazhan Duiwai Zhijie Touzi de Zhanlue Zhongdian ji Duice' (Expand China's Direct Investment Overseas: Strategy and Policy), *Guoji Maoyi* (Intertrade), 9 (1990), 46–7.

Wu Yongxun, 'Ye Tan Bijiao Chengben Shuo' (My Thought on the Theory of Comparative Advantage), *Guoji Maoyi Wenti* (Issues in International Trade), 4 (1981), 25–6.

Xia Shen, 'Dangdai Guoji Ziben Liudong Xingeju yu Zhongguo de Duice' (The Pattern of Contemporary International Capital Flow and China's Response), *Waimao Jingji Guoji Maoyi* (Foreign Trade Economics, International Trade), 2 (1989), 56–61.

Xie Yixian, 'Bashi Niandai Zhongguo Duiwai Zhengce de Zhongda Tiaozheng ji qi Yiyi' (The Important Adjustments in China's Foreign Policy in the 1980s and Their Significance), *Qiushi* (Seeking Truth), 1 (1989), 35–40.

Xin Ping, 'Woguo Duli Zizhu de Heping Waijiao Zhengce Qude Fengshuo Chengguo' (China's Independent Foreign Policy of Peace Has Made Great Achievements), *Zhongguo Waijiao* (China's Foreign Affairs), 2 (1986), 4–5.

Xing Shugang, Li Yunhua and Liu Yingna, 'Sumei Liliang Duibi ji qi dui Bashi Niandai Guoji Jushi de Yingxiang' (The Changing Balance of Power Between the Soviet Union and the United States and Its Impact on the International Situation in the 1980s), *Guoji Wenti Yanjiu* (International Studies), 1 (1983), 25–31.

Xiong Huayuan, 'Zhou Enlai yu Yafei Huiyi' (Zhou Enlai and the Bandung Conference), *Dang de Wenxian* (Documentary Record of the CCP), 2 (1996), 86–91.

Xu Yi and Long Wuhua, 'Lun Zhongguo Gongchandang de "Yibiandao" de Waijiao Zhengce' (On CCP's Policy of 'Lean to One Side'), *Dangdai Zhongguoshi Yanjiu* (Studies of Contemporary History of China), 1 (1995), 32–6.

Xue Mouhong, 'Woguo Waijiao de Xinjumian' (New Situation and Prospect of China's Foreign Relations), *Hongqi* (Red Flag), 6 (1986), 19–24.

Xue Muqiao, 'Tantan Duiwai Maoyi Guanli Tizhi de Gaige' (A Few Words on the Reform of the Management of the Foreign Trade System), *Guoji Maoyi* (Intertrade), 3 (1986), 4–7.

Xue Yongjiu, 'Guanshui ji Maoyi Zongxieding yu Woguo Waimao Tizhi Gaige' (The GATT and China's Foreign Trade System Reform), *Guoji Maoyi Wenti* (Issues in International Trade), 1 (1988), 16–21.

Yang Shujin, 'Guoji Maoyi Quxiang, Tixi yu Zhongguo' (Trend and Structure of International Trade and China), *Shijie Jingji* (World Economy), 10 (1991), 1–10.

Yao Yunfang, 'Guoji Jinrong Xingshi he Zhongguo de Duiwai Jinrong Gongzuo' (The Current International Financial Situation and China's Foreign Finance), *Shijie Jingji* (World Economy), 8 (1982), 17–21.

Yi Baishui, 'Waimao Fazhan yu Waimao Tizhi Gaige' (The Expansion of Foreign Trade and the Foreign Trade System Reform in China), *Waimao Jingji Guoji Maoyi* (Foreign Trade Economics, International Trade), 2 (1988), 27–32.

Yuan Wenqi, Dai Lunzhang and Wang Linsheng, 'Guoji Fengong yu Woguo Duiwai Jingji Guanxi' (International Division of Labour and China's Economic Relations with Foreign Countries) *Zhongguo Shehui Kexue* (China Social Sciences), 1 (1980), 3–20.

Zhang Guang, 'Bashi Niandai Zhongguo Waijiao Zhengce de Zhongda Tiaozheng' (The Important Adjustments in China's Foreign Policy in the 1980s), *Waijiao Xueyuan Xuebao* (Journal of Foreign Affairs College), 1 (1992), 10–16.

Zhang Lizhi and Liao Xianchi, 'Shilun Guoji Jiazhi he Guoji Shengchan Jiage' (On the International Value of Labour and the Cost of International Production), *Zhongguo Shehui Kexue* (China Social Sciences), 4 (1987), 91–100.

Zhang Songtao, 'Guanyu Woguo Waimao Tizhi Gaige de Wenti' (On Questions Concerning the Reform of China's Foreign Trade System), *Guoji Maoyi Wenti* (Issues in International Trade), 5 (1989), 18–23.

Zhang Zuoqian, '1989 Nian Woguo Duiwai Jingmao de Fazhan' (The Development of China's Foreign Economic Relations and Trade in 1989), *Waimao Jingji Guoji Maoyi* (Foreign Trade Economics, International Trade), 3 (1990), 23–30.

Zhao Huisheng, 'Shi Lun Duiwai Maoyi yu Jingji Fazhan de Guanxi' (On the Relationship between Foreign Trade and Economic Development), *Shijie Jingji* (World Economy), 2 (1982), 64–72.

Zheng Tuobin, 'Gaige Kaifang Tuidongzhe Woguo Duiwai Jingji Maoyi de Fazhan' (Reform and Opening to the Outside World Gives Impetus to the Development of China's Foreign Trade), *Xinhua Yuebao* (New China Monthly), 12 (1987), 38–9.

Zheng Weizhi, 'Woguo Duli Zizhu de Heping Waijiao Zhengce' (China's Independent Foreign Policy of Peace), *Guoji Wenti Yanjiu* (International Studies), 4 (1984), 1–9.

Zhou Shude et al, 'Lun Woguo Chukou Xukezheng Zhidu de Gaige' (On the Reform of China's Export Licensing System), *Waimao Jingji Guoji Maoyi* (Foreign Trade Economics, International Trade), 3 (1989), 7–12.

Zhou Xiaochuan, 'Tan Waimao Tigai de Fangxiang, Jieduan, Yinan Wenti he Peitao Yaoqiu' (On the Direction, Stages, Problems of Foreign Trade System Reform and Other Coordinated Reforms), *Guoji Maoyi* (Intertrade), 2 (1988), 12–18.

——, 'Dui Waimao Tizhi Gaige de Renshi yu Tansuo' (Thoughts and Observations on Foreign Trade System Reform), *Waimao Jingji Guoji Maoyi* (Foreign Trade Economics, International Trade), 4 (1990), 39–43.

Zhou Xiaochuan and Yang Jianhua, 'Shixing Zengzhishui Shi Zhengge Jingji Tizhi Gaige zhong de Zhongyao Buzhou' (The Introduction of Value Added Tax Is an Important Step in Reforming the Economic System), *Guoji Maoyi* (Intertrade), 9 (1989), 7–12; and 10 (1989), 18–22.

Zhu Tongshu and He Jiabao, 'Ye Tan Lijiatu Bijiao Chengben Shuo' (On Ricardo's Theory of Comparative Advantage), *Shijie Jingji* (World Economy), 1 (1982), 8–15.

Zhu Zhongdi, 'Bijiao Chengbenshuo de Lilun Quexian' (A Critique of the Theory of Comparative Advantage), *Shijie Jingji* (World Economy), 11 (1981), 25–33.

Index

Abyssinia, 15
Academy of Military Science, 170
Acheson, Dean, 21, 52, 53
Adjitorop, Jusuf, 131
Afghanistan, 31, 53, 78, 150
African National Congress (ANC), 115
agricultural reform, 201, 230
Alaska, 224
Algeria, 30, 216
alienation
   between China and Soviet Union, 138
   definition of, 43–5
   in international society, 42–46
   of China, 46–58 *passim*, 59, 62, 102, 156–57
   of Third World, 42
Ambrose, Stephen, 22
Amin, Samir, 118
Amnesty International, 188
Angola, 30
anti-colonialism, 47, 113
'anti-Sovietism'
   in Chinese foreign policy, 144
Anzus agreement, 23
APEC Business Advisory Council (ABAC), 240
arms control, 151–177 *passim*, see also *arms transfer control*, and *arms sale*
   and China at UN, 155, 159–61
   and China before 1980, 154–58
   and China's socialisation, 151, 176
   and China's strategic studies community, 157, 158, 162
   China's accession to major treaties, 151, 158
   Chinese policies towards, 127, 151, 154–55, 158, 159–60
   conventional, 159, 160, 161
   in Asia Pacific, 175–6
   multilateralism in, 167, 168
   special responsibility of superpowers for, 161
   White Paper on, 170, 175

arms control and disarmament (ACD), see *arms control*
arms sale, 150, 166–168
   of China to Third World, 166
arms transfer control, 165, 167–73, see also *arms control*
   China's behaviour in, 167
   transparency in, 173
Armstrong, David, 42, 44, 61, 177
Aron, Raymond, 25, 42, 43, 45, 68
ASEAN Regional Forum (ARF), 251
Asia Pacific Economic Co-operation (APEC), 195, 196, 225, 238, 240, 241, 242, 246
   and China, 238–42
   and liberalisation, 240
   and open regionalism, 241
   Australia's approach to, 238–39
   Bogor Declaration, 241
   Osaka Action Agenda, 241
Asia Watch, 188
Asian Development Bank (ADB), 195, 214
   China's membership in, 195, 214
   loans to China, 214
Association of Southeast Asian Nations (ASEAN), 130, 239, see also *Southeast Asia*
   relations with China, 130, 135
   reservations on China in APEC, 239
Atlee, Clement, 52, 53
Australia, 23, 24, 69, 76, 199, 200, 224, 238, 239 approach to APEC, 238–39
   CITIC in, 224, see also *China International Trust and Investment Corporation (CITIC)*
Austria, 40
Autumn Uprising, 1927, 109

B share, 217
Bai Xiangguo, 89
Bailey, Kathleen, 171

Index 331

Baker, James, 239
balance of power, 13, 14, 60, 110, 179
  and ideology in international
    relations, 69
  and strategic triangle, 60, 67
  and World War I, 13, 14
balance of terror, 110, 111, 157, 158
  China's acceptance of, 111
Bamboo Curtain, 19
Bandung Conference, 30
  and China's Third World policies,
    37
  and nationalism, 37
  China at, 36–38
Bangladesh, 79
Bank of China (BOC), 211, 215, 229
  as Chinese government borrowing
    window, 215
  bond issues, 216, 217
  in Luxembourg, 211
Bank of Communications, 215
Barkte, Wolfgang, 40
Barnett, Doak, 89
Beijing Review, 93, 163, 186, 202, 216,
    218; see also *Peking Review*
Belgium
  loans to China, 212
Berlin Crisis, 1948, 17, 47
Berlinguer, Enrico, 133, 134
Bhutto, Z. A., 78
bipolarisation, 17, 33, 64
Bolivia, 14
Bosnia, 148, 150
Boumedienne, H., 77
Boutros-Ghali, Boutros, 149, 169
Boxer indemnities, 89
Brandt, Willy, 63, 136
Brazil, 199, 200
  trade with China, 117
Bretton Woods system
  collapse of, 69
Brezhnev, L. I.
  and Sino-Soviet reconciliation, 100
Brezhnev Doctrine, 65
Britain, 14, 15, 16, 21, 23, 31, 32, 34,
    35
  and recognition of PRC, 21
  and treaty system, 15
Bucharest Conference, 26, 56

Bull, Hedley, 3, 30, 42, 44, 60, 244
Burma, 53, 79, 128
Burmese Communist Party (BCP), 130
Burundi, 74
Bush, George
  and American arms sale to Taiwan,
    173

Cairo, 19
Cairo Conference, 1943, 15
Cambodia, 30, 53, 130, 150
Canada, 24, 146
capital inflow, 208, 209, 211; see also
    capital outflow and *global capital
    market*
  and China's commercial borrowing,
    214–18
  and China's international equity
    placements, 217–18
  and economic interdependence, 221
  and foreign investment, 218–221;
    see also *investment, foreign*
  and inter-governmental loans,
    212–13
  and international bond issues,
    215–17
  and sale of Chinese stocks, 218
  and World Bank loans, 212–14
  into China: four paths of, 211; two
    major sources of, 213
  to OPEC countries, 211
capital outflow, 210, 221–25; see also
    capital inflow and *global capital
    market*
  and China's multinationals, 223–4
  and China's service of debt, 222
  and China's purchase of US
    Treasury bonds, 224–5
  Chinese statistics of, 222–23
  from China, 209, 221–22;
    unaccounted for, 222;
    unrecorded, 225
Carter, Jimmy, 186
Central Military Commission, 157, 170
  and arms sale, 170
Ceylon, 30
Chemical Weapons Convention
  China and, 160
Chen Chu, 81, 142

Chen Yi, 34, 53, 57, 66, 140, 141
  denunciation of UN, 140
Chengdu, 218
Chiang Kai-shek, 15, 25, 50
China
  abstention from UN Resolution 678, 147
  admission into UN, 73–76
  aid to Third Word countries, 40, 116–17, 210
  alienation from international society, 46–58 *passim*, 102, 156–57, 244; and historical experience with the West, 102; and arms control policies, 156; and foreign policy behaviour, 245
  and arms build-up in Asia Pacific, 176
  and European system of states, 9–14, 244
  and international borrowing, 89, 97, 208–21 *passim*
  and MTCR, 154, 162, 171, 176; see also *Missile Technology Control Regime (MTCR)*
  and multilateral diplomacy, 46, 48, 53, 58, 76, 79–83
  and NGO, 80
  and revolution in international relations, 115
  and Southeast Asia, 114, 127–30, 135
  and universality of international society, 71
  and world economy, 83–91, 94, 118, 123, 243, 246
  armed conflict with Soviet Union, 64, 65, 66, 109
  arms acquisitions of, 175–76
  as a revolutionary power, 5, 56–57, 92
  as spokesman of Third World, 82
  at UN, 79–83, 95
  cessation of atmospheric tests, 154
  economic aid programme, 40, 78
  economic integration of, 194–244 *passim*
  exclusion from international organisations, 20, 71
  expansionism of, 38, 54
  export of nuclear technology, 167
  first resident diplomatic mission in London, 10
  foreign investment in, see *investment, foreign*
  foreign policy objectives of, 105; see also *Chinese foreign policy*
  in 'angry isolation', 26
  in post-Cold War international society, 2, 6, 244–51
  international legitimacy of, 71, 102 denial of, 76
  isolation of, 18–20, 26
  membership in IMF and World Bank, 90–91, 195–96
  military spending of, 173–76
  missile sales of, 166–67
  multiple identities of, 250
  opening of, 4, 98
  opposition to peacekeeping, 141–42
  participation in international organisations, 80, 225–43, *passim*
  political liberalisation in, 101–2
  radicalisation of domestic politics, 38
  Republican Revolution in 1911, 13
  socialisation of, 6, 72, 94, 101, 126–27, 192–93, 245; and changing perceptions, 102–6
  subjection in world politics, 10
  trade embargo against, 22, 29, 39, 49, 53
'China Breakthrough', 62, 66–73 *passim*, 95; see also *United States: policies towards China*
  and balance of power, 67, 68
  and changing philosophy of American foreign policy, 68
  and China's socialisation, 72–3
China's strategic interests in, 66
'China card', 67, 99
China factor, 59
  and global balance of power, 66
  in Soviet-American relations, 67
China International Trust and Investment Corporation (CITIC), 211, 215, 216, 224

Index

as official window for commercial borrowing, 215
in Australia, 224
international bond issuing, 215–16
China Investment Bank, 215
China National Chemicals Import and Export Corporation (CCIEC): see *Sinochem*
China Non-ferrous Metal Industrial Company, 224
ChinCom, 23, 24
Chinese Academy of Social Sciences, APEC Policy Research Centre at, 241
Chinese Communist Party (CCP), 1, 26, 27, 33, 34, 50, 104
and East European Communist Parties, 137
and export of revolution, 133
and ideology in international relations, 127–38, *passim*
and inter-Party relations, 116, 127, 131–4, 138
at Bucharest Conference, 56
Central Propaganda Department, 188
International Liaison Department, 134, 135, 137
relations with CPSU, 26, 56, 137–38; see also *Communist Party of Soviet Union (CPSU)*
relations with non-Communist Parties, 135–36, 137
relations with revolutionary movements, 54, 127, 128, 135
secret agreements with other Parties, 129
struggles within, 125
Third Plenum of the Eleventh Central Committee, 88, 96, 119
and reforms and opening, 197
Twelfth National Congress, 132, 133, 137
Chinese foreign policy, 31–41, 75–83, 126–27
and Asia-Afro world, 30
and national liberation movements, 30, 113, 114, 127
basic objectives of, 99, 100
de-radicalisation of, 107

human rights in, 177–78, 180–83, 189–92
ideology in, 103, 114, 132, 134–38
in 1949, 33–36
independent, 99, 100, 107, 124, 144, 248
isolationism in, 31–41
towards arms control, 150–76
towards peacekeeping, 138–50
towards Third World, 116–7
Chinese People's Political Consultative Conference (CPPCC), 18, 34
Chinese world order, 7–9
and European expansion, 2, 3
collapse of, 9–10
Churchill, Winston, 15, 16
Clinton, Bill
first meeting with Jiang Zemin, 240
Coca Cola, 220, 221
CoCom (Paris Co-ordinating committee for Exports of Strategic Materials), 23, 24
Japan in, 23, 24
colonialism, 185
Committee on Disarmament
China at, 158
Communist Party of the Soviet Union (CPSU), 56, 134, 137; see also *Soviet Union*
and Sino-Soviet dispute, 55–56
relations with CCP, 26–7, 137; see also *Chinese Communist Party (CCP)*
Twentieth Congress of, 26
Communist Party of Thailand (CPT)
CCP's support for, 129
comparative advantage
and David Ricardo, 120
debates in China on, 120–21
Comprehensive Test Ban Treaty (CTBT), 152, 176
China's approach to, 162–65
Conference of Disarmament (CD), 164
Confucianism, 8, 184
Confucius, 96
Congo
peacekeeping in, 141
containment, 20, 21, 25
in Asia, 20, 52, 53

co-operative security, 179
Cuba, 30
cultural relativism
 and human rights, 182, 183, 184
Cultural Revolution, 18, 27, 33, 56, 57,
  62, 66, 73, 96, 123
 and China's 'revolutionary
  isolation', 18
 and interruption of trade with
  Europe, 87
 China's emergence from, 62
 foreign policy initiatives after, 66
 radicalism in, 27
Czechoslovakia, 35
 Soviet invasion of, 63, 65

Dalian, 215
de Cuellar, Javier Perez, 146
De Gaulle, 63
de-alienation, 45, 46, 59, 60, 93
 and changes in international system, 45–46
 of China, 58, 59, 92, 125, 158
decentralisation, 197, 232
 in foreign trade reform, 230–31
de-colonisation, 20, 47, 113–15, 128
 and 'anti-colonial revolution', 113
 and PRC's diplomacy, 30
 and structural changes of
  international system, 47–48
defence industry
 and military-industrial conversions, 174
Democracy Wall, 186
 and human rights discussions in
  China, 186, 187
democratic peace
 theory of, 249
democratisation, 248, 250
 in international relations, 110–11
Deng Xiaoping, 1, 26, 34, 72, 89, 97,
  98, 99, 105, 106, 124, 125, 129,
  138, 197, 198, 227
 and arms sale, 170
 at UN General Assembly, 1974, 79
 on CCP's inter-Party relations, 133
 on China's diplomatic relations with US, 77
 on dangers of war, 109
 on economic opening, 197
 on Euro-Communism, 133
 on independent foreign policy, 99
 on international economic order, 104, 118
 on peace and development, 105
 rise and fall of, 96, 129
 tour of Southeast Asian nations, 129
 visits to France and Japan, 79
dependencia theory, 118
Der Derian, James, 42
détente, 69, 100, 105, 111, 112
Dian Bien Phu, 156
diplomacy; 113, see also *dual track diplomacy*
 economic, 100
 globalisation of Chinese, 76–79
 multilateral, 25, 46, 76; and Third
  World, 76; China and, 79–83;
  China's exclusion from, 48, 53,
  58, 76
 transformation of, 165
disarmament; see *arms control*
Dittmer, Lowell, 26, 185, 191
domino theory, 52, 65
Donnelly, Jack, 184
dragon bonds market
 China's on, 217
dual track diplomacy, 128–31 *passim*;
  see also *diplomacy*
 China's pursuit of, 129
 demise of, 130–31
Dulles, John Foster, 21, 54
Dumbarton Oaks Conference
 China at, 15
Dunkel, Arthur, 236

EC (EEC), 69, 204, 213, 215, 216, 238
 economic co-operation with China, 84
economic integration, 94–95, 125, 194–96
 and capital flows, 196, 208–9, 221–24
 and China in international economic
  institutions, 225–43 *passim*
 and trade, 197–207
 as a contested idea, 195
Ecuador, 231

Egypt, 30, 37, 146
  relations with China, 30
Eisenhower, Dwight, 21, 55
  and nuclear threat against China, 54, 156
  meeting with Khrushchev, 55
Emperor Qian Long, 8
Engles, 123
English school in International Relations, vii, 3, 4
Ethiopia, 78
Eurobond market
  China on, 216, 217
Euro-Communism, 133, 134
Europe, 9, 40, 111, 133
  division of, 17
  Eastern: and recognition of China, 21; collapse of Communism in, 138; in Sino-Soviet dispute, 27; indebted industrialisation in, 211; trade with China, 205
  Western: arms sales to Iran and Iraq, 167; trade with China, 29, 39–40, 87
European expansion, 9, 11, 12
  and China, 10, 14
  and global international society, 12
exchange rate, 228, 232, 235
  unification of, 236
Export-Import Bank of Japan, 218

Fairbank, John King, 62, 244
Family of Nations, 2, 3, 5, 11, 13, 15, 18, 53, 93, 252
  China in, 16, 93
Fan Guoxiang, 168
Feeney, William, 83
Finland, 74
five principles of peaceful co-existence, 37
Ford, Gerald, 77
Foreign Trade Law, 1994, 236
France, 14, 24, 30, 31, 74
  accession to NPT, 163
  and major arms control treaties, 153
  recognition of PRC, 23, 30
  Socialist Party of, 136
Frank, Andre Gunder, 118
Fujian, 215, 216, 230
Fukuyama, Francis, 179

G7, 213
  sanction against China, 213
'Gang of Four', 96, 97, 129
Geldenhuys, Deon, 19, 42
General Agreement on Tariffs and Trade (GATT), 195, 196, 225, 226, 229, 232, 233, 238, 240
  China as an observer in, 195
  China's membership in, 1, 3, 229–38 *passim*; and Taiwan, 237; and trade liberalisation, 230–36; application for, 1986, 195, 232; politicisation of, 236–37
  Uruguay Round, 236
  Working Party on China, 235
Geneva 18-Nation Disarmament Conference
  China's refusal to participate in, 155
Geneva Conferences, 31, 53
  PRC's participation in, 36–7
Germany, 23, 164
  alienation of, 45–46
  East, 146
  West, 23, 24, 40; China's bond issues in 215–16; Social Democratic Party of, 136
Gilpin, Robert, 23
Gittings, John, 59
global capital market; see also *capital inflow*, and *capital outflow*
  and China before 1970, 210
  and China's integration in world economy, 196, 208
  China's engagement with, 89–90, 210–25
global governance, 179
globalisation
  of China's market, 221
  of Chinese diplomacy, 76–79, 91, 127, 245
Goldstein, M., 216
Gorbachev, Mikhail, 112, 138
'Great Leap Outward', 57, 73, 87–88
Greater China, 239
Grotious, Hugo, 43
Gu Mu, 210
Guangdong, 215, 230
Guinea, 30
Gulf War, 1991, 139, 147, 166, 172

Guoji Jingrong Xinxi Bao
(International Financial News),
224
Guoji Shangbao (International
Business Journal), 235
Gurtov, Melvin, 114, 115

Haiti, 148
Halliday, Fred, 127, 178, 249
Harding, Harry, 53, 200
Hawke, Bob
and launch of APEC, 239
on APEC without China, 239
Hegel, 43
Henkin, Louis, 183, 184
Hinton, Harold, 38
Hitler, 46
Ho Chih-min, 31
Hong Kong, 52, 195, 216, 217, 223
and APEC, 239
and foreign investment in China,
211, 221
China's investment in, 223
re-exports from, 205
Shougang in, 224
tourists from, 207
Hong Kong Business, 222
Hongqi, 117; see also *Red Flag*
Hosoya, Chihiro, 42
Howe, Geoffrey, 7
Hu Shih, 185
Hu Yaobang, 99, 102, 106, 125, 129,
133, 136
on CCP's inter-Party relations, 132
on independent foreign policy, 99,
116
Hua Guofeng, 79, 96, 97, 131
Huan Xiang, 120, 123
Huang Hua, 19, 81, 119, 123, 142, 143,
159
Hubei, 214
human rights, 127, 177–193, *passim*,
246, 247
abuses in China, 189
and American policy towards China,
186
and China's political socialisation,
177–178, 192–193
and cultural relativism, 182, 184
and (non-)intervention, 179, 180,
183, 249
and sovereignty, 180, 183, 249
as bourgeois ideology, 186
as norms in international society,
177, 179, 192, 249
China's White Paper on, 180–83,
249
China's participation in international
regimes, 178, 189, 190–91
China's position on, in 1979,
186–87
governed by European standards,
187
idea of: accepted in China, 192; and
Marxism in China, 185–86; in
China's political culture post-
1949, 185–86; popularised in
China, 188
in Chinese foreign policy, 177–78,
189–93
in Chinese tradition, 184–85
principle of universality, 145, 182,
183, 184; China's acceptance
of, 192; China's denial of, 187
studies in China, 180, 188
human rights exception
China as, 180, 193
Human Rights Movement
in China in 1920s, 185
Hunt, Michael, 33
Huntington, Samuel, 3, 248

Iceland, 74
ideology, 27, 55, 127–38 *passim*, 214
and Chinese foreign policy, 132
and relations between Communist
Parties, 136
in international relations, 102, 245;
and human rights, 183
in inter-Party relations, 127–28,
134–38
International Atomic Energy Agency
(IAEA), 154
International Bank of Reconstruction
and Development (IBRD); see
World Bank
International Labour Organisation
(ILO), 36

Index

International Monetary Fund (IMF), 1, 19, 36, 195, 204, 205, 215, 226, 228, 238, 246
  and devaluation of RMB, 228
  and revaluation of Chinese economy, 1, 194
  and Taiwan, 90, 227
  China's membership in, 1, 19, 90–91, 94, 228
  China's participation in, 226–29
  offer of loans, 211–12
India, 21, 37, 216, 217, 220
  and recognition of PRC, 21
  Congress Party of, 137
Indonesia, 216, 217
  withdrawal from UN, 140
inter-dependence, economic, 111, 124, 118–125, 203
Intermediate-range Nuclear Forces (INF) Treaty, 161
international bond markets; see also *global capital markets*
  China on, 215–17
  developing nations on, 216
International Civil Aviation Organisation (ICAO), 82
international Communist movement, 26–7, 134, 135, 136
International Covenant on Civil and Political Rights, 191
International Covenant on Economic, Social and Cultural Rights, 191
International Development Agency (IDA), 212, 213, 229
international division of labour, 196, 204, 232
  and foreign investment, 221
  China's participation in, 196, 198, 199, 208
  theoretical debate on, 121–22, 198, 199
international economic organisations, 3, 196, 212, 214 226, 227, 228; see also *GATT, IMF, World Bank* and *WTO*
International Finance Corporation (IFC), 229
International Fund for Agricultural Development (IFAD), 214

International Institute of Strategic Studies (IISS), 151
international law
  China's first application of, 10
International Olympic Committee, 19
  China's exclusion from, 19
international society; see also *international system*
  alienation in, 44–46
  China's alienation from, 41–42, 48–58, 61
  China's anomalous position in, 18–19, 60, 244
  China's entry into, 11–15
  definition of, 4, 44
  homogeneity of, 2, 127, 249
  of economies, 250
  post-Cold War, 2, 6, 178–80, 244–51
  state's alienation in, 42–6
  theoretical insight of, 248
  theory of, 3, 5
international system, 3, 17, 20, 23, 27, 28, 31, 32, 38, 126; see also *international society*
  American hegemony in, 23
  and China's alienation, 47–48
  and European expansion, 9
  and Revolutionary China, 141
  changing nature/structure of, 68–71
  China's perception of, 102–7
  Euro-centric view of, 29
  of East Asia, 9
  post-war, 17
  prohibitive nature of, 46
  structural changes of, 46–47; and Third World, 110
  transformation of, 13
  two camps in, 27
investment, foreign, 19, 88, 93, 211
  and capital flow into China, 218
  and US, 211
  in China, 194, 211, 218–21
investment, outward
  from China, 222–25
Iran, 78, 150, 167
  China's arms sale to, 166, 167
Iran-Iraqi War, 166

Iraq, 30, 55, 147, 150
  China's arms sale to, 167
isolationism, 19, 20, 31–41 *passim*
  economic, 39, 41
  in PRC's foreign policy, 31–4, 41
Israel
  arms transfer to China, 175
Italian Communist Party, 133, 134
Italy, 78, 79

Jacobson, Harold, 227
Japan, 11, 15, 16, 63, 64, 65, 66, 69, 76, 78, 146, 164, 194, 212, 215, 216, 217, 218, 221, 224, 225, 239
  alienation of, 45–46
  and Cocom, 23, 24
  and Greater East Asian Co-prosperity Sphere, 46
  as PRC's leading trade partner, 29
  invasion of Manchuria, 15
  investment in China, 221
  loans to China, 86, 90, 212
  normalising relations with China, 77
  peace treaty with Taiwan, 24
  policies towards PRC, 24–25
  rise of, 63, 64, 112
  trade agreement with China, 84
  trade with PRC, 24, 85–86
Jiang Zemin, 240, 241
  first meeting with Clinton, 240
Johnston, A. I., 157, 163, 164
joint venture law, 198, 210, 230
Jordan, 55

Kaifang, 197, 198, 199, 230
  as a fuzzy concept, 197
  clearer orientation of, 198
Kang Sheng, 134
Kaunda, Kenneth, 77
Kennan, George, 20
Kennedy, John F., 25
Kent, Ann, 182, 185
Khrushchev, N., 26, 55–6
  and détente with the US, 55
  and Sino-Soviet relations, 26, 55–6
  meeting with Mao Zedong, 55–6
  secret speech of, 1956, 26
  visit to the US, 56

Kim, Samuel, 80, 138, 147, 149, 185, 191
King George III, 8
King Juan Carlos, 77
Kissinger, Henry, 20, 62, 64, 66, 75
  on changing American foreign policy, 68
  secret visit to China, 62, 65
  talk with Zhou Enlai, 65
Korea
  North, 31, 52, 53, 142
  South, 216, 239; diplomatic relations with China, 240
Korean Armistice Agreement, 57
Korean War, 20, 21, 22, 25, 31, 141–42, 148, 156
  and American policies towards China, 22, 52–3, 71
  and China's alienation, 52–3
  and Cold War in East Asia, 21
  impact on Sino-American relations, 53
Kuomintang (KMT), 21, 22, 33, 34, 35, 36, 48, 50, 51
Kuwait, 147, 166
  Iraqi invasion of, 172
  loans to China, 212

LaFeber, Walter, 21
Lampton, David, 244
Lardy, Nicholas, 203, 205, 218, 221, 234, 237
Latin America, 30, 211
  indebted industrialisation in, 211
Law of the Sea, 93
League of Nations, 13, 14, 15
  China's membership in, 13, 14
  Covenant of, 13
lean-to-one-side, 34, 35, 49, 51, 64
Lebanon, 55
Lenin, 13
Lewis, John, 170
Li Daoyu, 148
Li Lanqing, 235
Li Luye, 146
Li Peng, 124, 162, 178, 183
Li Qiang, 88, 89, 90
Li Xiannian, 79
Liang Qichao, 185

Liang Yufan, 144
Liberal-Democratic Party (LDP), 24
Lie, Trygve, 36
Lin Biao, 66
  fall of, 96
  removal of, 87
Lin Qing, 139
Liu Bochen, 34
Liu Shaoqi
  secret visit to Moscow, 34
Lord Macartney, 8
'loss of China', 48, 49
Luo Longji, 185
Luxembourg, 211

MacArchur, General Douglas, 52, 53
MaCarthyism, 22
Macau, 207, 211, 221
MacFarquhar, Roderick, 101
Malaya, 52
Malaysia, 78, 79, 128, 130
  relations with China, 130
Malik, Adam, 81
Malta, 78
Manchuria, 15, 16
Manila Pact, 23
Mansfield, Mike, 65
Mao Zedong, 17, 18, 33, 34, 35, 39, 47, 50, 54, 55, 62, 65, 66, 67, 71, 72, 75, 78, 84, 88, 95, 96, 97, 98, 108, 114, 129, 157
  and 'China Breakthrough', 65–67, 71–72
  and Chinese foreign policy in 1949, 33–36
  and lean-to-one-side policy, 21, 34, 49
  death of, 129
  and removal of leftist influence, 115
  legacies of, 109
  meeting with Khrushchev, 55–56
  meeting with Stalin, 21
  on American policies in Chinese civil war, 50, 51
  on 'intermediate zone', 29, 47
  on war and peace, 108–9
  visit to Moscow, 21
  world view of, 95, 96–97
Marx, Karl, 43, 116, 119, 120, 121, 123

Marxism, 121, 185
  and human rights idea in China, 185
Marxism-Leninism, 114
Masayoshi, Ohira, 77, 86, 212
Mayall, James, 37, 249
McNamara, Robert, 227
Middle East, 63, 65, 117, 142, 143, 172, 173
  arms transfer to, 172
  peacekeeping in, 143, 146
Miller, J. D. B., 77
Ming Dynasty, 8
Ministry of Agriculture, 215
Ministry of Commerce, 229
Ministry of Finance, 215, 229
Ministry of Foreign Affairs
  and arms sale, 170
Ministry of Foreign Economic Relations and Trade (MOFERT) [now Ministry of Foreign Trade and Economic Relations (MOFTEC)], 170, 215, 229, 232, 235
  as government borrowing window, 215
Mintoff, Dom, 78
Missile Technology Transfer Control Regime (MTCR), 152, 154, 162, 168, 170–72
  and China's arms transfer, 176
  and China's defence of missile sales, 171–72
  China's criticism of, 154
  China's pledge to abide by, 162, 171
Mitterrand, François, 136
Mongolia, 31
Moore Stephen
  in China, 218
Morgan Stanley
  opening office in China, 218
Morocco, 30
Moscow Conference, 56
Mozambique, 30, 79
Multifibre Agreement (MFA), 195
  and China, 232
multilateralism, 151, 155, 158, 167, 168, 196, 225, 242, 246, 250
  and China in arms control, 155–58
  and China's membership in GATT/WTO, 238

multilateralism – *continued*
  in international security and China, 175–76
  in arms control, 246
multinational corporations, 209, 211, 220, 221, 224
  and foreign investment, 211, 220
  and investment in China, 221
  from China, 223, 224
  in *Fortune Global 500*, 223

Namibia, 146, 150
Nanjing, 9, 15, 34
Nankai University
  APEC Studies Centre at, 240
Nathan, Andrew, 177, 249
National Defence University, 170
national liberation movements, 30, 113, 115, 127, 128; see also *de-colonisation*
  and CCP, 127
  China's support of, 38, 113, 114
National People's Congress, 114, 201, 211
national self-determination, 13
nationalism, 47
  assertive, 144
  collective, 37, 69
North Atlantic Treaty Organisation (NATO), 17, 23, 47, 49, 71, 74, 76, 111
Naughton, Barry, 234
Ne Win, 129
neo-colonialism, 142
Nepal, 79
Netherlands, the, 223
New International Economic Order (NIEO), 70, 93, 103, 115, 119
New York Times, 74
New Zealand, 23, 24, 223
Nie Rongzhen, 66
Nietzsche, Friedrich, 41
Nigeria, 146
Nikko Securities
  in China, 218
Nish, Ian, 42
Nitze, Paul
  and NSC68, 52
Nixon, Richard, 20, 24, 26, 54, 58, 62, 63, 65, 66, 77
  and the Vietnam War, 63
  meeting with Mao, 71
  on his visit to China, 65
  visit to Beijing, 62
non-government organisations (NGOs), 188
  China's participation in, 80
  critiques of China's human rights policy, 188
Non-Proliferation Treaty (NPT), 152, 153, 154, 162–65, 176
  China's accession to, 152, 165
  China's approach to, 162–5; and strategic studies community in China, 163
  China's denunciation of, 57, 154
Norway, 74
NSC 41, 21, 22
NSC 68, 21, 52
nuclear-free zone, 154, 159

October Revolution, Russian, 51
Organisation for Economic Co-operation and Development (OECD), 1, 206
  China's trade with, 206
Oksenberg, Michel, 227
Organisation of Petroleum Exporting Countries (OPEC), 68, 211
Opium War(s), 9, 48
Ordinance Ministry, 174
Ostpolitik, 63
Ottoman Empire, 11

Pacific Economic Co-operation Council (PECC), 194, 241
Pakistan, 78, 79, 171, 218, 220
  China's missile sale to, 167, 172
  People's Party of, 137
Palestinian Liberation Organisation (PLO), 115
Paris Peace Conference, 14
  China at, 14
Partial Test Ban Treaty (PTBT), 152, 153, 154
  China's approach to, 162–65
  China's denunciation of, 57, 154
Pax Americana, 62, 68
  end of, 63, 66
Pax Sinica, 54

Index

peace movement, 100, 111
   China resuming contacts with, 111
peacekeeping, 127, 246
   and Gulf War, 1990–91, 147
   China's changing policy towards, 138–50 *passim*; and Korean War, 141–42
   China's participation in, 146
   Chinese casualties in, 146–47
Peking Review, 140; see also *Beijing Review*
People's Bank of China, 215, 229
People's Daily, 26, 77; see also *Renmin Ribao*
People's Liberation Army (PLA), 33, 51, 174, 175
   and arms sale, 170
   and defence spending, 174, 175
PERM-5 talks, 168, 173
   and arms transfer control, 168, 172; consensus on, 172
Persia, 11, 13, 15
Pham Van Dong, 31
Philippines, the, 23, 79, 128
PKI [the Indonesian Communist Party], 131
   relations with CCP, 131
Poland, 33, 35
Pollack, Jonathan, 20, 70
Poly Technologies (Baoli Gongsi), 170
Pompidou, George 77
Portugal, 76
People's Republic of China; see *China*
Prussian-Danish War, 10
Pudong, Shanghai
   foreign banks in, 218

Qian Qichen, 148, 160, 164, 239
Qiao Guanhua, 75, 81, 97
Qing Dynasty, 8

Razak, Tun Abdul, 78
Reagan, Ronald, 100, 112, 143
   and Sino-American relations, 100
realpolitik, 176
Red Flag, 26; see also *Hongqi*
Register of Conventional Arms, 166
Renmin Ribao, 97, 108, 140, 160, 161, 221; see also *People's Daily*

Renminbi (RMB), 201, 217
   convertibility of, 236, 241
   devaluation of, 228, 234, 235
   overvaluation of, 230
Reykjavik
   Soviet-American summit at, 161
Ricardo, David
   and theory of comparative advantage, 120
Romania, 69, 78
Roosevelt, Franklin, 15, 16
Rosenau, James, vii
Rousseau, Jean, 43
Ruggie, John, 151, 167, 180
Rusk, Dean, 49
Russia; see also *Soviet Union*
   as a treaty power in China, 10
   China's arms procurement from, 175
   end of treaty rights and privileges in China, 14
   trade with China, 205
Rwanda, 148

Samurai bonds
   Chinese issues of, 217
Saudi Arabia, 167
   China's missile sale to, 167, 171
Scalapino, Robert, 52, 115
Schmidt, Helmut, 77
seeking truth from facts, 125
self-reliance, 19, 32, 39, 40, 87, 93
   as China's development strategy, 118
Senghor, Leopold, 78
Shambaugh, David, 248
Shandong, 14
Shanghai, 215, 218
   Coca Cola in, 220
   foreign banks in, 218
   Foreign Exchange Swap Centre in, 234
   stock exchanges in, 217
Shantou, 198, 230
Shaw, Martin, 45
Shenyang, 51
Shenzhen, 198, 230
   foreign exchange swap centre in, 234
   stock exchanges in, 217
Shichor, Y., 147

Index

Shirk, Susan, 232, 237, 242, 250
Shougang, 224
   transnational operations of, 224
Siam, 15
Singapore, 79, 223
Sino-American ambassadorial talks, 31, 37
Sino-American relations, 86
   confrontations in, 18, 31
   difficulties in, 100, 143
   normalisation of, 86; and China's membership in IMF and World Bank, 95, 226; and China's membership in GATT/WTO, 238
   rapprochement in, 38, 61, 62, 66, 67, 71, 245
   uncertainties in, 95–96
Sino-British trade
   1949–1959, 39–40
Sino-centrism, 8
Sinochem, 223–24
   as a multinational, 224
   dealings in oil futures, 223
Sino-Indian border war, 54
   Soviet policy towards, 56
Sino-Japanese Treaty of Peace and Friendship, 89
Sino-Soviet Alliance, 21, 26, 31, 36, 49, 95
   collapse of, 56
Sino-Soviet polemics, 18, 26, 27, 55–56, 64, 134, 248
Sino-Soviet split, 64, 248
socialisation, 126–193 *passim*
   in post-Cold War international society, 178–80
   of China, 60–64, 73, 94, 101, 102; and human rights issues, 180, 192–93; and foreign policy adjustments, 126, 248–49; as a revolutionary state, 193
   of revolutionary state, 61
Solomon Brothers
   in China, 218
Somalia, 148
South Africa, 30
Southeast Asia, 54, 127–30; see also *Association of South East Asian Nations* (ASEAN)
   and China, 128
   and containment, 23–24
   and dual track diplomacy, 127–30
   Communist insurgencies in, 130
   Communist Parties of, 129
South East Asian Treaty Organisation (SEATO), 23
'Soviet Social Imperialism', 67
Soviet Union, 15, 16, 60, 64, 66, 67, 130; see also *CPSU, Sino-Soviet alliance, Sino-Soviet polemics, Sino-Soviet split*
   alienation of, 45–46
   and arms control, 159, 161, 169
   and China's alienation, 55–56
   and recognition of PRC, 21
   arms sale to Third World, 166, 167
   border clashes with China, 64, 65, 66, 109
   collapse of, 1, 46, 67
   collapse of Communism in, 138
   economic aid to China, 19, 118
   invasion of Czechoslovakia, 63, 65
   nuclear threat against China, 65, 156
   offer of credit to China, 210
   strategic balance with US, 63
   trade with China, 27, 28, 29
Spain, 76, 77
Special Committee on Peacekeeping Operations, 141, 146
special drawing rights (SDRs), 212, 227
Special Economic Zones (SEZs), 198
   and foreign trade system reforms, 230
Sri Lanka
   Unified Nationalist Party of, 137
Stalin, 21, 46, 112, 120
   meeting with Mao Zedong, 21
   on war and revolution, 112
standard of 'civilisation', 12
   and non-European states, 12
State Administration for the Management of State-owned Assets, 221
State Administrative Committee on Military Products Trade (SACMPT), 170
State Commission for Foreign Investment Control, 210, 211

State Commission for Imports and Exports Control, 211
State Commission of Science, Technology and Industry for Nations Defence (COSTIND), 170
State Council, 194, 206, 210, 223, 230, 231
  and arms sale, 170
  and laws and regulations on foreign investment, 219
State Education Commission, 229
Strategic Arms Limitation Talks (SALT), 64
Strategic Arms Reduction Talks (START), 176
strategic triangle, 60, 67, 92, 93–94
  and global balance of power, 60
  demise of, 67
Sudan, 30
Summers, Larry, 194
Sun Yat-sen, 13, 185
  and the Republican Revolution, 13
Sweden, 74
Syria, 30
  China's missile sale to, 167

Taiwan, 21, 22, 23, 25, 33, 52, 71, 90, 207, 227, 239
  and APEC, 239
  and GATT, 237
  foreign investment from, 211, 222
  Matador missiles in, 23
  US arms sales to, 173
Taiwan Strait Crises, 31, 53, 55
  and Khrushchev, 55
  and nuclear threat against China, 54, 156
Talbott, Strobe, 2
Tanaka, Kakuei, 77
Tanzam Railway, 210
Tanzania, 74, 79
Thailand, 79, 128, 216, 218, 231
Third World, 30, 68, 76, 82, 97, 103, 105, 110, 117
  and decolonisation and revolutions, 114
  and collective nationalism, 69
  and democratisation of international relations, 110–11
  and South-South co-operation, 116
  China's changing policy towards, 116, 117
  China's endorsement of revolutions in, 113
  revolutions in, 115
  rise of, 69
  and multilateral diplomacy, 76
three worlds theory, 97, 103, 108
  China abandoning, 104
Tiananmen, 147, 163, 177, 187, 188, 192, 203, 213, 234, 236, 239
Tianjin, 52, 215
Tibet, 53, 54
Time, 73
Tong Zhiguang, 235
Trade, foreign, 19, 84–89, 93, 196, 197–208
  and economic reforms in China, 197
  and GDP, 200, 202, 203
  and inter-dependence between China and world economy, 203, 208
  before 1979, 39–41
  growth and trade reform, 199–203
  patterns of, 203–6
  service trade, 206–7
  deficit of, 207
  fluctuations of, 201
  government intervention in, 201
  imports and exports, 205
  liberalisation of, 201
  rapid expansion of, 199
  re-orientations of, 28, 29
  with non-Communist countries, 40
  with Western Europe, 87
  trade system reform, 200, 225–38 *passim*; see also *trade, foreign*
  and China's GATT/WTO membership, 229–38
  and macroeconomic policies, 231, 233
  and tariff, 231
  contract responsibility system in, 234
  trade plans in, 234
Treaty of Nanjing, 9
Treaty of Peking, 10
Treaty of Rarotonga, 152
Treaty of Tianjin, 9, 10

Treaty of Tlatelolco, 152
Treaty of Wangxia, 10
Treaty of Whompoa, 10
treaty system, 9–10, 11, 12, 15
    end of, 12, 15
tribute system, 7, 8, 9–10
Truman Doctrine, 20, 21, 49, 50
Truman, Harry, 20, 21, 48, 49, 50, 52
Tuchman, Barbara, 62
Turkey, 231

U Thant, 72, 75
Ukraine, 175
United Nations Conference on Trade and Development (UNCTAD), 119
United Nations Disarmament Commission, 158
United Nations Disengagement Observer Group (UNDOF)
    China's participation in, 146
United Nations Educational Scientific and Cultural Organisation (UNESCO), 36
United Nations Food and Agriculture Organisation (FAO), 36, 82, 214
United Nations Fund for Population Activities (UNFPA), 214
United Nations Human Rights Commission (UNHRC), 190
United Nations International Children's Emergence Fund (UNICEF), 214
United Nations (UN), 15, 245
    admission of PRC, 1971, 72, 73–76, 155
    and arms transfer control, 166
    and Korean War, 142
    China at, 73–76
    China's revaluation of, 145
    exclusion of PRC from, 4, 17, 18, 25, 31, 53, 59, 246
    peacekeeping operations of, 138–149 *passim*
    universality of, 72, 76
United Nations Development Programme (UNDP), 214, 226
    China's approach to, 90, 226
United Nations Fund for Population (UNFP), 90

United Nations Industrial Development Organisation (UNIDO), 90
United Nations International Children's Emergency Fund (UNICEF), 90
United Nations Observation Group in Lebanon (UNOGIL), 142
United Nations Operation in the Congo (ONUC), 142
United Nations Special Session on Disarmament (UNSSOD), 159, 160
United Nations Transition Assistance Group in Namibia (UNTAG)
    China's participation in, 146
United States, 15, 16
    agreement on market access with China, 236
    and arms control, 159, 161, 169, 173
    and China's UN membership, 24–5
    and Chinese revolution, 50–1, 52
    and containment in East Asia, 22–25, 52–53
    and missile exports, 171
    and peacekeeping, 141
    and the treaty system in China, 15
    arms sale to Third World, 166
    as the dominant power in international system, 23, 49
    China's tacit strategic alignment with, 144
    confrontations with China, 18, 31, 244, 248
    investment in China, 221
    mutual accommodation with China, 69–70, 245
    nuclear threats against China, 54, 156
    policies towards China, 20–26, 39, 49–50, 52–53, 63–73
    rapprochement with China, 38, 61, 62, 66, 67, 71, 245
    security treaty with Japan, 23
    trade with China, 84, 85, 86–87
Universal Declaration of Human Rights, 182, 186, 188
Urquhart, Brian, 149

Van Ness, Peter, 114, 115
Versailles Treaty
    China's refusal to sign, 14

Index 345

Vietnam, 130
  invasion of Cambodia, 130
  North: at Geneva Conference, 31
Vietnam War, 23, 31, 37, 63, 65
Vincent, John, 184, 186, 249
Vyshinsky, A., 21

Wallenstein, Immanuel, 118
Wang Juntao, 188
Ward, Angus
  detention and expulsion of, 51–2
Warsaw Pact, 111
Watson, Adam, 44, 243
Weber, Max, 101, 126
Wei Jinsheng, 188
Whiting, Allen, 27
Wight, Martin, 42, 60, 165
Wiseman, Henry, 145
Woodrow Wilson, 13
Woolcott, Richard
  visit to Beijing, 239
World Bank, 19, 90–91, 94, 194, 195, 211, 213, 220, 221, 228, 230, 238
  and Taiwan, 227
  China's membership in, 1, 19, 95, 228
  China's participation in, 226–29
  offer of loans, 211, 212, 213
  on China's foreign trade, 200
  on China's opening and reforms, 200
  Resident Mission in China, 213, 228
  revaluation of Chinese economy, 1, 194
  suspending lending operations to China, 212
World Food Programme (WAF), 214
World Health Organisation (WHO), 36
World Trade Organisation (WTO), 225, 225, 229, 237, 240, 246, 251
  China's membership in, 1, 236–38, 240, 246, 247; and Taiwan, 237

Wu Xueqian, 130
Wu Yi, 235

Xiamen, 198, 230
Xinhua, 88
Xu Xiangqian, 66

Yalta Conference, 16
Yangtze River, 51
Yankee bonds, 217
Ye Jianying, 66
Yemen, 30
Yu Mengjia, 146
Yugoslavia, 84
Yugoslavian Communist League, 133
  relations with CCP, 138

Zaire, 31, 79
Zambia, 77, 79
Zhao Ziyang, 99, 102, 117, 125, 128, 129, 135, 136, 154, 158, 198
  at UN General Assembly, 107
  on China's opening, 198
  on ideology in international relations, 128
  on independent foreign policy, 99, 105
  on objectives of Chinese foreign policy, 99
  on UN, 145
Zheng Tuobin, 232
Zhou Enlai, 21, 55, 65, 67, 72, 74, 75, 78, 79, 81, 84, 88, 96, 113, 128
  and China's bilateral diplomacy, 78
  and China's membership at the UN, 36
  at Bandung Conference, 30, 37, 53
  death of, 129
  denouncing the UN, 57, 140
  talk with Kissinger, 65
Zhuang Yan, 143
Zhuhai, 198, 230
Zimbabwe, 30
Zongli Yamen, 10